Palgrave Studies in the History of Finance

The study of the history of financial institutions, markets, instruments and concepts is vital if we are to understand the role played by finance today. At the same time, the methodologies developed by finance academics can provide a new perspective for historical studies. Palgrave Studies in the History of Finance is a multi-disciplinary effort to emphasise the role played by finance in the past, and what lessons historical experiences have for us. It presents original research, in both authored monographs and edited collections, from historians, finance academics and economists, as well as financial practitioners.

More information about this series at
http://www.palgrave.com/gp/series/14583

Lilia Costabile · Larry Neal
Editors

Financial Innovation and Resilience

A Comparative Perspective on the Public Banks of Naples (1462–1808)

palgrave
macmillan

Editors
Lilia Costabile
University of Naples Federico II
Naples, Italy

Larry Neal
University of Illinois at
Urbana–Champaign
Urbana, IL, USA

Palgrave Studies in the History of Finance
ISBN 978-3-319-90247-0 ISBN 978-3-319-90248-7 (eBook)
https://doi.org/10.1007/978-3-319-90248-7

Library of Congress Control Number: 2018942887

Cover illustration: Fondazione Banco di Napoli
Cover design by Laura de Grasse

Printed on acid-free paper

This Palgrave Macmillan imprint is published by the registered company Springer Nature Switzerland AG
The registered company address is: Gewerbestrasse 11, 6330 Cham, Switzerland

Foreword

The papers collected in this volume, sagely edited by Lilia Costabile and Larry Neal, deal with the rise of modern banking in Europe between the sixteenth and the eighteenth century. As is well known, this was a period of remarkable financial innovation. New banking practices were coming to the fore, and different ways were being defined to deal with the turbulence that, mostly as a consequence of wars and natural disasters, recurrently hit the financial systems of the European states.

The diffusion of bank lending and the emergence of fractional reserve banking were particularly noteworthy, especially in England and in the Netherlands, with banks starting to create money beyond the stock of metallic currency coined by the mints. It is fascinating to read of the important contributions to this financial innovation provided by the "public" banks that were founded towards the end of the sixteenth century in the Kingdom of Naples. From the essays presented in this book, it appears that many crucial innovations were initiated by the Neapolitan banks ahead of others and with better results than elsewhere.

Much is rightly said about the role played by the *fede di credito*, a highly liquid and negotiable bill of credit whose circulation was backed by its very nature as a deposit certificate. No less interesting is the widespread, though carefully motivated, granting of uncollateralized loans, as we can read from the incredible records maintained in the three hundred rooms of the *Archivio storico del Banco di Napoli* (the Historical Archive of the Bank of Naples). Moreover, the possibility of recurring to cash credits provided to customers who could use them "whenever needed" formed an early version of overdrafts based on paper circulation. These innovations produced new, highly liquid means of payment, which circulated in a multiplicative manner and with a relatively weak link to the underlying metallic reserves.

But this was also a period of great economic shocks that significantly affected the financial systems of all major European countries. It is this succession of episodes of financial innovation and crises that led to the *de facto* or *de jure* assignment to central banks of exclusive or shared responsibility for price stability, financial stability and the overhaul of the payment system. In the case of the banking system developed in Naples, two developments are interesting to observe.

The first is that much of this (useful) financial innovation took place in spite of the orthodox regulatory framework that owing, amongst others, to religious principles, did not explicitly allow the new practices. Crucial, then, were the roles played by the banks in exploiting existing loopholes and by the regulating authorities' "benign neglect", allowing for the circumvention of the rules, both religious and those imposed by the kingdom. We must remember, in this perspective, that the Kingdom of Naples was a kingdom without a king "in residence", governed in those years by a succession of Viceroys.

The second development concerns the measures taken by these regulatory authorities to counteract the banking crises that inevitably occurred over the period. The resilience of the system was supported by the complex set of responses that combined bailing in of credits, capital bailouts and regulatory forbearance in ways that still characterize much of the conduct of political and control authorities today.

As Soren Kierkegaard once observed, "Life can only be understood backwards…". The historical essays and considerations on the rise of modern banking and on the associated development of various forms of central banking that we are offered in this book certainly help to foster this understanding. Perhaps in studying this period and the facts examined in these essays we may begin to observe a closer correspondence between the three classic functions of money (as a unit of account, a store of value and a medium of exchange) and the three main functions of central banks (preserving monetary stability, financial stability and maintaining a safe and well-functioning payment system).

The recognition of the crucial role of central banks has not been a smooth process. The consequences of the Great Financial Crisis of

2007–2008 have been such that, after a few decades of oversight, financial stability considerations have returned to be an issue to which central banks, albeit not necessarily singlehandedly, must devote their most careful attention. Much talk is therefore dedicated today to measures of a "macroprudential" nature, to curb excesses in lending and in the rise of asset prices. Furthermore, to ensure price stability, while keeping the returning spectre of deflation at bay after the inflationary genie had been successfully put back in the bottle, we have had to resort to measures which have not been applied much in the past or, as it is common to say nowadays, are simply "unconventional".

We have been confronted again with what a quarter of a century ago Amartya Sen aptly called, in his Paolo Baffi lecture on Money and Finance (*Money and Value: On the Ethics and Economics of Finance*, Banca d'Italia, 1991), "a dissonance between the low image of the practice of finance and the high social contribution it undoubtedly makes". I believe that it is fair to conclude that much has been achieved over the last ten years, within the Financial Stability Board and the Basel Committee on Banking Supervision, with the introduction of substantial regulatory changes aimed at reducing the frequency of financial crises and increasing the resilience of our banking and financial systems.

More can and should be done to strike the right balance between allowing financial innovation to flourish and at the same time preventing it from endangering financial stability. The history of the Neapolitan banking system, which is traced in the pages of this book, reminds us that it is possible, albeit laborious, to achieve this balance in order to provide the "high social contribution" of finance that Sen alluded to. At the same time, we must remember that financial innovation can allow for a more efficient allocation of risk but also entails dangers, both intrinsic and related to the greater interdependence of financial systems. This is particularly pertinent at a time when issues such as the potential benefits of adopting various forms of "Fintech", not to mention the uncertain future of "crypto-assets", are being widely debated.

Life can, indeed, only be understood backwards, and history, whether long ago or more recent, is a strong reminder of Kierkegaard's statement. We should also recall, however, that his statement concluded with "… but it must be lived forward". And what is the future if not the realm of innovation and uncertainty? How can we successfully reconcile these two major variables?

Perhaps we may conclude by observing that, with reference to all future developments in the financial system and its supervision and regulation, necessary rules and (flexible) backstops included, one further lesson again should be drawn from the history of the rise of modern banking in Naples. In their ability to create new liquidity, "inside money" as at some point it became referred to, the instrument created by the Neapolitan banks, widely circulated and trusted, was the "*fede di credito*". In Italian, the word *fede*, which comes from the Latin *fides*, means, at the same time, "trust" and "belief". In English, we find the same root in "confidence", as well as in "fiduciary" money. The main challenge, thus, for future financial innovations and their accompanying regulatory measures, is exactly how to preserve and increase confidence, trust, in the way the financial system and the authorities, not just central banks, that regulate and supervise it, operate. To respond to this challenge, the efforts and attention of all the parties involved are being and should continue to be dedicated.

Rome, Italy

Ignazio Visco
Governor of the Bank of Italy

Preface

The papers collected in this volume originated as presentations for "The Rise of Modern Banking in Naples, A Comparative Perspective", a conference held in Naples on June 15–17, 2017 with generous support from the Fondazione Banco di Napoli, the Università degli Studi di Napoli Federico II, and the Banca d'Italia. The purpose of the conference and this follow-up publication was to call the attention of international scholars to the remarkable innovatory achievements of the Neapolitan banking system in the early modern period of European history. The vast archival collection of the Banco di Napoli Foundation, a collection that should be classified as a UNESCO cultural site, provides the basis for further research into the accomplishments of these early modern banks.

The conference participants were impressed by the way the early Neapolitan banks, faced with similar systemic challenges to those that confront today's global financial system as it adjusts to the global economy of the twenty-first century, innovated to create the nucleus of a modern banking system. Credit and financial markets interacted with international banks to create the Great Financial Crisis of 2007–2008 and, consequently, opened a new stage in the continuing discussion of what banking systems and central banks should do in general. Contributors to that discussion have turned increasingly to comparisons with other financial systems and, especially, to historical examples of successful recoveries from systemic crises in the past, sometimes in the very distant past. The apparent success of the Neapolitan banking system in the early modern period motivated all of the conference participants to explore more deeply the linkages amongst financial innovation, financial instability and the recipes for resilience that were eventually discovered by regulatory authorities in Naples during sixteenth to nineteenth centuries. That period saw the beginning phases of the eventual transition from metal-based to paper-based monetary systems, a transition that may be analogous to the transition from paper-based to electronic record-based monetary systems today. The Neapolitan banking system takes central stage in our inquiry because it was both innovative and resilient in the face of the recurrent crises it went through, some of which originated in exogenous shocks, some of their own making, or determined by a combination of exogenous and endogenous causes.

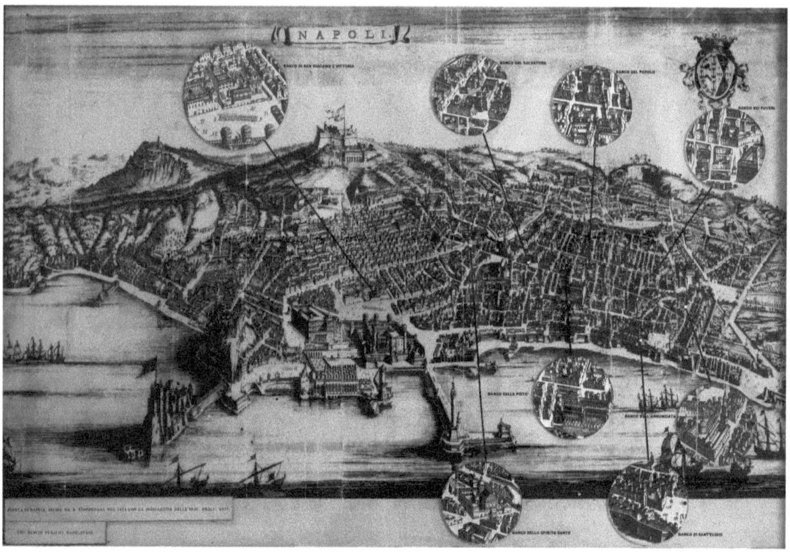

Fig. 1 Map of Naples with the names and locations of the public banks of Naples, 1653. Gravure by Bastiaen Stopendaal

Originally created as auxiliary departments of various charitable institutions in Naples (*luoghi pii* in Italian), the seven, later eight, public banks of Naples were spread across the city as shown in Fig. 1. The original seven received their formal charters from the government of Naples when the demands for war finance by Philip II of Spain increased in the last quarter of the sixteenth century while the last one emerged in response to the pressures placed by the finances of the Thirty Years' War. As shown in Chapter 3, however, some of the charities engaged in banking long before they received official approval. The earliest loan found to date in Naples was issued in 1462. We end their history in 1808 when the remaining banks were consolidated under Napoleonic rule.

Faced as group by repeated economic shocks, including further wars, political revolutions, outbreaks of plague and repeated earthquakes (Vesuvius

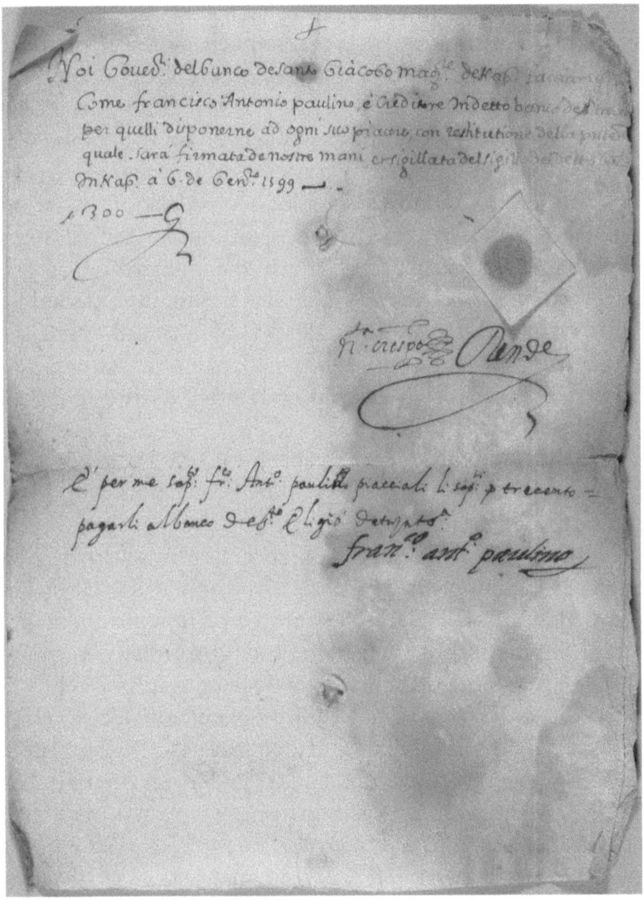

Fig. 2 Example of a *fede di credito*. Banco di San Giacomo. *Fede di credito* for 300 ducats from 6 January 1599, to Francisco Antonio Paulino, who transferred the certificate on the same day to the Banco di Sant'Eligio

has erupted over 50 times since AD 79), they created a financial system that provided the people of Naples the resiliency they needed to recover each time, and they performed this important service for over three centuries.

They began by transforming their paper records of deposits (*fedi di deposito*) into negotiable bills of credit (*fedi di credito*), as shown in Fig. 2. These paper documents, signed and stamped by the bank's teller, enjoyed widespread circulation. Although the regulatory system discouraged loans to private individuals (save for no-interest loans on pawned objects) and repeatedly issued laws prohibiting these loans, all the banks made loans at moderate rates of interest with the implicit approval of the religious and state authorities. Even loans unsecured by collateral appeared in the early decades of the seventeenth century. Their innovations, ratified by both church and state authorities, enabled credit in Naples to expand while anchored by a trustworthy system of paper money. They provided, in fact, the first example of a fiduciary circulation based on readily negotiable paper in the Western world. Throughout the eighteenth century, Neapolitan banks actually exceeded the monetization of all other European economies, including Holland for sustained periods of time, though not England, the eventual leader of financial capitalism.[1] The chapters in Part I, "The Rise of Modern Banking in Naples", explain in detail how the charitable organizations scattered through the city of Naples managed to achieve this.

Together, the public banks of Naples created a stirring example of how a banking system can, with proper motivation and governance, rebound from exogenous shocks to continue to perform vital financial services for the public they serve. Further, as the seven original banks were all founded as supplements to the charitable works of philanthropic foundations, they provide a useful example of how problems of opportunistic behaviour by bank managers and government regulators may be overcome in order to sustain the fiduciary responsibilities of banks to their depositors. While Italians rightly take credit for developing and exploiting the possibilities of bank finance from the Renaissance onward, most historiography focuses on banks in northern Italy, especially Florence, Genoa and Venice. Missing from recent treatments that claim to have general coverage is any mention of the remarkable performance of the public banks of Naples, which in many ways outperformed the

[1] William Roberds and François R. Velde, Chapter 17, in Wolfgang Ernst and David Fox, ed., *Money in the Western Legal Tradition*, Oxford University Press, 2016.

well-known banks in northern Italy.[2] To highlight both the achievements of the public banks of Naples and their lessons for financial resiliency, we focus on financial crises and how they were overcome in Naples in contrast to other European financial systems.

The introductory Chapter 1, "The Pattern of Central Bank Development: Past, Present and Future" by C. A. E. Goodhart, provides an excellent motivation for the need to find new innovations that can provide the necessary resiliency to overcome the inevitable challenges that banking systems everywhere will face in the near future. Based on his career with the Bank of England and, more recently, writing the official history of the Basel Group's successive attempts to agree on a common regulatory structure for international banks, Goodhart gives an authoritative overview of the present challenges confronting the global (and Italian) financial system. His chapter highlights the recurrent responsibilities of monetary authorities to respond effectively to economic shocks and provide the effective means for recovery and the way they have evolved in the past.

The first major financial crisis that confronted the early public banks of Naples for which the archives of the Bank of Naples have ample documentation occurred in 1622. Chapter 2, "The Public Banks of Naples Between Financial Innovation and Crisis" by Lilia Costabile and Eduardo Nappi, highlights how the banks in Naples introduced substantial innovations in banking techniques and then survived the monetary reforms imposed on them in 1622 with the help of regulatory forbearance by both the government and the church. The following chapters fill in the historical context in which the public banks emerged before 1622 and then continued to thrive afterwards. All seven original banks started from the responses of charitable foundations to earlier crises as described in Chapter 3, "Before the Public Banks: Innovation and Resilience by Charities in Fifteenth-Century Naples" by Rosalba Di Meglio. Chapter 4, "Between Charity and Credit: The Evolution of the Neapolitan Banking System (Sixteenth–Seventeenth Century)", by Paola Avallone and Raffaella Salvemini, explains how the banks grew at the expense of existing private banks, which had been initiated frequently by opportunistic merchants with foreign connections.

[2](For example, Larry Neal, *A Concise History of International Finance: From Babylon to Bernanke*, Cambridge UP, 2015 or Youssef Cassis, Richard S. Grossman, and Catherine R. Schenk, editors, *The Oxford Handbook of Banking and Financial History*. Oxford: Oxford University Press, 2016.)

Chapter 5, “The Investments of the Neapolitan Public Banks: A Long Run View (1587–1806)”, by Francesco Balletta, Luigi Balletta and Eduardo Nappi, provides a quantitative overview of the dramatic recoveries of the banks, taken as a systemic whole, after each major crisis that followed right up to the conquest of Naples by Napoleon’s armies in 1808.

The papers in Part I are based partly on new archival research leading to exciting novel findings and partly on materials retrieved over many years and by numerous scholars from the historical archives of the Bank of Naples. The Historical Archive of Banco di Napoli is housed in the sixteenth-century Palazzo Ricca in Via dei Tribunali and in the adjacent Palazzo Cuomo in the ancient quarter of Naples where it occupies more than 300 rooms filled with millions of documents. For centuries, the archives were hardly accessible to scholars, unorganized and neglected. Extensive efforts to modernize the collections in recent decades, however, have restored the archives now for regular and convenient access. Figures 3 and 4 show the remarkable improvement for just the archive of the Banco del Santissimo Salvatore, but all the archives have undergone comparable renovation.

There are two sections of the archive: the Patrimoniale and the Apodissario. The Patrimoniale has all the books dealing with the internal

Fig. 3 The archive of Banco del Santissimo Salvatore before the reorganization

Fig. 4 The archive of Banco del Santissimo Salvatore after the reorganization

administration of the eight original public banks, the management of their patrimonial assets, their directors' decisions, etc.. The Apodissario, which is much larger, contains the Master Books and the Giornali Copiapolizze where the customers' accounts were registered and copied. The Master Books include as well the accounts that the banks opened to receive deposits and make payments, whether with the bank itself, its founding charity, other customers, or with other banks. Moreover, the *fedi* and *bancali* issued by the banks are kept in the Apodissario archive, which served as legal proof of the individual transactions by clients. The Apodissario also contains the *Pandette* (alphabetic indexes of the customers' names) and the *Squarci di Cassa* (the daily journals in which cashiers entered their cash transactions), and other books. It is easiest to work with the administrative books in the Patrimoniale, but the occasional references there to interesting innovations can only be verified by following up the references to the relevant parts of the Apodissario archive, where the directors' decisions were carried out and documented. Figure 5, also used for the book cover, shows the organization of the relevant documents.

After focusing on the development of the public banks unique to Naples, it is natural to make comparisons with other financial systems in Europe to see how they responded to the same shocks in 1622, which were caused by the full mobilization of European belligerents to finance their efforts in the Thirty Years' War. Chapter 6, "The Variety of Financial Innovations in European War Finance during the Thirty Years' War (1618–1648)" by Larry Neal, introduces this section. The following chapters, "Public Banks and State Finance in Florence and Venice", by Luciano Pezzolo, and "Conflicts, Financial Innovations, and Economic Trends in the Italian States during the Thirty Years' War", by Giuseppe De Luca and Marcella Lorenzini, highlight the respective difficulties that the other leading Italian financial systems faced and then stumbled, despite having superior initial advantages over the banks in Naples. Chapter 9, "Experimenting with Paper Money during the English Civil Wars and Interregnum: Monetisation Versus Securitisation, 1643–1663" by D'Maris Coffman, argues that the basis for England's later success was laid in fact by the financial innovations undertaken by the English Parliament during the Civil War, but were stymied by the pressing political pressures that led to successive regime changes.

Part III continues the analytic arc by comparing lessons learned about public banks in the rest of Europe over the next century and a half. Chapter 10, "Neapolitan Banks in the Context of Early Modern Public Banks", by François R. Velde, compares the innovations and their resiliency made in the various financial systems that emerged throughout Europe over the period 1648–1808. The following chapters take up "The Institutional Foundations of Successful Public Borrowing—Models of Public Banks in Habsburg Austria and Habsburg Naples 1700–1800", (Clemens Jobst), "John Law: A Twenty-First Century Banker

Fig. 5 The Apodissario archive for Banco di San Giacomo. Hanging from the ceiling and on the table: *Filze* of *bancali* (*fedi di credito* and *polizze*). On the shelves, from top to bottom: first, second and third shelf: *bancali*; fourth shelf: *Pandette* (note-books containing indexes of customers' names); fifth shelf: *Giornali Copiapolizze*, both *di cassa* and *di banco* (copy-books, registering payments in cash and by transfers between accounts in the bank's books); bottom shelf: the Master Books. Historical Archive of the Bank of Naples. Bank of San Giacomo, end of eighteenth century.

in the Eighteenth Century?" (Antoin E. Murphy), and "The Bank of Amsterdam's Search for Success and Stability" (Stephen Quinn and William Roberds). Each focuses on the possibilities and difficulties that emerged in their respective countries, all of which were quite aware of the role played by the public banks in Naples, but each had to deal with their uniquely different political institutions. None of them, moreover, managed to match the accomplishments of the Neapolitan banks before they were forcibly consolidated in 1808 under Napoleonic rule.

Part IV, finally, comes back to original start of the analytic narrative. Chapter 14, "Banks, Financial Markets and the Development of International Currencies", by Barry Eichengreen, suggests ways that today's policy makers and thinkers could use the historical experience of the public banks of Naples to reflect on how to deal better with the ongoing problems stemming from the financial crisis of 2007–2008. In particular, it is interesting that the public banks of Naples, all issuing paper credits denominated in the local currency, which did not undergo further changes after 1622, did not create an international currency for general use in foreign trade like the currencies created in Genoa, Venice and Florence. Chapter 15, "Public Banks, Public Orientation and the Great Financial Crisis of 2007–2008" (Gerald Epstein and Devika Dutt), explores just how smaller banks focused on local community service rather than financing long-distance trade, managed to survive the latest financial crisis, which was very much international in scope. Finally, Chapter 16, "Profit and Non-profit Motives in the Public Banks of Naples: An Old Model in Modern Perspective" (Adriano Giannola), concludes by suggesting that to restore public confidence in the modern banking system we need to re-create the motivations and governance structures of the early banks of Naples that were owned by charitable organizations (*luoghi pii*). There may even be some lessons worth taking away for current policy issues.

The chapters in Part I begin by describing in detail how the public banks as a group responded to their first systemic shock, the monetary reform imposed on them by the Spanish Viceroy in 1622. Their creative response, sanctioned in due course by the Viceroy and even by religious authorities, set the stage for their continued existence until the Napoleonic conquest in 1808. Their ability to respond as a group, however, arose from a very long history of financial experiments earlier, typically as supplements to the philanthropic activities of their mother institutions. Over time, a cooperative system of governance emerged that included mutual clearing of payments and regular monitoring of each other's performance. Viewed as a system, the public banks of Naples continued to outperform banking experiments in the rest of Europe, continuing to expand their leverage for the benefit of the consumers and businesses of Naples throughout the eighteenth century. Comparing other financial systems in Europe in retrospect, all of which tried to cope with similar challenges as those in Naples, but which all ended with alternative strategies, the resiliency of the system of public banks in Naples remains a remarkable achievement. We hope this book can stimulate a new series of studies that will integrate the experience of Naples as a substantial part of the history of modern banking.

Please go to the following link for a video about the Historical Archive of the Bank of Naples: https://vimeo.com/149590614.

Naples, Italy
Columbus, USA

Lilia Costabile
Larry Neal

Contents

Notes on Contributors

Paola Avallone is Director of Research of Institute of Studies on Mediterranean Societies (ISSM)—Italian National Council of Research (CNR). She was managing director of the same institute from 2013 to 2015. She is in the scientific board of the *Annual Seminar of Doctoral Studies in History and Economy in the Mediterranean Countries* of ISSM and of the annual publication *Rapporto sulle Economie del Mediterraneo*. She is editor in chief of ISSM E-book series *Strumenti e Documenti per la Storia del Mezzogiorno*. She is specialized in economic history of southern Italy, credit and banking history, insurance history, school history, tourism history.

Recent publications: *Accounting Crimes: The Case of the Neapolitan Public Banks* (17–18th Centuries), in *The Accounting Historians Journal*, 2017; *The Neapolitan Credit Model. The Banking System in Pre-unification Southern Italy*, in *Annales Mercaturae*, 2016; *Il credito*, in P. Malanima e N. Ostuni (eds), *Il Mezzogiorno prima dell'Unità. Fonti, dati, storiografia*, Soveria Mannelli, 2013.

Francesco Balletta has been Full Professor of Economic History at the University of Naples "Federico II" from 1980 to 2011 and Head of Department from 1990 to 2011. Since 2011, he is Professor of Economic History at the University of Rome "La Sapienza"—Unitelma. He is Chief Editor of Rivista di Storia Finanziaria. He published over 40 books and 80 articles on the economic and financial history of Italy, with a special focus on southern Italy and Naples.

Luigi Balletta received a Ph.D. in Economics from Yale University in 2010 and a Ph.D. in Mathematics for Economic Analysis and Finance from University of Naples "Federico II" in 2006. He has been Lecturer in Economics at the University of Palermo from 2008 to 2017. Since 2017, he is Lecturer in Economics at the University of Naples "Federico II". His research focuses on economic theory, innovation, and the history of banking.

D'Maris Coffman is the Professor of Economics and Finance of the Built Environment at University College London and Director and Head of Department of the Bartlett School of Construction and Project Management. Her current research interests span financial history, infrastructure economics and finance, and climate change economics.

Lilia Costabile is Full Professor of Economics at the University of Naples Federico II. She received her Ph.D. at the University of Cambridge, where she is also Life Member of Clare Hall. In 2016, she received the Prize of the President of the Italian Republic, awarded by the Accademia dei Lincei, for her research in Economics. A member of the Academic Council of the European Association for Financial and Banking History, she is currently involved in a project on "Minimalism and Activism in Central Banking: Lesson from the History of Economic Thought" funded by the ECB through ESHET (the European Society for the History of Economic Thought), of which she is currently a Council member. She has published widely in academic journals, including the *Economic Journal*, *Cambridge Journal of Economics*, etc. and is the author of a book on *Malthus: Sviluppo e ristagno della produzione capitalistica*, as well as the editor of *Istituzioni e sviluppo economico nel Mezzogiorno*, and *Institutions for Social Well-Being: Alternatives for Europe.*

Giuseppe De Luca is Professor of Economic History at the University of Milan and holds a Ph.D. in Economic and Social History from the Bocconi University. He has been visiting professor in several Spanish universities and has recently devoted his research effort to the interplay between finance and economic growth, and to the evolution of infrastructure financing. He is co-editor with Youssef Cassis and Massimo Florio of *Infrastructure Finance in Europe: Insights Into the History of Water, Transport, and Telecommunications* (Oxford University Press, 2016), and his other recent publications include "Informal Credit and Economic Modernization in Milan (1802–1840)" *Journal of European*

Economic History (2013); "Milanese Finance, 1348–1700", in *Handbook of Key Global Financial Markets, Institutions, and Infrastructure* (2013); and "Between Theory and Reality: Economic Crises and the Historiography of Early Modern Europe", in *Merchants in Time of Crisis (16th to mid-19th Century)* (2015).

Rosalba Di Meglio is a Research Fellow in Medieval History at the Dipartimento di Studi Umanistici of the University of Naples Federico II. She obtained her university teaching qualification as an associate professor in 2013. She got her first degree (Laurea) in Lettere Moderne in 1998 and her Ph.D. in History in 2004, and then obtained a Postdoctoral Degree. She was also a Research Fellow at the Istituto Italiano per gli Studi Storici in 1998–2000. She has studied the religious history of Naples during the Angevin and Aragonese periods. She wrote extensively on this subject and participated in many national and international conferences and research projects. Her publications include *La Disciplina di S. Marta: mito e realtà di una confraternita 'popolare'*, in G. Vitolo and R. Di Meglio, *Napoli angioino-aragonese. Confraternite, ospedali, dinamiche politico-sociali*, Salerno 2003; *Il convento francescano di S.Lorenzo a Napoli. Regesti dei documenti dei secoli XIII–XV*, Salerno 2013; *Ordini mendicanti, monarchia e dinamiche politico-sociali nella Napoli dei secoli XIII–XV,* Raleigh, N.C., 2013.

Devika Dutt is a Ph.D. candidate at the Department of Economics of the University of Massachusetts Amherst and a Research Assistant at the Political Economy Research Institute. Her dissertation is on the Political Economy of the Cost of Foreign Exchange Intervention, in which she discusses direct and indirect costs of foreign exchange intervention in the context of the institutions of the global monetary system, and its differential impact on advanced and emerging economies. She is also interested in publicly oriented financial institutions and their effect on the economy and the financial system as a whole.

Barry Eichengreen is George C. Pardee and Helen N. Pardee Professor of Economics and Political Science at the University of California, Berkeley, Research Associate at the National Bureau of Economic Research and Research Fellow of the Centre for Economic Policy Research. Two of his books (related to the subject of his chapter in this volume) are *Exorbitant Privilege: The Rise and Fall of the Dollar and the Future of the International Monetary System* (Oxford, 2011) and *How*

Global Currencies Work: Past, Present and Future (with Arnaud Mehl and Livia Chitu—Princeton, 2017).

Gerald Epstein is Professor of Economics and a founding Co-Director of the Political Economy Research Institute (PERI) at the University of Massachusetts Amherst. Epstein has written articles on numerous topics including financial crisis and regulation, alternative approaches to central banking for employment generation and poverty reduction, capital account regulations and the political economy of central banking and financial institutions. Epstein has worked with numerous UN agencies including the ILO, UNDESA, UNDP and UNCTAD on the topics of macroeconomics and monetary policy in developing countries. His most recent edited volume is: *The Handbook of the Political Economy of Financial Crises*, Oxford University Press, 2013 (co-edited with Martin Wolfson). In recent years, he has been the recipient of two INET grants, one to study the "social efficiency" of the financial system and a second to look at the distributional impacts of quantitative easing. He has also won the Samuel F. Conti Faculty Fellowship Award from the University of Massachusetts Amherst.

Adriano Giannola is Full Professor of Economics of Banking at the University of Naples Federico II, and President of: SVIMEZ, *Associazione per lo sviluppo dell' industria nel Mezzogiorno; Fondazione di Comunità (Community Foundation of the Historical Center of Naples)*. He has been President of: *Istituto Banco di Napoli-Fondazione* (2000–2013); *Teatro Stabile di Napoli-Teatro Na*zionale (2011–2015); *ARISCOM Insurance Company* (2015–2017).

C. A. E. Goodhart was trained as an economist at Cambridge (Undergraduate) and Harvard (Ph.D.). He then entered into a career that alternated between academia (Cambridge, 1963–1965; LSE, 1967/68; again 1985-date) and work in the official sector, mostly in the Bank of England (Department of Economic Affairs, 1965/66; Bank of England, 1968–1985; Monetary Policy Committee, 1997–2000). He has worked throughout as a specialist monetary economist, focussing on policy issues and on financial regulation, both as an academic and in the Bank. He devised "the Corset" in 1974, advised HK on "the Link" in 1983, and RBNZ on inflation targetry in 1988. He has written more books and articles on these subjects throughout the last 50 or 60 years than any sane person would want to read.

Clemens Jobst is Lead Economist at the Oesterreichische National bank and Research Affiliate at CEPR. He has studied at the University of Vienna and the University of Illinois at Urbana-Champaign and earned his doctorate from Sciences Po Paris. His research has been published in the *Cambridge Journal of Regions, Economy and Societies*, the *Economic Journal*, the *European Review of Economic History* and the *Journal of Economic History* among others. In 2016, he has published a history of the Austrian National Bank: *The Quest for Stable Money. Central Banking in Austria 1816–2016*.

Marcella Lorenzini is Research Fellow at the University of Milan. Her research interests focus on the dynamics of informal credit markets in early modern Europe. She is co-editor with D'Maris Coffman and Cinzia Lorandini of the volume, *Financing in Europe: Evolution, Coexistence and Complementarity of Lending Practices from the Middle Ages to Modern Times* (Palgrave Studies in the History of Finance). Her latest publications include "Infrastructure Financing in the Early Modern Age: The Beginning of a *Little Divergence*" in *Infrastructure Finance in Europe: Insights Into the History of Water, Transport, and Telecommunications*, ed. Y. Cassis, G. De Luca and M. Florio (2016), and "Not Only Land: Mortgage Credit in Central-Northern Italy in the Sixteenth and Seventeenth Centuries", in *Land and Credit: Mortgages in the Medieval and Early Modern European Countryside*, ed. C. Briggs and J. Zuijderduijn (2018) (with G. De Luca). Email: marcella.lorenzini@unimi.it.

Antoin E. Murphy is a Retired Professor and Fellow Emeritus of Trinity College, Dublin. He is a specialist in the history of economic thought and was a joint managing editor of the *European Journal of the History of Economic Thought*. His books include *Richard Cantillon: Entrepreneur and Economist* (Oxford University Press, 1986, re-print 1989); *John Law: Economic Theorist and Policymaker* (Oxford University Press, 1997); *The Genesis of Macroeconomics* (Oxford University Press, 2009); *The Fall of the Celtic Tiger Ireland and the Euro Debt Crisis* (Oxford University Press, Oxford and New York, 2013), co-authored with Donal Donovan.

Eduardo Nappi is the Director of the Historical Archive of the Bank of Naples, where he has been working since 1963. He reorganized vast sections of the archive and studied its papers over the course of almost sixty years. His publications include "Aspetti della società durante la peste del 1656", 1980; "Nuovi documenti sulle origini e sui titoli del Banco di Napoli" (with Domenico Demarco), 1985; "Banchi e finanze della repubblica Napoletana", 1999; "Dai numeri la verità. Nuovi documenti sulla famiglia, i palazzi e la Cappella dei S.Severo", 2010. Some of these are downloadable at http://www.eduardonappi.com/.

Larry Neal is Emeritus Professor of Economics at the University of Illinois at Urbana-Champaign, and Research Associate of the National Bureau of Economic Research, and co-editor of the 2-volume *Cambridge History of Capitalism*, and the 4-volume *History of Financial Crises*. His books include *The Rise of Financial Capitalism: International Capital Markets in the Age of Reason*, *"I Am Not Master of Events": The Speculations of John Law and Lord Londonderry in the Mississippi and South Sea Bubbles*, and *A Concise History of International Finance: From Babylon to Bernanke*.

Luciano Pezzolo is Associate Professor of Early Modern History at the Department of Humanities of the Ca'Foscari University of Venice. His main fields of interest are financial and military history in the early modern age, on which he has published extensively.

Stephen Quinn is a Professor of Economics at Texas Christian University. He wrote his dissertation under Professor Larry Neal at the University of Illinois at Urbana-Champaign. In recent years, he has published numerous articles on the Bank of Amsterdam with William Roberds.

William Roberds is a Research Economist and Senior Adviser at the Federal Reserve Bank of Atlanta. He wrote his dissertation under Lars Peter Hansen at Carnegie-Mellon University. His research with Stephen Quinn has focused on the Bank of Amsterdam and its role in the evolution of central banking.

Raffaella Salvemini is the First Researcher of Institute of Studies on Mediterranean Societies (ISSM)—Italian National Council of Research (CNR). She has been an Adjunct Professor at the University of Molise in History of Insurance and Social Security. She is responsible for national and international projects. Her research interests lie in the social and economic history of southern Italy in the modern age with particular attention at the administration and management of Neapolitan hospitals; the relationship between assistance and credit; the education and training of human capital; abandoned childhood. Recent publications: *Tra necessità e quotidianità: la gestione della povertà a Napoli nell'Ottocento preunitario* in Proposte e ricerche, 2014; *L'assistenza*, in P. Malanima, N. Ostuni (eds.), *Il Mezzogiorno prima dell'Unità. Fonti, dati, storiografia*, Soveria Mannelli.

François R. Velde is a Senior Economist and Research Advisor in the Economic Research Department at the Federal Reserve Bank of Chicago. Velde's primary research on monetary history and monetary theory has been published in numerous journals. His research topics include medieval currency debasements, the monetary history of the USA, dollarization in Argentina and the macroeconomics of the French revolution. In 2002, Velde and Thomas Sargent co-authored the book *The Big Problem of Small Change* (Princeton University Press), which studies how monetary systems in Western European economies evolved in response to recurring shortages and depreciation of small change. Prior to joining the Chicago Fed as an economist in 1997, Velde was an Assistant Professor of Economics at Johns Hopkins University. He is currently a Visiting Lecturer at the University of Chicago. Velde earned an undergraduate degree at the École Polytechnique in France and a Ph.D. in Economics at Stanford University.

List of Figures

List of Tables

CHAPTER 1

The Pattern of Central Bank Development: Past, Present and Future

C. A. E. Goodhart

1 Introduction

Commercial banking developed in Italy by the fifteenth century. The public banks of Naples were in the forefront of that development. Since then, they, and the practice of banking worldwide, have been undergoing a continuous process of development, partly in response to the changing structure and needs of the macro-economy and partly in response to crises, some manmade, e.g. in the guise of wars and political disturbances, and some not, e.g. natural disasters such as plagues and earthquakes.

The early Italian banks introduced many crucial innovations, such as lending on the basis of collateral and the use of bills of exchange. The public banks of Naples had a special role in this regard, since they developed a flexible form of deposit certificate, the *fedi di credito*, based on currency, or other assets placed with them, that were flexible, redeemable and transferable, and, arguably, also the first recorded instances of cash credit overdraft facilities (see Chapter 2, Sect. 5 by Costabile and Nappi). These remarkable innovations are described at greater length in several of

C. A. E. Goodhart (✉)
Financial Markets Group, London School of Economics, London, UK

L. Costabile and L. Neal (eds.), *Financial Innovation and Resilience*, Palgrave Studies in the History of Finance,
https://doi.org/10.1007/978-3-319-90248-7_1

the subsequent chapters, notably Chapters 2–4, and their balance sheets (1587–1806) are reported in Chapter 5 (F. Balletta, L. Balletta and E. Nappi).

In particular, the paper by Avallone and Salvemini, Chapter 4, not only describes why the public banks in Naples, connected to large charities,[1] became preferred to private bankers (mostly managed by foreigners, e.g. Genoese), but also records why the *fedi di credito* were so popular. Silver coins were subject to clipping and their other transactions costs, e.g. ensuring safety, weight, forgery, etc., were also greater than those of the *fedi di credito*. Such coins were also subject in many regions to periodic debasement, following by inflation, and then 'crying down' to halt such inflation, all of which led to a greater demand for the paper of stable public banks (see Neal, Chapter 6). And, of course, there were usually many different coins in circulation at any time, whose value varied continuously against each other. One of the main roles of public banks, such as the Bank of Amsterdam (see Chapter 13 by Quinn and Roberds) was to provide a more stable and efficient medium of exchange, notably for bills of exchange, than could be obtained through the use of coins of shifting values.

Not all the developments that have occurred in the banking industry since then have been as beneficial as the *fedi di credito*. The charitable impulse that was associated both with the Neapolitan banks and with several other early Italian banks, such as the Monte de Paschi di Siena, is now somewhat conspicuous by its absence. Under the Amato-Carli Act of 1990, there was an attempt in Italy to restore the role of non-profit organisations, in the guise of Banking Foundations, in the governance of the newly privatised banks, as recorded by Giannola, Chapter 16; but this model has not been entirely successful. Many would argue, however, that the shift of investment banking in the USA from partnerships to limited liability companies and the switch of housing finance from mutual associations (S & Ls in the USA, Building Societies in the UK) to regular commercial banks have been deleterious in effect. Epstein and Dutt, Chapter 15, note that non-profit-maximising banks have not been

[1]This charitable connection provides the main theme of Chapter 3 by Di Meglio, "Before Public Banks: Charity, Welfare and the Economy in 15th Century Naples." This is based on the archival records of the SS. Annunziata Hospital, and, through these, shows how a charitable hospital also gradually developed a banking function.

as pro-cyclical as shareholder banks, and argue that a larger share of public sector or stakeholder banks would provide a beneficial diversification for the financial system.

Whereas bank intermediation has, on balance, been enormously beneficial, (lending to keen borrowers, providing a liquid and safe source of financial assets, running the main payment systems, smoothing out the jagged fluctuations of cash flow, etc.), there is one facet of its activities that remains of persistent concern, which is that bankers, being normal human beings, and their banks tend to amplify the inherent cyclical fluctuations of our economy. During good times, profits are high; asset prices rise; borrowing gets repaid; defaults are low; and bankers tend to lend more, thereby reinforcing the boom. And when the bust occurs, the amplification feedback mechanism goes into reverse.

Particularly during the boom period, this amplification process can threaten price stability and also the adherence of the local paper currency to an external standard of value, such as the gold standard or a pegged exchange rate. Although several of the early Central Banks, such as the Bank of England and Banque de France, were founded to help finance their country's war expenditure, a role that remained paramount during major wars, e.g. in the Napoleonic era, WWI and II, these nationally pre-eminent banks soon became accorded with the quasi-political task of managing the monetary and banking system as a whole, so as to maintain price stability.

The greater the power of the issuer of local currency, the less its value is needed to be strictly tied to its metallic content in gold, silver or copper, i.e. seigniorage will be greater. As Eichengreen shows in Chapter 14, the US dollar, the linchpin of the international monetary system, no longer has any firm link to a precious metal. He argues that, historically, the conditions supporting an international currency, besides its metallic content, were size, stability, liquidity and power. Several of the early Italian City States—Genoa, Florence, and Venice—had the attributes that made their currencies widely acceptable in international trade. The Neapolitan silver *ducato* was not so used; Eichengreen suggests that this may have been owing to some political limitations.

Just as the following Chapters record the evolving patterns of commercial banking in Naples, and more widely in Europe, so it is the purpose of this Chapter to analyse and record the changing pattern of Central Banking. The history of Central Banking, as I have outlined

Table 1 History of CBs has swung between periods of Consensus and Uncertainty

	Consensus	*Uncertainty*
1873–1914	Gold standard Real Bills Doctrine Lender of Last Resort (LOLR)	
1914–1933		Break-down of GS Break-down of Real Bills Doctrine Unemployment and inflation
1934–1970	Fiscal (Keynesian) dominance CB subject to Finance Ministry Financial repression Interest rates used for BoP, otherwise low	
1971–1990		Stagflation Monetarism vs Keynesianism Liberalisation and Financial Crises
1990–2007	Independent CBs Inflation Targets Great Moderation	
2008–		Great Financial Crisis Financial Instability Deflation

previously (Goodhart 2015), can be divided into periods of consensus about the roles and functions of Central Banks, interspersed with periods of uncertainty, often following a crisis, during which Central Banks (CBs) are searching for a new consensus. The timeline is roughly as follows (Table 1).

Most monetary historians, and this book is about monetary history, will be familiar with these key aspects of CB history. It may, however, be worthwhile emphasising a couple of features from this history, which have become less familiar during recent decades. These are, first, the Real Bills Doctrine and the second is the conclusion of much analysis into the onset of the depression in the USA in 1929–1933, that this was largely caused by excessive competition in the banking and wider financial systems, since that lowered profit margins and encouraged a riskier reach for yield. Many of the more stable banking structures, including most likely the public banks of Naples, have been cartelised.

2 The Real Bills Doctrine

Prior to the twentieth century, most government deficits were incurred by the need to finance war. Almost by definition, war is not productive, so monetary finance of wartime expenditure was inherently inflationary. So, banks, and especially Central Banks, tried to avoid purchasing government paper, beyond the minimum necessary to satisfy politicians' willingness to extend their Charter. Moreover, until the middle of the nineteenth century, the rulers of many European states were either unwilling or unable to repay all the debts that occurred to finance their wars, employing various forms of default, either strategically or under duress. Consequently, the better established banks often had more credibility and a better record of repayment than their rulers. This was one reason why in several countries debt management was largely delegated to the Central Bank.

Larry Neal argues in Chapter 6 that Bartolomeo d'Aquino's establishment of the final public bank, the Banco del Santissimo Salvatore in 1640, was motivated essentially by the need to manage the outstanding public debt (most of which he had purchased at fire sale prices in the previous years from the original holders). Thereafter, it became recognised as the government's bank, but existed harmoniously with the original seven public banks, at least after the Masaniello revolt was repressed.

Moreover, absent wartime, rulers during these early centuries often ran a surplus, and there was not always a large stock of short-dated public sector debt, through which to operate in order to manage the money market. So, the preferred liquid asset for money market operations, and for Central Banks' open market operations, became bills of exchange, short-dated credit instruments drawn by the borrower, and, when accepted, became a two-name bill. Here, the main distinction was between real bills, largely drawn by industry based on trade and inventory, and speculative bills, which were drawn largely for the purpose of purchasing assets, which were hoped to rise in price.

The basic idea was that the volume of real bills would rise and fall with the volume of output and trade, so that the monetarisation of real bills would not lead to inflation; according to the quantity theory of money, where $MV=PY$, the Real Bills Doctrine would bring about a close positive correlation between movements in M and Y, leaving P stable. Similarly, real bills would be self-liquidating, since, being based on trade and production, the borrower would always be able to repay the bill from the proceeds of the sales involved in the trade and sale of goods in process. In contrast, the repayment of speculative bills would depend on the course of asset prices, which, being uncertain, meant that they were much more subject to default.

One of the key founders of the Federal Reserve System, Paul Warburg's enthusiasm for "real bills" may have been based on his experience of mutual monitoring of other bankers' acceptances in Germany, with ultimate recourse to borrowing against short-term acceptances from other banks, ultimately from the Reichsbank. Perhaps the Banco del San Salvatore performed this lender of last resort function in the case of Naples.

A great virtue, therefore, of this doctrine, was that it unified the conduct of monetary policy to maintain price stability with the maintenance of financial stability. After the collapse of the Real Bills Doctrine, this unification has fallen by the wayside with both the objectives of price stability and financial stability being seen as separate, requiring largely differing instruments, and sometimes even potential conflict.

The reason why the Real Bills Doctrine failed during the interwar period was that it was inherently procyclical. When the US economy went into a nosedive after 1929, trade and production declined by so much that the volume of real bills declined very sharply. There were not enough real bills left to provide the Federal Reserve System with a sufficient basis to expand the money supply and counter the Depression. As is well known, the operational mechanism of the Fed had been based on the Real Bills Doctrine, and Friedman and Schwartz (1963) and Allan Meltzer (2003) both blamed the adherents of Fed staffers to the Real Bills Doctrine for their incapacity to undertake sufficiently expansionary monetary policy during that period. Indeed, more generally, adherents of the Currency School of monetary policy have always been strongly antagonistic to the Real Bills Doctrine, whereas adherents of the Banking School tended to make it a core plank of their policy proposals, prior to the inter-war disaster, and have had something of a soft spot for it even afterwards, although now clearly recognising its basic flaw.

3 The Dangers of Excessive Competition in Banking?

Whenever there is a crisis, there is an immediate surge of studies to explain the causes of that disaster. There were a number of studies done in the US in the 1930s, whose general conclusion was that a prime cause of the financial crisis had been excessive competition in financial markets, thereby driving profit margins down, and causing bankers to search for yield, quite largely by taking on riskier assets and riskier clients.

One reason for the resilience of the Neapolitan banks as a group may have come from a cartel-like arrangement among them, as they recognised each other's *fedi di credito* and accepted them as deposits. A large part of the daily work of the clerks was to redeem notes of other banks that they had accepted.

Although there was no equivalent inter-war financial crisis in the UK, the economic downturn was again partly attributed to the same cause, excessive competition. Consequently, both industrial and financial strategy during the 1930s largely involved the attempt to corral industrial and financial groups into cartels, whether formal or informal, with the aim of reducing pricing competition and restoring profit margins to a level that would maintain the solvency of the firms involved, whether financial or industrial. As recorded, for example, in Sayers' history of the Bank of England (1976), much of Montagu Norman's role during this period took the form of being cheerleader for such industrial and financial reorganisation into cartel-like structures.

It is, at least, possible that one of the reasons for the very low level of bank failures and financial crises during the subsequent period, 1934–1970, was that excessive competition in the banking sector was constrained, and profit margins remained comfortable. As has been frequently remarked, the growing liberalisation of financial markets during and after the 1970s was often the precursor of subsequent financial crises, in some part because competition, if unchecked, could lead to a combination of declining profitability and growing risk-taking. It is notable that the countries that survived the Great Financial Crisis (GFC) (2008/2009), such as Sweden, Canada and Australia, had domestic retail banking markets that were largely oligopolistic in character, without much competition from foreign banks. Nevertheless, the earlier views that competition in this field could be both excessive and dangerous have not only been disregarded in recent years, but largely turned on their head, insofar as most current commentators seem to believe that start-up challenger banks provide an unalloyed benefit to the macro economy.

4 How Did the Great Financial Crisis (GFC) Occur?

As is now quite generally accepted, one of the failings of Central Banks that led up to the GFC was their failure to appreciate Minsky's analysis (1986) that (macroeconomic) stability would lead to financial instability.

Thus, there were some generally accepted myths prior to 2007, which central bankers and financial regulators were as prone to hold as commercial bankers, commentators and other outsiders. These myths were:

> Price stability, plus Basel Capital Adequacy Ratio requirements, would guarantee solvency;
>
> With solvency thus guaranteed, liquidity will always be available via wholesale markets;
>
> That maturity mismatch in the banking system can be ignored.

The tendency of regulators to take financial stability for granted was reinforced by the mindset of current mainstream macro-economists. In their case, the predominant macro-economic model, the Dynamic Stochastic General Equilibrium (DSGE) model, assumed a world of representative agents who never ever defaulted. Since they never defaulted, lending to them was as riskless as lending to the government. There was, therefore, no need for banks, since the riskless agents could borrow and lend amongst themselves at the single current, riskless interest rate. Accordingly, the whole panoply of financial intermediation, default risk and concern about financial stability was simply airbrushed out of the standard mainstream models. In such models, the GFC simply could not occur. Thus, mainstream economists on the whole paid as little, or less, attention to financial stability issues as regulators.

There were, of course, other problems with invalid beliefs, notably the belief, widely held amongst both bankers and credit rating agencies that a widely geographically diversified portfolio of US mortgages would not be risky, since the probability of a significant decline in US housing prices, over the whole country, was extremely unlikely.

Commentators, especially perhaps journalists, like to attach blame to individuals, or sets of individuals, accusing them of venality, and other human flaws. On this account, the main reasons for the GFC were common failures to appreciate the extent of risk that had been building up in the system, a failure that was common to those in authority, to economists, as well as to those more typically bearing the brunt of blame, such as bankers and credit rating agencies.

5 Where Do CBs Stand Now?

The GFC exposed considerable shortcomings in the role of Central Banks, particularly a failure to give sufficient weight to the role of financial stability. So, most CBs now have an expanded mandate, to give more weight, perhaps equal weight, to financial stability as to price stability. If you have two objectives that are separate, the Tinbergen Rule requires two sets of instruments to achieve greatest efficiency. This has led to the growth and use of macro-prudential measures of various kinds. In addition, the depth of the 2008/2009 crisis led to official interest rates falling to the zero lower bound (ZLB). Since this was not, of itself, sufficient to restore either the major advanced economies to the target inflation rate (usually 2 per cent), nor led to a satisfactory recovery in real output, there was an additional need for unconventional monetary policies, largely connected with increasing the size of the CB balance sheet, i.e. QE in various forms.

Since there is a considerable overlap between *macropru* measures and monetary policy on the one hand, and *macropru* and *micropru* control measures, on the other, there has been some tendency for all three to be concentrated in the Central Bank. But *macropru* and QE both involve, in many cases, interventions into politically sensitive areas, such as intervention in housing and other markets, and interaction with debt management more broadly. Even though Central Banks have taken the initiative in expansionary policies to help our economies recover, in some large part because of constraints on the use of fiscal policy, they have run into criticism about whether their powers have become excessively broad, and their accountability insufficient.

As a result, there are now voices challenging Central Bank independence (CBI); the state of confidence amongst Central Banks that their role is clear, that their instruments can be successfully calibrated to achieve their mandated targets, and that they are confident that they know exactly how and what to do, is slipping.

Antoin Murphy in his later Chapter 12 invokes an analogy between the collapse of faith in bankers and central bankers after the GFC in 2008 and the collapse of faith in John Law and the Mississippi System in 1720. Both involved houses of cards based on the belief of ever-rising

Table 2 Compromise outcome

Date	*Crisis*	*Radical proposal*	*Compromise outcome*
Early 1800s	Suspension of GS	Ricardo's Currency Board	Bank Charter Act 1844
1929–1933	Collapse of US Banking System	Chicago Plan	Glass-Steagall
1970s	Stagflation	Monetarism	Pragmatic Monetarism
Now	Collapse of Banking Systems	Narrow Banking	Ring-fencing and?

asset prices, but both demonstrated the power of finance and monetary management (and mis-management) to affect the 'real' economy.

One feature of financial crises is that they tend to generate radical proposals for reform of the system, which, when subject to wider discussion, tend to lead to a compromise outcome, as set out in tabular form in Table 2.

5.1 *Do We Need to Rethink Monetary Policy?*

The fact that monetary policy has not (yet) been successful in bringing about a strong recovery after the GFC 2008/2009 has suggested that there may be a need to rethink, at least some aspects of, monetary policy. There are various different elements of this, as follows:-

5.2 *Raise the Inflation Target?*

If the ability of monetary policy to restore satisfactory growth and prevent deflation has been limited by hitting the ZLB, or the effective lower bound, then one suggestion that has been put forward is to raise the normal inflation target from 2 per cent to, perhaps, 4 per cent. This runs into a number of difficulties as follows:

If the current problem is that CBs cannot hit 2 per cent, what is the point of raising the target, at least now, to 4 per cent?

Whereas quality changes and technical innovations meant that 2 per cent can be viewed as, in practice, close to price stability, the same could not be said of a target of 4 per cent. The latter would undoubtedly mean that inflation, and inflationary expectations, would be built into the system.

If the politicians and CBs change the target now to suit policy in the current conjuncture, would that not make it more likely that they would change the target in future to get a better chance of meeting their current objectives? In short, would not a change in target lower the credibility of the whole exercise?

5.3 *Lean Versus Clean*

The GFC was caused by a financial crisis, notably, the interaction of bank credit expansion with a housing price bubble. Financial factors that lead to potential crises do not appear in CBs' mandates or professed objective reaction functions. So, the question is now often raised whether CBs should lean against financial asset booms and busts, and expand their reaction function to incorporate some measures of credit and asset prices. This suggestion contrasts with the view that CBs should focus solely on inflation and the output gap, trusting in their ability to clean up in the aftermath of financial crises.

This debate continues with economists, such as Borio at the BIS, suggesting that the authorities should lean against financial cycles, opposed by economists such as Lars Svensson, who argues that the case for doing so has not been satisfactorily made.

But this debate has been largely put to one side by the development of macro-prudential policies, additional to, and separate from, the general official short-term interest rate. The generally accepted idea now is that CBs should try to use such macro-prudential instruments relatively aggressively first. Only if these are seen to fail, or to be unusable in practice, might it then be worthwhile to reconsider the mandate of the CB, whether to include leaning against financial cycles.

5.4 *Why so Ineffective?*

If we are to rethink monetary policy, we need to know why it has failed to restore satisfactory growth, despite being more expansionary and accommodating than ever before in history. There are many potential answers to this. One of these is that a combination of demography, with a worldwide sharp improvement in the ratio of workers to dependents, and the opening-up of China and Eastern Europe to the world's trading system, introduced a huge positive supply-shock to the labour force.

This weakened labour bargaining power, reduced the natural rate of unemployment, and imposed continuing and severe downward deflationary pressures on the world. But this shock is now coming to an end, and may even reverse, as the baby boomers move into retirement, and migration from the agricultural interior in China to the manufacturing coast also comes to an end. If so, the continuing deflationary trends of the last 30 years, or so, may now reverse, bringing about a return to more inflationary, and previously normal, conditions.

Another, not-mutually exclusive explanation, is that the failure of central bank expansionary policies to succeed fully was partially due to the weakness of the transmission mechanism through commercial banks, as a combination of raised capital requirements, lower profitability, and massive fines for improper prior behaviour weakened the banks and led them to be ever more cautious in extending loans, leaving excess reserves unused.

A third explanation is that labour-saving technology has been largely responsible for the weakness of wages and labour bargaining power. As is well known, there is considerable disagreement about the extent and direction of technological innovations over future decades.

5.5 *What if Another Downturn?*

One of the major concerns about current monetary policy is that it has largely used up all likely available instruments. Interest rates have remained rock bottom and central bank balance sheets have expanded enormously, to a degree that worries many commentators. Also, public sector debt ratios have continued to rise despite attempts at austerity, and the worsening dependency ratios and rising costs of health care suggest that such public expenditures are likely to increase as a proportion of GDP. This makes it more difficult to envisage aggressive Keynesian countercyclical measures. In this context, with both monetary and fiscal policies largely exhausted, how could we offset a future recession? It is not easy to see how this could be done.

Whereas a faster renormalisation of interest rates would give greater head-room for cuts in the face of future recessions, the increases in such rates, particularly with the massive debt overhang that has already occurred, could, of itself, tip our economies back into the recession which we might have such difficulty in countering.

5.6 *Where Are CBs Now?*

Let us contrast the state of CBs in the Great Moderation with that now following the GFC (Table 3).

Furthermore, CBs have, as noted earlier, been allocated a second objective, that of maintaining financial stability. This has led to a dilemma. If the associated powers of undertaking micro-prudential supervision and applying macro-prudential instruments are allocated to an institution other than the Central Bank, then the CB will have responsibility of financial stability without being in control of either the information or the instruments needed to achieve that. On the other hand, if the CB is given responsibility for micro supervision and macro-prudential instruments, then the width of its power has extended so far that democratic legitimacy is called into question. Moreover, the application of macro-prudential instruments, at least in some cases, can take the CB into fields such as the housing market and debt management, which are both politically sensitive and more normally within the remit of the Ministry of Finance, rather than the CB. Either way, the previously straightforward and relatively simple delegation of responsibility for controlling inflation, via the use of a single instrument, i.e. the short-term interest rate, has now become much more complicated and subject to debate.

So, the future of the Central Bank in our economies now appears far more uncertain than it was during the splendid decades of the 'Great Moderation'. However, the future cannot, perhaps fortunately, be forecast. The present conjuncture for central banks looks somewhat unstable, but how their future may develop remains opaque.

Table 3 Contrast in role of CBs

	Focus	*Instruments*	*Confidence*	*Independence*
GM	Narrow: Price stability	Single: Interest rate	High	Undoubted
GFC	Broader: Price stability Financial stability	Many: Interest rate UMP, unconventional monetary policy Macro-Pru Stress tests Resolution	Groping	At some risk

References

Friedman, Milton, and Anna J. Schwartz. 1963. *A Monetary History of the United States, 1867–1960.* Princeton, NJ: Princeton University Press.

Goodhart, Charles, and Jensen, Meinhard. 2015. Currency School Versus Banking School: An Ongoing Confrontation. *Economic Thought* 4 (2): 20–31. ISSN 2049-3509.

Meltzer, Allan. 2003. *A History of the Federal Reserve "Volume 1, 1913–1951".* Chicago: University of Chicago Press.

Minsky, H.P. 1986. *Stabilizing an Unstable Economy.* New Haven and London: Yale University Press.

Sayers, R.S. 1976. *The Bank of England, 1891–1944.* Cambridge: Cambridge University Press.

PART I

The Rise of Modern Banking in Naples

CHAPTER 2

The Public Banks of Naples Between Financial Innovation and Crisis

Lilia Costabile and Eduardo Nappi

1 Introduction

In 1600, seven public banks were active in Naples, the capital city of a kingdom that was then part of the Spanish empire. Chartered as "public banks" by the Viceroy between 1584 and 1600, they had already been in operation as the deposit branches of some charitable institutions for many decades, and, in the case of the Holy House of the Santissima Annunziata, for over a century (Silvestri 1953; Demarco and Nappi 1985; Vicinanza 2006; Di Meglio, Chapter 3 in this book). These institutions were two charitable pawnbrokers (Monte di Pietà and Monte dei Poveri), four hospitals (Incurabili, S. Eligio, S. Giacomo e Vittoria, Santissima Annunziata) and one charity offering shelter to indigent young women (Casa dello Spirito Santo). Because of these roots, the public banks were also called the "banks of the charities" (*banchi dei*

L. Costabile (✉)
Dipartimento di Scienze Politiche,
Università di Napoli Federico II, Naples, Italy

E. Nappi
Archivio Storico del Banco di Napoli, Naples, Italy

L. Costabile and L. Neal (eds.), *Financial Innovation and Resilience*, Palgrave Studies in the History of Finance,
https://doi.org/10.1007/978-3-319-90248-7_2

luoghi pii in Italian). Later, in 1640, the flour-tax farmers created the only for-profit public bank in the Neapolitan system, the Banco del SS. Salvatore. Between the second half of the sixteenth century and the first decades of the seventeenth century, the banks of the charities initiated a pattern of financial innovation, crisis and recovery that was to be the mark of their resiliency over the course of the centuries to come.

These banks were financial innovators: they created the first circulating deposit certificate in the form of *fedi di credito* and their ancillary instruments, *polizze*. These negotiable means of payment started to circulate widely as money in the last decades of the sixteenth century, giving rise to the first example of a paper *circulation* in the Western world. This innovation transformed the nature of banking and changed the determinants of the money supply, because traditional deposit and lending activities became relatively independent of both the metallic base, and illiquid "ledger money". This epochal change also enabled these banks not merely to increase the velocity of circulation of money, but also to *expand* the money supply through the creation of loans. One of their channels of creating credit was through the innovative instrument of cash credits.

These financial innovations had consequences that the banks themselves had to learn how to master through the traumatic experience of banking crises, particularly the first, cataclysmic crisis of 1622, which had all the marks of a modern financial crisis: a scramble for "high-powered" (metallic) money, an attempt by the banks to restore reserves by calling in loans, refusing to roll-over existing ones and resorting to selling assets (Schwartz 1986). But these efforts were not enough: with their very existence at risk, the banks worked together with governmental authorities to introduce a package of remedies, including bail-in, bail-out and temporary "nationalisation" measures that saved their life and, in conjunction with further innovations, brought them back on a growth path at the beginning of the 1630s. Their experience in these foundational, "heroic" decades of their life provided a blueprint for the resolution of future banking crises.

This chapter tells the story of this first cycle of financial innovation, financial fragility, public intervention and new financial innovation. With their subsequent life marked by recurrent crises, nevertheless the public banks of Naples continued to expand and collectively became one of the largest banking systems in Europe (Velde, Chapter 10 in this book).

2 A Look at the Data

Detailed information on the size and composition of the public banks' operations is provided by their Master Books (*Libri Maggiori*), copybooks (*Giornali copiapolizze*), *Pandette* (registers of customers' names) and other books maintained in the Historical Archive of the Bank of Naples (ASBN).

From these books, we can get information on the number of customers served by the banks. For example, in 1611, 35,345 people held accounts in the seven public banks, about 13 per cent of an estimated population around 270,000 people. Assuming four dependants for each customer, these figures mean that the public banks provided their services to about 52 per cent of the Neapolitan population. Bank accounts held by women were 2920, about 8 per cent of total accounts.

A precious source of information is a database containing the banks' balance sheets (*bilanci apodissari*) from 1587 to 1863, parts of which we use in this paper. Nappi's archival research in the 1960s consisted in recording them, interpolating from adjacent years when a balance sheet was missing in the relevant Master Book.[1]

Balance sheets were drawn up twice a year as the banks' accounts were balanced. Because mid-year balance sheets are often missing, in Figs. 1, 2, and 3 and in Tables 1 and 2 we use end-of-year data drawn from the "debtors" side (registering the banks' active operations) of these balances. The "creditors" side registered the banks' passive operations. The "debtors" and "creditors" sides always balanced, or showed small residuals of the decimal order.

Figure 1 illustrates the public banks' circulation between 1587 and 1708. It underwent many cycles over the course of the seventeenth century. The most important crises were concomitant with:

- the monetary reform of 1622;
- the "Masaniello uprising" in 1647;
- the Black Death in 1656;
- the end of century crisis.

[1] Franca Assante, now a Professor of Economic History, collaborated sometimes. Balletta (2008) presents these balance-sheets data.

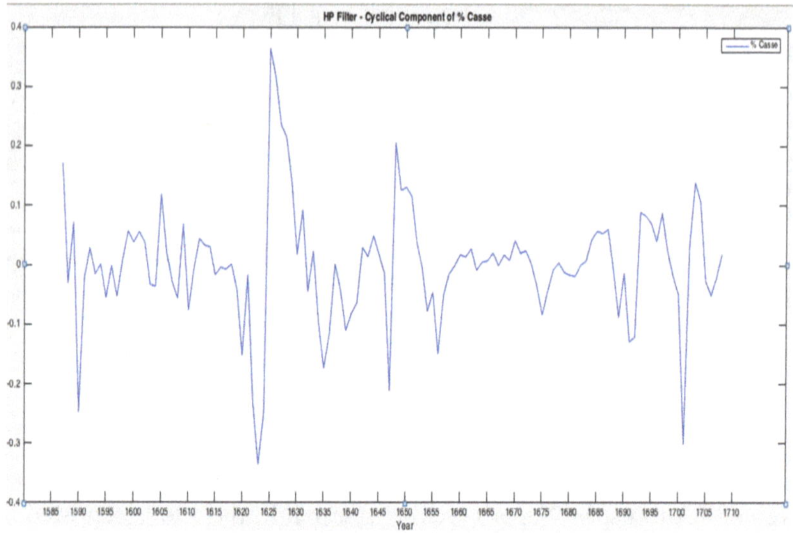

Fig. 1 Circulation—Cyclical component. *Source* Historical Archive of the Bank of Naples, Apodissario, All banks, *Libri Maggiori*, end-of-year balance sheets, 1587–1708

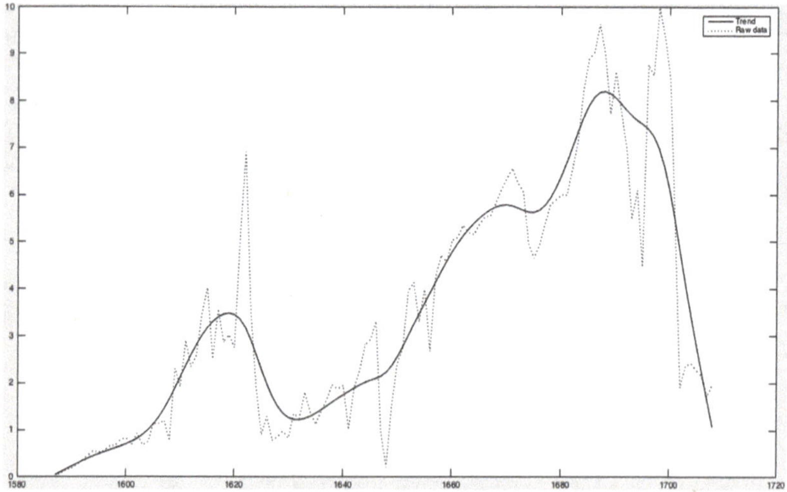

Fig. 2 Circulation—Trend. *Source* Historical Archive of the Bank of Naples, Apodissario, All banks, *Libri Maggiori* (Master Books), end-of-year balance sheets, 1587–1708

Table 1 All banks—reserves as percent of circulation

All banks—Reserves as percent of circulation (averages)	
1600–1620	16,443
1600–1609	24,669
1610–1620	13,963

Source Historical Archive of the Bank of Naples, Apodissario, All banks, *Libri Maggiori* (Master Books), end-of-year balance sheets, 1600–1620

However, as Fig. 2 shows, these crises were severe enough to create a dramatic downward change in the *trend* of bank circulation on only two occasions: in 1622 and, much more dramatically, at the end of the century. Leaving this second episode for future analysis, we focus on the period 1587–1630, when the seeds of future developments were sown.

Figure 2 also shows that the first expansion in the public banks' circulation was already on course in 1587 and went on up to 1622, favoured by the final crisis of the private banks concluded in 1604, when the remaining Genoese bankers (Spinola, Grimaldi and Ravaschieri) closed down their banking businesses and transferred their accounts to the Pietà bank. The Genoese, however, remained as rich and powerful merchants (Dauverd 2015, pp. 55–80), still able to influence the Kingdom's monetary policy in the next decades (see Section 6 below).

In the second decade of the seventeenth century, the public banks underwent further, dramatic expansion. Their circulation was slightly above five million ducats in 1621. To give an approximate idea of the purchasing power of this sum: in 1620–1621, an unskilled worker in the building sector had to work about five days to earn just above a ducat. Put differently, the public banks' circulation could have bought about 22 million work-days from these workers.[2]

Having reached a peak at almost seven million ducats in 1622, the public banks' circulation collapsed in 1623, remaining at around

[2]In 1621, the public banks circulation was exactly D. 5,132,411.00. In 1620–1621, one *carlino* (the tenth part of a ducat) had a silver content of 2.495 grams (Muto 1992, p. 160). In 1620–1621, the daily wage of an unskilled worker in the building sector was on average the equivalent of 5.75 grams of silver. Wage data for Naples and their conversion in silver equivalents are from Robert Allen's website, at the following address: https://www.nuffield.ox.ac.uk/People/sites/Allen/SitePages/Biography.aspx.

one million ducats for almost a whole "lost decade", with a trough at D. 780.962 in 1629. Growth resumed gradually in the 1630s.

Table 1 provides further information on the banks' policies. Between 1600 and 1620, their reserves/circulation ratio (R/C) was low, decreasing and highly variable.

With money creation well in excess of their reserves, it appears that the public banks neither considered their reserves as a constraint on their circulation, nor did they apply a rule of proportionality between the two. The interesting questions, then, are as follows: firstly, how could over-expansion have come into existence at all, given that the regulatory system in force at the time discouraged and often prohibited most active operations? Secondly, if not a proportionality rule, what criteria did these banks adopt for managing their money supply? Thirdly, what channels and techniques allowed them to create money? Here is where financial innovation comes in. "Rules and loopholes – it has been argued – coexist in every legal text and in every regulatory system". Financial innovation often consists in "what we may call circumvention or avoidance behaviors" (Kane 1988, p. 332). In order to answer the above-mentioned questions, then, we must first explore the innovative foundations of the Neapolitan banking system in their unique new form of money; and then go on to study how they used it to circumvent regulations through their innovative channels and techniques of money creation.

3 The Public Banks' Paper Circulation

3.1 Fedi di Credito, *Predecessors of Modern Banknotes*

The public banks of Naples accepted deposits and issued *fedi di deposito* and *fedi di credito*. Deposits were *irregular*, meaning that the banks were not obliged to give back the same coins, but only coins of equal value.

Fedi di deposito served as receipts of deposit or to certify that money was kept in escrow for settling transactions between customers, such as property purchases.[3]

Fedi di credito, more important for our present purposes, were negotiable instruments, and enjoyed widespread circulation. On receiving a deposit, the

[3]The first *fede di deposito* we know of was issued by the Annunziata bank on 20 September 1564 in favour of Domitio Caracciolo for D. 30.000, to pay for the purchase of a piece of land in Atripalda (Demarco and Nappi 1985, p. 25).

bank's Governors (called Protectors at the Pietà) acknowledged their debt by issuing a *fede di credito* stating the amount owed, and their obligation to honour the payment by giving back cash at any time.[4] The bank's officials wrote down and signed *fedi di credito*, and then stamped them with the bank's dry seal.[5] These instruments then circulated by endorsement (*girata*), with signatures by both the payer (the bank's depositor) and the payee.[6] The oldest *fede di credito* we know of was issued by the Pietà in 1573. Figures 4, 5, 6, 7, and 8 at the end of this chapter present some examples of *fedi di credito*.

Typically, a *fede di credito* had the following form: "We, the Governors of the Bank... [Bank's name], certify that ...[customer's name] is our creditor for the amount of Ducats..., which s/he will be able to dispose of at her/his will on restitution of the present *fede*, signed and sealed". The depositor could use the *fede* as a means of payment by writing on the same sheet of paper: "And for me please pay Ms./Mr.... and this is for...", typically followed by the reason for paying.

These motivations for payment were usually very detailed. Because *fedi di credito* had notarial value in case of judicial controversies, the banks kept forever both these original documents and their copies (in *Giornali copiapolizze*). This is why the Historical Archive, with its (literally) millions of documents kept in the three hundred rooms of Palazzo Ricca and Palazzo Cuomo, offers an incredible wealth of information on the economic, social, familial, cultural, artistic dimensions of life, over a time span extending from the second half of the fifteenth century to the end of the twentieth century.

[4] *Fedi di credito* were issued on depositors' demand: on depositing money, the depositor only asked for a *fede di credito* if s/he needed one for making payments. For instance, we found that on 9 February 1615, the Pietà issued *fedi* for D. 848, equal to 21 per cent of the money received as deposits (ASBN, Apodissario, Pietà, *Giornale Copia Polizze di Cassa*, matr. 65, f. 72).

[5] *Fedi di credito* were handwritten documents until 1749 when the Spirito Santo introduced a printed form.

[6] In addition to these circulating notes, sometimes referred to as free *fedi di credito* (*libere*), there were other categories: "conditioned *fedi di credito*" (*fedi conditionate*) could only be cashed on the occurrence of some specified conditions or after a certain date; *judicial fedi* were issued by the bank on receiving sums deposited on judicial order. The banks profited from the long delays before the judges eventually ordered the conversion of these *fedi* into cash.

Fedi di credito were divisible. If depositors had to make smaller payments than the full amount of their *fedi*, they would use *polizze* (or *polise* in older Italian) drawn on the original *fedi di credito*, thus remaining in credit with the bank for the excess value. The *fede* would then become a *madrefede*, documenting all deposits and withdrawals (see Fig. 6). Unlike *fedi di credito*, *polizze* did not mention the Governors and were signed only by the payer. However, the banks' officials often endorsed them as "*notate in fede*" *(n.f.)*, meaning they were registered on a *madrefede* and duly covered by a cash deposit.[7] *Fedi di credito* and *polizze* were collectively called *bancali*.

On receiving a *bancale*, the endorsees would simply go to the issuing bank, or to any other bank in the system, to have them converted into cash or credited in their own accounts; alternatively, they may make another *girata*. The last endorsee would then go to the bank either to redeem the amount in cash or to have it credited in his/her account.[8]

These chains of payments were sometimes quite long, acting as a multiplier. For example, we found a *fede di credito* for one hundred ducats, issued by the Banco dello Spirito Santo in favour of Giacinto Antinori on May 5, 1706 and extinguished on July 14 of the same year, having passed through the hands of seven people after him. Thus, this *fede di credito* financed transactions for 700 ducats in about two months, with a velocity of circulation of almost 3.5 per month (see Fig. 7).

Beyond the description of the instrument, the conceptual substance of the operation is of interest here. The *fede di credito* stated both that the original depositor had deposited X ducats at the bank, and that s/he was trustworthy, just because s/he was in credit with the bank for that amount of money (*fede* in Italian means both statement and trust). This "statement of trustworthiness" is what enabled the payers to transfer their credit towards the bank to the payees.

The payees accepted *fedi* because they were the bank Governors' debt. At no stage in the chain of payments were the original depositors considered responsible or their presence required, either formally or informally. What conferred the *fede di credito* its main feature, namely its *liquidity* (general acceptability) was the bank's promise to pay.

[7] *Polizze* were usually written on pieces of paper of uniform quality and size, suggesting that they were issued by the banks and delivered to their customers on their request.

[8] *Bancali* were then extinguished and, together with many others, would form a *filza*.

To clarify, compare this instrument with other non-metallic means of payment commonly used at the time: ledger money and bills of exchange.

Ledger money (also called book-entry money), the time-honoured procedure of transferring obligations in books of accounts, was already recognised by the Roman Law as an extinction of the debtor's obligation (Usher 1943, p. 95). Widely used by banks in Barcelona, Venice and Amsterdam, it was an *illiquid* means of payment, because it "had not taken the form of paper money that passed from hand to hand" (Lane and Mueller 1985, p. 62) and required the simultaneous presence at the same bank of both the payer and the payee, or their formally appointed agents, in order to have the operation registered in the bank's books (Van Dillen 1934; Luzzatto 1934, esp. p. 46; Usher 1943).

As for bills of exchange,[9] these were issued by one of the trading partners, i.e. a private individual, and only later, possibly, accepted by a bank. Consequently, creditors only accepted bills drawn by debtors they knew and trusted personally. This bond of trust, however, did not extend to the whole community. Put simply, if I know you and trust you, I may well accept your bills of exchange. But if I try to pass them on to third parties as a means for discharging my own obligations towards them, they will refuse them unless they also directly know you and trust you. In other words, short chains of trust can only feed, so to speak, short chains of transactions. By contrast, trust becomes generalised if all the actors in a community know and trust the issuing institution.

The Neapolitan public banks were well respected, powerful institutions that took responsibility for their own paper notes, and guaranteed their convertibility into cash. This is why their notes were money, the liquid means of payments *per excellence*. Moreover, the banks' acceptance of each other's notes and their interbank clearing system (*riscontri*) reduced costs for their customers, as they were free to choose their bank according to convenience and location. This system helped them to create a demand for their notes, and thus to enhance their liquidity, and the viability of the system as a whole.

[9]We refer to domestic bills of exchange. The Neapolitan banks also dealt with bills for long-distance trade, which merchants credited in their bank accounts (De Rosa 1955). On foreign bills of exchange, see De Roover (1953), Neal (1990), Flandreau et al. (2009). Costabile (2015, 2016a) studies early seventeenth-century debates on the effects of foreign bills of exchange on the balance of payments in Naples and in England.

In short, the Neapolitan public banks initiated the *circulation* of paper money in the Western world, thus marking the beginning of a new era in banking practices, in advance of similar developments in other parts of Europe, such as Genoa, Sweden and England. The Genoese *biglietto di cartulario*, imitated from the Neapolitan *fede di credito*, was introduced in the third decade of the seventeenth century (Felloni 2010; Roberds and Velde 2016, p. 329). Swedish banknotes, firstly introduced in 1650, were suspended in 1664 and only reintroduced in 1701. In England, the goldsmith-bankers started to issue circulating notes around the middle of the seventeenth century. The main difference with the Swedish and English notes was that, unlike these, the Neapolitan *bancali* were not anonymous, having the names and signatures of both the payer and the payee written on them. The main similarity was that they circulated widely as means of payment.

3.2 *The Three Pillars of Trust*

The public banks introduced a fiduciary circulation (*fede* and *fiducia* mean faith and trust), thanks to a combination of political, economic, social and historical factors that coalesced to form the three pillars of trust: (i) the good reputation and the patrimonial assets of the banks' shareholders, the charities; (ii) the banks' professional services; and, last but not least (iii) a political factor, namely support by the state. As the great theoretician Ferdinando Galiani stated: "it is a praiseworthy fruit of virtue that faith alone bestows value; it has transformed into precious money mere sheets of paper which are otherwise worthless" (Galiani 1750 [1751] pp. 324–325).[10] Let us briefly consider the three pillars of trust.

(i) The charities enjoyed generalised trust, thanks to the assistance they provided to the sick, the poor and the needy. On this basis, they had established a system of social control going back, in some cases, to the Middle Ages (Vitolo and Di Meglio 2003). Also, very importantly, they owned substantial patrimonial assets, used as collateral for their banks' debts. In 1702, for example, when the Annunziata bank failed, the Holy House of the Annunziata (the hospital) paid for its debts, if only reluctantly and under judicial ordinance.

[10] On Galiani's theory of money, see Costabile (2016b).

(ii) Professionalisation played no minor role. For instance, the banks offered some protection of deposits from judicial seizure, as they honoured *fedi* issued on seized accounts. The reasoning was that, once the original depositor had passed on the instrument to the payee, the latter, not the former, was legally the owner of the money (Rocco 1787, Part II.III, pp. 114–115).

(iii) Finally, support by the state was of paramount importance.[11] For example, on 31 July 1549, the Viceroy Pedro de Toledo established a "privilege" by which the population should prefer the Monte di Pietà over any other lender for loans upon pledge up to four ducats (raised to 10 ducats by the Viceroy Granvela). Later, in 1553, a more comprehensive Vice-royal edict ordered that the population should always prefer the not-for-profit banks ("*banchi senza lucro*") over those for-profit ("*banchi con lucro*") (*Prammatica III De Nummulariis*, July 17, 1553, Giustiniani 1804, 8, p. 130). As these developments show, the Spanish kings were slowly shifting their support away from private, mostly Genoese financiers to the ascending Neapolitan banks. This shift, however, did not come without contradictions or second thoughts, as the Court was not sure whether it should rather establish alternative institutions more directly under state control. For example, in the 1570s, Philip II proposed to found a new bank in Naples, with the purpose of "obtaining some noticeable service of money lent at no interest for some long period of time by the person obtaining the grant", as he wrote to his Viceroy in Naples in a letter dated January 22, 1574 (quoted in Silvestri 1952, pp. 1–2). Time seemed ripe for the project in 1580, when a pool of private banks (Olgiatti, Grimaldi, Citarella & Rinaldo, Colamazza & Pontecorvo) offered the Vice-royal Court a multi-year loan at very good conditions in exchange for a twenty-year bank monopoly. Among the Neapolitan charities, only the Monte della Pietà managed to obtain permission to stay open. But the other charities, led by the Holy House of the Annunziata, joined together to forestall the monopoly project, by offering loans to the

[11] Not surprisingly for a Catholic country, protection by the Church was also important. To mention just some examples: in 1517, the Consiglio Lateranense approved that Charity Lombards could earn interest at 6.5 per cent to cover their costs; in 1552, Julius III approved the statute of the Neapolitan Monte della Pietà (De Rosa 2004, p. 58); in 1586, Sistus V recognised one of the fraternities at the origin of the Bank of the Poor (*Banco dei Poveri*), etc.

> Court at even better conditions. The monopoly project failed for the time being, but resurfaced again in 1598, under the aegis of rich Genoese merchants. Again, the project was blocked when the whole population backed the charities' protests, in a rare display of unity at a time when class conflicts were deep and epidemic (Villari 2012). Popular pressure thus led the Court to fully recognise the banks of the charities as the backbone of the Kingdom's financial system, a clear victory for the ascending local bourgeoisie.

The 1622 crisis would soon prove how much these banks and the government needed and supported each other. Meanwhile, as their approach to regulation shows, their relationship oscillated between tension, complacency, and role-playing.

4 Regulation and Rule Circumvention

Vice-royal edicts (*Prammatiche*[12]) and the banks' charters, themselves subject to Vice-royal approval, regulated banking operations. All the public banks had formal permission to accept deposits and issue *fedi di credito*. As for their active operations, the authorities tried to restrain them within narrow limits, making exceptions just for loans to themselves, and for small charitable loans. Nevertheless, as we shall see, they accepted compromises, and the orthodox model of banking never ruled in reality.

Loans to private individuals. These loans, called *accomodi*, mostly took the form of overdrawn accounts (*conti debitori*). A specific technique, *introiti vacui* (empty takings), consisted in writing *fedi di credito* uncovered or only partially covered by deposits. Another technique consisted in "making good" *polizze*, that is, paying cash out to their bearers or crediting their accounts, although the payer's account did not contain enough money for the payment. These practices were always considered as fraudulent. Vice-royal edicts at first tried to contain, then to eradicate them, eventually resorting to the death penalty ("morte naturale") for cashiers if they "credited people who do not own the money" (*De Nummularis*, Pram. VI March 31, 1603 and VIII, December 14, 1701, Giustiniani 1804, 8, pp. 132–133, 136–6; Pramm. XIII *De Bancis*, May 29, 1728, Giustiniani 1804, 3, pp. 64–67).

[12] See the collections by Varius (1772) and Giustiniani (1804).

Some of the banks' charters confirmed this prohibition. For example, in 1580, the Viceroy Juan de Zunica, Count of Miranda, on behalf of King Philip II, provisionally accepted the Annunziata's request for a bank license, but only on condition that it should not:

"make, order, sign or in any way permit that either in the House or in its name deposit certificates [*fedi di deposito*] be made, or any person be paid any sum whatsoever above what they actually and truly own and for which they are creditors with the House" (Tortora 1890, p. 123, quoting the original document).

The Annunziata adopted this formulation in its charter (1587), followed in 1589 by the Banco di Santa Maria del Popolo, owned by the Incurabili Hospital, and by the Banco dello Spirito Santo in 1590.

Small *gratuitous* loans upon pledge to the poor and the needy by the two pawnbrokers, Pietà and Poveri, were permitted because of their charitable nature, and also because the pledged objects (made of gold, silver and sometimes cloth) were considered to be as good as *specie*, as the banks could always sell them and use the proceeds to restore their reserves. These loans were supposed to be small, but the banks lifted the ceiling on their credit potential, either by means of ambiguous formulations in their charters, or by other means. The Banco dei Poveri's charters, for example, blurred the lines between small loans to poor inmates, which were the bank's official mission, and sizeable loans to wealthy merchants. Its first charter, submitted for Vice-royal approval in 1585, allowed the bank to make gratuitous loans upon pledge up to D. 5 (raised to D. 10 in the second charter) "unless the quality of the person or the importance of the case" justified greater amounts. The second charter, submitted in 1612, clarified the bank's right to accommodate frequent and "fruitful" depositors, as well as the bank's shareholder (Monte dei Poveri) up to D. 200, plus another D. 200 if the majority of the Governors agreed (Anonymous 1750, pp. 93–94).[13]

On its part, the Pietà managed to obtain separate permission from the authorities. On 27 April 1612, the Viceroy Lemos sent a letter to the bank's Protectors. Written on behalf of King Philip III, and duly impressed with the Royal seal, this letter, while imposing the condition that loans should now be agreed upon by the Protectors at their formal meetings rather than left to their individual initiative, in fact gave the Viceroy's blessing to the bank's loans, and lifted any quantity ceiling

[13]Vice-royal approval for the Poveri charters arrived after many years, allowing the bank to rely on its self-made charters in the interval.

on them. The Pietà's Protectors immediately had the letter sewn to the first page of their *Libro degli Accomodi. 27 April 1612–29 December 1617* (from now on: *Book of Accommodations*), as a proof of the legitimacy of their loans, and, that very day, started to register them in this book (ASBN, *Patrimoniale,* Banco della Pietà, matr. 361). Interestingly, the Viceroy's letter was not attached to the bank's official *Libro delle Conclusioni.* The Protectors preferred to keep this letter, and the whole *Book of Accommodations* below the radar, also because their loans went to a selected section of the bank's customers: members of the aristocracy, high public officials, rich merchants and exchange dealers, in addition to some of the bank's own officials and employees. We return to this fascinating source for the public banks' activities in the next section.

Another widely used escape route for the banks were *compre di annue entrate con patto di retrovendita.* These *compre* disguised the loan as an asset purchase with a buy-back clause, and the interest as a temporary transfer of revenue (Avallone 1997, pp. 56–57). *Compre* were just another example of the banks' financial engineering abilities.

Loans to the banks' founding institutions. Banks were prohibited from making loans even to their own founding institutions, namely the charities, for whatever cause "even of maximum urgency", as we read in the charter of the Banco del Popolo (Tortora 1882, p. 232).

Loans to other banks. The regulatory system prohibited *riscontri* and prescribed that no bank should either open accounts with other banks or accept their *bancali* (Charter of Popolo, 1589, Tortora 1890, pp. 70–71; Pramm. XI and XIII *De Bancis,* June 22, 1635, and May 17, 1728 respectively, Giustiniani 1804, 3, pp. 62–63, 64–67). These acceptances in fact amounted to interbank loans. Moreover, because the lending banks' administrators considered *bancali* issued by other banks as part of their own cash reserves, they could easily overestimate their reserves. Here is an interesting example: in January 1617, the Governors of the Banco dei Poveri decided to claim back in cash only D. 4000 of their total credits towards the other public banks, and *not* to claim back the remaining D. 7414, because they thought they could recover and use this sum "at their will" at any moment (ASBN, Patrimoniale, Banco dei Poveri, *Libro delle Conclusioni,* 1616–1618, matr. 105). Thus, what the authorities tried to avoid, namely that reserves be made of paper rather than coins, was in fact a common practice, continuing in the following century (De Simone 1974, p. 56).

Loans to the Government and the City. For obvious reasons, these loans were not just exempted from prohibitions, but positively encouraged. For example, the Annunziata, followed by Spirito Santo and Popolo, was given permission in its charter to "use only one quarter" of its deposits, "and only for the operations [called] *compre*" with the Royal Court and the City of Naples, that is, to buy public debt instruments. Loans to the public institutions were also a common practice: in 1588, for instance, the recently licensed Pietà bank gave the Royal Treasury an interest-free loan of D. 5000 for one month (ASBN, Patrimoniale, Pietà, *Libro delle Conclusioni*, 1574–1593, matr. 232). However, loans to the public sector were a minor share of the banks' active operations, suggesting that they were able to keep some distance from the government.

Summing up. To its merit, the Neapolitan regulatory system was able to incorporate the novelty of the Neapolitan banks' fiduciary circulation and, so to speak, to canonise their *fedi di credito*. But it was reluctant to *formally* accept the banks' ability to create money over and above the available stock of specie. The prohibitions were so numerous that, had the banks complied, they would have been unable to operate as banks. But all regulatory systems present loopholes that regulatees are quick to exploit in their own interest. The Neapolitan system was no exception. The public banks' unstoppable *élan vital* as financial innovators, the inefficiencies of the policing system, the complacency of the public authorities and the ambiguities of baroque politics (Villari 1987) all contributed to transform them into a modern, money-creating banking system.

5 Money Creation: Criteria, Channels and Techniques

The banks' *Books of Deliberations*, sometimes called *Books of Secret Deliberations* (*Libri delle Conclusioni Segrete*) and, in the case of the Pietà bank, also the above-mentioned *Book of Accommodations*, keep the records of their governing boards' meetings, offering us a privileged observatory of their asset-management and lending policies.

The Pieta's *Book of Accommodations* deals exclusively with the Protectors' meetings devoted to deliberations about loans, and, for each loan, it reports the motivation, the typology, and the sum to be loaned. It offers the following information.

With regard to lending policies, the Protectors' main purpose was to attract the best customers to the detriment of competitors, in order to maintain the "concourse of deposits" in their banks and enlarge the scale of their business. They were also very mindful of the political and institutional status of their customers, because powerful customers could help them further the bank's interests. Consequently, they justified their generous loans to influential magistrates and other state officials, rich businessmen and cardinals with the recurring formula "because it is useful in the bank's interests" (*perché è utile in conto del banco*). Thus, while they motivated their lending policies with an ample spectrum of economic, political and, so to speak, diplomatic considerations, they never mentioned their reserves as a constraint.

On a yearly basis, the number of loans was as follows:

- 259 in 1612
- 288 in 1613
- 313 in 1614
- 306 in 1615
- 316 in 1616
- 356 in 1617

Table 2 illustrates their value and composition in each of these years.

The value of loans was around 30 per cent of the bank's total circulation in 1614, 1616 and 1617, with a peak at about 50 per cent in 1615 (data for the Pietà's circulation are missing for 1612 and 1613).

Loans were mostly granted to private individuals, with a very small share going to the government and to the City of Naples (this may be idiosyncratic to the Pietà, because the bank of S. Giacomo and Vittoria specialised in loans to the Court, and the Banco del Popolo in loans to the City).

Loans to the government were either gratuitous or onerous. The most common beneficiaries were the Royal Court, the Royal Treasury, the City of Naples and the Cassa Militare, an institution in charge of defence, war, police and public works expenditures. Loans sometimes took the form of uncovered *polizze*: on 12 June 1615, for example, the bank decided to accept a *polizza* for 507 ducats not covered by deposits in the account held by the Royal Treasury at the bank. The bank also bought government securities (assignments of tax revenues).[14]

[14]For a detailed study of public finances in Naples during this period, see Calabria 1991.

Table 2 Banco della Pietà—Value and composition of loans

a. Accomodi issued by Monte di Pietà, 1612–1617, ducats

Year	*Total*	*Gov't*	*Of which w/interest*	*Of which w/o interest*	*Private*	*Of which w/int.*	*Of which w/o int.*	*Of which "made good"*	*Of which cash credits*	*Of which other*	*Of which on pledge*
1612	131,447	0	0	0	131,447	7277	124,170	28,291	5200	82,394	8285
1613	257,534	0	0	0	257,534	107,777	149,757	17,477	18,190	107,964	6126
1614	158,959	4180		4180	154,779	55,810	98,969	13,408	12,450	67,258	5853
1615	377,744	40,570	40,000	570	337,174	189,523	147,651	24,934	5425	111,486	5806
1616	173,146	3950	0	3950	169,196	76,340	92,856	18,848	8300	57,714	7994
1617	172,165	15,041	15,000	41	157,124	114,063	43,061	4893	11,640	18,556	7972

b. Accomodi issued by Monte di Pietà, 1612–1617, as percentage of total

Year	*Total*	*Gov't*	*Of which: w/interest*	*Of which w/o interest*	*Private*	*Of which: w/int.*	*Of which w/o int.*	*Of which "made good"*	*Of which cash credits*	*Of which other*	*Of which on pledge*
1612	100.00	0	0	0	100.00	5.54	94.46	21.52	3.95	62.68	6.30
1613	100.00	0	0	0	100.00	41.85	58.15	6.79	0.76	41.92	2.38
1614	100.00	2.63	0	2.63	97.34	35.11	62.26	8.44	7.83	42.31	3.68
1615	100.00	10.74	10.59	0.15	89.26	50.17	39.08	6.6	1.43	29.51	1.53
1616	100.00	2.28	0	2.28	97.72	44.08	53.63	10.88	4.79	33.33	4.61
1617	100.00	8.74	8.71	0.02	91.26	66.25	25.06	2.84	6.76	10.77	4.63

continued

Table 2 continued

c. Total Accomodi as percentage of the circulation of Monte di Pietà

Year	*Total*
1612	–
1613	–
1614	27.98
1615	54.88
1616	31.83
1617	32.72

Legend: Gov't=Loans to Government; Private=Loans to the private sector; w/int=with interest; w/o int.=without interest

Source Historical Archive of the Bank of Naples, Patrimoniale, Pietà, ***Libro degli Accomodi*** *(27 April 1612–29 December 1617)*; Apodissario, Pietà, ***Libri Maggiori***, end-of-year balance sheets,1614–1617. Data for the bank's circulation in 1612 and 1613 are missing

Sums lent to private borrowers went from four ducats to much larger sums, in the order of the thousands and, in rare cases, the ten thousand ducats.[15] They were partly interest-bearing, partly interest-free, or gratuitous, loans.

With the exception of 1612, interest-bearing loans were a substantial and increasing share of total loans. The bank charged interest rates between 7 and 7.5 per cent, with two exceptions contemplating lower (6 per cent) or higher interest rates (8 per cent). Surprisingly, a small number of borrowers were offered to determine "in conscience" the rate they would pay.[16] Some of the onerous loans were mortgages. In many cases, but not always, the bank obtained a lien (*cautela*).

The share of gratuitous loans decreased over the years (from about 94 per cent in 1612 to 25 per cent in 1617). These loans were granted under the following headings:

(1) loans upon pledge, guaranteed by gold and silver objects; this typology was a small fraction of total loans;
(2) acceptances of *polizze* and *fedi di credito* not covered, or only partially covered, by deposits. On accepting them, the Protectors ordered that their officials must "make them good" or "write them in the bank's books", sometimes explicitly stating "although the money is not there"[17];

[15]The largest interest-free loan (forty thousand ducats) was granted in 1614 to two rich merchants, Giovan Battista and Francesco de Rinaldo, because they promised to make business with the bank at the Salerno fair next September.

[16]On 1 December 1614, the Marquis of Torrecuso ("because he will bring D. 5.000 cash into the bank"), obtained a loan of D. 50 "until Ash Wednesday and it is up to His Lordship to decide about the interest rate". On 27 October 1615, the Protectors ordered that "Mr. Giovan Battista della Marra, Duke of Macchia, be allowed to spend one thousand ducats" in excess of his credit with the bank. "As for the interest rate, this is left to the good judgment of His Lordship".

[17]Examples: (i) on 4 May 1612, the Protectors ordered that "the *polise* by *Signor* Cardinal Acquaviva be made good up to the sum of 300 Ducats"; (ii) on 4 June 1612, they accepted "the *fede di credito* written in favour of Mr. Giovan Tommaso Mastrillo on 25 May 1610, and transferred by him to Ottavio di Ragone, although the money is not there"; (iii) on 7 July 1615, the Protectors decided to make good a *polizza* of ducats 5637. *tarì* 1. *grana* 2 to the powerful Count of Mola, the Portuguese Michele Vaas, an advisor to the Viceroy, to settle an account with the Prince of Sansivierj (old Italian for Sansevero). This loan was motivated by the advantages that the Count had already brought, and may continue to bring to the bank.

(3) other interest-free loans[18];
(4) cash credits, which may be used by the customer "whenever the need may arise" (*"nell'occorrenze"*). Cash credits differed from the category recorded under point (3) above, because they were renewable or represented standing orders. They often, but not always, went to merchants.[19]

It may be worth opening a parenthesis on cash credits. Some part of the literature on banking attributes their invention to the Royal Bank of Scotland and considers that the merchant William Hog was the world's first recipient of a cash credit in May 1728.[20] But surely, Hog must leave pride of place to the merchant Stefano Rinaldo, to whom on 10 May 1612 the Pietà's Protectors granted permission to withdraw "one hundred ducats in our bank whenever the need may arise". He was followed on the 16th of the same month by *Signora Donna* Polissena Siscara, who obtained permission to withdraw up to D. 200 whenever the need may arise "because she is a punctual lady"; and then by a long series of customers.

This is not to claim that overdrafts were invented in 1612: they existed both in Naples and elsewhere in Europe long before this date. They were mentioned, for instance, in the *Book of Deliberations* of the Pietà's Protectors on 19 August 1577 and 10 March 1584 (ASBN, Patrimoniale, Pietà, *Libro delle Conclusioni*, 1574–159, matr. 232).[21] In

[18]Examples: (i) 12 June 1615: "Let Mr Ferrante della Quadra be granted a loan of D. 371 because this is useful and good in the interest of our bank"; (ii) 12 September 1614: "Because Vespasiano d'Amato brings D. 900 into our bank, let he be credited with about D. 1100"; (iii) 8 November 1616 "Let Albertino del Giudice receive a loan of D. 300, because he kept in this bank much idle money for very long time."

[19]For example: (i) "Let Livio Greco be allowed to spend up to D. 300 as he has promised to bring into our bank twelve-thousand ducats every year" (17 February 1615); (ii) "The Member of the Council Mr. Cesare Frezza may use and spend up to the sum of D. 200 whenever the need may arise, because he is a very punctual person, and usually brings useful benefits to this Holy House" (31 December 1614). Cesare Frezza was a member of the Sacro Real Consiglio, the Kingdom's supreme jurisdictional Court, with wide competence on civil and criminal issues.

[20]Checkland 1975, p. 63. See also The Royal Bank of Scotland's heritage website at: http://heritagearchives.rbs.com/rbs-history-in-100-objects/serving-our-customers/overdraft-authorisation-1728.html.

[21]In 1584, the Pietà's Protectors decided for the first time to keep a "little book" registering all their "accommodations". But we only found the *Book of Accommodations* for 1612–1617. Other similar books, if they existed, were possibly destroyed in the fire of 1786.

the rest of Europe, overdrawn accounts are found in the books of the banks of Catalonia, Venice and Germany from the fifteenth century onwards (Usher 1943, p. 333; Lane and Muller 1985, pp. 62–64; Geva 2016, p. 413). But overdrafts based on a paper circulation are of a different nature than in ledger-money systems. While an overdraft granted by, say, the Taula de Canvis in Barcelona or Banco di Rialto in Venice settled payments in the bank's books without bringing any circulating note into existence, by contrast in Naples banks made loans by creating new *fedi di credito*, thereby generating and expanding their *circulation* of *liquid* means of payment.

A short description of their lending techniques will help clarify this point.

Few days, or sometimes even just one day after the Protectors' deliberations, the bank's officials would write down the sums to be loaned on the deposit side of the borrowers' account in the Master book, adding a specific symbol to differentiate these loans from usual deposits. In the *Giornale copiapolizze*, the officials detailed the motivations for the loans, typically introduced by the formula: "and they [the Protectors] say this loan is for...". Once the loans were credited in their accounts, the borrowers could ask for and receive the corresponding *fedi di credito*, which they could then endorse to third parties. These loans would now be registered in the withdrawal side of the borrowers' accounts.

We followed several files from the deliberative stage in the *Book of Accommodations* to the loan disbursements and, beyond that, to the use to which the borrowers put their loans (often to pay for commercial transactions or sometimes for property purchases). These files consistently show that the bank made loans through the issuance of *new fedi di credito.*[22] Figure 8 reproduces one *fede di credito* issued by the Pietà as the vehicle for one of these loans.

This technique implies that, in making loans, the public banks did neither transfer money from their depositors' to their borrowers' accounts, nor did they lend out their cash reserves (the equivalent of modern "base money"), suggesting that the public banks' function was to *create* new

[22]For instance, on 15 September 1615, the Directors decided that: "Because Andrea Turturella keeps in our bank D. 2000 and also enjoys his usual accommodation of. D. 500, a *fede di credito* for D. 3000 shall be issued in his favour for the Salerno fair, because he promised to bring back the money in few days" (Pietà, *Libro degli Accomodi*, f. 103). The word "usual", also used for other customers, shows that some *accomodi* were standing orders.

money rather than *intermediate* or even *multiply* an already existing purchasing power. Moreover, it appears that their loans created deposits, because each new *fede di credito* (or *polizza* drawn upon it) would sooner or later go back to one of the public banks as a deposit. This lending technique offers interesting insights on the nature of banking activity and, specifically, on the relationships between loans, deposits and reserves, an issue still debated in the modern literature.[23]

These results antedate almost one century, to the end of the sixteenth century, the revolutionary bank practice of issuing "notes that certified the promise to provide a specified amount of precious metal or coin on presentation to the issuer, even though there had not been a previous deposit (…) [making] now possible to (…) increase the money and credit, since, in economic terms, money and credit were identical" (Siekmann 2016, p. 496).

Because these lending procedures weakened or abolished a causal link between metallic reserves and the money supply, we may conclude with Usher (1943 p. 12) that convertibility only meant that these banks were responsible for maintaining "a link between two relatively independent means of payment".

But, in the exuberant decades before the "great crisis", the public banks cared little about convertibility and hardly practised any form of prudential behaviour, unaware that the day of judgement was quickly approaching. As Fig. 3 shows, they made all active operations, whether forbidden or not, namely loans to both the private and the public sector; loans to their shareholders, the charities (in separate accounts called "our own", *nostri*, or *nostri di casa*); interbank loans; *compre*; plus, other operations like buying precious metals for coinage (Mint), discounting bills of exchange they later cashed in at trade fairs, etc. (See also the discussion in Balletta, Balletta and Nappi, Chapter 5 in this book).

When the monetary reform was announced in 1621, the banks tried to disinvest and recover as many of their loans as they could. This, again, can be read both in their *Books of Deliberations* and in their balance sheets, which show that their reserve/circulation ratio jumped to more

[23]E.g. Cannan (1921); Robertson (1926); Keynes (1930), vol. 1, Chapter 2; Schumpeter (1954), pp. 110–117; Murphy (1997), Chapter 9; Graziani (2003), Chapter 4; Goodhart (2010); McLeay et al. (2014).

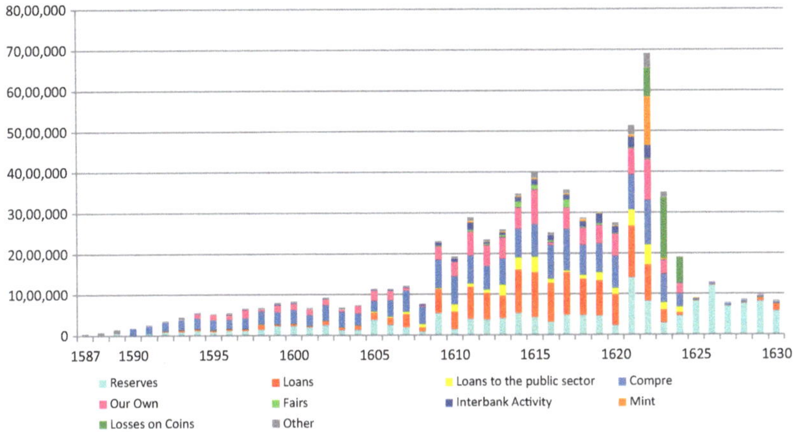

Fig. 3 All banks—Composition of circulation. 1587–1630. *Source* Historical Archive of the Bank of Naples, Apodissario, All banks, *Libri Maggiori*, end-of-year balance sheets, 1587–1630

than 27 per cent in 1621 (see also Demarco 1996, p. 259; De Rosa 1987). But that was too little and too late. They were largely overexposed when the reform finally struck in 1622.

6 Monetary Reform, Crisis and the Bank Rescue Package

6.1 *The Strange Case of the 1622 Monetary Reform*

In metal-based monetary systems, monarchs pressured by the needs of state finance debased their currencies in order to pay for the same purchases with a lower weight of silver or gold. Viceroy Zapata did the opposite: he increased the metallic content of the Neapolitan coin. Here is the evolution of the silver weight of one *carlino* (=1/10 of a ducat) (Muto 1992, p. 160):

1554 = gr. 2.991 silver
1620 = gr. 2.495
1622 = gr. 2.965

This was a very strange decision, given that the Neapolitan currency was already better than those of the Kingdom's trading partners according to several commentators. For example, already in 1587 the Camera della Sommaria (the ministry of economic and fiscal affairs) contended that the Neapolitan money flew out of the country because of its better intrinsic quality (Muto 1992, p. 162). Later, Gian Donato Turbolo, the head of the Royal Mint, repeatedly condemned the Vice-royal strong currency policy, and argued that, because Neapolitan silver and gold coins were better than those issued in other European cities, this policy hindered exports, only benefitting foreign rentiers (Turbolo 1629, pp. 304–316). Moreover, he argued, the face value of these coins did not even cover the cost of the metals imported for minting, implying an estimated loss of about D. 400,000 between 1607 and 1619 (ibid., pp. 311, 317). And, at the end of the nineteenth century, the well-respected historian Ludovico Bianchini confirmed that the Neapolitan coins "contained more silver than the corresponding Spanish coins" at the time of Philip III (1598–1621) (Bianchini 1839, pp. 352–353).

The 1622 monetary reform raised the silver weight of the *carlino* substantially, bringing it back roughly to its value in 1554, with the small difference to cover minting costs. And, although the official justification for reforming money had been the low intrinsic value of clipped and debased small change coins, all other coins were re-based in proportion (Bianchini 1839, p. 355). Because the face value of these coins was now below the market value of their silver weight, it was profitable to export or melt them. This opportunity did not escape smugglers: three months after the reform, in June, new coins were illegally exported on Genoese galleys, and two merchants, Gio. Batta Sauli and Gio. Maria Spinola, were arrested for this offence (Di Somma 1960, p. 55).

How can this unusual monetary reform be explained? We do not know. Possibly, one reason was the attempt to curb inflation, but this certainly was not the only cause. One way to get a clue about this issue is by exploring the reform's distributional consequences. All monetary reforms have winners and losers. Asking the question: *cui prodest*? may give us useful insights into this matter.

6.2 *Winners and Losers*

In this period, the pendulum of Vice-royal benevolence had swung in favour of the powerful "Genoese nation" again. In 1621, at the meeting of the Money Committee (*Giunta della Moneta*) established by Viceroy Zapata to discuss the lines of the coming reform, the Genoese consul Cornelio Spinola singled out (what he regarded as) the two causes of the Kingdom's economic and monetary problems: the bad quality of its currency and the public banks' operations. In a nutshell, the Genoese consul demanded that the authorities:

1. restrict "in-bank" payments as much as possible;
2. raise the intrinsic value of Neapolitan coins.

These proposals are not difficult to interpret: the Genoese businessmen demanded that their profits and rents be paid in metal coins rather than paper; and in a hard, not debased currency, because this meant higher purchasing power back home in Genoa and elsewhere in the Empire.

While Spinola wanted the burden of the reform to fall on nationals, by contrast the Neapolitan delegates, Ascanio Carafa, Geronimo Naccarella and Gian Tommaso Borrello (Protector of the Pietà bank) argued that the main burden should fall on the Genoese and on all other foreigners earning rents in the Kingdom. But they were too weak to reject the reform entirely (Colapietra 1973, pp. 40–41).

The Genoese nation had it its way eventually. On 2 March 1622, Viceroy Zapata introduced his monetary reform. It was almost a mortal blow for the public banks.

The edict (*Pramm. XX De Monetis*, Giustiniani, 7, pp. 275–280) prohibited the circulation in Naples of all bad coins of small denomination: *tre cinquine* and *zannette*, the latter also called *mezzi carlini* (*half carlini*). These debased coins must be substituted for by new coins, heavier in weight and better in alloy, some of which had already been minted. The banks' reserves of metal coins should be brought to the Royal Mint for re-coinage. The Vice-royal edict ruled that henceforth all economic actors (private individuals, banks and Royal institutions such as the Cassa Militare) should accept and pay out coins in weight and not "in number". The banks' cashiers were personally responsible under penalty of corporal punishments. Moreover, henceforth bills of exchange should be paid in new or in Spanish coins, while bank money was prohibited for that purpose. Jewellers could not use the precious metals without declaring their provenance and quantity in advance. The edict fixed bilateral exchange rates with all foreign coins. Finally, because a scarcity of cash was expected in the interval before new money was coined, a *moratorium* was introduced, meaning that debtors should not be "bothered" by creditors for 40 days at least in Naples and surrounding areas and 60 days elsewhere in the Kingdom.

Under threat of a run by their customers, the public banks closed for two days (2 and 3 March 1622), but the Viceroy ordered them to reopen immediately. On the other hand, he also ordered that creditors could only claim back 2/3 of their credits, and only in small daily amounts (D. 5 per day).

The Viceroy's "2/3 solution" was based on his calculation that the new circulation would reach the value of six million as the sum of: coins already minted, plus those to be minted out of the remaining 1/3 of bank reserves; some private holdings of old coins; coinage of silver bullion for the value of 3 million ducats expected from abroad. These calculations, however, soon proved to be wrong, for two reasons: firstly, bullion never arrived from abroad; secondly, the banks' reserves were well below their estimated value. Consequently, only 1.5 million ducats were minted of the planned 6 million, imposing a deflationary pressure on the Kingdom.

The banks knew they only had scarce reserves owing to their imprudent policies in the previous years. When, on 7 July 1622, the Viceroy's delegate Scipione Rovito ordered that they bring their reserves of old and foreign coins to the Royal Mint, their budget shortfalls were revealed. And the value of their reserves was further eroded by the reform itself, because the Mint accepted their coins by weight rather than tale. Further distributional issues arose, as depositors and other creditors wanted to be paid in the new, better coins, while the banks argued that having originally accepted deposits in the old coins they could not bear that burden. It was a dramatic situation for the public banks. Contemporary chronicles even reported rumours that they would be abolished (Palermo 1846, p. 295).

As their losses (estimated at D. 4,400,000) were swelling up, it was time for the government to come to their rescue.

6.3 *Too Big to Fail. A Blueprint for Crisis Resolution*

The authorities gradually realised that they had gone too far, as the banks' crisis was putting the stability of the whole financial system at risk. In modern language, they recognised the banks as too big to fail, and introduced a package of bail-in and bail-out measures designed for their survival. It was now their turn to show their financial innovativeness.

Bail-in measures were gradually incorporated in two edicts "on banks", issued respectively in November 1622 and April 1623. Both, and especially the second, ordered that a large share of the banks' debts be written-off at the expenses of their creditors.

As for bail-outs, an edict imposed a tax on all foreigners' rents, with the explicit purpose of rebalancing the burden of the monetary reform (Colapietra 1973, p. 44n.). Another edict in 1623 established a new tax on wine, of D. 1 per *botte* (=5232 litres).[24] The annual revenue capitalised at 6 per cent amounted to D. 773.871 capital. The banks used their shares of this capital to pay back two-thirds of their debts as required.

The authorities also experimented with a sort of nationalisation, or rather municipalisation, of one of the failing banks: Banco del Popolo was brought under municipal control and lost administrative autonomy until it returned under the Incurabili Hospital in 1636 (Filangieri 1940, p. 57).

All these measures did not save the public banks from a deep, prolonged crisis that was still on at the end of the 1620s. Only in 1628, one of them, the Pietà, had another innovative idea: to have its time-honoured, if illegal, practice of lending at interest legalised. The Viceroy formally agreed. All other banks followed suit, and their activities started to flourish again in the following decades.

7 Conclusions

We traced the genesis of modern banking to the invention of *fede di credito*, a new form of money that revolutionised both passive and active banking operations, an epochal step in the movement away from metal-based monetary systems. This genetic episode is instructive for both the history and theory of money and banking.

Historically, the Neapolitan public banks' multiple innovations, from their circulating note to cash credits, relaxed the liquidity constraint biting on the Kingdom's economic activity at a time when, like a leaking bucket, the country was forced to send abroad whatever amount of silver it coined in payment for profits, rents, taxes and "donations", with Gresham law adding to the plight of money outflows. But financial

[24]With the edict being re-issued in 1627 and 1658, the tax on wine was still in existence almost half a century later!

innovation, if not corrected by prudential behaviour, may be a mixed blessing, as economic theory has taught us ever since Adam Smith introduced his creative image of "the Daedelian wings of credit". Bank overexpansion, an endogenous factor of instability, coupled with the exogenous shock of monetary reform in 1622, determined a very deep, long banking crisis. Only the government's impressive bank-rescue package, together with new financial innovation, brought the public banks back on a growth path that, with ups and downs, would continue in the next two centuries until they merged in the Bank of the Two Sicilies, continued in the Bank of Naples after Italy's unification in 1861.

The Neapolitan public banks' experience also sheds light on some theoretical issues still debated by monetary theorists today. What do banks do? Do they substitute one type of money for another? Do they transfer money from lenders to borrowers? Do they "lend out" their reserves of base money, perhaps with multiplicative powers? Or do they *create* money through lending instead? The experience of the public banks of Naples, and especially their lending techniques, offer at least a tentative answer. These banks created new *liquidity* in the form of *fedi di credito* and thus released their money supply from the constraints of both base money and depositors' savings.

If a modern bank is defined by its ability to create money by issuing liquid means of payment, then we may locate in Naples the origins of modern banking.

References

Anonymous. 1750. *Regole e capitoli antichi e nuovi per lo regolamento della Congregazione del Sacro Monte e banco dei Poveri del SS. Nome di Dio*. Napoli: De Simone.

Avallone, Paola. 1997. Public Banks in Southern Italy. In *Banking, Trade and Industry. Europe, America and Asia from the Thirteenth to the Twentieth Century*, ed. Teichova et al., 50–68. Cambridge: Cambridge University Press.

Balletta, Francesco. 2008. *La circolazione della moneta fiduciaria a Napoli nel Seicento e nel Settecento (1587–1805)*. Napoli: Edizioni Scientifiche Italiane.

Bianchini, Ludovico. 1839. *Della storia delle finanze del Regno di Napoli*. Palermo: Stamperia di Francesco Lao.

Calabria, Antonio. 1991. *The Cost of Empire: The Finances of the Kingdom of Naples in the Time of Spanish Rule*. Cambridge: Cambridge University Press.

Cannan, Edwin. 1921. The Meaning of Bank Deposits. *Economica* 1: 28–36.

Checkland, S.G. 1975. *Scottish Banking. A History.* Glasgow and London: Collins.

Colapietra, Raffaele. 1973. Introduzione in Id. *Problemi monetari negli scrittori napoletani del Seicento.* Rome: Accademia Nazionale dei Lincei.

Costabile, Lilia. 2015. Monetary Analysis, Financial Innovation, and Institutions Before the Industrial Revolution: A Paradigm Case. In *Resources, Production and Structural Dynamics*, ed. Baranzini et al., 213–231. Cambridge: Cambridge University Press.

Costabile, L. 2016a. External Imbalances and the Money Supply. Two Controversies in the English 'Realme' and in the Kingdom of Naples. In *Antonio Serra and the Economics of Good Government*, ed. R. Patalano and S. Reinert, 166–190. London: Palgrave Macmillan.

Costabile, L. 2016b. The Value and Security of Money. Metallic and Fiduciary Media in Ferdinando Galiani's *Della Moneta. European Journal of the History of Economic Thought* 23 (3): 400–424. http://dx.doi.org/10.1080/09672567.2014.916730.

Dauverd, Céline. 2015. *Imperial Ambition in the Early Modern Mediterranean. Genoese Merchants and the Spanish Crown.* Cambridge: Cambridge University Press.

Demarco, Domenico. 1996. *Il Banco di Napoli. Dalle Casse di deposito alla fioritura Settecentesca.* Napoli: Edizioni Scientifiche Italiane.

Demarco, Domenico, and Eduardo Nappi. 1985. Nuovi documenti sulle origini del Banco di Napoli. *Revue Internationale d'Histoire de la Banque*, Librairie Droz, Genève, 30–31, 1–78.

De Rosa, Luigi. 1955. *I cambi esteri del Regno di Napoli dal 1591 al 1707.* Napoli: Banco di Napoli, Biblioteca del "Bollettino dell'Archivio Storico".

De Rosa, L. 1987. Il Banco dei Poveri e la crisi del 1622. Chapter VI in Id., *Il Mezzogiorno Spagnolo tra crescita e decadenza*, 128–165. Milano: Mondadori.

De Rosa, L. 2004. L'Archivio del Banco di Napoli e l'attività dei Banchi Pubblici Napoletani. *Revista Espanola de Historia de la Contabilidad* 1 (December): 55–66.

De Roover, Raymond A. 1953. *L'evolution de la lettre de change, XIVe -XVIII ^{e} siècles.* Paris: Armand Colin.

De Simone, Ennio. 1974. *Il banco della Pietà di Napoli. 1734–1806.* Napoli: Institut International d'Historire de la Banque.

Di Somma, Carlo. 1960. Il Banco dello Spirito Santo dalle origini al 1664. *Università degli Studi di Napoli, Biblioteca degli Annali dell'Istituto di Storia Economica e Sociale*, n. 2.

Felloni, Giuseppe. 2010. 1407. La fondazione del banco di S.Giorgio in AA.VV. *Gli anni di Genova*, Giuseppe Laterza e figli (edizione digitale, giugno 2015).

Filangieri, Riccardo. 1940. *I banchi di Napoli dalle origini alla costituzione del Banco delle Due Sicilie (1539–1808).* Napoli: Banco di Napoli.

Flandreau, Marc, Galimard, Christophe, Jobst, Clemens, and Pilar Nogués-Marco. 2009. Monetary Geography Before the Industrial Revolution. *Cambridge Journal of Regions, Economy and Society* 2 (2) (July): 149–171.

Fox, David, and Wolfgang Ernst. 2016. *Money in the Western Legal Tradition. Middle Ages to Bretton-Woods*. Oxford: Oxford University Press.

Galiani, Ferdinando. 1750 [but 1751]. *Della moneta. Libri Cinque*. Napoli: Giuseppe Raimondi.

Geva, Benjamin. 2016. 'Bank Money': The Rise, Fall, and Metamorphosis of the 'Transferable Deposit'. In *Money in the Western Legal Tradition. Middle Ages to Bretton Woods*, ed. Fox and Ernst, 359–386.

Giustiniani, Lorenzo. 1804. *Nuova Collezione delle Prammatiche del Regno di Napoli*, t. 8, Napoli, Stamperia Simoniana.

Goodhart, Charles. 2010. Money, Credit and Bank Behaviour: Need for a New Approach. *National Institute Economic Review* 214 (1): F73–F82.

Graziani, Augusto. 2003. *The Monetary Theory of Production*. Cambridge: Cambridge University Press.

Kane, Edward J. 1988. Interaction of Financial and Regulatory Innovation. *American Economic Review* 78 (2): 328–334. *Papers and Proceedings*.

Keynes, John M. 1930. *A Treatise on Money, Vol. 1: The Pure Theory of Money*, as reprinted in *The Collected Works of John Maynard Keynes, Vol. 5*. London: Macmillan, St. Martins Press for the Royal Economic Society, 1978.

Lane, Frederic C., and Reinhold C. Mueller. 1985. *Money and Banking in Medieval and Renaissance Venice, Vol. 1, Coins and Moneys of Account*. Baltimore: Johns Hopkins University Press.

Luzzatto, Giuseppe. 1934. Les banques publiques de Venise (siècles XVI-XVIII). In *History of the Principal Public Banks*, ed. Van Dillen, 39–78. Dordrecht: Nijoff.

McLeay, M., Radia A., and Thomas R. 2014. Money Creation in the Modern Economy. *Bank of England Quartely Bulletin* 54 (1): 14–27.

Murphy, Antoin E. 1997. *John Law. Economic Theorist and Policy-Maker*. Oxford: Clarendon Press.

Muto, Giovanni. 1992. *Saggi sul governo dell'economia nel Mezzogiorno Spagnolo*. Napoli: Edizioni Scientifiche Italiane.

Neal, Larry. 1990. *The Rise of Financial Capitalism. International Capital Markets in the Age of Reason*. Cambridge: Cambridge University Press.

Palermo, Francesco (ed.). 1846. *Narrazioni e Documenti su la Storia del regno di Napoli dall'anno 1552 al 1667* raccolti e ordinati da F. Palermo, Firenze, Vieusseux.

Roberds, William, and François R. Velde. 2016. Chapter 17: "Early Public Banks, I: Ledger-Money Banks"; Chapter 22: "Early Public Banks II: Banks of Issue". In *Money in the Western Legal Tradition*, ed. Fox and Ernst, 321–355, 465–488.

Robertson, Dennis H. 1926. *Banking Policy and the Price Level.* London: P.S. King and Son.

Rocco, Michele. 1787. *De' banchi di Napoli e della loro ragione*, Vol. I - II- III, Napoli: Presso i fratelli Raimondi.

Schwartz, Anna. 1986. Real and Pseudo-Financial Crises. In *Financial Crises and the World Banking System*, ed. F. Capie and E.G. Wood, 11–31. New York: Macmillan.

Siekmann, Helmut. 2016. Deposit Banking and the Use of Monetary Instruments. In *Money in the western Legal Tradition*, ed. Fox and Ernst, 489–531.

Silvestri, A. 1952. Sui banchieri pubblici della città di Napoli dalla costituzione del monopolio alla fine dei banchi dei mercanti. *Bollettino dell'archivio storico del Banco di Napoli* 1: 1–4, Napoli.

Silvestri, A. 1953. Sull'attività bancaria napoletana nel periodo aragonese. *Bollettino dell'archivio storico del Banco di Napoli*, 6, Napoli.

Schumpeter, Joseph A. 1954. *History of Economic Analysis.* London: George Allen & Unwin.

Tortora, Eugenio. 1882. *Raccolta di documenti storici e delle leggi e regole concernenti il Banco di Napoli.* Napoli, Stabilimento Tipografico del cav. Giannini.

Tortora, E. 1890. *Nuovi documenti per la storia del Banco di Napoli.* Napoli, A. Bellisario e C.- R. Tipografia De Angelis.

Turbolo, Gian Donato. 1629. *Discorso sopra le monete del Regno di Napoli*, as reprinted in Colapietra, 1973, 298–376.

Usher, Abbot Payson. 1943. *The Early History of Deposit Banking in Mediterranean Europe, Vol. 1. Part. I. The Structure and Functions of the Early Credit System. Part II. Banking in Catalonia*, 1240–1723. New York: Russel & Russel.

Van Dillen, Johannes Gerard. 1934. The Bank of Amsterdam in Id. (ed.), *History of the Principal Public Banks*, 79–123. Dordrecht: Nijoff.

Varius, Domenico Alfeno. 1772. *Pragmaticae Edictae, Decreta, Interdicta Regiaeque Sanctiones Regni Neapolitani*, vols. 2 and 4. Napoli: Cervoni.

Vicinanza, Monica (ed.). 2006. *Napoli: Petruccio Pisano 1462–1466.* Athena: Acerra.

Villari, Rosario. 1987. *Elogio della dissimulazione. La lotta politica nel Seicento.* Roma-Bari: Laterza.

Villari, R. 2012. *Un sogno di libertà. Napoli nel declino di un impero. 1585–1648.* Milano: Mondadori.

Vitolo, Giovanni, and Rosalba Di Meglio. 2003. *Napoli Angioino-Aragonese. Confraternite, ospedali, dinamiche politico-sociali.* Salerno: Carlone editore.

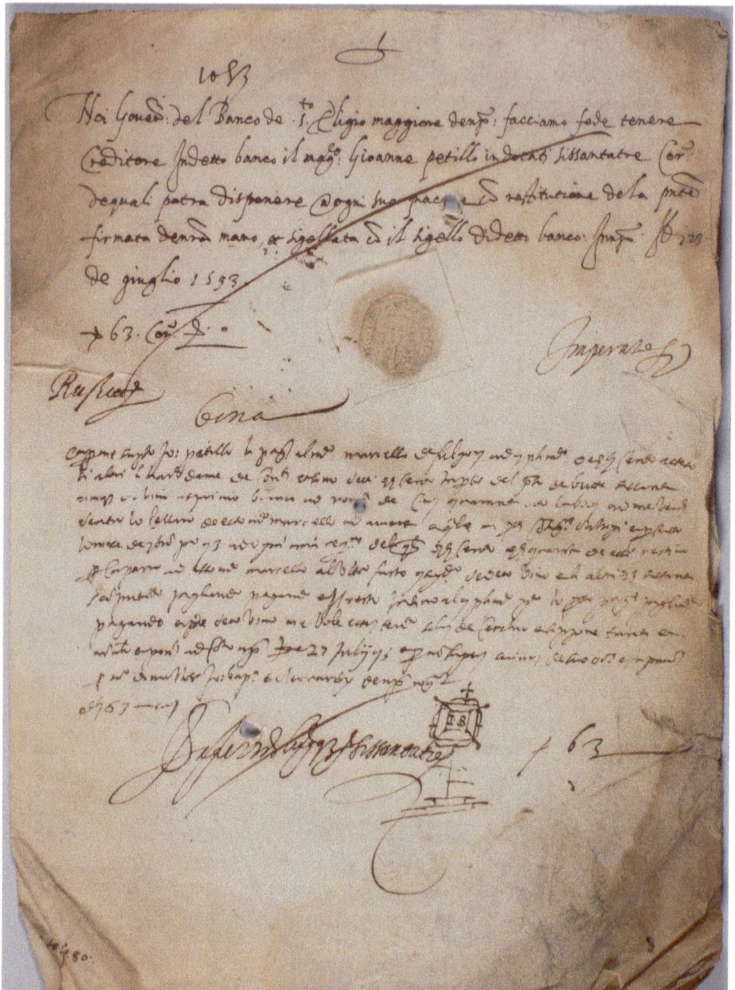

Fig. 4 Banco di S. Eligio. *Fede di credito* issued on June 23, 1593 to Giovanni Petillo. "We the Governors of the Bank of St Eligio certify that the Magnificent Giovanni Petillo is creditor in our bank for 63 ducats, which he will be able to dispose of at his will on restitution of the present *fede*, signed by his hand and sealed with the seal of the above said bank. Signed on 23 June 1593." Mr. Petillo transfers the sum to Marcello de Fulgure towards a total of 100 ducats as a down payment for 70.5 barrels of white wine *asprinio* sold from his cellars

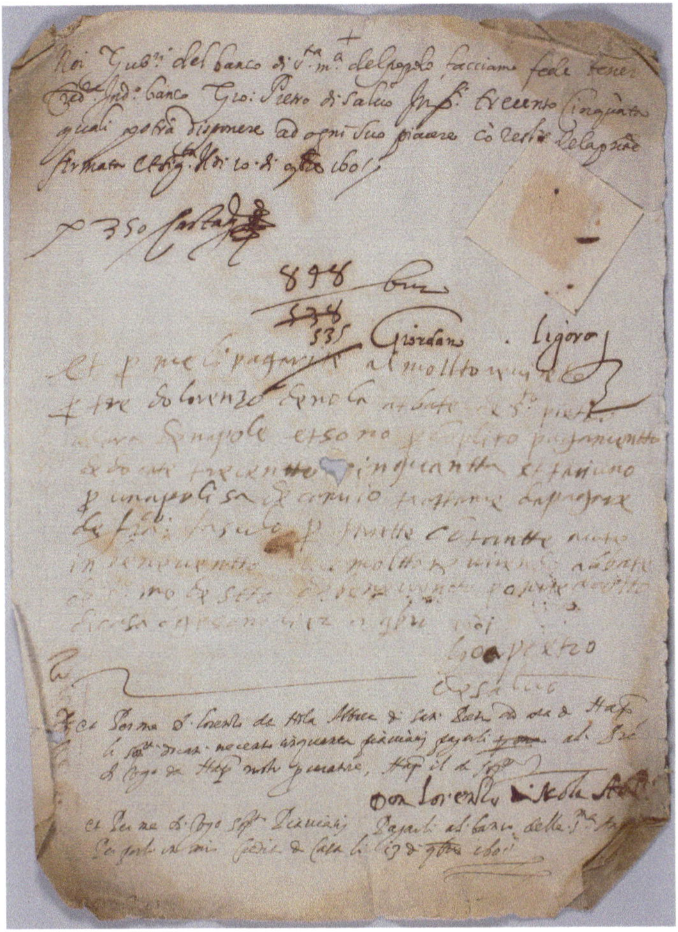

Fig. 5 Banco del Popolo. *Fede di credito* issued on November 10, 1601. "We the Governors of the bank of Santa Maria del Popolo certify that Giovanni Pietro di Salvo is creditor in our bank for 350 ducats that he will be able to dispose of at his will on restitution of the present [*fede*], signed and sealed". Giovanni Pietro di Salvo asks the bank to transfer the sum to Lorenzo da Nola, the Abbot of the monastery of S. Pietro ad Aram, and explains that he received the sum via a bill of exchange from Francesco Fasulo on behalf of the Abbot of Santo Modesto di Benevento, as part of a total payment of 350 ducats and one *tarì*. Father Lorenzo transfers the sum to Father Ugo da Napoli, the Abbey's attorney, who finally deposits the *fede* in his own account at the Banco dell'Annunziata

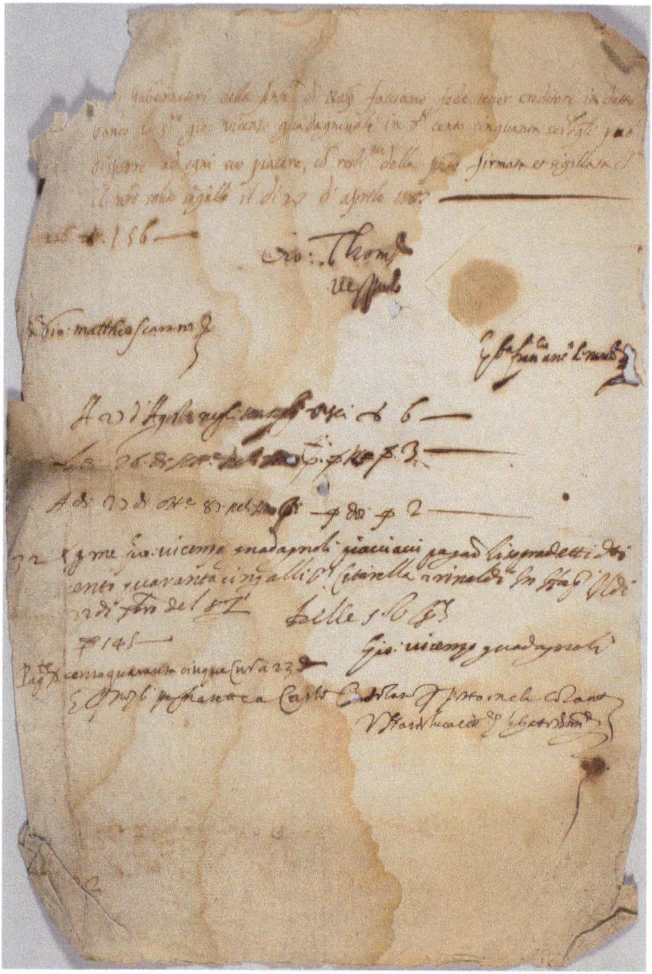

Fig. 6 Banco dell'Annunziata. *Fede di credito* issued on 20 April, 1587 in favour of Giovanni Vincenzo Guadagnoli. The Governors of the Bank certify that Mr. Guadagnoli is creditor in their bank for 156 ducats, of which he will be able to dispose at his will on restitution of the *fede*, signed and sealed. Guadagnoli later issued three payment orders: for 6 ducats on 27 August, for 3 ducats on 26 September, and for 2 ducats on 27 October. The *fede di credito* was now called a *madrefede* because it registered these payment orders. On 22 December of the same year, Guadagnoli transferred the remaining 145 ducats to two gentlemen, Citarella and Grimaldi, the owners of a private bank

(a)

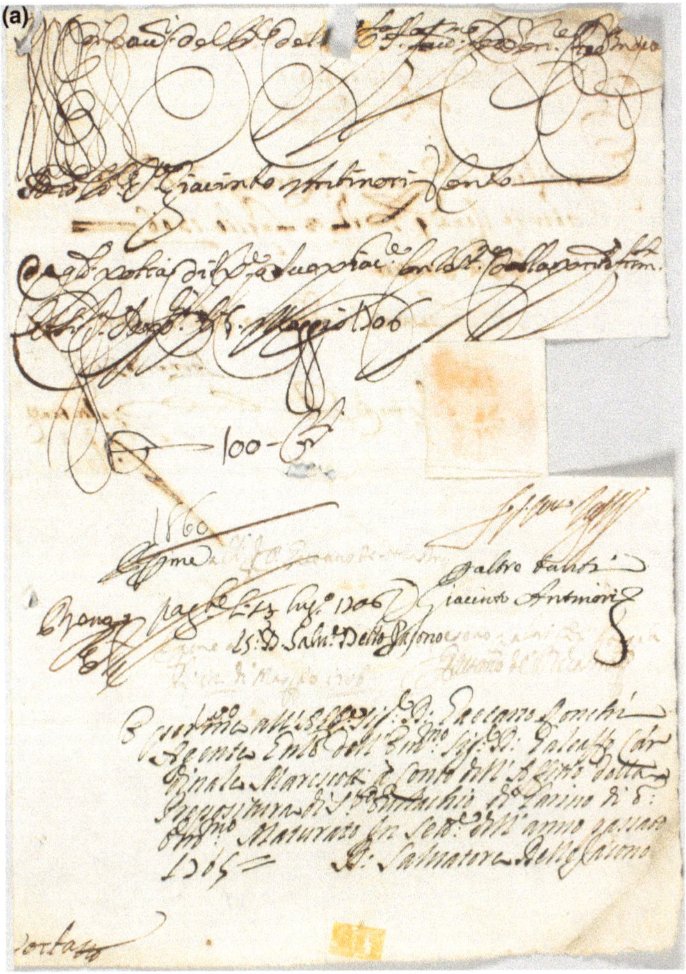

Fig. 7 Banco dello Spirito Santo. *Fede di credito* for 100 ducats released on May 5, 1706 to Giacinto Antinori, who transferred it to Gaetano De Nicastro on May 12, 1706. De Nicastro then transferred the entire sum to Salvatore dello Jacono who passed it on to Gaetano Ronchi, who was Cardinal Marescotti's agent. On 29 June, Ronchi transferred the sum to the Cardinal, who in turn transferred the 100 ducats to Leonardo Libri in Rome on 3 July. Leonardo Libri finally transferred the sum to Domenico Perrelli. The *fede di credito* was finally brought back to the Bank of the Spirito Santo and extinguished on 14 July 1706

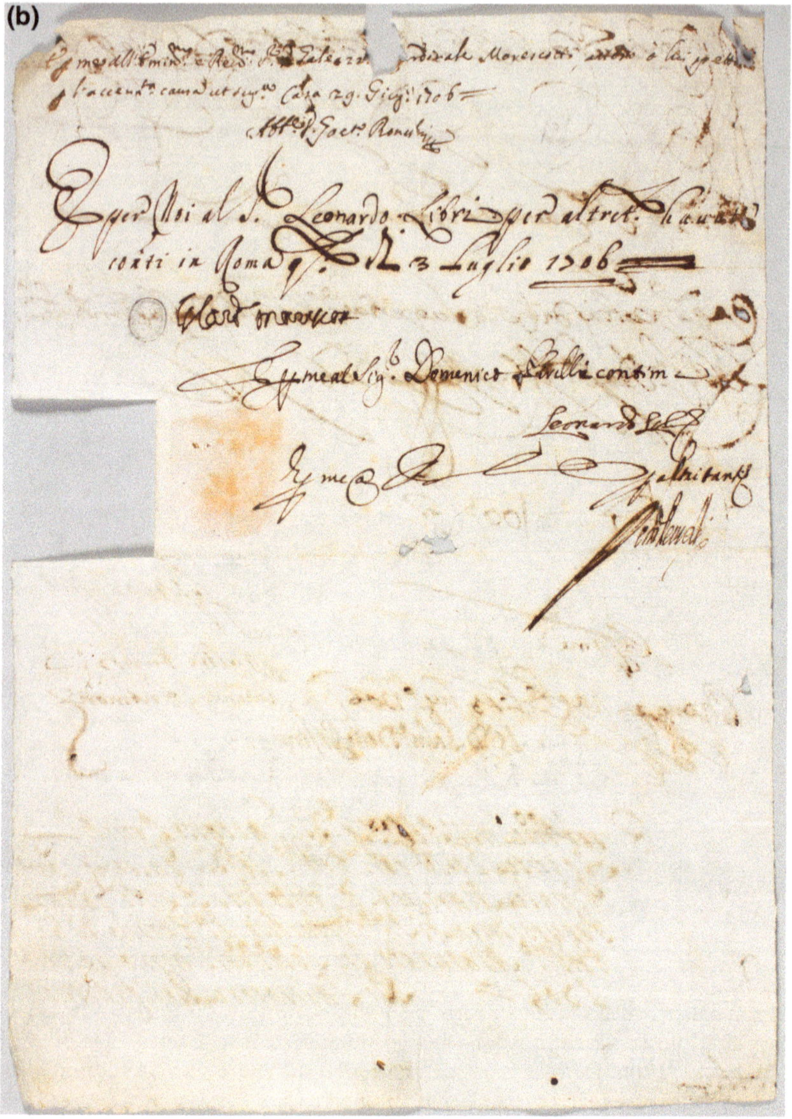

Fig. 7 (continued)

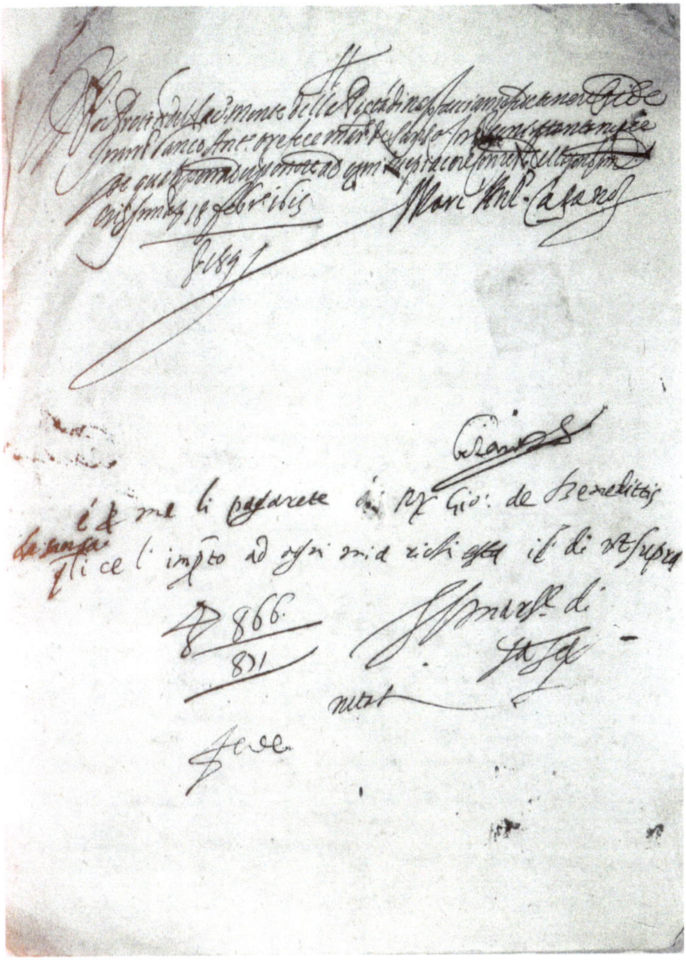

Fig. 8 Banco della Pietà. *Fede di credito* released on February 18, 1615 to Antonio Orefice, Marquis of Sansa. "We, the Protectors of the Monte della Pietà of Naples certify that Antonio Orefice, Marquis of Sansa, is our creditor for 189 ducats, which he shall be able to dispose of at his will on restitution of the present [*fede*] signed and sealed". The day before, the Board of Protectors of the Pietà had deliberated this loan to the Marquis, and had their deliberation registered in the bank's *Book of Accommodations* (*Libro degli Accomodi*). The Marquis's account at the bank was accordingly credited with the sum, and the Marquis promptly transferred the sum to Giovanni De Benedictis di Sansa

CHAPTER 3

Before the Public Banks: Innovation and Resilience by Charities in Fifteenth-Century Naples

Rosalba Di Meglio

1 Introduction

The Middle Ages, as is well known, is the age when the religious dimension was closely intertwined with all the other aspects of public and private life, implying that the distinction between the political-administrative organisms and the ecclesiastical institutions we are accustomed with today has very little correspondence with the medieval reality. Thus, welfare services, now considered to be the main task of national government and local administrations, were carried out then as well, and sometimes mainly, by churches, monasteries, confraternities and cathedral chapters. Charitable activities were not conceived of as a simple, provisional work of substitution for political power, but as an *opus pietatis*, that is to say, a duty of the Christian. The church exercised charity either directly, through the institutions that it created and

R. Di Meglio (✉)
Dipartimento di Studi umanistici,
Università di Napoli Federico II, Naples, Italy
e-mail: rosalba.dimeglio@unina.it

L. Costabile and L. Neal (eds.), *Financial Innovation and Resilience*, Palgrave Studies in the History of Finance,
https://doi.org/10.1007/978-3-319-90248-7_3

managed, or indirectly, by channelling in this direction and supporting the activity of the laity, who obviously were led to think of their charitable work as a religious obligation.

During the last centuries of the Middle Ages, imbued like the previous centuries with strongly felt religious ideals, the crisis of the fourteenth century, in addition to triggering a series of economic processes that had positive repercussions on society (Epstein 2006), had a great influence on the ideological level. The crisis forced a series of resilient and innovative responses by individuals and groups towards their charitable efforts. It was then that an "ideology of charity" developed that involved men and women of all social categories: artisans, merchants, nobles, feudal lords and monarchs. Among charitable works, great importance was attached to founding and supporting hospitals. At the time they provided a range of free services that went far beyond the purely curative sphere, which was the least important aspect and sometimes inexistent: care for abandoned children, lonely old people, widows, orphaned girls without dowries, pilgrims, the poor and the needy, for whom hospitals offered shelter, accommodation, alms in the form of food and clothing, care and certainties for the future of young children (Albini 1993, 1997, 2002, 2016; Piccinni and Vigni 1989; Piccinni 2008, 2012). Hospitals thus became "charitable companies," places where faith became concrete by good works. On the one hand, the rich found the incentive to give, and in many cases give of themselves through the act of oblation, a term that refers to the idea of offering oneself and one's property to the institution, putting oneself at its service. On the other hand, the poor found practical help to cope with the precarious nature of their existence. In the case of hospitals, charity ended up taking on a twofold nature and became exponential: the hospital, which received secular help through bequests and donations, also performed charitable works by providing assistance to the poor and outcasts (Piccinni 2012).

2 Two Neapolitan "Charitable Companies": The Hospitals of S. Eligio and SS. Annunziata

Two Neapolitan hospitals provide examples of "charitable companies." Founded fifty years apart with aims that were not completely identical, their histories ran parallel to each other and at one point intertwined so that they shed light on each other's roles in many ways (Vitolo 2003, 2016). This is particularly significant in the case of the hospital of S. Eligio al Mercato, whose archive has been almost completely lost, while, with the unfortunate exception of the fourteenth and fifteenth century, the archive of the hospital of SS. Annunziata is largely intact (Mauri Mori 1967, 1969; Marino 2015). Giovanni Vitolo, who deserves recognition for paving the way for a new phase of research on Neapolitan hospitals and religious life in the city in general, inspiring recent work by young scholars (Vitolo and Di Meglio 2003; Marino 2015; Vitolo et al. 2016), has managed to set the two foundations within the political, economic and social context of Angevin Naples. As the first real capital city in a modern sense, Angevin Naples witnessed a period of rapid growth, which had already been underway during the Swabian period. Indeed, the colonies of foreign merchants operating in the area of present-day Piazza Mercato are a clear reflection of this process (Vitolo 2003).

They included a colony of French merchants who in 1270 founded the confraternity and hospital of S. Eligio, initially for the benefit of their fellow nationals, but very soon afterwards for all those who lived in an area that was to become the main commercial and productive centre of the city. By contrast, the foundation of the confraternity-hospital of SS. Annunziata was a wholly Neapolitan initiative and had a slightly different social function. It was set up in 1318 by members of the royal court and families of the *Seggio* (Seat) of Capuana, but soon came to resemble the confraternity-hospital of S. Eligio both in terms of activities and organisation, as well as, and above all, in terms of the social background and relations with political and religious power (Imperato 1629; D'Addosio 1883; De Maio 1973; Vitolo and Di Meglio 2003; Marino 2004).

The most important finding of Vitolo's work regards the identification of the governance of the two hospitals which, like the large contemporary hospital complexes in other main Italian cities such as Siena (Piccinni 2012), Milan (Albini 1993) and Messina (Santoro 2016), was formed by members of the merchant and business class, as well as members of the professions and the royal bureaucracy. In general, the administrators, known as masters and governors, were four or five (rarely nine), of whom one was designated by a noble *seggio* (seat), usually the noble seat responsible for the territory, the others by certain sections (*ottine*) of the *seggio del Popolo*.[1] There were five administrators at the Annunziata,

[1]The *seggi* were clan-organisations of the society on a territorial basis, namely each seat had influence on a district of the city. There were five noble *seggi* in the second half of fourteenth century in Naples: Capuana, Nido, Montagna, Porto and Portanuova. Who was not part of the noble *seggi*, constituted the *seggio del Popolo*, that is, a vast aggregation that, divided into territorial districts called *ottine* (twenty at the beginning of the fifteenth century, then became twenty-nine during the century), included the rest of the population.

of which, as early as 1339, one was from the *seggio* of Capuana and four were from the *seggio del Popolo*, which shows how it was the exponents of the working classes who had the professional skills to make it work. The nobles of the *seggio* of Capuana had more than anything else only the role of representation. However, there were guarantee mechanisms that provided, for example, in the case of the Annunziata, the rule according to which for the validity of the decisions, a majority of at least three members out of five was necessary, including the representative of the *seggio* of Capuana, so that the four of the Popolo alone were not enough to make a majority (Imperato 1629; Muto 1982, 1983). By comparing the lists of the grand masters and governors of the Annunziata and S. Eligio, Vitolo also managed to show how, by gaining respect for their management capacities, they passed from one hospital to another on more than one occasion, contributing in all likelihood to the uniformity of their organisation (Vitolo 2016). This clearly does not imply that the huge gaps in the records for S. Eligio can be filled by automatically applying the information from the sources related to the hospital of SS. Annunziata. However, in a broad sense and by proceeding with due caution, it is possible to identify several elements they had in common, which can be summarised as follows.

1. Secular confraternities in new settlements outside the city walls founded both.
2. They both established privileged ties with the monarchy, albeit for different reasons. S. Eligio's ties existed from its very foundation, having obtained the land from Charles of Anjou who was particularly sensitive, as was only natural, to requests from his fellow Frenchmen; SS. Annunziata's ties were due to the fact that it was situated in an area held in particular regard by Queen Sancia as part of her initiatives designed to combat prostitution.[2]
3. The association with the monarchy naturally conferred immediate prestige on the new foundations and thus attracted the attention of the aristocracy, the city and other parts of the kingdom. A steady

[2]The church of SS. Annunziata was built during the reign of Robert of Anjou and orders were given on 15 December 1318 to expropriate a vegetable garden belonging to Tommaso Coppola for this purpose. The church received many donations, thanks to the intervention of Queen Margaret of Durazzo who, on 21 October 1404, donated three

flow of donations ensued which led to the creation of considerable property assets that also included many feudal properties (Gambini de Vera d'Aragona 2013).

4. One unexpected consequence, but which is particularly significant for appreciating the capital's significance as a reference point for the entire kingdom, was the imitation process set in motion by the two Neapolitan institutions. Hospitals named S. Eligio and Annunziata sprang up in various other cities, sometimes as a direct result of the wishes of Angevin rulers (Vitolo 2003; Marino 2004).

plots of land next to the church of SS. Annunziata: one for the construction of the sacristy, one to create a garden and, lastly, another plot of unbuildable land to keep the church separate from surrounding residential buildings. Queen Margaret, furthermore, after being cured of a serious illness, donated the town of Lesina and its lagoon on 6 November 1411. On 5 May 1417, her daughter, Queen Joanna II, also granted the church and hospital of SS. Annunziata all the rights under her jurisdiction regarding the church of Maddalena and two dilapidated hospitals at Sudatorio in Agnano, with the obligation of restoring them to look after the poor who came there for spa treatment; on 2 April 1418, she also commissioned Urbano Cimmino to buy numerous houses situated in Naples, in *rua Novella* and *rua Francesca* and at *Foro Magno*, in order to donate them to the church of SS. Annunziata, so that the incomes deriving from them could be used for the dowries of unmarried girls who were guests of the Santa Casa. On 15 July 1420, Joanna donated the fiefs of Vignola, Massafra and Fasanella. On 25 April 1423, she donated an inn at Pendino di S. Agostino in Naples. On 2 September 1424, she donated the area of the Lavinaio in Naples and in 1433, she laid the foundations of the new hospital of SS. Annunziata whose construction had become necessary because the original building was no longer sufficient for hospital requirements and for providing welfare and treatment. On 8 June 1426, she donated another inn to the institution; on 20 April 1429, she donated a plot of land in Pozzuoli and many houses in *rua Catalana* in Naples, as well as two plots of land in Somma Vesuviana. One of the plots situated at the so-called Old Market (*Mercato Vecchio*) was purchased and donated by the queen to the Santa Casa with the undertaking to make an annual consignment of 60 *tomola* of wheat (a *tomolo* was a unit of measurement that corresponded to about 55 litres) to the monks of S. Francesco a Salerno, who had to celebrate mass for the soul of her mother Queen Margaret. In 1423, Joanna granted the privilege of discretionary management with royal consent so that the Santa Casa could keep, own and accept feudal lands. Lastly, in 1424, she granted tax exemption to the director of works for the complex of the Santa Casa (Gaglione 2009). There is far less information about the hospital of S. Eligio: besides being granted land for building work in 1270 by Charles I of Anjou and an income of 7 gold ounces (*once*) per annum the following year, we know of a donation of land made in 1279 by the same monarch for extension work to be done on the institution. Further extension work is recorded in 1304 when the hospital of S. Eligio was amalgamated with the hospice for the war wounded founded by Charles II who, in 1305, also donated 30 *once* for the work (Vitolo 2003; Gaglione 2009).

5. The fame of the two Neapolitan hospitals also spread because both were authorised to collect alms throughout the kingdom: the collecting of alms represented one of their sources of funding, which was authorised through an official tendering procedure.

Both hospitals were given permission to set up two public banks in the late sixteenth century: SS. Annunziata in 1587 and S. Eligio in 1592 (for the bibliography on this subject, see the papers in this book, especially Chapter 2 by Costabile and Nappi, Chapter 4 by Avallone and Salvemini and Chapter 5 by F. Balletta, L. Balletta and E. Nappi). However, research by Alfonso Silvestri (1953), Domenico Demarco and Eduardo Nappi (1985), recently confirmed by work by Gemma Colesanti and Salvatore Marino (2016), has, in my opinion, clearly shown that the hospital of SS. Annunziata, while not running a public bank along the lines of private banks authorised by Angevin monarchs, began to engage in banking activities much earlier. It received deposits, granted loans, made investments with the money of depositors and paid interest in the central decades of the fifteenth century, in ways not dissimilar to those widely documented for other Italian cities from as early as the fourteenth century. The best-known example, both because it is well documented and because it has recently been the subject of a series of studies by Gabriella Piccinni and her students using the latest historiographical approaches and techniques, is that of the hospital of S. Maria della Scala in Siena.

3 The Sources of SS. Annunziata

Similar banking activity is demonstrated for SS. Annunziata by two sets of documents: first, the protocol of the notary Petruccio Pisano, which dates to the period 1462–1477 (published not entirely by Monica Vicinanza in 2006 and subsequently in 2009, and deposited at Archivio di Stato di Napoli). Pisano's protocol is almost entirely devoted to the hospital (of the 267 documents, 249 were compiled for the Annunziata, while only 18 documents were compiled for private individuals). The second set of documents contains the oldest administrative records of the SS. Annunziata (kept in the historical archives in Naples: Archivio Storico Municipale di Napoli, Sezione Real Casa Santa dell'Annunziata: Liber B, Liber C, Liber E, Liber K, all still unpublished).

The Pisano protocol contains the oldest document that records a loan made by the church of Annunziata, a loan previously unremarked by historians. On 19 July 1462, the masters and governors of the institution,

Gotofredo Caracciolo, Giovanni Geremia and Francesco de Apenna, rented out land in Somma Vesuviana belonging to the hospital *ad bene laborandum* to Nardello de Martino. The land measured about 5 *moggi* (1 *moggio* is 3380 square meters) and was rented to Nardello for 5 years starting on the following 1 August, on condition that he improve the yield of the land, cultivating it appropriately and that each year he give the masters and the governors half of the harvests for the Annunziata. According to the same document, Nardello, *pro bene laborando et cultivando dictam terram*, received a loan from the masters and governors *de pecunia dictarum ecclesie et hospitali* of 20 *tarì*, which he undertook to pay back to the masters within 5 years of the lease (Vicinanza 2006, doc. no. 12). It is an interesting document because it shows how the practice of granting loans by the hospital probably began. In other words, it was linked to the need to activate a flow of microcredit to support tenant farmers not only for their own interests but also for the benefit of the hospital. Beginning from 1462, documents granting loans are a constant feature in the protocol kept by Petruccio Pisano (Vicinanza 2006, docs. nos. 21, 31, 34, 41, 48, 62, 123, 130; Vicinanza 2009, docs. nos. 174, 186, 191, 196, 207, 209).

However, it is not certain that the document dealing with the concession of land in Somma Vesuviana is the oldest document indicating a loan made by the Annunziata. An inventory of documents of the hospital archive compiled in the modern era notes an abstract of a deed of 3 February 1455 drawn up by the notary Antonello di Flumeri with which Don Gennaro Cerella, the procurator of the hospital, granted a loan of 8 ounces (*once*) to a man called Francesco, about whom nothing else is known (Archivio Storico Municipale di Napoli, Sezione Real Casa Santa dell'Annunziata, *Inventario antico*, ff. 702v–703r; Marino 2015, doc. no. 217; Sangiovanni 2016). This document is very important not only because it anticipates the start of the hospital's credit activity by about eight years, but above all, because the amount of the sum disbursed (eight ounces were a considerable sum) is proof of the hospital's financial capability, obtained thanks to the donations of which it was a frequent beneficiary, a key feature of the institution's active role.[3]

[3]In the same inventory of documents of modern era, there is an abstract of a document dated 16 February 1430, with which Antonello Brancaccio declares he is indebted towards the Annunziata. Lacking the original document, the brevity of the abstract and its contents do not authorise us to hypothesise that at the time the Annunziata was already carrying out lending activities (Archivio Storico Municipale di Napoli, Sezione Real Casa Santa dell'Annunziata, *Inventario antico*, f. 562v; Marino 2015, doc. no. 121; Colesanti-Marino 2016).

An even more important documentary source consists of the *libri d'amministrazione* (administrative books), which constitute a series of archives of which four volumes have so far been discovered:

Liber B related to the years 1481–1482
Liber C related to the years 1483–1484
Liber E related to the years 1489–1492
Liber K related to the years 1507–1510[4]

There is an extremely plausible case to be made for the existence of a *Liber A* which has not yet been found, related to the previous years (1479–1480?). They are all written by the same author—Ambrosio Abate from Naples—who belonged to a family linked to the institution from its origins; as many as five members of his family acted as governors in different years:

Giovanni Antonio 1348
Nardiello 1368–1369
Marino 1429
Rainaldo 1453
Lionello 1480, 1485, 1490

In the invocation (*invocatio*) that opens Liber C, he defines himself as *razionale de tucte le intrate et exite et de omne cunto* (f. 1) due to the hospital of the SS. Annunziata, in other words, the person who was in charge of running the institution's funds and who must have gained a certain level of expertise considering that he was active for about twenty years.

He states that he will note down all the revenues and expenditures *deposite et debite fatte e che si faranno dal 1 luglio alla fine del mese di giugno dell'anno successivo* (Liber C, f. 1). The volumes were therefore supposed to keep records of the cash flow movements of the hospital regarding a single year beginning on 1 July when the governors were appointed. However, for obvious practical reasons, they also ended up keeping records of operations related to the years prior to and following the year in question.

[4]This book has recently been found in the Archivio Storico Municipale di Napoli, Sezione Real Casa Santa dell'Annunziata. I would like to thank Giuliana Buonaurio, the archivist at the Archivio Storico Municipale in Naples, for pointing out the discovery to me.

These volumes present various interpretative uncertainties because they have several elements in common with traditional inventories of goods and books of revenues and expenditures of monasteries. One example is the opening part of the book for the years 1481–1482, with two pages containing lists of a series of properties defined as *concesse a diverse persone vita loro durante* (granted to various people during their lives), which in reality comprise two types of properties on which the institution made no money at the time when the register was drawn up: properties donated with the clause that they would belong to the hospital only after the death of their respective usufructuaries who were not required to pay anything to the SS. Annunziata; properties for which the institution had received a significant sum from an individual through an agreement drawn up before a notary as long as the said person could use it for the rest of his life as a usufructuary. This practice clearly stemmed from the hospital's need to have liquidity. The index preceding Liber B defines it as the *Libro Maggiore*, a double-entry ledger registered in the name of people or institutions with accounts at the hospital. Their accounts may have been opened directly by the deposit of sums of varying amounts for which, if legally bound, they received interest, or by others, as in the case of an employer who opened it on behalf of an employee. An account was usually accompanied by other types of registers for which there are precise references in this book: there are references to a *librecta*, a *libro di Gabriele* and a *Libro rosso*. The latter, with its name that evokes volumes of a statutory nature, was an extremely lengthy text of over 500 pages. There are references also to the next book Liber C for the following years. The volume ends with the sum of the revenues and expenditures of the institution.

With Liber B, which, as already mentioned, was probably preceded by a Liber A, the book-keeper (*razionale*) Ambrosio Abate was codifying a book-keeping structure that would become the standard at the SS. Annunziata and would be copied in the volumes of subsequent years. The accounting structure provided guarantees for both the institution and the depositor, who could go to the hospital and contact the bookkeeper who wrote the sum in the entries for revenues in the cash register. The entry in the register acted as a record of the signed contract and could have been sufficient as a guarantee for the depositor. However, it is extremely likely that a deposit certificate or receipt (*poliza*) was issued. Only one example remains, however. It is randomly bound within *Liber B*, dated 7 July 1478, issued by the vicar of an annex of the Annunziata in his own name and on behalf of the five masters of the SS. Annunziata to the person who had collected the alms that were due to it. Although it is still not clear when receipts began to be issued, these ledgers, which already represented a guarantee for the depositor, certainly began to be kept by the late 1470s.

However, even as early as a decade beforehand, the Annunziata had provided significant guarantees to those who deposited money with its bank since the aforementioned notary Petruccio Pisano (Vicinanza 2006, 2009) was in its employ. His protocol reveals the turnover of the hospital, linked partly to its immense moveable and immoveable property and, to the same extent, to the circulation of money that its administrators were able to promote. The money circulation was so extensive that, for a fifteen-year period (the protocol covers the period 1462–1477), it required the exclusive services of the notary whose "public trust" (*publica fides*) made other instruments superfluous. When it became necessary to have more detailed information about the hospital's turnover, formal archives were compiled that made it possible to monitor the institution's accounts. This led to the creation of the *Libri Maggiori* (ledgers) drawn up by the hospital bookkeeper (*razionale*) Ambrosio Abate. They are a precious source of evidence, not just for the running of the bank, but above all, because they provide a tangible way of analysing the Neapolitan society that revolved around it.

It is not possible to go into full detail in this paper. To give an idea of the importance of the theme and a basis for my concluding remarks, I shall merely highlight several points. Firstly, it must have been an activity that did not begin in a carefully planned way but in the wake of long-standing practice. There would have been many examples in the rich monastic network of Naples of this practice such as the deposit of precious objects and coins at a religious institution that inspired the trust of the depositor. In the case of the SS. Annunziata, this practice would sometimes have involved a notarial act.

The existence of a series of ledgers covering a period spanning almost twenty years (1481–1510) provides the opportunity, using a wide-ranging interpretative approach, to gain considerable information normally obtained by specific types of sources: the type, social background and variation through time of the clientele (in the broadest sense of the term, and therefore even occasional clients), the size and movement of the deposited sums, the interest received with the relative variations over time, the network of relations with other banks, and the type of loans granted by the hospital.

The Liber B—studied using a diachronic approach, that is, combining the data with the data from the later volumes—provides evidences of great interest and confirms, through comparative study, the data from the same period as that from the *Giornale del Banco Strozzi*, published by Alfonso Leone in 1981 (Leone 1981) and subsequently the subject of an incisive analysis by Mario Del Treppo in a remarkable essay written in 1986 (Del Treppo 1986). A comparison of the two data sets reveals once again the image of Naples during this period, which is being confirmed at a historiographical level. Once the serious material wounds caused by the twenty-year war of succession following the death of Joanna II (1373–1435) had begun to heal during the Aragonese era, the city began to undergo a period of political, administrative and economic reforms the like of which would not be seen until the unfortunately equally brief period of the reign of Charles III of Bourbon during the mid-eighteenth century. The reforms were inspired and accompanied by an extraordinary circle of Italian and foreign intellectuals and economic players that the monarchy managed to assemble. However, they were not sufficient, as was the case elsewhere, to eliminate the social unrest and pockets of poverty that characterised large cities during this period. Monarchs were not directly involved, but they did provide support for institutions that gave alms and granted small loans designed to set up new activities or to ensure their continuity. However, when it came to the banking activity of hospitals of the size of Annunziata—although the same may also be true for S. Eligio—a ledger (Liber B) offers an insight into the world of the poor and the needy, but also into society in general, because in one way or another—through deposits, loans, donations, bequests, voluntary or paid work—all the city's social classes and important religious institutions played a part.

Liber B offers a wealth of information concerning the bank's customers. There are about 350 names including private individuals and organisations for the year 1481, which doubled in number during the period 1489–1492, a clear sign of the significant increase that this sector of the hospital's activity enjoyed within the space of a few years. Unlike the Banco Strozzi, the hospital did not act as a bank for, or on behalf of, the administrative and financial organs of the state, even though Queen Joanna, wife of Ferrante, and two notaries of the court of Vicaria had accounts there. Other depositors included the main feudal lords of the kingdom such as Onorato Gaetani (Count of Fondi), Antonio de Guevara (Count of Potenza), Pirro del Balzo (Count of Venosa), Scipione Pandone (Count of Venafro), the Sanseverino family with Polissena (Countess of Ariano), and Geronimo (Prince of Bisignano), as well as members of Neapolitan families who belonged to the *seggio*, such as the Della Marra family, the Caracciolo family, the Carafa family, with Cardinal and Archbishop Oliviero. There were also monasteries (San Festo, Santa Maria di Donnaromita), convents (San Domenico, Sant'Agostino) and religious institutions (Santa Maria Maggiore, the *staurita* [a lay association] of Sant'Arpino a Forcella). Although unremarked until now, Lorenzo dei Medici was an exceptional occasional client, together with his business partners. Two Jews, Allegans and Iosef, may have also have been owners of a bank.

The fact that the scope of the hospital's banking activity went beyond the confines of the city is also demonstrated by the 18 accounts registered in the names of friars (*preceptors*) who were in charge of 18 preceptories of the hospital order of Sant'Antonio di Vienne scattered throughout the kingdom (from Gaeta and Chieti to Scalea) and even in Sciacca in Sicily. They found it useful to avoid moving the money but to circulate it through the bank of the SS. Annunziata.

Strikingly, there is also a significant group of depositors from Pozzuoli, who clearly formed after the hospital of S. Marta di Tripergole, founded by Charles II of Anjou near Pozzuoli, was amalgamated with the SS. Annunziata in 1477: the operation must have met with a warm reception from local population, encouraging them to place their trust in the Neapolitan institution.

Most of the deposit accounts, however, were registered in the name of people who were members of the lowest levels of the economic and social life of the city and who undoubtedly benefited from the microcredit that the hospital was able to grant: they were mainly cobblers and tailors who probably did considerable work for the institution, but also leather-workers, smiths, masons, swordsmiths, saddlers, lime-makers (*calcarari*), barbers, painters, apothecaries, millers, inn-keepers, charcoal burners (*carbonari*) and haberdashers who deposited a few ducats and *tarì*. It is interesting to compare them with the clientele of the Banco Strozzi, which included artisans but also comprised goldsmiths, silversmiths and jewellers who do not feature among the depositors of the Annunziata.

There are numerous joint accounts: some are in the names of people who were related to each other, while other joint account holders were probably business partners. There are also names of the heirs of the deceased who inherited the rights on deposits.

In terms of the number of registered operations, the majority are accounts registered in the name of the masters of the hospital, which were not their own personal accounts but were used to deposit sums paid into the hospital and from which they withdrew what was necessary to keep it running. It was the office of the *mensariato*, that Francesco Imperato in 1629 describes with these words: « Li governatori del Popolo esercitano il mensariato, ciascun' di lor' il suo mese ordine successivo, nel qual han pensiero di esigere da debitori, e pagar' di contanti, e per banchi à creditori, notriccie, officiali, ministri e altre sorti di persone » [« The governors of the Popolo exercise the duty of mensariato (comptroller), they take turns monthly, and in their month in office they take care of getting money back from debtors, and of paying cash or "in bank" creditors, nurses, officials, administrators and other kinds of people »] (Imperato 1629). At the end of the volume, where there are lists of the revenues and expenditures of the hospital, the so-called *redde rationem*, the only figures are the sums paid and spent by the masters, who carried out the office of *mensariato*. Only the masters of the *seggio del Popolo* held this office, which shows how diversified were their roles, which included strong management skills. The master of the *seggio* of Capuana had more than anything else only the role of representation.

A particularly interesting example is the account of the master Loise di Gaeta, who was also an owner of a bank in his own right, with the *doganiere* (customs office) Francesco Palmeri, through which payments and withdrawals of funds were made at the bank of the Annunziata. Loise of Gaeta had been several times governor of the hospital and in the Liber B is among those who hold the office of the *mensariato*. Moving money around without actually touching it was one of the main needs of medieval merchants, especially in the case of long distances. However, even those who acted on a local scale were interested in having instruments that enabled them to transfer sums from one account to another or to facilitate payments without using cash: this practice is documented at Genoa from the twelfth century or at Siena in the fourteenth century. "The model is collaborative rather than competitive" as wrote Gabriella Piccinni, given that even for an owner of a private bank, passing one's operations through the bank of a prestigious hospital meant guaranteeing greater security for his clientele (Piccinni 2012). Loise of Gaeta and Francesco Palmeri were not the only private bankers to work in collaboration with the Annunziata: very active were the family of de Penna, originally from the Amalfi Coast, of which five members (Paolo, Francesco, Piscopo, Raffaele and Giovanni Paolo) several times served as governors between 1390 and 1497. Among them, Piscopo de Apenna ran a bank that collaborated with that of the Annunziata. This is demonstrated by a document dated 27 July 1470 (Vicinanza 2006, no. 140; Sangiovanni 2016) with which Andrea Scarlata of Caltabellotta *procurator insulae Siciliae* collects at the Piscopo bank 150 Venetian ducats deposited on 26 October 1466 at the bank of the Annunziata *inter quoddam marsuleum de coiro rubeo legatum et sigillatum*, in a moment of lack of liquidity for the Annunziata.

As time went by, even only a few years later, other new features began to appear which show that this was a phase of managerial reinforcement of the institution through the opening, as became necessary, of accounts registered in the names of specific business activities. Liber E for the period 1489–1492 has the following accounts opened in the name of:

- the building of the women's hospital, founded by Onorato Gaetani in 1468 behind the chapel of Santi Quaranta of the church of SS. Annunziata,
- the confraternity of SS. Annunziata,
- the cash of SS. Annunziata,
- the hospital,
- the Bank of the Treasury (*Cassa del Tesoro*) of the Sacristy.

Other accounts are in the names of the fiefs of the hospital.

It was an age of organisational experimentation during which new features coexisted with traditional practices. It is worth emphasising that this took place in a city with extremely lively socio-political dynamics. With regard to the history of social services and welfare, it is safe to say that the Middle Ages in Naples, but also elsewhere in Italy, was coming to an end with the same degree of creativity with which it had begun: initially, a new world was being created, very arduously and on the basis of the heritage of the ancient world, based on Christian values; however, in the late fifteenth century, even more painfully after the crisis of the fourteenth century, new institutions were being founded which would hopefully be able to increase collective and individual well-being. A great test of resilience.

References

Albini, Giuliana. 1993. *Città e ospedali nella Lombardia medievale*. Bologna: Clueb.

———. 1997. La gestione dell'Ospedale maggiore nel Quattrocento: un esempio di concentrazione ospedaliera. In *Ospedali e città. L'Italia del Centro-Nord, XIII–XVI secolo*, a cura di A.J. Grieco and L. Sandri, 157–178. Firenze: Le Lettere.

———. 2002. *Carità e governo della povertà (secc. XII–XV)*. Milano: Edizioni Unicopli.

———. 2016. *Poveri e povertà nel Medioevo*. Roma: Carocci.

Colesanti, Gemma, and Salvatore Marino. 2016. L'economia dell'assistenza a Napoli nel tardo Medioevo. In *L'ospedale, il denaro e altre ricchezze. Scritture e pratiche economiche dell'assistenza in Italia nel tardo medioevo*, a cura di Marina Gazzini e Antonio Olivieri, Reti Medievali Rivista, 17, 1 (2016). http://rivista.retimedievali.it.

D'Addosio, Giovan Battista. 1883. *Origine, vicende storiche e progressi della Real S. Casa dell'Annunziata di Napoli*. Napoli: Antonio Cons.

De Maio, Romeo. 1973. L'ospedale dell'Annunziata, «il megliore e più segnalato di tutta Italia». In Id., *Riforme e miti nella Chiesa del Cinquecento*, 241–249. Napoli: Guida.

Del Treppo, Mario. 1986. Il re e il banchiere. Strumenti e processi di razionalizzazione dello stato aragonese di Napoli. In *Spazio, società e potere nell'Italia dei Comuni*, ed. G. Rossetti, 229–304. Napoli: Liguori.

Demarco, Domenico, and Eduardo Nappi. 1985. Nuovi documenti sulle origini e sui titoli del Banco di Napoli. In *Revue internationale d'histoire de la banque*, 30–31 (1985), 1–78, ora in D. Demarco, *Il Banco di Napoli. Dalle casse di deposito alla fioritura settecentesca*, Napoli 1996 (Opere di Domenico Demarco, 5), 9–99.

Epstein, Stephan R. 2006. I caratteri originali. L'economia. In *L'Italia alla fine del Medioevo: I caratteri originali nel quadro europeo*, ed. F. Salvestrini, 381–431. Firenze: University Press.

Gaglione, Mario. 2009. *Converà ti que aptengas la flor: profili di sovrani angioini, da Carlo I a Renato (1266–1442)*. Milano: TuttiAutori.

Gambini de Vera d'Aragona, Mauro. 2013. Un singolare barone del Regno: la Reale Casa dell'Annunziata di Napoli, peculiarità giuspubblicistiche dei feudi di un antichissimo ente assistenziale laico napoletano. In *Napoli Nobilissima*, VI ser., vol. IV, 177–196.

Imperato, Francesco. 1629. *Discorso intorno all'origine, regimento e stato della gran Casa della Santissima Annunziata di Napoli*. Napoli: Longo.

Leone, Alfonso. 1981. *Il giornale del banco Strozzi di Napoli (1473)*. Napoli: Guida.

Marino, Salvatore. 2004. *Ospedali e città nel Regno di Napoli. Le Annunziate: istituzioni, archivi e fonti*. Firenze: Olschki.

———. 2015. *L'Archivio dell'Annunziata di Napoli. Inventari e documenti (secoli XII–XIX)*. Salerno: Laveglia & Carlone.

Mauri Mori, Giuseppe. 1967. *Pergamene dell'Annunziata. 1194–1400*. Casavatore (Napoli): Stagrame.

———. 1969. *Pergamene dell'Annunziata. 1400–1450.* Casavatore (Napoli): Stagrame.

Muto, Giovanni. 1982. Forme e contenuti economici dell'assistenza nel Mezzogiorno moderno: il caso di Napoli. In *Timore e carità. I poveri nell'Italia moderna*, ed. G. Politi, M. Rosa, and F. Della Peruta, 237–258. Cremona: Annali della Biblioteca statale e Libreria civica di Cremona.

_____. 1983. Tra «Hombres de negocios» e banchi pubblici: progetti di autonomia finanziaria nello stato napoletano (secoli XVI–XVII). *Studi Storici Luigi Simeoni*, 33 (1983), 85–101.

Piccinni, Gabriella. 2008. Il sistema senese del credito nella fase di smobilitazione dei suoi banchi internazionali. Politiche comunali, spesa pubblica, propaganda contro l'usura (1332–1340). In *Fedeltà ghibellinaaffari guelfi. Saggi e riletture intorno alla storia di Siena fra Due e Trecento*, a cura di G. Piccinni, 209–289. Pisa: Pacini.

———. 2012. *Il banco dell'ospedale di Santa Maria della Scala e il mercato del denaro nella Siena del Trecento.* Ospedaletto (Pisa): Pacini Editore.

Piccinni, Gabriella, and Vigni, Laura. 1989. Modelli di assistenza ospedaliera tra Medioevo ed età moderna. Quotidianità, amministrazione, conflitti nellìospedale di Santa Maria della Scala di Siena. In *La società del bisogno. Povertà ed assistenza nella Toscana medievale*, a cura di G. Pinto, 131–174. Firenze: Salimbeni.

Sangiovanni, Laura. 2016. Il cartulario di Petruccio Pisano. In *Quaderni dell'Archivio storico. Istituto Banco di Napoli. Fondazione*, 245–344. Napoli: Istituto Banco di Napoli. Fondazione.

Santoro, Daniela. 2016. Investire nella carità. Mercanti e ospedali a Messina nel Trecento. In *L'ospedale, il denaro e altre ricchezze. Scritture e pratiche economiche dell'assistenza in Italia nel tardo medioevo*, a cura di Marina Gazzini e Antonio Olivieri, Reti Medievali Rivista, 17, 1 (2016). http://rivista.retimedievali.it.

Silvestri, Alfonso. 1953. Sull'attività bancaria napoletana durante il periodo aragonese. Notizie e documenti. In *Bollettino dell'Archivio storico del Banco di Napoli*, vol. VI.

Vicinanza, Monica. 2006. *Napoli. Petruccio Pisano.* Parte prima: 1462–1466. Napoli: Edizioni Athena.

———. 2009. *Napoli. Petruccio Pisano.* Parte seconda: 19 aprile 1467-17 agosto 1468. Salerno: Laveglia & Carlone.

Vitolo, Giovanni. 2003. L'Ospedale di Sant'Eligio e la piazza del Mercato. In *Napoli angioino-aragonese: confraternite, ospedali, dinamiche politico-sociali*, ed. G. Vitolo and R. Di Meglio, 39–176. Salerno: Carlone Editore.

———. 2016. L'immigrazione francese a Napoli. La governance dell'ospedale di Sant'Eligio (secc. XIII–XV). In *Ut sementem feceris, ita metem. Studi in onore di Biagio Saitta*, ed. P. Dalena and C. Urso, 287–297. Acireale and Roma: Bonanno Editore.

Vitolo, Giovanni, and Rosalba Di Meglio. 2003. *Napoli angioino-aragonese: confraternite, ospedali, dinamiche politico-sociali.* Salerno: Carlone Editore.

Vitolo, Giovanni, et al. 2016. *Città, spazi pubblici e servizi sociali nel Mezzogiorno medievale.* Salerno: Laveglia & Carlone.

CHAPTER 4

Between Charity and Credit: The Evolution of the Neapolitan Banking System (Sixteenth–Seventeenth Century)

Paola Avallone and Raffaella Salvemini

1 Introduction

Ever since the publication of Michele Rocco's work in the second half of the 1700s (Rocco 1785), mainstream studies on the birth and spread of Neapolitan public banks have been marked by an emphasis on two factors: on the one hand, the technical characteristics of the document that typified these institutions for more than two centuries—viz.,

Introduction, Section 5 and conclusions are common; Sections 2 and 6 are to be attributed to Raffaella Salvemini; Sections 3 and 4 are to be attributed to Paola Avallone. This contribution is part of the research activities carried out within the framework of the PRIN2015 Project "At the origins of Welfare (XIII–XVI century). Medieval and modern roots of the European culture of assistance and forms of social protection and solidary credit." University of Siena, University of Parma, CNR-ISSM (Naples).

P. Avallone (✉) · R. Salvemini
National Research Council (CNR) – Institute of Studies on Mediterranean Societies (ISSM), Naples, Italy

L. Costabile and L. Neal (eds.), *Financial Innovation and Resilience*, Palgrave Studies in the History of Finance,
https://doi.org/10.1007/978-3-319-90248-7_4

the certificate of credit—on the other, the fiscal requirements of the Kingdom of Naples, which was increasingly strangled by money requests from Spain and cash shortages. Even the most recent studies in domains ranging from the history of accounting to that of economic thought (Coronella et al. 2016, pp. 368–399; Costabile 2016, pp. 166–190) have faithfully adhered to this prevalent and well-established methodological approach.

However, an institutional fracture such as that which led to the rise of public banks must necessarily be the final result of a longer process, especially in the economic domain. As one of the foremost students of banking and finance in the Kingdom of Naples, Luigi De Rosa, has observed: "The economic organism shows more inertia when organizing a response to stimuli and impetuses to innovate, and in any case its path towards change is never linear" (De Rosa 2010, pp. 83–85).

The several generations of scholars who have dealt with banks in Naples and in the Italian South have favoured literature and sources, which start from the singling out and testing an initial model to arrive at a final model, dwelling on the major issues that determined this transition. In doing so, however, they overlook some important intermediate stages. It is on one of these that we focus here. We will trace the relationship between public banks and the "mother" institutions that spawned them to explain not only the origins, but also the evolution of a singular project. Indeed, differently than in other nations—where they arose with the sole objective of profit—in the Kingdom of Naples banks were established by "non-profit" institutions striving, with much difficulty, to find a middle road between charity and credit. These institutions ultimately came up with a unique model in its kind.

We will start from the period of the Spanish Viceroyalty (1502–1707), briefly dwelling on political action to alleviate poverty and, more specifically, on the supply and demand of services offered by lay charities in Naples. We will then show how, at a time of severe economic straits for the Kingdom and the charities during the second half of the sixteenth century, banking took its place among a broad range of economic, financial, and credit activities. The need for new financial resources led some Neapolitan charities to diversify their services by offering and opening public banks. Finally, we will retrace the difficulties encountered by these institutions striving to make charity coexist with banking, and the consequent decision to separate the two to avoid compromising not only the said institutions, but the whole economic, financial, and credit system of the Kingdom.

2 The Charity Plan

In his Teatro Eroico of 1692, speaking of monasteries, conservatories, hospitals, pawnshops, and other institutions engaged in charitable activities in his time, D. A. Parrino wrote that "this is only a minimal part of the Christian charity of Neapolitan Citizens, there being no pious work they neglect" (Parrino 1730, p. 23). There was thus no spiritual or material need that could not be met by the charity of this array of institutions. But let us look at the organization of charitable assistance in Naples.

Starting from the Spanish takeover in the sixteenth century, the population grew in the Kingdom, and even more in the capital. Masses of poor people moved to Naples, as well as nobility and property owners. Of course, not all were guaranteed a job. The rate of demographic growth recorded in the city—which grew from ca. 115,000 inhabitants at the beginning of the sixteenth century to about 280,000 in 1606—was much higher than the actual potential for economic growth of the local industries, of productive sectors such as silk-growing, or of the trading circuits activated by grain, oil, and wine distributions. In this particular conjuncture—at least as far as we can tell from the chronicles of the time—more and more people were forced to wander around the town looking for a job, or merely for hospitality and charity. Many had moved to Naples because they thought that it would be easier to earn a few coins there, if only by begging at church doorsteps or knocking on hospital doors (Palermo 1846, p. 247).

But the high number of indigent people posed a threat to public order. Laws against vagrants and jobless were therefore issued—first only against foreign ones, later against Neapolitan ones as well—although with meagre results. Craft workshops were urged to take in and train the poor. Initially, the laws equated vagrants to delinquents, introducing the concept of a "stable job" as the only way for a foreigner—and eventually for a Neapolitan, as well—not to be mistaken for a vagrant, an idle person, and prosecuted as such (Salvemini 2000, pp. 297–298).

How many were the indigent? It is hard to say. According to a very tentative estimate, the percentage may have been around 15–20 per cent of the population. Commenting on the condition of the population in his *La Città del Sole*, published in 1602, Tommaso Campanella writes: "in Naples there are three hundred thousand souls, and fifty thousand do not have a job" (Campanella 1941, p. 76). This gap between the demand and the supply of labour in Naples at the time is confirmed by the studies of S. Woolf and B. Pullan on the numbers of the unemployed in other areas (Woolf 1988; Pullan 1978, pp. 981–1047).

Private, lay, and religious charity played an important role in meeting the poor's need for help and relief. Thanks to bequests and donations, an elaborate aid system was set up, revolving around multifunctional structures capable of satisfying every need. The management of charity could rely, on the one hand, on the support of the city government, which provided grain supplies and watched over public health, on the other on that of the Spanish court, which granted various benefits to charities, including alms, franchises, tax exemptions, and jurisdictional privileges.

Crafts corporations were also involved in bringing support and succour to this complex galaxy of indigent people, notably by promoting the building of churches and, above all, of lay institutions such as male and female conservatories. E. Bacco reports that in 1606 in Naples there were 5 male conservatories housing 762 boys and 16 female ones housing 2208 women. Then there were *monti dotali* (dowries funds), *monti di pietà* (pawnshops), orphanages, and ten hospitals (Bacco 1609, p. 128).

Four of these hospitals, along with the Spirito Santo Conservatory for girls at risk, experimented with the combination of charity and banking. Among the other hospitals there were the Casa Santa di Sant'Eligio, which included a conservatory and a hospital for women established back in 1270; the Casa Santa dell'Annunziata, founded in 1318, with an orphanage for abandoned infants and males and females affected by common ailments; the Casa Santa degli Incurabili, founded in 1520 to assist incurable patients of both sexes; and the Hospital of San Giacomo degli Spagnoli, established in 1540 at the behest of Don Pedro de Toledo for the Spanish military.

These were very wealthy institutions, and well connected within the city's political, economic, and financial fabric. Thanks to the great trust they enjoyed, their assets, deriving from alms and generous bequests, increased enormously. The assets of these institutions were the so-called assets of the poor, a sort of fund for the indigent, which both lay and religious administrators relied upon, as well as the Spanish court and the city government. This fund was regarded as a common property, which should be made available to the collectivity, through the charitable works undertaken by these institutions, and to the state that obliged these institutions to finance state works through the purchase of public debt securities. This wealth attracted the state and city administrations, as well as private citizens, who were among their largest debtors. Growing financial difficulties throughout the long Spanish occupation had forced the state to borrow more and more. The interest rates it offered to investors were such that investments in public debts were preferable to any other form of investment (De Rosa, pp. 57–67).

3 The Credit and Financial System

These charitable institutions were true holdings *ante litteram*. On the one hand, they served as social shock absorbers by providing services such as alms, dowries, food and milk for foundlings, accommodation, clothing, medical care, education, and interest-free loans on pledge; on the other, they operated as true businesses, producing and selling consumption commodities, lending money to the state, the city, and private individuals, and offering deposit services. Along with private citizens such as notaries, tenderers, and nobles, they formed the base of the virtual pyramid of the financial and credit system of the Kingdom of Naples in the sixteenth century, reinvesting profits from their activities or their revenues in profitable activities.

At the time, however, the most conspicuous share of the financial and credit market was held by a group of merchants who supplemented their main line of work by providing banking services. They invested their profits in loans—especially to the Vice-royal Court, which was always looking for funding for the wars it was involved in the motherland—and also offered deposit services (Table 1). N. Toppi provides the following, not exhaustive list of the bankers who operated in Naples between 1516 and 1604 (Toppi 1655, pp. 49–50).

To these banks, G. Petrone adds Michele Coriel, Gian Vincenzo and Giannandrea del Solaro, Ravaschiero and Pinelli, Raphael Galsareno, Acciaiuoli, Giulio Comeres, Andrea Agostino, Nicolò de Mare and his associate (Petrone 1871, p. 13). In addition to these, there were the Jewish bankers, at least until 1541, when they were definitively banned from the Kingdom. N. Ferorelli reports that in the late fifteenth century, in the city of Naples alone, there were the following Jewish banks: the Compagnia of Joan Francesco Guindaczo—called Diodato until 1497,

Table 1 Private bankers in Naples from 1516 to 1604

Names of bankers	*Years (from–to)*
Ravaschiero	1516–1579
Vaglies	1519–1534
Marruffo e Oria	1529
De Mare e Citarella	1533–1570
Lomellino e Pallavicino	1535–1546
Galzarano e Vidal	1536–1547
Sommoya	1542
Serra e Vivaldo	Unknown dates
Larcaro e Imperiale	1544–1551
Spinola e Mare	1551
de Montenegro	1559–1576
Turbolo e Comeres	1567 and following
Bannini e Neri	1569–1577
Gentile	1596–1599
Coney e Comeres	1570–1573
Turbolo	1570–1576
Grimaldi	1571–1588
Citarella e Rinaldo	1572
Olgiati e Solaro	1573–1580
Composta e Corcione	1573–1580
Turbolo e Caputo	1576–1580
Calamazza e de Pontecorvo	1576–1582
Casola e Marrocco	1582 and following
Cimino	1578–1581
de Leone e Bonaventura	1579 and following
Olgiatti	1578–1597
Coneglio	1580
de Belmosto	1580
Bifoli	1581
Casola, Baccara e Borrella	1578 and following
Vollaro, Solaro e Composta	1582–1596
Incurabiles	1583–1588
de Centurione	1591–1596
Spinola, Mare e Grillo	1592–1595
Lorenzo e Sebastiano Mari	1595–1598
Talano e Mari	1596–1598
Spinola, Ravaschiero e Lomellino	1596–1603
Turbolo e Caputo	1602–1604
Franco e Spinola	1604

when he converted to Christianism—and Jacob de Angelo, a citizen of Cosenza; the Compagnia of Ferrera Nescas and Salomone Nactan; the Compagnia of Jacob de Elia and Sabato di Lucca; and the Jew Moises. His is the last name mentioned by Ferorelli, who adds, however, that "there were doubtlessly many others" (Ferorelli 1990, p. 146).

According to Toppi, overall there were more than 5000 cashbooks, registers, and other documents, most of which are lost. To get a sense of the elaborate accounting practices of the time, we can look at the only surviving criminal trial from the Collaterale funds in the Naples State Archives, relative to the failure of the Vollaro, Solaro e Composta bank.[1]

From the names of the bankers, we gather that the credit market was all concentrated in the hands of foreigners (as it was in Spain) (Brancaccio 2001, p. 59; De Rosa 2004, pp. 55–56). But that is not all: when in 1549 a *prammatica* (law) issued by Pedro de Toledo obliged all who wanted to provide banking services to pay a security deposit of 40,000 ducats in Naples, and 15,000 in the Province (De Sariis 1795, p. 200), the lists of vouching subjects (*plegi*) indicate that most were Genoese. Quite a few Lombards, Venetians, Catalans, Spanish, and Neapolitans are also mentioned, often as associates of the Genoese. Throughout the sixteenth century, new banks opened in Naples as soon as others closed down. It is estimated that during that period on average nine private banks were open at the same time.

The obligation to pay a security deposit was imposed following the many bank failures due to the economic crisis that had struck not just the Kingdom of Naples, but Europe as a whole. This crisis was determined by a serious drought, whose first harbingers are recognizable in 1534 (De Rosa 2002, p. 58). The agricultural crisis spread to credit and finance as a matter of course. The hike in grain prices impacted all strata of the population, especially those who lived just above the poverty line. These were increasingly forced to turn to usurers, since in the meantime many bankers had had to declare bankruptcy for having financed the Court's purchases of grain subsequently sold at lower prices (De Rosa 1987, pp. 44–70). To complete the picture of these economic difficulties, a decree expelling the Jews from the Kingdom was issued in 1533 and enacted in 1541. This caused the cost of money to rise even further, since "Christians started to do worse than the Jews" (Bianchini 1971, p. 325). These were the years

[1] Archivio di Stato di Napoli (ASN), Consiglio Collaterale, Carte diverse, Processi penali del Collaterale, n. 339.

of the rule of Don Pedro de Toledo, who was well aware of the social conflicts that hunger could spark. To prevent this danger and alleviate the hardship of the poor, in 1539 the foundation of the Monte di Pietà (pawnshop) in Naples was authorized, which granted free loans on pledge for sums below 10 ducats. All this, however, was not enough to quell the crisis, which was further aggravated by the many requests of money from Spain. As soon as private banks were opened, they were invited to supply the Vice-royal Court with money to be sent to Spain. Part of these sums was drawn from the clients' deposits. But the Court was not merely unable to pay back the borrowed sums by the due time; above all, it was unable to pay the high rates of interest. Hence the depositors' assault on the banks' reserves, prompted by fear of a default of the Court and the consequent failure of the banks themselves. For these reasons, the *prammatica* of 17 July 1553 raised the security deposit to 100,000 ducats, whether the bank was opened in Naples or in the Province (De Sariis 1795, p. 200).

The most interesting passage in this *prammatica* concerns precisely the Monte di Pietà, which by then had evidently been operative for some time. The *prammatica* warned all who wished to avail themselves of bank services that "the depositaries of the said non-profit Banks should always be preferred to the other profit-making depositaries" (De Sariis 1795, p. 200). Thus, all money depositors started to turn to the only "non-profit depositary" of the time, that is, the Monte di Pietà. The Monte had been prompted to launch its banking services by the many requests for loans on pledge coming from the population, which was increasingly crushed in the vise of usury: "To increase the said work, the Deposits Bank was introduced, where very significant quantities were deposited and are deposited every day, whereby the said holy institution was made and is made, and was maintained and is maintained."[2]

4 The Fede di Credito and the Offering of New Services

The Monte's success as a bank mainly depended on its use of the *fede di credito* (certificate of credit). This was a paper document, originally manuscript, later on, well into the eighteenth century, printed. It bore the bank's chirograph, emblem, stamp and seal, and was signed by the

[2] Archivio Storico del Banco di Napoli (ASBN), Monte della Pietà, Archivio Patrimoniale (AP), Conclusioni, conclusione del 9 febbraio 1585, m. 232, f. 163v.

cashier. It declared that the depositor was the bank's creditor, and that the bank was under the obligation to pay back the equivalent value of the deposit in cash (*tantundem*, not *eadem res*).

Actually, *fede di credito* were not a novelty. Even before the appearance of public banks, charities, notaries, or private bankers issued *fede di deposito* (certificates of deposit), i.e. documents simply attesting that money had been deposited. *Fedi di deposito*, in their turn, where distinguished in: judicial certificates of deposit, against a numeraire deposit to be released only by order of a magistrate; plain certificate of deposit, against a numeraire deposit to be returned to the depositor upon request; certificates of term deposit or of deposit under condition, against a numeraire deposit to be made available by a given term or when a certain condition was fulfilled. In all three cases, a trust relationship was established between the depositor and the depositary. Every deposit was recorded in a master book, usually called Libro Maggiore.

Fedi di deposito became *fedi di credito* when they became endorsable. Holders of such certificates could claim their deposit at any time or use the certificates for any commercial transaction. In the latter case, they would pay by endorsing the certificate or issuing other certificates—called policies—for part of the deposit in favour of their creditors.

The technical characteristics of the *fede di credito* described so far, however, do not in themselves account for its popularity. In his work *Della Moneta* (1750), Ferdinando Galiani singled out three causes for the success of public banks—and hence of the *fede di credito*, the document that epitomized them—in the Kingdom of Naples: (1) the decline of metal coinage due to forgeries and the practice of "clipping"; (2) the so-called price revolution from the late 1500s onwards; (3) the material advantage of not having to use metallic coins, which were heavy and dangerous to carry, but lightweight paper documents that were hard to forge.

The material usefulness of the *fede di credito* is almost self-explanatory. Other aspects of the question deserve more attention. The decline of coinage had begun to be felt in the Italian South around the mid-sixteenth century, when complaints began to circulate about "clipping" (*tosatura*) of coins, that is, the shaving off of metal from their circumference. From 1565 onward, the government repeatedly took measures against clipping, mainly by reinforcing control of ports and frontier posts to limit the illicit traffic of coins or silver. Between 1564 and 1567, large quantities of silver were introduced in the Kingdom to be transformed into coins. But coins, as soon as they were minted, were brought out of the Kingdom, forged, or clipped. The coins that went out of the Kingdom were sent to Spain—which ruled the Italian South for all of two centuries—to pay for its wars or other needs of the Court; to Rome, because of the many sources of revenue the Papal States had in the Kingdom; and to Genoa, Florence, or Venice, the cities of residence of the subjects who had lent money to the Neapolitan Court. The incessant importation of silver and the consequent minting of new coins from the late sixteenth century onward did not solve the problem of the scarcity of metal money, which continued to be clipped and brought out of the Kingdom, with additional negative impacts on exchange rates.

As to the second cause Galiani mentions, i.e., what is known as the "price revolution," it consisted of an inflationist trend prevailing all over Europe as a consequence both of the introduction of precious metals from the Americas into the European market and of population growth in the course of the sixteenth century. This inflation brought with it an increase in the prices of all consumption goods. It spared land rent, but severely affected the business world, and especially credit, partly because it caused a devaluation of the numeraires that banking operations were transacted in. In the Kingdom of Naples, inflation was further increased by the borrowing policy adopted by the government to participate in Spain's wars. To repay its creditors, the state habitually ceded its revenues to them, in the form of the taxes or duties imposed on the products imported or consumed in the Kingdom. Thus, in order to offer guarantees to its creditors, the state often devised new taxes, to the serious detriment of the population, whose purchasing power was increasingly curtailed. Furthermore, the state had often found itself in the condition of being unable to pay its creditors and having to declare bankruptcy, reducing interest rates to the disadvantage of all who had invested in public debt.

In order to increase its depositors, the Monte di Pietà, besides using the *fede di credito* as a payment tool, strove to diversify its services to the public. By 1577 (the first instructions to this effect date from this year), the service of "*Accomodazione per i depositanti ordinari e continui*" was introduced, that is, the possibility for depositors to obtain "short term" loans, with or without interest. The other main charities in town had already been offering this service previously (Salvemini 2011, pp. 190–191). For sums up to 50 ducats, the authorization of the bank's *Mensario Protettore* (one of the Governors of the Monte) sufficed; for sums from 50 to 100 ducats, besides the authorization of the *Mensario*, the approval of another Protector was required; for sums above 100, the loan had to be discussed by the congregation and approved by at least four Protectors. If the applicant deposited a pledge, the procedure was simplified; any Protector could then authorize the loan, as long as it did not exceed 50 ducats. The sum could be repaid in several instalments if the pledge was divisible. Of course, not all categories of depositors could benefit from this service; the clergy, for example, were excluded from it, because they could not be tried in secular and lay courts.[3]

This policy gave the hoped-for results, drawing more and more clients to this non-profit institution, created to help people in need, whereas private bankers' sole objective was profit. Besides, trust in private bankers was declining because of a common malpractice among them to pay with policies taken out on other bankers instead of cash when they did not have enough money in their coffers. They thus covered one another by shifting their debts back and forth among themselves. Therefore, to avoid cash shortages, at the end of 1579 the Viceroy Juan de Zuniga forbade compensations between bankers (De Sariis 1795, p. 200).

5 Towards a New Structure of the Credit and Finance System

Losses due to coin clipping and the Court's constant requests for loans caused bank failures to increase—as was also happening elsewhere, outside of the Kingdom (Palermo 1846, p. 291). An attempt to reconvert public rent in the 1570s, involving the Florentine banker Francesco Biffoli, who had his office in Naples, had been fruitless. Therefore, in 1580, four banking companies, Olgiatti e Grimaldi, Citarella e De Rinaldo, Colamazza, and Pontecorvo seized the opportunity to request a 20-year monopoly on banking services, until 1600, demanding that "no other banks, desks, or depositaries be established in Naples,[4] nor any other means of transferal of cash transactions, except for the Monte della Pietà" (Tortora 1890, p. 118). The concession holders had promised to lend 400,000 ducats, at an interest of 6.5 per cent a year. This money

[3] ASBN, Banco della Pietà (BP), AP, Conclusioni, m. 232, ff. 163–164v.

[4] Biffoli was commissioned by the Royal Court to bring 400,000 ducats to Naples to convert into "*reali castigliani*" worth 11.5 grana, to repurchase government debts sold to private individuals at a rate of over 8 per cent (Archivo General de Simancas (AGS), Visitas de Italia, legajo 24, libro 1, f. 45v).

could have been used to redeem many state revenue sources that had been sold at less advantageous rates. A long epistolary exchange between the Viceroy and Philip II, from 26 May 1580 to 15 September 1583, preserved in double copy at the National Library of Naples, reveals that the King had some misgivings about the bankers' proposal. What worried him was not so much the downfall of the banks to be suppressed, but rather the danger that the granting of the control of the Viceroyalty's credit market to a handful of speculators for 20 years might pose to the state and the citizens. To win Philip over, the applicants even proposed increasing the sum to 600,000 ducats. The need for cash for royal expenses ultimately outweighed the king's concerns, and the monopoly was granted.

The excluded bankers, however, did not stand by and watch; one protest followed the other, and the monopoly was cancelled (Tortora 1890, pp. 118–119; Silvestri 1951, pp. 1–35; 1952, pp. 1–35). The Monte di Pietà also sent a memorandum to the King expressing its concern about the effects of the monopoly, which had caused a decline in its deposits. Herein it was argued that "in the said charities, everyone has always been and is free to deposit their money, as it stands to reason that every individual is freely entitled to manage his own money and deposit it where he pleases, with charitable institutions or with public or private persons" (Tortora 1890, pp. 119–122). The problem was not merely that the Monte had been accepting free deposits for years, but especially that it had been accepting judicial deposits, which, being subject to be released under the terms of a sentence, or after a certain date, could be employed for free loans upon pledge and other activities. With the monopoly, not only the Monte but all the other charities accepting deposits would have lost this source of funding for their activities. The Casa Santa dell'Annunziata echoed the Monte's concern. Invoking its statute, it stressed that it had always received judicial deposits of money and released certificates of deposit that had been regularly submitted and accepted in the Neapolitan royal courthouse. It hence requested, and was granted, to retain its right to accept money deposits and issue credit certificates on them (D'Addosio 1883, pp. 513–515).

But there were other, more important reasons behind the request by the Annunziata—and later on the other charities in the capital as well—to ask for recognition of their role as depositaries. From 1580 onward, the conditions of the population of the kingdom worsened due to catastrophic events. These included bad harvests and droughts in the earlier half of the 1570s, and then again in 1584, 1585, and 1591, and epidemics in 1562, 1578, and 1580. On top of that, there were price hikes and an increase of fiscal pressure. The city's charities struggled to meet the needs of the indigent. The expenses of hospitals increased, due, on the one hand, to the increasing poverty of the population, on the other, to constant price increases.

This situation is very clearly reflected in the visit made by Lope de Guzman on behalf of the Court to the main city hospitals, starting in 1582. The aim of his investigation was to highlight criticalities not only in administration and accounting, but also in the wealth these places commanded, which the Court coveted.[5]

De Guzman ascertained that the Annunziata assisted up to 1000 poor daily, and provided upkeep for 7000 wet nurses. Direct expenses to finance the actions of this charity had increased remarkably, from 130,000–140,000 ducats to 170,000 ducats a year. Revenues, instead, which had previously amounted to 95,000 ducats, had declined, since the delicate moment the economy of the Kingdom was going through had taken its toll on the collection of alms and rents in the city. In the meantime, expenses for administration and employees' salary had increased. Debt thus absorbed revenue. An especially critical factor was the drop of trust, which threatened to cause a reduction of bequests. The Casa Santa di Sant'Eligio faced similar problems. In the last decades of the century, due to an increase in the number of destitute orphan girls it housed, works had been undertaken to enlarge the conservatory. To expand the building so that it could hold up to 1000 orphans, 40,000 ducats had been spent. Expenses for the salaries and upkeep of the priests, clerics, and minister officers were high; so were the upkeep costs of the orphans and the ill, as well as maintenance costs. To meet the growing demand for charity, the governors of the Casa Santa di Sant'Eligio had already turned to the city administration of the Seggio del Popolo, which included four out of five of the governors of the charitable institution. The sum they had been granted, however—1500 ducats, and 7000 ducats of rent—was insufficient to cover either ordinary expenses, which amounted to 20,000 ducats a year, or the extraordinary ones for the expansion of the conservatory building. The situation of the

[5] Lope de Guzman arrived in Naples in October 1581, sent by King Philip II as General Visitor to investigate the corruption of public officials of the Kingdom (Bulifon 1932, p. 50).

Conservatory of the Spirito Santo and the Casa Santa degli Incurabili was similar. The youngest of the hospitals, that of San Giacomo established in 1540, was in a less alarming but nevertheless difficult condition.[6] At any rate, all five of these institutions saluted the authorization to open a public bank as an opportunity to recover from their current straits.[7]

Some of the reasons that led the Court to grant permission to open a public bank in the most pious places in the city clearly emerge from Guzman's visit itself. First of all, it is worth recalling that the reform of the statutes in the 1540s requested by Don Pedro De Toledo concerning the hospitals of the Incurabili and the Sant'Eligio, and in the case of the new hospital of San Giacomo, was, thanks to the royal patronage, a containment of the power of the local church to the advantage of the lay administrators, who represented the city's economic and even royal power. Guzman in his visit focused on the benefits that the pious sites would enjoy from the presence of the *super partes* "Homo de la corte," already present at the Incurabili. But another aspect that legitimized the operation was the opportunity of some of these assistance institutions to operate with ease in the economic and financial fabric. In fact, regarding the Annunziata and S. Eligio, Guzman expanded the old function of collecting deposits that were entrusted to their cash desks, as they were considered secure, issuing *fedi di deposito* or policies signed by the Governor on duty, an expression of municipal power.[8]

They thus all decided to found public banks after the example of the Monte di Pietà, one after the other: the Casa Santa and Ospedale dell'Annunziata in 1587, the Casa Santa e Ospedale degli Incurabili in 1589, the Casa Santa e Conservatorio dello Spirito Santo in 1590, the Casa Santa e Ospedale di Sant'Eligio in 1596, and the Casa Santa e Ospedale di San Giacomo degli Spagnoli in 1597.

[6] AGS, Visitas de Italia, legajo 24, libro 3, pp. 118–125, 153.

[7] In a note written by Avv. Gorgoglione in 1645, who opposed the separation of the Hospital of the Incurables from the Banco di S. Maria del Popolo, which we will see later, he argued that the causes that led the "Pious Places" to open a bank were two: "the first for the utility that comes from it [...], the second for the convenience that it provided; since the large Pious Houses, for the important negotiation and administration of inheritances and dowries, which they hold, it is necessary to have one's own Bank in order to maintain different accounts, which the other banks cannot do." It is interesting, therefore, also the accounting usefulness itself of having a bank for a better and rational administration of assets (Tortora 1890, pp. 79–80).

[8] AGS, Visitas de Italia, legajo 24, libro 3, pp. 21, 158.

In only ten years, the charities' banks won the trust of both the citizens and the Court. Thus, when—after the umpteenth default of the bankers Mari, Olgiatti, and others—the Genoan banker Francesco Saluzzo applied for authorization to open a "bank for deposit of individuals," to be called "Depositeria Generale," in Naples,[9] with branches in all the other provinces and in other towns in the Kingdom, the deputies of the *piazza dei nobili* (noblemen) of the city rose in strong opposition, arguing that "this benefit should be left to the banks of the pious places rather than to foreigners, whose only aim was profit" (Bulifon 1932, p. 68; Silvestri 1952, p. 7).[10] By this time, the notion was spreading that foreigners were essentially speculators, who brought cash money, already so scarce, out of the Kingdom through the various sources of revenue they had accumulated in years of mercantile and banking activities. Scaramelli, a Venetian diplomat residing in Naples, expressed the concern that the Genoese alone were "acquiring the best not only of Naples, but of the Kingdom, as well", having accumulated a rent of all of 1,200,000 ducats, of which 150,000 were revenues from fiefs, 900,000 came from mortgaged property, and the rest from 13 to 16 per cent rates of interest on various loans (*Corrispondenze diplomatiche veneziane da Napoli* 1991, p. 141).

In 1600, the bank of the Monte di Poveri was created to issue loans on pledge first to debt prisoners, then to any who requested them (De Rosa 1958b, pp. 5–29; De Rosa 1958a, pp. 49–78; Avallone 1995). The new century thus opened with a new structure of the credit and financial market. It was no longer private bankers who stood at the apex of the pyramid, but the public banks of charitable institutions. The singularity of the paper circulation system of these banks made a widespread impression, drawing attention and admiration from foreign observers in the Kingdom, the same ones who lamented the ease with which the "minutes" used for payments elsewhere in Italy could be forged (Palermo 1846, p. 228).

[9]The request to open a depository had been put forward by Antonio Belmosto to settle his claim against the Court following the conversion of the public income of 1594. However, he ceded this D. 30,000 privilege to the banker Saluzzo (*Corrispondenze diplomatiche veneziane da Napoli* 1991, p. 141).

[10]Biblioteca Nacional de Madrid, manuscrito n. 6722, ff. 39–40.

6 The Difficult Coexistence of Credit and Charity

But what happened to the charitable institutions? What benefits did they derive from this combination of charity and credit? What guarantees did they provide to depositors? The original plan was that the granting of credit and the investment of deposited capital in public rent should be a means to support the charitable activities of each mother institution by increasing its revenues and assets.[11]

As their statutes prescribed, the money deposited in the new banks should only be used in transactions with the state and the city and only the income earned from these investments could be used for charity activities. As a safeguard for depositors, it was strictly forbidden that the deposited money be used to support the charitable institution itself (Tortora 1890, *Nuovi documenti*, p. 83).[12] There are documents, however, showing that it was very hard for the charities not to take advantage of the deposited money to cover their high maintenance costs. Between 1597 and 1619, the Casa Santa di San Giacomo found it increasingly hard put to meet its costs. To reassure depositors, on 16 February 1620 the board of governors of the charity and of the bank signed a contract with the bank for a loan of 80,000 ducats, refundable at an annual instalment of 3200 ducats. The hospital could not suspend yearly payments for any reason whatsoever, not even in case of "natural calamities such as war, plague, or any other hindrance or fortuitous, divine, humane, contingent, rare, unusual or unexpected circumstance."[13] In case of insolvency of the present or future administrators of the Casa Santa, the payment would be demanded from the tenants of the homes and shops the charities owned.

The situation for the banks and their mother institutions worsened after an attempt by the government to regain possession of its sources of fiscal revenues through the conversion of public rent in 1594 (De Rosa 1987, pp. 71–88), the Belmosto operation. The most serious problem remained the alteration of coins. In substance, the real value of

[11] See, for example, what the Venetian diplomat resident in Naples, Giovanni Carlo Scaramelli, says about the Conservatory of the Spirito Santo, namely that the bank had been opened for the benefit of the charity institution (Corrispondenze diplomatiche veneziane da Napoli 1991, p. 205).

[12] ASBN, Banco di San Giacomo (BSG), AP, Miscellanea, m. 228, ff. 55–58.

[13] ASBN, BSG, AP, Miscellanea, mm. 225 e. 228.

circulating money was less than its nominal value. The problem went back to as early as the first half of the sixteenth century. In 1537, the value of all silver coins had been increased by 20 per cent because the ducat—the ancient currency of the Kingdom of Naples—had increased by 12 *carlini* due to forgery and clipping. Based on this ratio, the following smaller subdivisions had been created: *spezzati* (also known as *tarì*), *carlini*, *zannette*, and the *quarto di carlino* or *cinquina*.

All measures taken to protect the Neapolitan currency were fruitless. In 1609, legal course was maintained only for *zannette* and *tre cinquine*: all the other coins were to be withdrawn from circulation and taken to the Mint to be exchanged on a weight basis. In substance, any losses of value caused by coin clipping would be borne by the possessors of the coins. The measure was immediately revoked due to protests from several quarters; the situation, however, needed to be dealt with once and for all. The coins could not keep circulating as they were, as they were harming commerce by incessantly causing hikes in prices and foreign currency exchange rates. In March 1622, the Viceroy Cardinal Zapata issued a *prammatica* ruling that all low-denomination coins used in small trade—*zannette*, *tre cinquine*, and all other clipped or forged coins that did not have the right weight—should be withdrawn from circulation and replaced by new coins that were being minted, partly thanks to the initiative of some storeowners who had committed themselves to introducing silver for a value of 3 million ducats into the Kingdom.

Unfortunately, as is known, only 1,500,000 of the 6 million ducats to be replaced had been coined. This reflected on the banks, which all the creditors flocked to with their certificates, requesting them to be changed into the new currency. The banks, however—which had themselves been obliged by the Viceroy to send their metallic currency to the Mint for changing—resisted these requests, since the money in their coffers amounted to only a small part of the value of the circulating certificates. The reason for this was that, on the basis of a calculation of average deposit time, no less than 75 per cent of the deposited money had been put back in circulation. Part of these deposits had been loaned to the Court. Others had been used for charitable works or to pay the wages of the increasingly numerous personnel of the charities.

The banks were thus forced to close down. But their function was too important for the economy of the Kingdom, and especially for the government, which could request loans from them at any time. The Viceroy thus intervened in their favour, inviting them to reopen and granting them a moratorium. It was decreed that creditors could not be paid back more than 5 ducats per day, and until they had regained 2/3 of their credit.

In the meantime, only half of the new currency had been minted. Because of the loss of value in the exchange of the old coins with the new ones, the increasing scarcity of cash coin, and the inadequacy of the measures adopted against the trade and export of the new coins, the Cardinal's operation was ultimately an out-and-out failure. The consequences were further stagnation of small trade, drought, hunger, and popular exasperation.

Of course, to face this situation the banks tried to demobilize all their investments. They suspended all their social endeavours, as well as all interest free loans on pledge, and made cuts to their staff employed in banking activities (De Rosa 1958a, pp. 49–78). Furthermore, they decided to cover their ordinary management costs by charging interests on loans on pledge. Between 1628 and 1629, the banks were authorized to draw from their deposits of money sums ranging from 30,000 to 40,000 ducats to employ them for loans on interest, which would be used to cover the banks' ordinary management expenses.[14] Furthermore, for the Banco dello Spirito Santo, the condition for opening a pawn shop was a new and more rational reorganization of the governance of the charity institution divided into "four parts: Church, Conservatory, House and Bank." In substance from that moment the charity institution would have been "guarded" by a "Junta or Commission" of 7 people who would have been chosen to include a noble aged not less than 50 years, a lawyer and five bourgeois elected, including a foreigner merchant all aged not less than 35 years. Thus, every privilege of government of the charity went to the administration of the City of Naples (Tortora 1890, p. 84).

This reorganization did not suffice to pay off the banks' debts and bring their relationship with their mother institutions back to normality. Not even the Viceroy's decision, in 1623, to impose a new tax on wine of one ducat per barrel to refund part of the banks' losses on *zannette* helped

[14]ASBN, BP, AP, Libro maggiore di terze, m. 92, f. 172; Banco dei Poveri (BPOV), AP, Documenti di scritture diverse, m. 224, inc. 4; Banco del Santissimo Salvatore (BSS), AP, Libro maggiore di terze, m. 8, f. 32. Only the Banco di S. Maria del Popolo opened its loan at interest cash in 1648, when it obtained permission from the Viceroy for a capital of d. 6000 (Tortora 1890, p. 80).

them to make up for their deficits.[15] The privileged funding relationship went on for a few more years, causing concern among the depositors. This concern was probably shared by the state, which was anxious to appropriate the resources that were going from the banks to the charities they depended from in the form of loans or subsidies. The state needed those resources in order to cover the increasingly onerous costs of public administration. In 1636, on the occasion of the second bankruptcy of the bank of San Giacomo, the two institutions separated and administrative management was entrusted to two different councils of governors. In 1645, it was the Casa Santa degli Incurabili's turn to separate itself from the Banco di Santa Maria del Popolo. According to Tortora, in this case it was the bank that had taken advantage of the enormous wealth of the hospital, putting the latter's stability at jeopardy (Tortora 1890, pp. 76–78).

As to the two banks established to loan money at zero interest, that is, the Monte di Pietà and the Monte dei Poveri, the question of their relationship with their respective mother institutions was never raised, since their loans were guaranteed by pledges, which could be sold if needed. Actually, the Protectors of the Monte di Pietà had addressed the issue long before. In 1574, since there had been "a large increase both in gracious loans on pledge to the poor and in money deposits in the coffer of the said Monte," the decision was made to separate both the budget and the offices of the two administrations, which were lodged in two different apartments and placed each under the control of a Protector.[16]

Under certain aspects, the relationships between the charities of Sant'Eligio, Spirito Santo, and Annunziata and their respective banks were different. Their system of government, unlike the banks of San Giacomo and of Popolo where management was entrusted to a council of governors different from the charity institutions, continued to be unique (Salvemini 2000, pp. 311–313). The bankruptcy of the Banco dell'Annunziata in 1702, on the other hand, is due to a lack of definition of relations or competences between charity institution and credit institution. The Casa Santa to cover its huge expenses continued to use the Bank's *apodissary* deposits.[17]

[15] Only the Banco dell'Annunziata received nothing because it was unable to present the loss account (Tortora 1890, p. 253).

[16] ASBN, BP, AP, Libro di Conclusioni, Conclusione del1 giugno 1580, ff. 89–89v.

[17] D'Addosio writes that Casa Santa had an exposure towards the Bank for D. 1,802,450 (D'Addosio 1883, p. 250).

The fact that the banks were born to support the charitable institutions was so much acclaimed in the public opinion of the time that when the Banco dell'Annunziata failed, in the dispute between the creditors and the credit evaluation commission, the creditors argued that they should have recourse to the goods of the Casa Santa, since the Bank was set up to support its charity activities (Tortora 1890, p. 263).

7 Conclusions

As we have seen, as far as the Casa Santa di San Giacomo, the Casa Santa degli Incurabili, and the Casa Santa dell'Annunziata are concerned, the original plan to combine charity and credit by establishing public banks foundered. The Casa Santa di Sant'Eligio and the Conservatory of the Spirito Santo fared better. There were several reasons for these different outcomes, and especially for the decision of the governing boards of the first three institutions to put an end to the project. On the one hand, there were the interests of the clients, who were worried by the withdrawals from the bank's deposits for the upkeep of some of the cities' main charities, on the other, those of the state, which until the French takeover continued to draw on the banks' deposits to meet its own financial needs.

The main institutions engaged in the struggle against poverty were hard put to conciliate assistance and credit because they were themselves in need of funding to survive. The way they approached this problem is distinctive of the history of Neapolitan charitable institutions. As far as we know, no other cities—with the exception of Rome, where the Archiospedale established the Banco del Santo Spirito—devised a strategy similar to the one adopted in Naples, based on public banks.

The capital city of the Italian South thus gave a unique contribution to the reform of the management of pious institutions engaged in assisting the poor and the ill. The experiments conducted, starting from the second half of the 1500s, by some of the city's major lay foundations can be regarded as an original model, moving towards a resilient banking system, capable of holding up through crises, exogenous shocks, etc. This system endured for two centuries, until the French takeover, when the foundation was laid for the rise of modern banks, first with the creation of the Banco di Corte and then with that of the Banco dei Privati (the two banks were later fused in the Banco delle Due Sicilie, which eventually became the Banco di Napoli). It was also under the French that we see the first signs of the rise of the welfare state, notably the centralization of social policies under the newly created Consiglio Generale degli Ospizi and the state's levying of taxes to partly finance public assistance services.

The parallel may seem rash, but we find that the Amato Act of 1990 on banking foundations reflected a similar difficulty in finding the right balance between the credit and the assistance sector. The Amato Act sparked a long debate on the nature of banking foundations and on the need to distinguish the activities of banks from those of their foundations, ascribing to the latter an important role in the non-profit sector. The search for new solutions to the crisis of the welfare state prompted reflections on the possible role of banking foundations. Contrarily to modern-age practice, it was decided that banks should now establish foundations having their own resources and management, and engaged in providing public utility services, distinct from the profit-making activities of the bank.

References

Archivo General de Simancas. *Visitas de Italia*, legato 24, libri 1, 3.

Archivio Storico del Banco di Napoli. *Banco della Pietà*, Archivio Patrimoniale, Libro di Conclusioni, m. 232; Libro maggiore di terze, m. 92.

———. *Banco dei Poveri*, Archivio Patrimoniale, Documenti di scritture diverse, m. 224.

———. *Banco di San Giacomo*, Archivio Patrimoniale, Miscellanea, mm. 225, 228.

———. *Banco del Santissimo Salvatore*, Archivio Patrimoniale, Libro maggiore di terze, m. 8.

Archivio di Stato di Napoli, *Consiglio Collaterale*, Carte diverse, Processi penali del Collaterale, n. 339.

Avallone, P. 1995. *Stato e banchi pubblici a Napoli a metà del '700. Il Banco dei Poveri: una svolta*. Napoli: Edizioni Scientifiche Italiane.

Bacco, E. 1609. *Il regno di Napoli diviso in dodici provincie*. Napoli: appresso Gio. Giacomo Carlino e Constantino Vitale.

Barzazi A. (ed.) 1991. *Corrispondenze diplomatiche veneziane da Napoli. Dispacci*, vol. III (27 maggio 1597–2 novembre 1604). Roma: Istituto Poligrafico e zecca dello Stato.

Bianchini, L., 1839. *Della storia delle finanze del Regno di Napoli: libri sette*. Palermo: dalla Stamperia di Francesco Lao. For the note we used the reprint ed. Luigi De Rosa 1971. Napoli: Edizioni Scientifiche Italiane.

Biblioteca Nacional de Madrid. *manuscrito* 6722.

Biblioteca Nazionale di Napoli. *Sezione manoscritti*, manoscritti XV.B.11; XI.A.22.

Brancaccio, G. 2001. *Nazione genovese: consoli e colonia nella Napoli moderna*. Napoli: Guida Editori.

Bulifon, A. 1932. *Giornali di Napoli dal MDXLVII al MDCCVI*, vol. I, ed. N. Cortese. Napoli: Società Napoletana di Storia Patria.

Campanella, T. 1941. *La Città del Sole*, ed. N. Bobbio. Torino: Einaudi.

Coronella, S., L. Santaniello, M.E.C. Scelfo, and C. Monda. 2016. I Banchi Pubblici Napoletani e la gestione economica della peste del 1656. Il caso del Monte della Pietà. Storie di banche e di istituzioni finanziarie in una prospettiva economico-aziendale. In *Proceedings of the XIII Convention of the Italian Society of Accounting History*, Mantova.

Costabile, L. 2016. External Imbalances and the Money Supply: Two Controversies in the English "Realme" and in the Kingdom of Naples. In *Antonio Serra and the Economics of Good Government*, ed. S. Reinert and R. Patalano. London: Palgrave Macmillan.

D'Addosio, G. 1883. *Origine, vicende storiche e progressi della Real S. Casa dell'Annunziata di Napoli*. Napoli: per i tipi di Antonio Cons.

De Rosa, L. 1958a. Il Banco dei Poveri e la crisi economica del 1622. *Rassegna Economica* 1.

———. 1958b. Le origini curialesche del Banco dei Poveri (1563–1608). *Bancaria Review of the Italian Banking Association*.

———. 1987. *Il Mezzogiorno spagnolo tra crescita e decadenza*. Milano: Mondadori.

———. 1998. Immobility and Change in Public Finance in the Kingdom of Naples (1649–1806). *The Journal of European Economic History* XX–VIII. For the quote we used the translated reprint in De Rosa, Luigi. 2010, *Sulla banca, la finanza e la moneta, Scritti di L. de Rosa*, vol. 1. Soveria Mannelli: Rubettino, Ed.

———. 2002. *Gli inizi della circolazione della cartamoneta e i banchi pubblici napoletani nella società del loro tempo (1540–1650)*. Napoli: Istituto Banco di Napoli.

———. 2004. L'Archivio del Banco di Napoli e l'attività dei banchi pubblici napoletani, *De Computis, Revista Española de Historia de la Contabilidad*, n. 1.

De Sariis, A. 1795. *Codice delle leggi del regno di Napoli, Del pubblico commercio interiore per terra e per mare, e della pubblica sanità*. Libro ottavo. Napoli: presso Vincenzo Orsini, 1795, p. 200.

Ferorelli, N. 1990. *Gli Ebrei nell'Italia meridionale dall'età romana al secolo XVIII*, reprint ed. F. Patroni Griffi. Napoli: Dick Peerson.

Galiani F. 1750. *Della Moneta, libri cinque.* Napoli: presso Giuseppe Raimondi.

Palermo, F. 1846. *Narrazione e documenti sulla storia del Regno di Napoli dall'anno 1522 al 1667 raccolti e ordinati con illustrazioni.* Firenze: Gio. Pietro Viesseux.

Parrino, D.A. 1730. *Teatro eroico, e politico de' governi de' viceré del Regno di Napoli dal tempo del re Ferdinando il Cattolico fin all'anno 1683.* Napoli: per Francesco Ricciardo.

Petrone, G. 1871. *De' banchi di Napoli*, libri 2. Napoli: Raimondi.

Pullan, B. 1978. Poveri, mendicanti e vagabondi (secoli XIV–XVII). In *Storia d'Italia Einaudi, Annali I, Dal feudalesimo al capitalismo.* Torino: G. Einaudi.

Rocco, M. 1785. *De' banchi di Napoli e della lor ragione.* Napoli: Fratelli Raimondi.

Salvemini, R. 2000. Operatori sociali, operatori economici: gli enti di assistenza napoletani in età moderna. In *Povertà e innovazioni istituzionali in Italia. Dal Medioevo ad oggi*, ed. V. Zamagni. Bologna: Il Mulino.

———. 2011. La gestione delle Annunziate in età moderna. Il caso di Aversa e Cosenza. In *Ritratti di famiglia e infanzia. Modelli differenziali nella società del passato*, ed. G. Da Molin. Bari: Cacucci Editore.

Silvestri, A. 1951. *Sui banchieri pubblici napoletani dall'avvento di Filippo II al trono alla costituzione del monopolio: notizie e documenti.* Napoli: Bollettino dell'Archivio Storico del Banco di Napoli, tomo 3.

———. 1952. *Sui banchieri pubblici nella città di Napoli dalla costituzione del monopolio alla fine dei banchi dei mercanti. Nortizie e documenti.* Napoli: Bollettino dell'Archivio Storico del Banco di Napoli, tomo 4.

Toppi, N. 1655. *De origine omnium tribunalium.* Napoli: tipografia Onofrio Savi.

Tortora, E. 1890. *Nuovi documenti per la storia del banco di Napoli.* Napoli: Bellisario e c.

Woolf, S. 1988. *Poveri e assistenza nell'età moderna.* Laterza: Roma-Bari.

CHAPTER 5

The Investments of the Neapolitan Public Banks: A Long Run View (1587–1806)

Francesco Balletta, Luigi Balletta and Eduardo Nappi

1 Introduction

In this chapter we analyse the deposit and lending operations of the eight Neapolitan public banks for the period 1587–1806. These banks were established in Naples between 1539 and 1640 to substitute for private bankers (De Rosa 2002, pp. 437–439). The eight banks were: Pietà (established formally in 1584), Poveri (1587), Annunziata (1587), Popolo (1589), Spirito Santo (1590), S. Eligio (1592), S. Giacomo and Vittoria (1597) and Salvatore (1640). Seven of the eight banks sprung from charities and religious organizations, interested in using the large endowments they had accumulated through donations and legacies

F. Balletta
University of Rome "La Sapienza" – Unitelma, Rome, Italy

L. Balletta (✉)
Università di Napoli Federico II, Naples, Italy

E. Nappi
Historical Archive of the Bank of Naples, Naples, Italy

L. Costabile and L. Neal (eds.), *Financial Innovation and Resilience*, Palgrave Studies in the History of Finance,
https://doi.org/10.1007/978-3-319-90248-7_5

of the nobles and wealthy. Only one, the Banco del Salvatore, was not linked to a charity. Tax farmers (the administrators of the excise tax on flour) established it to facilitate collecting the tax and distributing the proceedings to their investors.

The Banco dell'Annunziata failed in 1702, the others survived until 1809, when they were closed or merged into the Banco delle Due Sicilie. They operated within the city walls and they dominated the banking market in Naples as an oligopoly until the merging of 1809. The banks collected deposits issuing an instrument called *fede di credito* or *fede di deposito*, a certificate in the name of the depositor, which was used to make payments via endorsement. The *fede di credito* was widely trusted, and it was accepted as near-money because it constituted legal proof of payment and because it allowed people to overcome the difficulties in using the Kingdom's coinage. Chronic problems were due to repeated specie devaluations, coin clipping, and a shortage of silver diverted to finance Spain's military campaigns.

For 220 years, from 1587 to 1806, at half-year frequency, we reconstruct the circulation of *fedi di credito*, i.e. the deposits at the banks, both in nominal and in real per capita terms, along with the lending activity of the banks. To shed light on the banks' lending activities, we categorize the various investments according to their characteristics and their destination. As the banks were located in distinct districts within the city walls, we also analyse the movement of their operations and relate them to the movement of the population. To this end, we grouped the 12 districts of Naples into 3 areas (North, South and Quartieri Spagnoli), each with its own socio-economic profile, where one or more banks operated.

Our objective is twofold. First, we wish to trace the quantitative history of the public banks in Naples, highlighting their extraordinary resilience in the face of many crises (caused by economic and political events, often exogenous to the activities of the banks themselves), thanks to their ability to learn and to the innovations introduced by the rulers and by their administrators. Second, by analysing lending activities we shed light on the role that the public banks played in the economic development of Naples, trapped as it was by many feudal institutions, the unfair collection of taxes due to tax farming and the confusion of the fiscal system based mostly on consumption taxes.

Before moving to the analysis of the banks' operations we trace the demographic profile of Naples in the seventeenth and the eighteenth centuries.

2 The Population of Naples During the Seventeenth and the Eighteenth Centuries and the Geographical Location of the Banks

Data on the population of Naples for this period are uncertain, but nonetheless progress has been made in the understanding of its demography using parish data. We rely mainly on Petraccone (1974), in particular regarding the subdivision in districts and areas, and other sources. We report the available data points in Table 1 and we stress that we are mainly preoccupied with picking up long run trends.

At the beginning of the seventeenth century population grew relatively fast, reaching 267,973 inhabitants at the 1606 census (Petraccone 1974, p. 13) and 250,000 in 1645 (Galanti 1969, I, p. 120). Then a major population event, the plague of 1656, hit the city hard. It is difficult

Table 1 Available data on the population of Naples (in parenthesis the percentage for each zone)

Years	*North*	*South*	*Quartieri Spagnoli*	*Total*
1593	108,086 (50.7)	55,642 (26.1)	49,459 (23.2)	213,187
1596	114,683 (50.7)	59,038 (26.1)	52,478 (23.2)	226,199
1606	130,771 (48.8)	71,281 (26.6)	65,921 (24.6)	267,973
1645	122,000 (48.8)	66,500 (26.6)	61,500 (24.6)	250,000
1655	146,400 (48.8)	79,800 (26.6)	73,800 (24.6)	300,000
1657	49,950 (33.3)	51,300 (34.2)	48,570 (32.5)	150,000
1688	60,182 (33.3)	61,773 (34.2)	58,767 (32.5)	180,722
1707	79,461 (37.1)	65,732 (30.7)	68,871 (32.2)	214,064
1742	115,136 (39.4)	79,301 (27.1)	97,759 (33.5)	292,196
1770	141,031 (40.1)	79,484 (22.6)	131,183 (37.3)	351,698
1790	156,373 (40.1)	88,147 (22.6)	145,498 (37.3)	390,018

Sources Beloch (pp. 118–121), Galanti (Tomo I, p. 120; Tomo II, pp. 251–253), Petraccone (1974, pp. 135–139), Romano (1909, p. 122 et seq.)

to assess its exact impact, but starting from a population of 300,000 in 1656 (Riaco 1658, pp. 244–245), many reconstructions agree that its impact was to halve the population. Thus we attribute a population of 150,000 to Naples right after the plague. This number, coupled with slow growth in the subsequent years, is consistent with the estimate reported by Petraccone (1974, p. 135) of 180,722 inhabitants in 1688. In the following years, population started to grow at a faster pace, also fuelled by immigration of the rural poor and the nobles: the former attracted by better job prospects and better chances to obtain bread due to public provision of wheat stocks (*annona del grano*), the latter by the many fiscal privileges given to the residents of the capital (Romano 1909, p. 12 et seq.; Coniglio 1951, pp. 55–56). The population finally reached 351,698 in 1770 and 390,018 in 1790 (Capasso 1883, p. 121; Beloch 1994, p. 121). During the eighteenth century there were moments of demographic setbacks, although none comparable to the plague of 1656, due to popular uprisings in 1741, the plague in Messina in 1743, and the famine of 1764 (Venturi 1973, pp. 437–438; De Rosa 1958, p. 169). As a consistency check, we remark that interpolating our point data returns a series that broadly agrees with the yearly series for the period 1767–1797 reported in Romano (1976, p. 204).

To assess the geographical distribution of banking activities we partition the city of Naples into three areas, each with its own socio-demographic characteristics (Petraccone 1974, p. 181), and its specific banks (see Fig. 1).

The North area, where Pietà, Poveri, Popolo, Annunziata and Salvatore operated, had a strong presence of nobles, clergy, well-off bourgeoisie and their many service people, servants and maids (Petraccone 1974, pp. 227–230). The South area, where S. Eligio was the only bank, had many productive activities with artisans, merchants and transport workers (Petraccone 1974, pp. 79–80; Maiello 1986, pp. 49–50). The Quartieri Spagnoli (i.e. the Spanish quarters, due to the barracks housing the Spanish military during the sixteenth and first half of the seventeenth century), where S. Giacomo and Spirito Santo were located, was characterized at first by a strong presence of the military, but later on it saw the in-migration of many well-off nobility and bourgeoisie, together with their servants, who moved from the more densely populated North and South areas to escape epidemics (Petraccone 1974, pp. 74–93).

The data in Table 1 document the long-run movement of the population of Naples within the city. At the beginning of the seventeenth

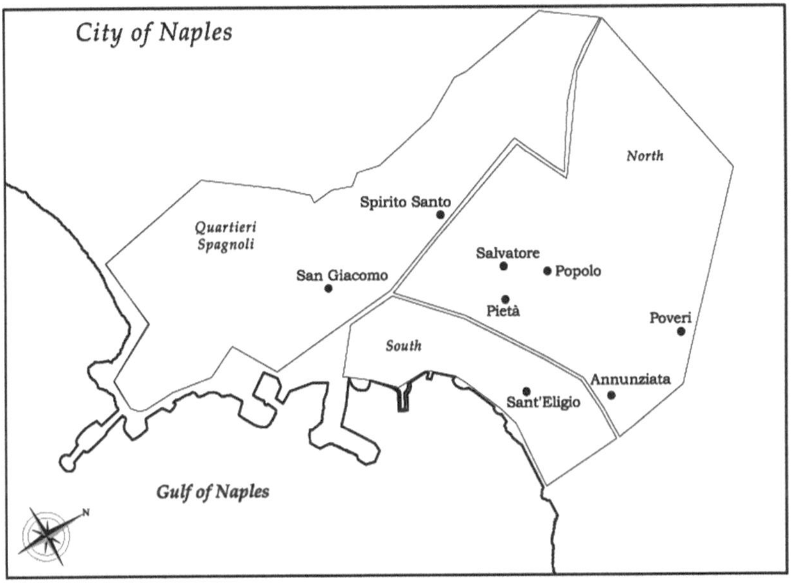

Fig. 1 Division of Naples in three areas (North, South and Quartieri Spagnoli) and the location of the banks. For the attribution of specific districts to each zone and for more details on population data, see Petraccone (1974, p. 181)

century over half of the population was concentrated in the North area, while the rest spread more or less evenly across the two other zones. The plague affected disproportionately the more densely populated area of the North, acting as an immediate equalizer and also inducing a long run movement from the North and the South toward Quartieri Spagnoli. At the end of the eighteenth century the Quartieri Spagnoli and the North housed 37.3 and 40.1 per cent of the total population, respectively.

The geographical location of the banks is relevant as Neapolitans rarely left the neighbourhood where they lived. As Pasquale Villari notes: "the people of one neighbourhood spend half their lives without going to another neighbourhood" (Cavour 1954, p. 41, our translation). Referring to the location of the banks within the city, Luigi De Rosa noted that they "served a certain area and we must conclude that this strategy contributed to the formation of a stable, and therefore solid, customer base" (De Rosa 2002, pp. 1516–1517, our translation).

3 The Structural Evolution of Neapolitan Public Banks (1587–1806)

All eight Neapolitan public banks except one sprung up from charities and religious organizations for the philanthropic purpose of helping the poorest families with loans (Gifuni 1801, pp. 1–10; Demarco 1963, p. 11; De Rosa 2002, pp. 509–515). This initial purpose was ever present in the discourse over their role for the economy of Naples. Before opening a public bank, the charity typically accepted deposits through a simple *cassa di deposito*. The trustworthiness of the charitable institutions, however, enabled them to transform their receipts for deposits (*fedi di deposito*) into bills of credit (*fedi di credito*) when pressed to do so by their clientele or patrons, as described above in Chapters 2–4. Most had become banks in practice before their official recognition and formal authorization by the Viceroy. Our records do not begin therefore until 1587, well after their banking activity had begun. After the Monte di Pietà received the first recognition as a public bank for its Banco della Pietà in 1584, the other charities hurried to ask for the same authorization. When their banks received official authority as well, they collected deposits through issues of *fedi di credito*, transferred funds across accounts, and granted loans (Demarco 1996a, p. 50). Although they were recognized as public banks and supervised by publicly appointed delegates, the charity still owned the bank and kept the profits. Their accounting methods did not change significantly throughout the seventeenth and eighteenth centuries, while they provided their services almost exclusively within the city of Naples.

In 1702 Banco dell'Annunziata went bankrupt, with estimated total losses of 4 million ducats (Demarco 1996b, pp. 36–37). The residual assets of the bank, by order of Viceroy Medina Coeli (1695–1702), were transferred to the Banco dei Poveri (Demarco 1996b, pp. 34–35). In the eighteenth century, the banks went through other difficult moments, all of which they were able to overcome. At the end of the century, however, the political events were such that the 200-year history of resilience to adversities collapsed.[1]

[1] For a more detailed chronicle of cycles in the history of the banks, see Balletta (2008).

The difficulties started at the end of the eighteenth century with the outbreak of the French Revolution, and the military mobilization by European rulers worried by the consequences of a war with France (Cusumano 1887, p. 81; Demarco 1986, 1996a, p. 63). The King of Naples, Ferdinand IV of Bourbon, needed money to finance the army. He turned to the banks, which between 1792 and 1793 lent approximately 2 million ducats to the Crown. At the same time, poor wheat harvests forced the city of Naples to ask for loans to provide wheat to the population. Because of the increased demand for loans, the banks were forced to issue *fedi* not backed by actual inflow of metallic coins. The same scarcity of metallic coins led borrowers to repay in *fedi* and not in metal, leading to a progressive deterioration of the banks' reserves. Naturally, this brought about an increase in prices.

But the troubles of the banks were only beginning. In September 1794 the King appointed a *Giunta dei banchi*, a committee that put them under strict tutelage and imposed many limits to their operations. Henceforth, the banks had to be conceived not as distinct entities owned by charities, but rather as different desks of a single Banco Nazionale, which had to serve the interests of the nation (Tortora, pp. 329–331). The banks continued to keep separate internal organizations and accounting books but the centralization measures took away their autonomy and independence (Maiello 1980, pp. 42–43). When Ferdinand fled to Sicily at the end of 1798, he took with him most of the reserves of the banks. The Neapolitan Republic (29 January 1799–23 June 1799) then employed the banks to collect taxes and make payments, but the situation deteriorated rapidly (Nappi 1999, pp. 87–88). When the Republic ended, the banks closed for three months. With the return of Ferdinand in May 1800 the nominal value of *fedi* issued during the Republic was voided, so that reimbursements took place at very uncertain and plummeting market rates. In the years that follow the banks went through a period of reorganization, leading to their final merging into the Banco delle Due Sicilie in 1809 (see Fig. 2).[2]

[2]At the time of Italy's unification the Banco delle Due Sicilie became Banco di Napoli, which was one of the issuing banks of the Kingdom of Italy, showing a fundamental continuity in the history of fiduciary money in Naples.

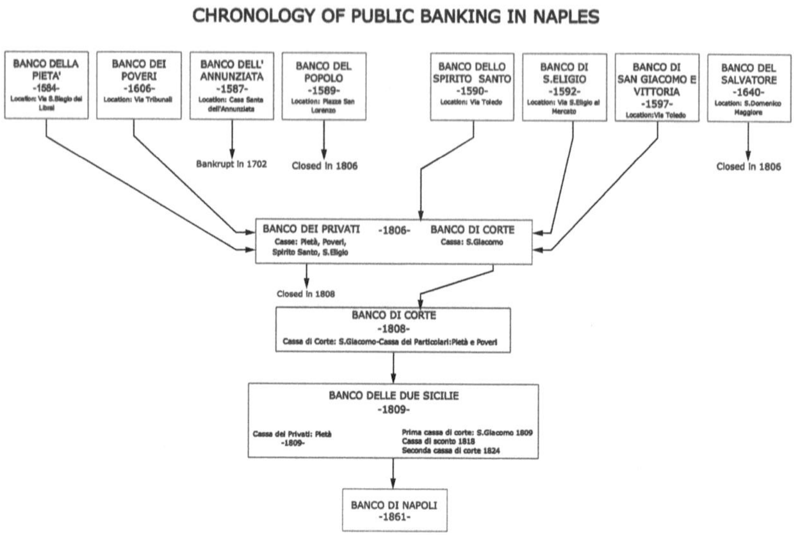

Fig. 2 The history of public banking in Naples

4 DATA: THE BALANCE SHEETS OF THE BANKS

From the large documentation produced by the eight Neapolitan banks, we quantified 220 years of their deposits and circulation of *fedi di credito* as well as the uses to which the banks put the money they collected from their depositors. For each bank, the starting year of our available data coincides with the date of their establishment, except for Pietà, whose documentation starts in 1611, and Poveri, which starts in 1605.

The main archival resource used in our research is the *Libro Maggiore* of the *apodissario*, where the banks recorded their transactions keeping a different account for each client, and the related *pandetta*, which was an alphabetic index with the names of the clients and the page of *Libro Maggiore* corresponding to that account. Included in the accounts of the *Libro Maggiore* are the accounts for the *Cassa Maggiore* (i.e. the "big till", where the banks recorded the amounts of specie deposited in the bank's vault), the *Cassa Piccola* (i.e. the "small till", that is the account used to keep track of the money used for the everyday operations of withdrawals and deposits) and the accounts opened to the charity that created the bank and to the bank itself for its operating needs (Demarco 2000, p. 204; De Simone 1974, pp. 49–56).

Table 2 The "ristretto" balance sheet of Neapolitan public banks

Creditori	*Debitori*	
Creditori Apodissari	Cassa Maggiore	Reserve
	Cassa Piccola	
	Conto dei pegni	Investments
	Conto delle Compre	
	Conto dei Prestiti	
	etc.	
Depositi		Circulation

Twice a year for most years, but sometimes three times or one time per year, the banks closed the account books, computed the balance for each account and reported the related *ristretto* (condensed) balance sheet at the end of the *Libro Maggiore* (Table 2). In the *Creditori* section there was the balance of the accounts of the bank's depositors, the bank's total liabilities. In the *Debitori* section there was the balance of the accounts of the debtors to the bank, which included the aggregate investment accounts for the amounts loaned using different instruments and going to different uses together with the balances in the *Cassa Maggiore* and *Cassa Piccola,* the bank's total assets. The two sides had to balance, so one can read this document as showing the ability of the bank to satisfy its creditors for deposits, either with cash or with the amounts loaned to third parties (Rocco 1785, pp. 8–10; Demarco 2000, p. 210).[3] Our archival research consisted in recording and reconstructing the Debitori section of this balance sheet, which sometimes was missing from the Libro Maggiore and therefore had to be reconstructed from the single accounts.

From the balance sheet we obtain the circulation of *fedi di credito*, which corresponds to the deposits in the bank. The cash in the two *Casse* constituted the reserves. The difference between circulation and reserves, which represents the part of deposits not held as reserves, corresponds to our definition of investments of the bank. The categorization and quantification of the balance of the investment accounts, of which examples are the *Conto Pegni* (pawns) and *Conto Compre* (explained below), allows us to obtain a quantitative long-run view of the investment policy of the

[3] A word of caution, however, as this document cannot be exactly compared to a modern balance sheet, as the investment accounts often included sums that were committed to a particular destination but not yet used.

Neapolitan banks. The end result is a dataset for the period 1587–1806 at half-year frequency that contains, for each bank, in addition to the circulation and reserve, also the amounts invested in the major investment categories (described below). We use this dataset in the following sections to trace the quantitative history of the public banks in Naples.

5 The Collection of Deposits

The public banks in Naples were able to grant loans thanks to the money they collected through the deposit service, for which the banks did not charge a fee or pay interest. In fact, the preferred payment method for commercial transactions was not specie but the *fede di credito* or *fede di deposito* guaranteed by the bank. The reason for this was the dismal quality of metallic coins subject to coin clipping, silver shortage and the fact that the *fede* constituted legal proof of payment. The client could nonetheless deposit the sum with the bank but not ask for a *fede* (Demarco 2000, p. 191). With the issuing of a *fede* the depositor could use the money deposited issuing a *polizza*, that is a payment order addressed to the bank holding the deposit (Tortora 1888, p. 142). Whenever on a *fede* different sums were added and withdrawn it was called the *madrefede*.

The *fede di credito* could be transferred via endorsement, which could be *per altrettanti* or *per causa*, the difference being that for the latter the reason of the transfer was noted. Quite importantly, the banks mutually accepted each other's *fedi* (see Sect. 6) (Rocco 1785, p. 25; Somma 1844, pp. 237–238; Demarco 2000, p. 200). Whenever specific needs by public institutions arose—such as wars, famine, earthquakes—the banks issued *fedi a vuoto di introito*, that is, without actual cashing in the related sum of money, thereby making unsecured loans (Rocco 1785, p. 100; Demarco 2000, p. 200). At the end of the eighteenth century large amounts of *fedi a vuoto* were issued, which caused a crisis of confidence for which a radical reform was needed. At the beginning of the nineteenth century many *fedi* were withdrawn from circulation and destroyed.

The analysis of the quantitative evolution of aggregate circulation and reserves allows us to periodize the history of the public banks, which we will use for the rest of the paper. In Fig. 3 we report the time series of circulation and reserves and in Table 3 we compute long-run nominal

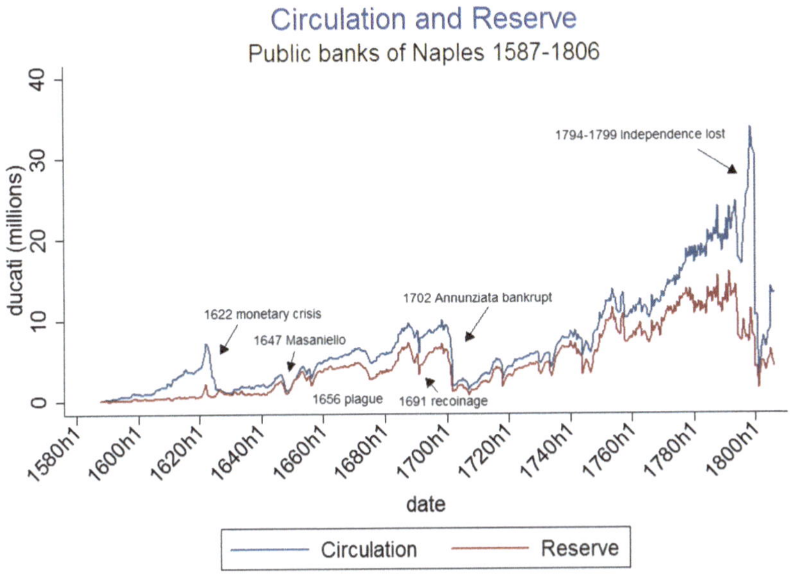

Fig. 3 Aggregate circulation and reserve of the public banks of Naples

averages, also including investments.[4] The first period, which runs from 1587 to 1622, is characterized by a strong growth in activities, partly due to the sequential entry on the market of the successive banks, and partly due to a rather aggressive policy of issuing *fedi*. The period 1611–1622 is notable. Circulation averaged 3.94 million ducats, 4.5 times the circulation over the period of the banks' foundation (1587–1610). The reserves of 0.65 million ducats were leveraged just over 6 times to provide loans of 3.29 million ducats. The monetary crisis of 1622, which was partly exogenous to the activity of the banks, found them unprepared and overexposed, so much so that their survival seemed at risk (see Chapter 2 in this volume).

[4]For most of the time period in analysis the public banks formed the bulk of the banking market in Naples. As the deposits in the public banks could be used as a mean of payment through the *fede di credito*, aggregate circulation is also a measure, in modern terms, of the difference between M1 and M0.

Table 3 Aggregate circulation, reserve and investments of the public banks in Naples, averages in million ducats

	Balance sheet composition public banks of Naples		
Years	*Circulation*	*Reserve*	*Investments*
1587–1610	0.86	0.20	0.66
1611–1622	3.94	0.62	3.29
1623–1655	2.25	1.47	0.78
1656–1701	6.61	4.51	2.09
1702–1750	5.24	3.94	1.30
1751–1793	15.40	10.68	4.72
1794–1799	24.24	8.45	15.79
1800–1806	8.81	4.21	4.60

This event seems to have temporarily undermined the confidence of Neapolitans in the banks. Until the plague of 1656, circulation fell to an average of 2.25 million ducats, a number also influenced by the Masaniello uprising of 1647 which momentarily hit the banks hard enough to cause bank runs and the temporary closure of some. On the other hand, the banks seem to have learned from the crisis and moved towards a more prudent management, keeping an average reserve of 1.47 million ducats, over 65 per cent of circulation. In the long run this strategy seemed to pay. The plague of 1656 slowed down the activity of the banks but it did not cause a major crisis. The second half of the seventeenth century is characterized by slower growth, with two crises corresponding to the Messina uprising (1674–1678) and a new re-coinage (1691), but the crisis of 1622 seems to be forgotten: circulation averaged 6.61 million ducats and reserves 4.51 million ducats, 68 per cent of deposits.

However, the death of Charles II of Spain and the outbreak of the War of Spanish Succession marked the beginning of a new profound period of crisis. In just three years, the banks lost approximately 79 per cent of their circulation (from 9.12 million ducats in the first semester of 1700 to 1.91 million ducats in the second semester of 1702) and reserves fell from 6.12 million ducats to 1.29 million ducats. One of the oldest banks, Annunziata, went bankrupt. The years that follow, spanning the Austrian domination (1707–1734) and the coming of Charles of Bourbon as the first King of Naples and Sicily (1734–1759), are characterized by a slow recovery, which took approximately 50 years to regain the pre-crisis level of circulation.

In the second half of the eighteenth century, especially after 1770, partly thanks to the expansionary policy of Ferdinand IV, the level of activity began rising again. Until 1793 circulation averaged 15.4 million ducats and reserves 10.68 million ducats. But at the end of the century, the events following the French revolution led to the final crisis of the banks. The military needs of the Crown coupled with the lost independence of the banks caused an abnormal jump in circulation (roughly doubling in the span of the six years between 1794 and 1799), fuelled most likely by the issuing of *fedi* without inflow of specie, a decrease in the reserve and a jump in investments. At the outbreak of the Neapolitan Revolution the King fled to Sicily taking part of the specie reserves of the banks with him. After the return of the King to Naples in 1800 the banks went through a period of reorganization, which lasted well into the nineteenth century.

The comparison across periods for such a long time span is made difficult by the changing of the demographic and economic conditions of the city of Naples. To offer a more thorough analysis, in Table 4 we attempt to convert values from units of account (*ducato*) into per capita

Table 4 Circulation and investments per capita, in grams of silver and *tomolo* of wheat (1 *tomolo* is approximately 56 kg)[a]

Years	*Circulation (per capita)*		*Investments (per capita)*	
	Silver (gr.)	*Wheat (t.)*	*Silver (gr.)*	*Wheat (t.)*
1587–1610	88.66	2.19	67.70	1.67
1611–1622	363.37	10.41	305.33	8.72
1623–1655	172.02	6.02	58.57	2.04
1656–1701	742.02	33.40	230.81	10.55
1702–1750	378.60	15.49	95.54	3.90
1751–1793	840.49	25.39	250.27	7.34
1794–1799	1155.80	21.64	757.91	14.12
1800–1806	407.07	6.77	213.47	3.55

[a]The silver equivalent is obtained using the series of grams of pure silver per carlino (1 ducato = 10 carlini) in the Allen (2001) dataset, available at http://www.iisg.nl/hpw/data.php#europe. The series for the price of wheat is taken from Faraglia (1878). The population data are obtained by interpolating the data in Table 1

values in silver (using the silver content of a smaller denomination coin, the *carlino*) and in per capita real values in terms of wheat. From Table 1 we recall that the plague was a major population event, approximately halving the population of Naples immediately and slowing down its growth in the decades that follow. It is interesting that we observe no such dramatic fall in the activities of the banks. On the contrary, the nominal values of circulation and investment increase. The obvious consequence is a jump in per capita values over the previous period, by a factor of approximately 5. A further consequence of taking into account real per capita values is that the level of circulation in the period 1751–1793 becomes comparable to the period 1656–1707, while investments are actually lower. Indeed, the two periods differ markedly in terms of population (see Table 1) and prices (the price of a *tomolo* of wheat is on average 1.19 ducats in 1656–1701 and 1.89 in 1751–1793). Finally, the numbers for the period of lost independence of the banks (1794–1799) show that, while investments doubled in real per capita terms over the average of the previous period, circulation actually fell, witnessing a severe disruption of the banking system.

As a final glimpse into the evolution of the banking market in Naples, in Table 5 we compute average market shares for circulation and investments and in Fig. 4 we show the distribution within the city. In all periods under consideration, market concentration remains quite stable. The number of "effective banks" (the inverse of the Herfindahl index) ranges from about 5.5 to 6, thus the market is slightly more concentrated than

Table 5 Market shares of circulation for each of the public banks in Naples and Herfindahl index (sum of market shares squared)

	Market shares—Circulation				
	1611–1622	*1623–1639*	*1640–1701*	*1702–1750*	*1751–1799*
Pietà	0.160	0.146	0.265	0.174	0.087
Poveri	0.025	0.103	0.09	0.132	0.098
Popolo	0.197	0.152	0.066	0.099	0.147
Annunziata	0.058	0.195	0.22	–	–
Salvatore	–	–	0.057	0.152	0.135
S. Eligio	0.193	0.16	0.072	0.111	0.122
Spirito Santo	0.205	0.095	0.103	0.20	0.155
S. Giacomo	0.162	0.149	0.127	0.132	0.255
Number of active banks	7	7	8	7	7
Herfindahl index	0.182	0.172	0.185	0.163	0.168

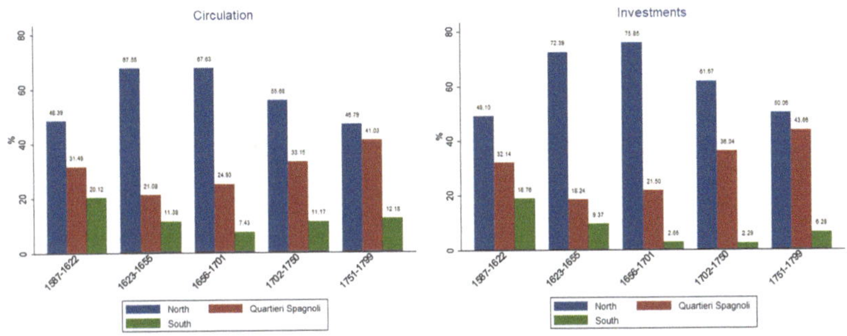

Fig. 4 Geographical distribution of circulation and investments within the city of Naples

what an equal share among the number of active banks would imply. However, the identities of the dominant firms change over time. Prior to 1622 the five dominant firms were Pietà, Popolo, S. Eligio, Spirito Santo and S. Giacomo, the first two leading the market in the North, while the last two roughly shared the Quartieri Spagnoli market. The city distribution roughly matched the distribution of the population.

After the 1622 crisis, activities became concentrated in the North until 1701. This is the more remarkable as the plague of 1656 hit the densely populated North harder than other areas. We note that Annunziata was the second largest bank for most of the seventeenth century (indeed, in 1701 right before bankruptcy it was the largest bank, with 35 per cent market share). Thus its bankruptcy was a true systemic event. The turn of the century marks the beginning of a long-run movement of activities back to Quartieri Spagnoli, which roughly matches the movement of the population shown in Table 1. This is coupled with the loss of the leading role of Pietà and the growth in activities of Salvatore, which entered the market as a minor player but became the fourth largest bank by the end of the century.

6 The Investments of the Banks

In this section we take a closer look at the investment policy of the public banks. We start by showing in Fig. 5 the evolution of the aggregate investment policy of the banks measured by the investment ratio (investments/circulation), and in Table 6 we compute long-run averages.

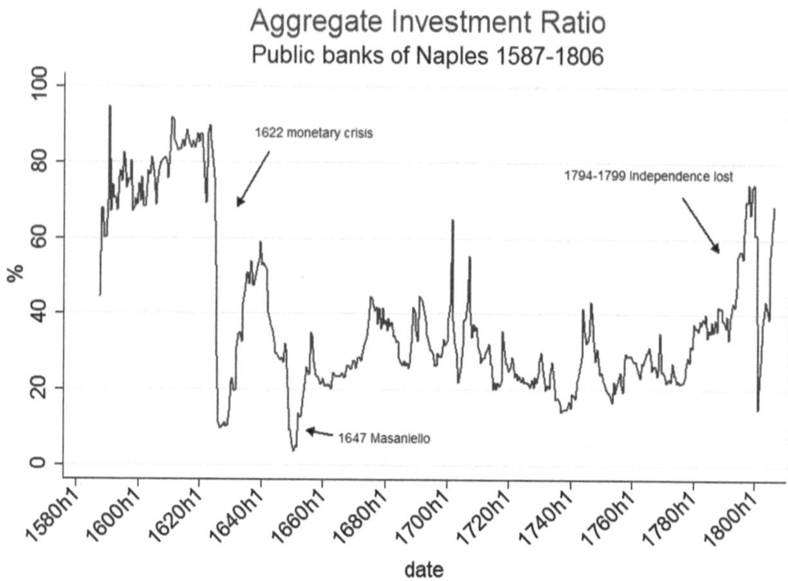

Fig. 5 Aggregate investment ratio (Aggregate investments/Aggregate circulation)

Table 6 Aggregate investment ratio (Aggregate investments/ Aggregate circulation)

Years	*Aggregate investment ratio public banks of Naples*
1587–1622	77.05
1623–1655	32.87
1656–1701	31.57
1702–1750	26.49
1751–1793	29.34
1794–1799	63.53

Prior to the crisis of 1622 investments averaged 77.05 per cent of circulation. The crisis is a turning point and marks a structural break in the policy of the banks. From a long-run perspective, the banks seem to learn that being overexposed leaves them vulnerable to exogenous shocks and they switch to a more prudent stance. There follows a long period of relative stability, with a peak at 65 per cent corresponding to the crisis of 1701 driven by the fall in reserves due to the bank runs surrounding the bankruptcy of Annunziata, and cycles around a long-run average of approximately 30 per cent. The picture also shows the abnormal increase in the investment ratio in the period 1794–1799, when in just a few years it jumps from approximately 40 per cent to 75 per cent.

The banks invested in a variety of directions. The final step is to break down the aggregate investments according to the characteristics and the destination of the loan. For the long period in analysis, we identified five major categories of accounts that appear in the Debitori section of the balance sheet: (a) loans granted against pawns; (b) *compre e ricompre di annuee entrate*; (purchase and re-purchase of public debt) (c) *prestiti, mutui* and *terze*; (d) loans to institutions; (e) current accounts of the banks with themselves and with the charity. In addition, we recorded other categories of investments which appear to be relevant in some specific time periods; (f) operations with the Mint; (g) operations with the fairs; and (h) debts of other banks for the mutual acceptance of *fedi di credito*.

(a) *Loans Granted Against Pawns*

The operation that mostly characterized the use of funds by the public banks of Naples was the loan against pawns of objects (such as jewels, plate or cloth). The duration of the loan could not exceed six months and it could be extended for a maximum of three years, hence it was mainly a short-term loan. At expiration the object was auctioned to the public if the owner had not already redeemed the object. Once subtracting the amount loaned plus interest and a commission for the bank, the proceeds were given back to the owner of the object (Filangieri 1940, pp. 185–201; Tortora 1888, pp. III–VII). Before the monetary crisis of 1622 only Pietà and Poveri granted small loans without interest against pawn, for objects of value not exceeding 10 ducats. The nature of this operation was mainly charitable as it was conceived to help the poor. After the crisis, the banks were granted formal permission to start a pawning operation charging interest for larger sums, with the purpose of covering the expenses for the deposit services (for which, we recall, the banks did not charge a fee). Since then, and until the final demise of the banks at the beginning of the nineteenth century, pawns were the "business-as-usual" operation that characterized the lending activity of the public banks of Naples.

(b) *Compre e ricompre di annue entrate*

At the time when the public banks were created, in Naples canon and civil laws prohibited charging interest, as it was considered usury. To circumvent the prohibition, the public banks entered in an operation called *compra e ricompra di annuee entrate* (literally, "buy and buy-back of yearly revenues") (Assante et al. 1972, p. 69; Filangieri 1940, pp. 45–46). The loan took the form of a contract whereby a rent (such as the proceeds from renting land, a house, or the proceeds from a tax) was bought (*compra*) against a buy-back pact (*ricompra*), which was the repayment of the loan. The capital value, and so the amount borrowed, was obtained by discounting the rent. In this operation the interest rate was somewhat implicit, being the rate at which the rent was discounted. The date at which the buy-back option expired was often absent, thus it was naturally a long-term investment. Moreover, the proceeds from the underlying rent could undergo significant variations, which made it a risky investment.

(c) *Prestiti, mutui* and *terze*

In addition to *compre*, the public banks granted also loans that were repaid at fixed intervals, which went under the names of *mutui* (the modern term for mortgages) and *terze*. The latter was a typical loan repaid in three installments per year (Easter, mid-August and Christmas). We will refer to both *mutui* and *terze* as generically *prestiti*, the name under which they were often referred to in the books. In these cases the interest rate was explicit, and the banks slowly moved toward this kind of lending during the second half of the eighteenth century.

Table 7 Interest rates on *compre* and *prestiti* of Banco della Pietà (Allocati 1966)

Years	*Interest rates on compre and prestiti*
1587–1622	7.4
1623–1656	7.04
1656–1702	6.4
1703–1750	5.8
1751–1799	3.8

In our dataset we only observe aggregate values at the closing of the accounts. To obtain a glimpse on the interest rates and on the individual *compre* and *prestiti* we can refer to the documents of Banco della Pietà published by Antonio Allocati (Allocati 1966, pp. 13–169).[5] In Table 7 we report average interest rates on *compre* and *prestiti* (with a positive rate). As we can see, the interest rate followed a decreasing path, going from above 7 per cent at the beginning of 1600 to below 4 per cent at the end of the eighteenth century.[6]

The documents also contain information on the rent backing the operation, the receiver of the loan and sometimes the intended use of the money. The vast majority of the operations was backed by income deriving from fiefs, houses and land, from *fiscali* (taxes collected by local authorities on behalf of the state) and *arrendamenti* (tax farming). Whenever loans were directed to individuals, in at least half of the cases they were members of the nobility. The money was used mainly to buy houses, land or feudal rights, for marriages and sometimes for charity (Allocati 1966, pp. 13–169; Demarco 1996a, pp. 23–24, 72; De Simone 1976, p. 90). It is noteworthy that among the 831 loans recorded by Allocati only one, in 1788 for 20,000 ducats, went to an industrial activity, the cloth factory of Piedimonte. Indeed, according to De Simone, the loans of the public banks were mainly "limited to the support of public finances and the nobility and bourgeoisie. There is no trace, even sporadically, of investments with merchants, artisans or manufacturers" (De Simone 2010, p. 102, our translation).

[5] The transcripts published by Allocati refer to 831 operations of Banco della Pietà for the time period 1540–1804.

[6] Although these data refer to only one bank and they do not include all its operations, they are broadly consistent with information from other sources to be taken as an indication of the most common interest rates charged in Naples. For example, the interest rates in the period 1751–1799 are consistent with the data for Banco della Pietà published by De Simone (1974). According to Demarco, in 1767 the Banco di Santo Spirito granted *mutui* at 4 per cent interest (Demarco 1996a, pp. 23–24). Maiello, in his study on the debts of the nobility, notes that for the second half of the 1700 the most common interest rates were 3.5–4 per cent (Maiello 1986, pp. 109, 122). Galiani claims that the interest rate in Naples around the time of his writing *Della Moneta* was between 3 and 5 per cent (Galiani 1750, p. 281).

(d) *Loans to Institutions*

The public banks granted loans to a variety of institutions, both public and private. They could be either general purpose loans or loans for specific objectives. Notably, we find accounts opened for generic loans to the Regia Corte, for the Viceroy first and then the King after 1734, and to the Eletti della Città, the administrators of the City of Naples. We also find accounts opened for more specific purposes such as public works within the city walls, the construction of roads and bridges in Calabria, Puglia and Terra di Lavoro, for public health, loans to hospitals and charities such as the Albergo dei Poveri and Monte dei Maritaggi. Among the loans granted for specific needs to the administrators of the City of Naples there are the ones for the *annona*, the old institute of public provision of basic goods to be distributed to shops for sale to the population (Balletta 2008, pp. 120–122; Capasso 1876, pp. V and VI). In Naples between 1500 and 1800 there was the *annona* for wheat and oil (Demarco 1996a, p. 69). These loans were without interest and the banks could not refuse to grant them because they were often imposed by a ruling of the King (Demarco 2000, p. 151). The liberalization of the wheat and oil market happened in 1804, and it was quite a relief for the banks not to be forced to finance the *politica annonaria* anymore (Bianchini 1839, p. 364; Demarco 2000, p. 152).

In the Kingdom of Naples, between 1500 and 1700, the majority of state and city taxes were collected through the system of tax farming, the *arrendamenti* (from the Spanish word *arrendar*, to rent). The individuals who paid the rent for tax collection were the *consegnatari* (Demarco 2000, p. 104; De Rosa 1958, pp. 90–95). The *arrendamento* on a tax could be divided into shares, whose capital value took the name of *partita di arrendamento*, which could be traded. Governors who were appointed by the Viceroy first and then the King managed the *arrendamenti* (De Simone 1983, pp. 725–726). In 1649 a sale of 56 *arrendamenti* (*in solutum et pro soluto*) took place to the *consegnatari*, who took the name of *assegnatari* since they became the owners of the tax rent, a transaction that very much resembles public debt (Galanti 1969, p. 113; De Simone 1983, p. 707). The banks had accounts opened to the governors of *arrendamenti*, where they recorded the inflow of proceeds from tax collection and the outflow of payments to the owners of the right to receive the rent. When there was a negative mismatch between inflows and outflows we find the sum in the Debitori section of the balance sheet, which could be interpreted as a loan to the administration of *arrendamenti* (De Rosa 1958, p. 89). After the failure to buy back these rights, by the Austrian government first and then by Charles of Bourbon, the system of *arrendamenti* was definitely abolished by the French government in 1806 (Somma 1844, p. 234; Demarco 2000, p. 121). It meant a significant loss for the banks which, in addition to the treasury service described above, had also invested a conspicuous amount of their own money in *arrendamenti* (Demarco 1996a, p. 118; Rapporto generale 1808, p. 20).

(e) *Current Accounts of the Banks with Themselves and with the Charity*

The financial relationship between a bank and the charity from which it was created was the same as the relationship with other institutions (Demarco 2000, p. 225). The banks opened an account in the Libro Maggiore that kept track of the cash flows for the current operations of the charity. Quite interestingly, the bank itself had an account in its own name, where it recorded its operating cash flow. At the end of the period, if the current account had a negative balance (outflows of money exceeded inflows), the event was interpreted as a loan that the depositors made to the bank and/or charity. In this case, the balance appeared as an asset in the Debitori section of the balance sheet (De Simone 1974, p. 50; Demarco 2000, p. 207).

In Fig. 6 we report the share of each of the main five categories of investments described above in total investments. In the first period of activity until the crisis of 1622, the public banks mainly invested in *compre* (50.43 per cent of aggregate investments) and a distant second in *mutui* and *terze* (12.42 per cent). At this time, the pawning activity was limited to small loans without interest by Pietà and Poveri. The crisis marks a clear turning point in the direction of investments. As we noted above, from 1628 on, the banks were granted permission to open a pawning activity against interest to finance the deposit service. From then on, pawns became the major category of investment, ranging from 40 to over 60 per cent of total investment. The figure also shows the anomaly of the period 1794–1799, when the banks cease to operate as usual, granting a disproportionate amount of *prestiti* (50.84 per cent) at the expense of pawns (14.54 per cent) and the share of loans to institutions doubles over the previous period.

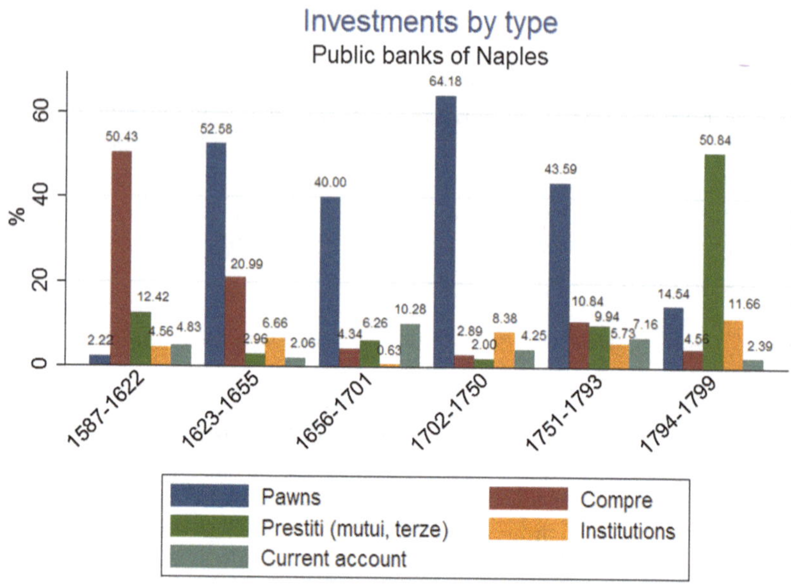

Fig. 6 Share of aggregate investments for the main five categories: Pawns, *compre*, *mutui* and *terze*, institutions and current account

(f) *Accounts Opened to the Mint*

During re-coinage operations, the public banks collected the coins from the public to be sent to the Mint for melting and creating new coins. The banks recorded the amounts sent for re-coinage in the accounts opened to the Mint. These operations are quantitatively relevant around two major episodes of re-coinage. For example, until the second semester of 1621 operations with the Mint averaged around 1 per cent of investments, jumped to 11 per cent in the first semester of 1622, and to 21 per cent at the end of 1622, only to fall back to 1 per cent at the end of 1624, when the re-coinage ended. The same behaviour is found around the re-coinage of 1688–1691. There were no Mint operations immediately before 1687, but they then peak at 19 per cent in the first semester of 1688, and disappear again by 1692.

(g) *The Operations with the Fairs*

In the Kingdom of Naples major fairs took place in Lanciano, Lucera, Aversa, Foggia and Salerno, where merchants from Lucca, Venice, Genoa, Sicily and Catalonia did business (Coniglio 1951, p. 116; Grohmann 1969, p. 79). During trading days, the public banks of Naples kept a desk for the exchange of *fedi*. A merchant could deposit a sum in Naples against a *fede* whereby the bank promised to repay the sum, even in a different currency, at the location of the fair. The repayment could then be made to the depositor or to others in his name. The advantage for the merchant was that he did not have to carry coins, which could be subject to theft (Ferrara 1935, p. 14; Demarco 2000, p. 300). In the balance sheets we find operations with fairs concentrated in the period 1611–1622, when they averaged at around 3 per cent of total investments.

After 1622 the operations related to internal currency exchange (that is, money exchange across different locations in the Kingdom) were prohibited as the profits from exchanging at less than face value was considered unjustified and thus usury (Di Somma 1960, p. 332). In reality, the banks did not comply with this prohibition. Proof of this is found in the accounts of S. Eligio and Popolo, where we find traces of operations at the Salerno fair between 1635 and 1645.[7]

(h) *Debts of Other Banks for the Mutual Acceptance of fedi di credito*

Among the Debitori accounts we also find accounts opened to other banks, which record the operations of mutual acceptances of *fedi*. This meant that clients had cashed in a *fede* issued at a different bank, which therefore became a debtor for the sum (the practice took the name of *riscontrata*). This operation required periodically clearing the sums with the other banks, and at the closure of accounts the residual balance was reported in the balance sheet. If, on the one hand, the mutual acceptance of *fedi* facilitated the circulation of *fedi*, on the other hand banks could hide these residual amounts in their reserves, thus artificially inflating their value above the amount of specie. To avoid this, in 1635 Viceroy

[7] Other examples of transgressions to this prohibition are found by Demarco in the documents of Spirito Santo (Demarco 2000, p. 180).

Table 8 Net position of each bank toward all other banks for the mutual acceptance of *fedi di credito* (values in ducats). Black: net creditor, red: net debtor

	1611	*1617*	*1622*
Pietà	38297	15260	65200
Poveri	3044	4052	–36874
Popolo	–69914	–15777	–119723
Annunziata	68143	52326	65429
S. Eligio	–5891	19548	–47649
S. Santo	8549	–30532	110787
S. Giacomo	–42227	–44877	–37169

Table 9 Value of *fedi di credito* cashed in at a different bank as a percentage of own circulation

	1611	*1617*	*1622*
Pietà	2.21	0.47	1.62
Poveri	5.19	3.64	10.69
Popolo	10.98	3.84	6.98
Annunziata	0.18	0	0
S. Eligio	3.28	0.45	5.64
S. Santo	8.83	5.18	0.81
S. Giacomo	9.76	8.56	4.09
Average	5.78	3.16	4.26

Monterey issued the first of a long series of prohibitions of *riscontrata* (Tortora 1888, p. 198). Nonetheless, for over two centuries the banks did not comply and kept accepting each others' *fedi*, but they did not show the sums explicitly in the balance sheets.

We find the accounts of other banks in the balance sheets until 1622. For the period 1587–1610 they constituted 1.87 per cent of investments, and the percentage grew to 5.23 per cent for the decade 1611–1622. From the balance sheets we can also deduce the individual positions of each bank toward other banks. In Table 8 we report the individual net positions for years in which complete data are available. As we can see, Pietà and Annunziata were net creditors of the system, while Popolo and Spirito Santo were clearly net debtors. To assess the quantitative relevance of these operations, we relate the debt at other banks to own circulation in Table 9. This percentage can be taken as an estimate of the fraction of the value of own *fedi* cashed in at another bank.

7 Conclusions: Resilience, Innovations and the Role of the Public Banks for the Economy of Naples

In this final Section, we conclude with three observations that help explain the survival of the banks for over two centuries and their role in the economy.

1. The first observation regards the legal status of the banks, which contained a mix of public and private components. Although the banks had the status of public banks subject to regal approval and supervision, until the end of the eighteenth century they remained clearly distinct and independent institutions. On one hand, public supervision helped consolidate the trust necessary for fiduciary circulation to take off. Public management of major crises like the bankruptcy of the largest bank in 1701, together with mutual assistance from other banks, also played a role in consolidating trust in the system as a whole. On the other hand, independence allowed them to actively resist excessive interference in their operations. As an example of active resistance toward impositions that would endanger their survival, in Sect. 6 we mentioned the non-compliance of the banks with the prohibition of mutual acceptance of *fedi* and with the prohibition of internal currency exchange. Their religious and charitable origins also granted them a powerful argument to refuse loans to the Viceroy and the King, appealing to their original purpose of helping the poor. We can speculate that, vis-à-vis the Viceroy and the King, the fragmentation of the banking market increased their collective bargaining power, perhaps because it was difficult to extract large resources from small entities, which moreover were linked to powerful religious and lay institutions. Indeed, before reaching deep into the reserves of the banks, Ferdinand IV claimed that all the disasters related to the bank management came from their being disjoined entities (Tortora 1888, p. 331). We saw that, contrary to the King's claim, the years that followed the lost independence saw an abnormal increase in the investment ratio and excessive monetization of military expenditures (through issuing *fedi a vuoto*).
2. The second observation relates more properly to the "business model" of the banks. We argue that the fear brought about by the crisis of 1622 led the banks to innovate by radically changing their

operations, in two ways that specifically contributed to their subsequent resilience. First, they maintained the investment ratio at a significantly lower level than the pre-crisis period. Second, they switched to a business model whereby the costs of the demand deposit service were covered by the proceeds of relatively small short-term pawn loans, rather than the long-term *compre*. Pawns constituted a much stronger collateral than uncertain rents. They allowed the banks to broaden their customer base and direct their lending to a relatively poorer segment of the population (although not the very poor, who were completely outside of the financial system). From a more ideological perspective, pawns lending was historically linked to the rhetoric of helping the poor, as two of the banks had a history of lending without interest for objects of less than 10 ducats value. Possibly this helped the popularity of the banks in such a religious city as Naples. We of course do not have definite proof that these two characteristics were the key to the survival of the public banking system in Naples. However, we are lucky enough to have available the counterfactual of the bankrupt bank, Annunziata. In Table 10 we compare its balance sheet data to the aggregate of other banks for the 25 years prior the crisis of 1701.

Indeed, we find that Annunziata maintained a much larger investment ratio (64.81 per cent compared to 25.52 per cent), invested much less in pawns (12.86 per cent compared to 55.62 per cent) and more in *prestiti* and *compre* (17.90 per cent compared to 11.25 per cent). We also find the share of current account much larger than the other banks, which is a sign that the difficulties of Annunziata were somewhat structural.

Table 10 Comparison of Annunziata with other banks, 1675–1701

	Annunziata (1675–1701)	*Aggregate other banks (1675–1701)*
Investment ratio	64.81	25.52
Pawns	12.86	55.62
prestiti and *compre*	17.90	11.25
Current account	21.19	6.46

3. The third and final observation relates to the role that the banks played for the economic development of Naples. While it is undisputable that the monetary service provided by *fedi di credito* greatly facilitated exchanges, the analysis of lending activities in Sect. 6 shows how the banks operated mostly in support of existing feudal institutions. Loans were directed for the largest part to unproductive activities. The instrument of *compra* made it easier to trade feudal rents, and indeed the beneficiaries were members of the nobility. The same success of the pawning activity implies that the public banks did little in terms of maturity transformation.

References

Allen, Robert. 2001. The Great Divergence in European Wages and Prices from the Middle Ages to the First World War. *Explorations in Economic History* 38: 411–447.

Allocati, Antonio. 1966. *Tipiche operazioni del Banco della Pietà in alcuni atti notarili dei secoli XVI–XIX*. Napoli: ESI.

Assante, Franca, et al. 1972. *L'Archivio Storico del Banco di Napoli. Una fonte preziosa per la storia economica, sociale e artistica del Mezzogiorno d'Italia*. Napoli: Banco di Napoli.

Balletta, Francesco. 2008. *La circolazione della moneta fiduciaria a Napoli nel Seicento e nel Settecento (1587–1805)*. Napoli: ESI.

Beloch, Karl Julius. 1994. *Storia della popolazione d'Italia*. Firenze: Le lettere.

Bianchini, Ludovico. 1839. *Della storia delle finanze del Regno di Napoli*. Palermo: Stamperia di Francesco Lao.

Capasso, Bartolomeo. 1876. *Catalogo ragionato dei libri, registri e scritture esistenti nella sezione antica dell'Archivio municipale di Napoli (1387–1806)*. Napoli: Giannini.

———. 1883. *Sulla circoscrizione civile ed ecclesiastica e sulla popolazione della città di Napoli alla fine del secolo XIII. fino al 1809*. Napoli: Tipografia della Regia Università.

Cavour, Camillo Benso. 1954. *La liberazione del Mezzogiorno e la formazione del Regno d'Italia, Carteggi a cura della Commissione Editrice*, vol. IV. Bologna: Zanichelli.

Coniglio, Giuseppe. 1951. *Il Regno di Napoli al tempo di Carlo V. Amministrazione e vita economico – sociale*. Napoli: ESI.

Cusumano, Vito. 1887. *Storia dei banchi della Sicilia*, vol. II, "I banchi pubblici." Roma: Loescher.

Demarco, Domenico. 1963. *Banca e congiuntura nel Mezzogiorno d'Italia*. Napoli: ESI.

———. 1986. Banca e credito in Italia nell'età del Risorgimento. *Revue Internationale d'Histoire de la Banque* 32–33: 1–53.

———. 1996a. *Il Banco di Napoli dalla débacle alla rinascita*. Napoli: ESI.

———. 1996b. *Il Banco di Napoli dalle casse di deposito alla fioritura settecentesca*. Napoli: ESI.

———. 2000. *Il Banco di Napoli. L'Archivio Storico: la grammatica delle scritture*. Napoli: ESI.

De Rosa, Luigi. 1958. *Studi sugli arrendamenti nel Regno di Napoli*. Napoli: Giannini.

———. 2002. *Gli inizi della circolazione della cartamoneta e i banchi pubblici napoletani nella società del loro tempo (1540–1650)*. Napoli: Istituto Banco di Napoli Fondazione.

De Simone, Ennio. 1974. *Il Banco della Pietà*. Napoli: ISTOB.

———. 1976. Case e botteghe a Napoli nei secoli XVII–XVIII. *Revue Internationale d'Histoire de la Banque* 12: 77–140.

———. 1983. Le scritture contabili di un arrendamento della città di Napoli. In *Studi in onore di Gino Barbieri*. Pisa: IPM.

———. 2010. Il Banco delle Due Sicilie. In *Il pensiero e l'opera di Domenico Demarco*. Milano: FrancoAngeli.

Di Somma, Carlo. 1960. Il Banco dello Spirito Santo dalle origini al 1664. *Annali dell'Istituto di Storia Economica e Sociale – Università di Napoli* 1: 1–96.

Faraglia, Nunzio Federico. 1878. *Storia dei prezzi a Napoli dal 1131 al 1860*. Napoli: Real Istituto di Incoraggiamento.

Ferrara, Francesco. 1935. *La girata della cambiale*. Roma: Editrice Foro Italiano.

Filangieri, Riccardo. 1940. *Storia del Banco di Napoli. I banchi di Napoli dalle origini alla costituzione del Banco delle Due Sicilie (1539–1808)*. Napoli: Banco di Napoli.

Galanti, Giuseppe Maria. 1969. *Della descrizione geografica e politica delle Sicilie (a cura di Assante Franca e Demarco Domenico)*, Tomo I e II. Napoli: ESI.

Galiani, Ferdinando. 1750. *Della moneta*. Napoli: Giuseppe Raimondi.

Gifuni, Gianbattista. 1801. *Compendio istorico della origine e fondazione del Monte della Pietà di Napoli de varj autentici documenti*. Napoli: Antonio Raimondi.

Grohmann, Alberto. 1969. *Le fiere del Regno di Napoli in età aragonese*. Bologna: Il Mulino.

Maiello, Carmine. 1980. *La crisi dei banchi pubblici napoletani (1794–1806)*. Genève: Droz.

———. 1986. *L'indebitamento bancario della nobiltà napoletana nel primo periodo borbonico (1734–1806)*. Napoli: Istituto per la Storia della Banca.

Nappi, Eduardo. 1999. *Banchi e finanze della Repubblica Napoletana*. Napoli: Istituto Italiano per gli Studi Filosofici.

Petraccone, Claudia. 1974. *Napoli dal '500 all'800*. Napoli: Guida Editori.

Rapporto generale sulla situazione del Regno di Napoli negli anni 1806–1807. Presentato al re nel suo Consiglio di Stato del ministro dell'Interno il 28 marzo 1808, Napoli.

Riaco, Carlo Francesco. 1658. *Il giudicio di Napoli. Discorso del passato contaggio rassomigliato al Giudizio Universale*. Napoli: Edition Playne.

Rocco, Michele. 1785. *De' banchi di Napoli e della loro ragione*. Napoli: Fratelli Raimondi.

Romano, Aurelio. 1909. *La città e il comune di Napoli (1331–1904)*. Napoli: Riccardo Ricciardi Editore.

Romano, Ruggiero. 1976. *Napoli: dal Viceregno al Regno*. Torino: Giulio Einaudi Editore.

Somma, Angelo. 1844. *Trattato de' banchi nazionali nel Regno delle Due Sicilie*. Napoli: Tipografia di Barnaba.

Tortora, Eugenio. 1888. *Nuovi documenti per la storia del Banco di Napoli*. Napoli: A. Belisario E.C. – R. Tipografia de Angelis.

Venturi, Franco. 1973. 1764: Napoli nell'anno della fame. *Rivista Storica Italiana* 85 (2): 394–472.

PART II

Comparative Perspectives on the Rise of Public Banks

CHAPTER 6

The Variety of Financial Innovations in European War Finance during the Thirty Years' War (1618–1648)

Larry Neal

1 Introduction

The public banks of Naples arose in the first instance to enable charitable organizations to meet the increased needs of their respective clienteles when they were struck by a crisis, whatever its cause (Di Meglio, Chapter 3). They expanded in number and size in response to repeated crises that occurred both before and after the 1622 monetary reform (Costabile and Nappi, Chapter 2; Avallone and Salvemini, Chapter 4; and Francesco, Luigi Balletta and Eduardo Nappi, Chapter 5). The 1622 monetary reform was imposed by the ruling Viceroy of Naples in response to the increased demands for war finance by Philip IV of Spain combined with the demands by foreign rentiers that their rents be paid in a hard, not debased, currency (Costabile and Nappi, Chapter 2). The intensification of the Thirty Years' War (1618–1648) began in 1622 at the end of the Twelve Years' Truce between Spain and the Dutch

L. Neal (✉)
University of Illinois, Urbana, IL, USA

L. Costabile and L. Neal (eds.), *Financial Innovation and Resilience*, Palgrave Studies in the History of Finance,
https://doi.org/10.1007/978-3-319-90248-7_6

Republic and the commitment by Spain to aid the Habsburg Emperor in Austria. Then began a series of financial repercussions that beset not only the public banks of Naples but also financial systems throughout the rest of Europe, repercussions that endured for the rest of the seventeenth century (Kindleberger 1991; Parker 1997). The war expenses for all the belligerents kept mounting, not least because of the need to incorporate the essential features of the ongoing "military revolution", which reached its full expression during the course of The Thirty Years' War (Parker 1996; Roberts 1967).

The initial finance problem for military leaders was to make the monthly subsidies promised to the troops on each side actually appear to them in usable form wherever they were posted. For example, Maurice of Nassau, commander of the Dutch Republic forces, promised Frederick V, the Protestant claimant to the Bohemian throne, 50,000 guilders monthly at the outset of the war in 1618. The guilders, however, had to be distributed among Frederick's troops in Bohemia as 25,000 thalers, which they needed to purchase their food, clothing, and shelter in the Palatinate or Bohemia. The Spanish troops opposing them in the Spanish Netherlands needed Flemish guilders for their pay but Philip III in Madrid had to satisfy them with silver pieces of eight from his treasure fleets arriving in Seville. It was up to Genoese merchant bankers to exchange the silver coins from Spain into fewer, more valuable gold coins for transshipment to the Spanish Netherlands. Once in Antwerp, the gold coins had to be converted again into silver guilders for local payments (Parker 1972). It became the task of assorted mint masters strewn along the Spanish Road stretching overland from Genoa to Antwerp to facilitate these exchanges, taking their commissions in return for their service. The number of independent mints proliferated throughout the mining districts of central Germany and their competition to satisfy the local demands for currencies as the various troops moved through their locality spawned the first set of financial innovations—repeated re-coinages in additional units of account.

2 Innovations by Mints

Experiments with new minting technology preceded the onset of the Thirty Years' War, possibly in response to a fall in the receipts of silver by the Spanish crown toward the end of the sixteenth century (Hamilton 1934), or to higher amounts retained in Spanish America (TePaske 1983, 2010), or to larger diversions by foreign merchants (Morineau 1985). Whatever the ultimate cause of the fall off in silver imports, Philip II introduced an *ingenio* to mill copper coins in 1596. His intent was to free more silver from small change coins so it could then be used to mint more large coins, which were more useful for war finance. Initially, the numbers of copper coins were limited to the amount of *vellón* coins they replaced from circulation, so no price inflation occurred (Sargent and Velde 2003, Chapter 14, pp. 231–247).

In one of the ironies of history that continue to bemuse historians, it was the attempt by Philip II to mint low denomination coins in copper that led to Sweden's rise to prosperity in the seventeenth century as it became the main supplier of copper to the Spanish authorities. Louis de Geer, a Dutch merchant based in Amsterdam but originally from the Spanish Netherlands, imported copper miners and metal workers from Walloon to Sweden. De Geer's profits from the copper trade made him the wealthiest man in the Netherlands and Sweden (Carr 1963). The revenues from copper exports to Spain in turn helped Axel Oxenstierna in Sweden to finance the armies of Gustavus Adolphus when he descended into northern Germany to reverse the tide of war in favour of the Protestants. The unintended consequences of Philip II's initiative to mint copper coins in Spain led to repeated failures of finance by his successors while it also enabled the eventual successes of their opponents—the Dutch Republic, the Bourbon dynasty, and northern European Protestants.

The successor regimes in Spain of Philip III (1598–1621) and Philip IV (1621–1665) increased the number of copper coins so dramatically that the larger denomination silver coins disappeared from circulation as well. The recurring spurts of inflation could only be curbed by decrees "crying down" the value of the coins, regardless of what they had previously been assigned. After several stops and starts for minting copper coins, Philip IV cried down both *vellón* and copper coins in 1628. But then he had to resume inflationary debasement in 1636, re-stamping first *vellón* and then copper coins to three times their previous value. In 1642, Philip then stopped the runaway inflation his earlier measure had caused by crying down both sets of coins by a factor of six. After the end of the Thirty Years' War, but with war still underway against France, Philip IV re-stamped the copper coins once again to make them worth four times their previous value in 1651, but then followed by crying the coins down by the same factor in 1652. Another bout of first re-stamping, then crying down, took place in 1658 and 1659, culminating in the final demonetization of the copper coinage along with the signing of the Peace of the Pyrenees in 1659 (Sargent and Velde 2003, Table 14.4, p. 252).

Sargent and Velde see these repeated "crying up", followed by "crying down", episodes as useful experiments for discovering the essential elements of what they term the "standard formula" for minting both large denomination and small denomination coins. The key element the Spanish state missed was to declare that small change coins would be legally convertible at face value into larger denomination coins, at least up to a relatively small amount. Even though the small change coins carried a face value higher than the market value of their metal contents, maintaining their legal convertibility even for low amounts would have kept larger coins in circulation while limiting the need to produce more token coins. In this way, Spain could have avoided the problem faced by Philip IV.

The successive experiments made by the Spanish authorities in Madrid as they searched in vain for the standard formula, however, had no learning effect upon their Habsburg allies headquartered in Vienna. Searching for some way to finance an army large enough to dislodge the Protestant rebels in Bohemia and then to reclaim the territories that had earlier been allotted to Protestant, mainly Lutheran, authorities and churches, Emperor Ferdinand II turned to the military-entrepreneur Albrecht Wallenstein in 1625. Already wealthy as a proven supplier of military forces in support of the Emperor, first in 1617 in the war against Venice, Wallenstein had enlarged both his domains in Bohemia, Moravia, and Upper Austria in 1622–1623, basically by enlisting the services of his talented financier, Hans de Witte (Ernstberger 1954).

Hans de Witte was a Protestant merchant who had left his family in Antwerp to pursue his fortune elsewhere, primarily in parts of Germany less hostile to even non-practicing Calvinists like him than the Spanish Netherlands. Eventually establishing himself as a wholesale trading merchant in Prague, Hans used his cousin Antoine de Witte, who had remained in Antwerp as a converted Catholic, as his chief correspondent. Their business flourished during the Twelve Year Truce (1609–1621) when traditional trade routes re-opened briefly. When war broke out, de Witte used his now well-established trading connections between Prague and Antwerp to supply Albrecht Wallenstein's army against the Protestant forces. So valuable were his logistical services that Ferdinand II, the Holy Roman Emperor, authorized him to organize a mint consortium in 1622, despite De Witte's Protestant origins and connections.

De Witte's mint consortium had imperial authority to re-mint coins throughout the territory controlled by Wallenstein's army, the largest deployed by any of the belligerents at the time. Even more daring was de Witte's deliberate inclusion of Jewish mint masters in his consortium, despite the religious zeal of the Emperor to eliminate both Jewish moneylenders and Protestants from his domains. The consortium's profits came from reducing the silver content of the replacement coins by first one-third, then one-half. Their efforts, combined with similar debasements by neighboring mints in Saxony and the Palatinate, created the infamous "Kipper–und Wipper Zeit" in central Germany. The sums generated by de Witte's consortium were huge by the standards of the time and they enabled Wallenstein to pay the wages and supplies of his ever-larger army without further assistance from either the Emperor or his Spanish ally. The mint consortium produced over 42 million guilders, 31 million by de Witte alone (Ernstberger, pp. 120–123).

The consequences of the serial debasements among the numerous mints scattered through the domains of the Holy Roman Empire, however, proved disastrous even for the original innovators. Very soon after the debasements, their political masters realized that their real revenues were reduced more than proportionally by the failures of their peasants and artisans to maintain their agricultural and industrial production in face of their rising costs and falling market demands. Countermanding the debasements by crying down the value of the existing coinage halted the inflation, but did not solve the continuing problems of war finance, even in Upper Austria and Bohemia (Jung 1976). A longer run solution came only with the creation of public banks, banks dedicated to maintaining the statutory value of the official unit of account locally and thwarting the incentives of mint masters in adjacent territories to debase competing coins (Kindleberger 1999; Schnabel and Shin 2018).

3 Public Banks

When Charles Kindleberger reviewed the history of public banks in Europe, he was struck by how many of them arose precisely to insure local merchants and governments from having to accept debased coinage from neighboring mints (Kindleberger 1999, "Currency Debasement"). The revolting provinces of the northern Netherlands were the prime example. With no established market for sovereign government debt, and with the difficulties of reaching common accord among the separate provinces and independent cities in revolt against Spanish authority for sharing the expenses of defense, the debasement of the metallic coins constituting the money supply for the Netherlands had been inexorable from the start of their revolt against Spain in 1568 (Fritschy 2017).

The strained finances of individual provinces led each of the 14 mints in the Netherlands (8 provincial and 6 municipal) to follow its own policy in the timing and extent of successive debasements. The numerous mints in the adjacent areas of the Spanish Netherlands and Westphalia took advantage of the resulting confusion in circulating coins to produce their own variants. Foreign coins were introduced as well by merchants from the British Isles and the Baltic and German city-states. By 1610, moneychangers in Amsterdam had to keep track of nearly 1000 different gold and silver coins. Bit by bit, but relentlessly, the price of silver rose on average 1 per cent a year in terms of the unit of account, the florin decreed by Charles V in 1544 but which had long ceased to exist as a coin (Dehing and t'Hart 1997, p. 40).

If the Bank of Amsterdam, established in 1609 at the beginning of the Twelve Years' Truce between the Dutch Republic and Spain, was modelled explicitly upon the Banco di Rialto in Venice, however, its main role was simply to facilitate wholesale payments among merchants, both local and foreign, as they settled accounts, just as in Venice. Protection from debased coins was achieved at first by paying withdrawals in the same coin the account holder had used in deposit. If those coins had been cried up or down in the meantime, however, their withdrawal would vary in value as well from the initial deposit. Indeed, Quinn and Roberds (2009) demonstrated that even though the Bank of Amsterdam tried repeatedly to establish a separate unit of account, the *schelligen banco*, for measuring its deposits and withdrawals, debasements of comparable coins in the Spanish Netherlands kept undercutting the Bank's authority.

Even in the revolting province of Holland, authorities kept changing standards until the Bank established an independent, fixed, standard on its own initiative in 1659, when the Netherlands had temporary respite from attacks by either Britain, Spain or France. The Bank of Amsterdam's standard remained set for the next 200 years, creating true "inside money" for the first time and setting a worthy example for modern central banks (Quinn and Roberds 2009). Mints also became stricter in maintaining the mint price of their coins in the Netherlands, which circulated at varying discounts to "bank money", the stable unit of account for the Netherlands thereafter. In this way, the public bank in Amsterdam managed to control the output of the mints still operating throughout the Dutch Republic. The Bank of Amsterdam had finally achieved permanently the goal sought by de Witte's mint consortium in Austria, but only after the conclusion of the Eighty Years' War between Spain and the Dutch Republic.

Kindleberger also noted that the presumed model for the Bank of Amsterdam, the Banco di Rialto in Venice founded in 1587, was not designed initially to protect depositors from currency debasements. Rather, it was promulgated as a secure alternative for depositors to the private banks, which had failed at alarming rates in the previous decade, culminating with the collapse of the largest private bank, the house of Pisani and Tiepolo in 1584 (Dunbar 1892, p. 319). The original Banco della Piazza di Rialto simply provided a substitute for the private banks that had lost the confidence of the Venetian public, the result of continued failures that culminated in the 1584 collapse. (The rise of the public banks of Naples in the same period coincided as well with widespread failures of private banks there.) It was the Banco del Giro established in 1619 that obliged foreign bills of exchange to be deposited and debited there, not the Rialto bank. Kindleberger remarks that in this sense Venice followed the example of Amsterdam, not the reverse. He further doubts that the Amsterdam bank was founded in anticipation of the trade boom that did occur after the truce of 1609.[1] François R. Velde, Chapter 10 compares the many other experiments with public banks that preceded and followed the Thirty Years' War in Europe. While public banks could become complements to existing mints by helping to stabilize their coinages, there was always the threat of mints becoming competitors under the pressure of war finance. Further, independence of a public bank from the policy goals of the existing government could never be assumed.

Kindleberger made no mention of the creation of seven public banks in Naples, a typical omission in the historiography of European finance to date. Their history, however, also reinforces Kindleberger's theme that fiscal pressures stimulated financial innovation. While the first bank started formally in 1539 when the *Monte della Pietà* opened a bank to the public, other charitable organizations in Naples opened banks as well in 1587, 1589, 1590, 1591, 1597 and 1600, all after a brief political revolt in 1585 (a response to fiscal demands imposed by Philip II). Only in 1640 was the last bank created, the Banco del Santissimo Salvatore, which despite its religious name was not founded for philanthropic reasons but rather to enable the collectors of the new flour tax to induce deposits

[1] The Dutch historian Clé Lesger (2006) makes a convincing argument that the prime motivation for establishing the Bank of Amsterdam in 1609 was to ensure that the massive flight capital from Antwerp after the closure of the Scheldt would remain under the political control of the local Amsterdam elite. The same argument can be made for the timing of the Bank of England in 1694, this time to maintain local control over capital imports from Amsterdam!

from the wider public (Tortora 1890; Avallone 1997). The role of this bank, however, is better discussed below in the sections dealing with issues of sovereign debt and the tax base committed to servicing the debt. Moreover, the tempestuous history of this bank illustrates the danger of establishing such a bank purely to placate one set of tax farmers (Tortora 1890, pp. 98–106). While San Salvatore held second place among the public banks in terms of circulation, it was next to last in terms of loans, and dead last in terms of annual revenue (Tortora 1890, pp. 105–106).

4 Public (Sovereign) Debt

Public debts had long been dealt with by southern European cities, especially in Italy and Spain. At first, they would be forced loans taken from the wealthiest citizens, as determined by a cadastral survey. The wealthy elite, provided they had control over the city's sources of revenues, could obtain secure income as interest paid regularly on their debt holdings. To meet later emergencies, not always caused by war, some cities found they could open subscriptions for new issues of debt that bore comparable levels of interest to the forced loans (Pezzolo 2014). The terminology for the long-term sovereign debts varied, according to the legal backing ascribed to them by city authorities. They typically were in the form of *rentes,* long-term obligations that assigned the annual revenues the city collected in various taxes levied on property or goods brought to market (Munro 2013). In Spain, these were called *juros,* as the issuing authority swore to continue paying annual interest from the taxes imposed for this purpose. Under duress from a warlord, the city authorities would lend an agreed amount, usually in exchange for a pledge of new privileges granted to the city.

In the case of Naples, Philip II's Viceroy extended the privileges of official recognition of the accounts of the various public banks for payment of taxes as part of the settlement to end the revolt of 1585. In return, the city authorities (composed mainly of feudal lords with extensive estates in the surrounding countryside) accepted new *juros* issued by the Kingdom of Naples. These bonds, modelled after the Castilian *juros,* but backed by taxes levied by royal authority in the kingdom, proved to be very popular with the local population. They were widely held up to the outbreak of the Thirty Years' War (Calabria 2002). It was only under the repeated demands upon the Viceroy by Philip IV that the issue of *juros* increased faster in Naples than the tax yields for the kingdom.

By 1640, when the last public bank was created in Naples, the search for sources of revenue to meet the demands upon the Viceroy led to repeated fire sales of royal assets. New creditors took over the collection of various revenues at huge discounts in return for providing immediate cash or material or men for the Viceroy to send on to Milan or Genoa. The most successful of the new tax farmers were a consortium headed by Bartolomeo d'Aquino. D'Aquino's success in turn appears to have depended upon finance from his agent in Genoa, the banker Giovanni Toffetti (Villari 1993, p. 95), who served as the prime conduit for moving Neapolitan resources to Milan and beyond (Villari 1993). But d'Aquino's rise to wealth and political influence also dated from his marriage in 1640 to Barbara Stampa from the leading banking and political family in Milan (De Luca 2012; Musi 1976).

The Banco del Santissimo Salvatore was also founded in 1640 when d'Aquino's consortium acquired the concession for collecting the tax on flour in the kingdom. While d'Aquino's biographer makes no mention of the creation of the bank, it is likely that Bartolomeo's brother, Tommaso d'Aquino, helped manage the affairs of the bank as well as those of their father's mercantile business, which remained very prosperous. Indeed, both Tommaso and Bartolomeo received noble titles, Tommaso as Duca di Casoli and Bartolomeo as Principe di Caramanico in recognition of their financial services to the Viceroy of Naples.

Both the creation of the bank and the marriage in 1640 laid the basis for d'Aquino's success in buying up other tax concessions, also at fire sale prices. In eight years from 1636 to 1644, he managed to provide the Viceroy 16 million ducats to send to Milan and Spain. He quickly became the wealthiest man in Naples, but in 1647 his increase in taxes on all fruits brought to the city led to a brief, but bloody revolt led by the fishmonger, Masaniello (D'Aquino 2017). In the course of the revolt, d'Aquino's mansion was destroyed, but he escaped with his life on promise of making restitutions, only to die in the plague of 1656. D'Aquino's efforts to combine management of the growing public debt by a combination of public banking and control over sources of tax revenues were surely heroic, but ultimately could not overcome the problem of economic distress that kept reducing all tax yields, whether on oil, flour, salt or silk (Villari 1993). If public banks were the key to solving the problem of competitive debasements by uncoordinated mints, then securing a reliable source of tax revenue was the key to solving the long-run problem of marketing sovereign debt.

5 Reliable Tax Sources

Indeed, d'Aquino's efforts at managing the repayment of the loans his consortium made to the Viceroy during the intensive period of financing the Thirty Years' War, starting in 1636, evolved over time to find new sources of revenue that the government could assign to the consortium. D'Aquino initially (1636–1640) claimed excise taxes on local consumer products, flour, wine, salt and oil. As those sources of revenue were depleted, the new loans were backed by claims on export products, silk from Calabria and export quality olive oil (Musi, pp. 26–28). In the final stages, starting in 1637 but increasing in scope up to the revolt in 1647, d'Aquino's group actually acquired the rights to preempt the payment of feudal obligations to local nobles throughout the Kingdom (Musi, pp. 37–38). The nobility were only too happy to regain their traditional claims on their feudal holdings while the new Viceroy managed a protracted default on the Kingdom's debts to d'Aquino and his partners, mainly to block the substantial payments owed to the Genoese (Musi, pp. 49–50). Ultimately, the traditional feudal rights of the Neapolitan nobility were restored, even as they lost their chance at gaining independence from the political power of Spain (Musi, pp. 53–54).

Much the same story of a financial innovation based on reliable sources of tax revenues and monitored by merchant bankers can be told for the Republics of Genoa and Venice (Luciano Pezzolo, Chapter 7), the Duchy of Milan (Giuseppe De Luca and Marcella Lorenzini, Chapter 8) and for the Commonwealth of England during the English Civil War (D'Maris Coffman, Chapter 9). In each case, the long-run benefits of the financial innovation undertaken in response to the immediate demands of war or revolution could not be sustained, due to political constraints that emerged after the initial emergency had been overcome.

6 Finances in Europe After the Thirty Years' War

The eventual workout of the Kingdom of Naples' financial obligations to Philip IV, therefore, resembled in many ways the financial resolution of the Fronde rebellion in France at the same time. The central authority of the ruling monarch was reasserted over the affairs of the city (Naples in Italy and Paris in France) while the basis of local taxes remained the same in both Naples (Bulgarelli 2015, pp. 66–67) and France (Beguin 2012), at least until the French Revolution and Napoleon's rule abolished feudal obligations and imposed central tax authority in both Italy and France.

The contrasting successes of the sovereign debts issued by various European city-states in other parts of Europe can largely be attributed to the control that the majority of their debt holders had over the collection of city-authorized taxes (Stasavage 2011). D'Aquino's efforts came close to achieving this goal in Naples during the Thirty Years' War but fell short due to circumstances very much beyond his control, although the earlier stabilization of the currency held up throughout the war, at least with respect to Milan (Musi, p. 21). In other city-states, the most successful guarantee for their debt service were indirect taxes, either excises collected on the domestic goods brought to market or customs duties levied on foreign goods imported from abroad or from neighbouring cities and countryside. The amount of revenue collected depended positively upon the number and income of the city's inhabitants. For entrepôt cities such as Genoa, Venice, Amsterdam, Hamburg or London, revenue could rise as well if overseas trade was forced by circumstances to go through the city's port. While the goods would be transshipped eventually, they would be stored in warehouses in the meantime where they were subject to taxes and storage charges, but also serving as collateral for mercantile loans.

Amsterdam clearly benefited from its central role in first, long-distance trade between the Mediterranean and the Baltic, especially during the Twelve Year's Truce, and second, in the ensuing period as its trade with both the West Indies and East Indies expanded at the expense of the Portuguese while Portugal was under the rule of Philip IV of Spain.[2] Excise revenues, previously levied solely within individual cities, now were levied throughout the province of Holland and were collected by the provincial authorities of Holland. As tax-receivers scattered through the province, they also had responsibility for managing the sovereign bonds held by local residents. The result was a felicitous harmony of interests of traders, tax collectors, and local bondholders, producing the basis for continued expansion of Holland's provincial debt, but easily serviced by the burgeoning tax revenues of the province (Fritschy 2003, 2017).[3]

[2] True, some of the Dutch financiers suffered losses during ill-considered speculations on tulips during the Tulip Mania of 1636–1637. I dismiss this episode as having no significance for financial history in Neal (2015, pp. 63–66). Cf. Goldgar (2007).

[3] Fritschy (2017) emphasizes that customs revenues were kept low throughout the Dutch Republic, which maintained Amsterdam's role as an international entrepôt.

The virtuous circle of regularly collected indirect taxes that served as backing for repeated issues of short-term sovereign debt with low interest rates in Holland had another unintended consequence. Unlike the case of Naples, Amsterdam and the other city-states that made up the United Provinces that broke away permanently from Spanish rule at the end of the sixteenth century did not create public banks of deposit for the purpose of lending at a profit. Instead, individual moneyed men (and women) were readily available to lend to worthwhile artisans or merchants (Gelderblom et al. 2016), while the needs of the urban indigents and even artisans were provided by municipal-financed charities (McCants 1997). Indeed, the Lombard bank in Amsterdam (Bank de Leening), formally established in 1614 by public subscription and finally financed by the municipal authorities in 1684, increasingly served a wide section of Dutch society as did the Municipal Orphanage (Burgerweehuis) (McCants 2007; Philopolis 1733). A similar story holds as well for the self-governing cities of Flanders and Brabant. Even under continued Spanish rule, their merchant elites had sufficient control of local taxes and sources of funds to make even an exchange bank as in Amsterdam and Hamburg unnecessary, much less public banks of deposit as in Naples (Aerts 2011).

By sharp contrast, the tax revenues collected by the Kingdom of Naples faltered repeatedly in face of revaluations of the coinage, poor harvests and competition from surrounding areas, especially Sicily (Calabria 2002). Debt had to be issued at a higher rate to compensate for falling tax yields. This was the situation when the Viceroy's government began to sell off an increasing number of the remaining royal assets, sometimes to local nobles, sometimes to foreign lenders especially from Genoa, and last of all to d'Aquino's consortium of tax farmers. In common with tax farmers in England, France, and central Europe, d'Aquino's partners raised their own finance through selling partial shares in the tax farm to depositors looking for some return on their savings. These outside investors were especially susceptible to new investment opportunities if their existing investments had been in the Kingdom's sovereign debt, which fell sharply in value throughout the last years of the Thirty Years' War (Calabria 2002).

The fate of tax farmers scattered around the periphery of Europe varied therefore with the prices and volumes of goods passing through their respective portals. The variety of experiences among sundry sources of taxable traffic led the most successful governments to auction off the rights to the varied tax farms in order to find the best composition of local expertise among the competing financiers (Johnson and Koyama 2014, 2017). Only when a central, unified system of tolls could be imposed on a more homogeneous set of ports could central government customs officials replace the tax farming. Only then could governments assure their debt holders that interest could be paid regularly at a fixed rate for the duration of the bonds. In the meantime, governments waging war needed the *ad hoc* services of financial intermediaries, who profited to the extent they could sustain financial innovations. And sustainability depended, in the final analysis, on political factors largely beyond their control.

Throughout the sixteenth and then well into the seventeenth century Genoese bankers dominated the network of European finance, including Naples. Their ability to deal in bills of exchange to finance large-scale trade between the Mediterranean and the Baltic was well-known and their "virtual" fair for clearing accounts, known as *Bisenzone*, dominated finance of trade and armies moving along the "Spanish Road" between Spain and the Netherlands (Pezzolo and Tattara 2008; Marsilio 2013.) Their success over the centuries of repeated crises in Europe, it would appear, owed much to their base in the corporation called the *Casa delle Compere e Banco di San Giorgio*, founded in 1408. The Casa was a joint-stock corporation with a well-defined governance structure based on its shareholders, who held the sovereign debt of the city of Genoa and were responsible for collecting the taxes assigned to repay the debt (Felloni 2006, 2014). Whenever and wherever Genoese bankers operated in Europe, their actions were coordinated through their respective accounts at the Casa di San Giorgio (Neal 2015, Chapter 3).

7 A Final Tour d'Horizon

The net results of the financing experiments performed by the European participants in the Thirty Years' War can be divided into three sets: one group of countries clearly failing to put a viable financial system together (Spain, Austria), another group fortunate enough to keep in place some solid parts to build upon later (Dutch Republic, Britain, France, Sweden), and the rest of Europe that continued to cope with reduced economic opportunities and uncertain political regimes thereafter (including Genoa, Milan, Naples and the Ottoman Empire).

In the cases of Spain and Austria, there were many proposals to implement some of the innovations that had succeeded in facilitating the finance of war by their opponents. The rulers of Spain, in particular, looked to the obvious success of the Casa di San Giorgio in Genoa and the public banks in Naples, and entertained seriously proposals to initiate similar banks. But all the proposed banks, whether they were to be imposed by royal fiat, or solicited from the individual cities of Castile, or initiated by forced loans from mercantile groups, came to nought due to political resistance by the Spanish nobles or city elites (Hamilton 1949). The case of Austria is the focus of Jobst, Chapter 11.

In the middle group, we can put the Atlantic maritime countries who managed to profit by tapping into the growing trans-Atlantic trade initiated by Portugal and Spain: France (Atlantic ports), the Netherlands, Great Britain, Denmark, Hamburg and Sweden. A century later, the United States of America would join them. Their respective paths to modern economic growth have been studied intensively so all this paper can add is to note that each of the potential maritime powers attempted in their own way to imitate in some respect the Genoese experiment in mobilizing finance, the Casa di San Giorgio. Each country, however, attempted to incorporate what its leaders saw to be the essential elements of the Casa for economic success but also to limit the possibilities that the new corporation could encroach on existing political powers.

The Dutch imitators for example, the VOC and WIC, each kept their governance in the hands of a board of directors, the Heeren XVII or XIX, who were politically appointed by the member cities rather than being elected annually by the shareholders votes as in Genoa (Felloni 2014). The interaction of the Dutch companies with the Bank of Amsterdam remained a matter of bilateral negotiation thereafter, as analysed by Quinn and Roberds (Chapter 13). The Tudor monarchs tried to keep royal power over their distant agents operating the royal chartered monopoly companies as well, until the Glorious Revolution in 1688–1689 asserted Parliament's authority instead (Dickson 1967). Even the brief experiment with financial innovations by the English Commonwealth had to await political developments before they came to fruition (Coffman 2013). French monarchs monitored closely their overseas companies after subsidizing them initially, which limited their entrepreneurial activities. Even John Law's later attempts to imitate the Genoese example for France was eventually aborted by political interventions (Murphy, Chapter 12). Much later, Hamilton's First Bank of the United States made sure that the Federal government had a substantial bloc of voting shares. Political, more than financial, constraints, limited the long-run success of the sundry efforts to imitate the Genoese example.

From smaller political states bordering the north Atlantic, the Danish, Swedish and Hamburg trading companies simply lacked the financial ability to provide either the naval protection that the Genoese had provided their Mediterranean and Black Sea outposts or the convoys that both Genoa and Venice had deployed in their Mediterranean trade. Ultimately, even the Dutch East India Company could not defend Amsterdam in the final Anglo-Dutch War of 1784. Nevertheless, the rising customs revenues that each Atlantic port enjoyed as ocean trade expanded allowed each to feel their modifications were fully vindicated and perhaps even Providential. Genoa and Venice, meanwhile, like Naples, lacked the increased tax revenues that expanding Atlantic trade generated for the Atlantic ports, but all three sustained their economies by relying on the financial resiliency provided by their financial systems, which successfully coordinated banking, public debt, and commercial finance with sound currencies (Pezzolo, Chapter 7). Milan proved eventually to be a special case by developing a manufacturing and mining sector, thanks to the resiliency of its financial system emerging from the trauma of Spanish domination (De Luca and Lorenzini, Chapter 8).

In contrast to these success, or partial success, stories, the efforts by Philip IV to raise *donations* from the kingdoms of Catalonia, Portugal, and Sicily comparable to those he managed to extract from Naples, led in each case to successful tax revolts. In Portugal, the revolt succeeded to the extent that it separated the kingdom of Portugal from the rule of Spain in 1640, a separation enduring to the present. The revolts in both Sicily and Naples were suppressed effectively, but only by conceding to local nobility further taxing authority previously reserved to the king. In each case, the newly empowered barons imposed further fees, taxes, or rents upon the inhabitants of their estates. The fiscal fragmentation by Philip IV of the composite state of Spain that had been governed more or less successfully by Philip II continued to be a problem for Spain thereafter (Stein and Stein 2000, Chapter 2). The revolt in Catalonia proved more difficult to suppress, aided as it was by intervention of France under the direction of Cardinal Mazarin, and appears to remain a problem for the fiscal unity of Spain to this day.

The "dream of liberty" (*il sogno di libertà*) for the city of Naples ended after the brief revolt of Masaniello in 1647–1648 and the seizure of d'Aquino's estates by the Viceroy. The Viceroy then followed the example of Olivares in Spain by alienating the remaining tax resources of the kingdom to the nobility of Naples in the surrounding provinces. Meanwhile, the public banks of Naples continued to deal with the fiscal emergencies that struck the kingdom in the future. These included repeated bouts of the plague, earthquakes, piracy, as well as dealing with the eventual replacement of the Habsburg viceroy with a Bourbon monarch, Charles I, Duke of Parma and Piacenza.

In 1734, Charles conquered the kingdoms of Naples and Sicily and reigned there as Charles VII of Naples and Charles V of Sicily until 1759, when he became Charles III of Spain. During his reign in Naples, one of the oldest of the public banks, Banco dei Poveri, caused a scandal by the misuse of the congregation's assets by the self-appointed directors. Charles intervened forcefully, creating new members of the congregation of electors and appointing directly the new governor of the bank from a list of three provided for his consideration by the reconstituted and expanded congregation of the confraternity responsible for the bank (Avallone 1995). Afterwards, while reigning as Charles III of Spain in Madrid (1759–1788), among his many reforms that brought back a measure of stability and prosperity to the Spanish empire was founding the Banco de San Carlos in 1782, which later became the Bank of Spain. Perhaps it was his experience dealing with the public banks of Naples, including his reform of the Banco dei Poveri, which enabled this enlightened monarch to adapt belatedly to the emerging world of financial capitalism.

References

Aerts, Erik. 2011. The Absence of Public Exchange Banks in Medieval and Early Modern Flanders and Brabant (1400–1800): A Historical Anomaly to be Explained. *Financial History Review* 18 (1): 91–117.

Avallone, Paola. 1995. *Stato e Banchi Pubblici a Napoli a metà del '700: Il banco dei Poveri: una svolta*. Napoli: Edizioni Scientifiche Italiane.

———. 1997. Public Banks, Trade and Industry in Southern Italy, Seventeenth to Eighteenth Century. In *Banking, Trade and Industry: Europe, America and Asia from the Thirteenth to the Twentieth Century*, ed. Teichova et al., 50–68. Cambridge: Cambridge University Press.

Béguin, Katia. 2012. *Financer la guerre au XVIIe siècle*. Paris: Champ Vallon.

Bulgarelli-Lukacs, Alessandra. 2015. Tax Evasion and Tax Avoidance in the Towns of the Kingdom of Naples (XV–XVIII Centuries). *Boetica Estudios de Arte, Geografía e Historia* 36–37: 49–71.

Calabria, Antonio. 2002. *The Cost of Empire: The Finances of the Kingdom of Naples in the Time of Spanish Rule*. Cambridge: Cambridge University Press.

Carr, Raymond. 1963. Two Swedish Entrepreneurs: Louis de Geer and Joel Gripenstierna. In *Historical Essays, 1600–1750, Presented to David Ogg*, ed. H.A. Bell and R.L. Ollard. London: Adam & Charles Black.

Coffman, D'Maris. 2013. *Excise Taxation and the Origins of Public Debt.* Houndmills, Basingstoke, Hampshire and New York: Palgrave Macmillan.

D'Aquino, Bartolomeo. http://www.napoligrafia.it/citta/1503-1734/crisi.htm. Accessed November 17, 2017.

Dehing, P., and M. t'Hart. 1997. Linking the Fortunes: Currency and Banking, 1550–1800. In *A Financial History of the Netherlands*, ed. M. 't Hart, J. Jonker, and J. Luiten van Zanden. New York: Cambridge University Press.

De Luca, Giuseppe. 2012. Trading Money and Empire Building in Spanish Milan (1570–1640). In *Polycentric Monarchies: How Did Early Modern Spain and Portugal Achieve and Maintain a Global Hegemony?*, ed. Pedro Cardim, Tamar Herzog, José Javier Ruiz Ibáñez, and Gaetano Sabatini. Brighton: Sussex Academic Press.

Dickson, P.G.M. 1967. *The Financial Revolution in England, a Study in the Development of Public Credit, 1688–1756.* New York: Macmillan.

Dunbar, Charles F. 1892. The Bank of Venice. *The Quarterly Journal of Economics* 6 (3): 308–335.

Ernstberger, Anton. 1954. *Hans de Witte: Finanzmann Wallensteins.* Wiesbaden: Franz Steiner Verlag.

Felloni, Giuseppe. 2006. *Genoa: A Series of Firsts.* Genoa: Brigati Glauco.

———. 2014. *Administration and Ethics in the Casa di San Giorgio (1407–1805): The 1568 By-Laws.* Firenze: Leo S. Olschki Editore.

Fritschy, Wantje. 2003. A 'Financial Revolution' Reconsidered: Public Finance in Holland During the Dutch Revolt. *Economic History Review* 56 (1): 57–89.

———. 2017. *Public Finance of the Dutch Republic in Comparative Perspective. The Viability of an Early Modern Federal State (1570–1795).* Leiden: Library of Economic History.

Gelderblom, Oscar, Joost Jonker, and Clemens Kool. 2016. Direct Finance in the Dutch Golden Age. *Economic History Review* 69 (4): 1178–1198.

Goldgar, Anne. 2007. *Tulipmania: Money, Honor, and Knowledge in the Dutch Golden Age.* Chicago and London: University of Chicago Press.

Hamilton, Earl J. 1934. *American Treasure and the Price Revolution in Spain, 1501–1650.* Cambridge, MA: Harvard University Press.

———. 1949. Spanish Banking Schemes Before 1700. *Journal of Political Economy* 57 (2): 134–156.

Johnson, Noel D., and Mark Koyama. 2014. Tax Farming and the Origins of State Capacity in England and France. *Explorations in Economic History* 51 (1): 1–20.

———. 2017. States and Economic Growth: Capacity and Constraints. *Explorations in Economic History* 64 (1): 1–20.

Jung, Heidelinde. 1976. The 'Kipper und Wipper' Period and Its Effects on Upper Austria. *Jahrbuch des Oberosterreichischen Musealvereines* 121: 55–65 (Trans. Rebekha Wilson for inclusion in Coffman and Neal (eds.). 2015. *The History of Financial Crises, vol. 1. The Early Modern Paradigmatic Cases.* London: Routledge).

Kindleberger, Charles P. 1991. The Economic Crisis of 1619 to 1623. *Journal of Economic History* 51 (1): 149–175.

———. 1999. Currency Debasement in the Early Seventeenth Century and the Establishment of Deposit Banks in Central Europe. In *Essays in History: Financial, Economic, Personal*, Chapter 4. Ann Arbor: University of Michigan Press.

Lesger, Clé. 2006. *The Rise of the Amsterdam Market and Information Exchange: Merchants, Commercial Expansion and Change in the Spatial Economy of the Low Countries, c. 1550–1630.* Aldershot, UK: Ashgate.

Marsilio, Claudio. 2013. European State Finance, Genoa, 1348–1700. In *Handbook of Key Financial Markets, Institutions, and Infrastructure*, vol. 1, ed. Gerard Caprio, 235–249. Oxford: Elsevier.

McCants, Anne E.C. 1997. *Civic Charity in a Golden Age: Orphan Care in Early Modern Amsterdam.* Urbana: University of Illinois Press.

———. 2007. Goods at Pawn: The Overlapping Worlds of Material Possessions and Family Finance in Early Modern Amsterdam. *Social Science History* 31 (2): 213–238.

Morineau, Michel. 1985. *Incroyables gazettes et fabuleux métaux: les retours des trésors américains d'après les gazettes hollandaises (XVIe–XVIIIe siècles).* London and New York: Cambridge University Press.

Munro, John H. 2013. 'Rentes' and the European Financial Revolution. In *The Handbook of Key Global Financial Markets, Institutions, and Infrastructure*, vol. I, ed. Gerard Caprio, 235–249. Oxford: Elsevier.

Musi, Aurelio. 1976. *Finanze e Politica nella Napoli del '600: Bartolomeo d'Aquino.* Naples: Guida Editori.

Neal, Larry. 2015. *A Concise History of International Finance: From Babylon to Bernanke.* Cambridge: Cambridge University Press.

Parker, Geoffrey. 1972. *The Army of Flanders and the Spanish Road, 1567–1659. The Logistics of Spanish Victory and Defeat in the Low Countries' Wars.* Cambridge: Cambridge University Press.

———. 1996. *The Military Revolution: Military Innovation and the Rise of the West, 1500–1800.* Cambridge: Cambridge University Press.

———. 1997. *The Thirty Years' War.* London: Routledge.

Pezzolo, Luciano. 2014. The *via Italiana* to Capitalism. In *The Cambridge History of Capitalism, Vol. 1, The Rise of Capitalism From Ancient Origins to 1848*, ed. Larry Neal and Jeffrey G. Williamson. Cambridge: Cambridge University Press, pp. 267–313.

Pezzolo, Luciano, and Giuseppe Tattara. 2008. "Una fiera senza luogo": Was Bisenzone an international Capital Market in Sixteenth Century Italy? *Journal of Economic History* 68 (4): 1098–1122.

Philopolis. 1733. *An Account of the Bank of Loan at Amsterdam, Commonly Called the Lombard*. London [The Making of the Modern World: Web: 30 October 2017].

Quinn, Stephen, and William Roberds. 2009. An Economic Explanation of the Early Bank of Amsterdam, Debasement, and the Emergence of the First Central Bank. In *The Origins and Development of Financial Markets and Institutions: from the Seventeenth Century to the Present*, ed. Atack and Neal, 32–70. Cambridge and New York: Cambridge University Press.

Roberts, Michael. 1967. The Military Revolution, 1560–1660. In *Essays in Swedish History*. London: Weidenfeld & Nicolson.

Sargent, Thomas J., and François R. Velde. 2003. *The Big Problem of Small Change*. Princeton, NJ: Princeton University Press.

Schnabel, Isabel, and Hyun Song Shin. 2018. Money and Trust: Lessons from the 1620s for the Digital Age. BIS Working Papers No. 698.

Stasavage, David. 2011. *States of Credit: Size, Power, and the Development of European Polities*. Princeton, NJ: Princeton University Press.

Stein, Stanley J., and Barbara H. Stein. 2000. *Silver, Trade, and War: Spain and America in the Making of Early Modern Europe*. Baltimore and London: The Johns Hopkins University Press.

TePaske, John J. 1983. New World Silver, Castile and the Philippines, 1590–1800. In *Precious Metals in the Later Medieval and Early Modern Worlds*, ed. J.F. Richards, 425–446. Durham: Carolina Academic Press.

———. 2010. *A New World of Gold and Silver*. Boston: Brill.

Tortora, Eugenio. 1890. *Nuovi documenti per la storia del banco di Napoli*. Napoli: A. Bellisario E.C. – R. Tipografia de Angelis.

Villari, Rosario. 1993. *The Revolt of Naples*, trans. James Newell with Assistance of John A. Marino. Cambridge: Polity Press.

CHAPTER 7

Public Banks and State Finance in Florence and Venice

Luciano Pezzolo

1 Bank and State Finance in Florence

Florence is rightly considered as one of the most developed financial areas of the Renaissance. Its merchant-bankers, who were widely involved in international and long-distance trade and in the church's financial system, were able to mobilize huge resources and transfer them across every place of the continent. Considering that the banking sector was one of the pillars of the Florentine economy, it is surprising to find that the role of bankers in the mechanisms of public finance in their city was marginal. While it is very likely that until the mid-fourteenth century banks were requested to advance money to the municipal treasury, after the consolidation of the debt following the establishment of the *Monte* (Fund) in the 1340s and the development of a solid tax system, the use of short-term loans became less pressing, at least until the early fifteenth century.

The heavy military commitments of the 1420s caused serious difficulties for the state financial system: the government increased the

L. Pezzolo (✉)
Department of Humanities, Ca'Foscari University of Venice, Venice, Italy

L. Costabile and L. Neal (eds.), *Financial Innovation and Resilience*, Palgrave Studies in the History of Finance,
https://doi.org/10.1007/978-3-319-90248-7_7

demand for forced loans and at the same time failed to pay interest regularly; many taxpayers-lenders encountered difficulties in funding the loans and the number of delinquent citizens expanded dramatically. In this context, the government returned to exploiting the practice of short-term debt to finance urgent needs.

Although it is not yet clear when the system took hold, research has shown that the floating debt represented one of the vital devices for financing urgent needs. First the *Officiali del Banco* (Bank's Officers) and later the *Officiali del Monte* (Monte Officers) were set up precisely to take responsibility for raising loans, which would be paid back relatively quickly. The officers could lend their money directly to the *Monte* or take charge of collecting sums from among various citizens at a lower rate and then lending to the government at a slightly higher rate. So, for example, Lorenzo Morelli, who in the 1480s held the position of *Officiale del Monte* on various occasions, received money between 9 and 12 per cent and lent to the government at 14 per cent (Goldthwaite 1996). The interest rate usually ranged from 12 to 14 per cent; the amounts assigned to repayment came from forced loans and, especially from the end of the fifteenth century, direct taxes (Molho 1971; Marks 1960). Unlike traditional loans, which offered an interest—if paid regularly—of 5 per cent, short-term loans were particularly attractive. In Renaissance Florence, a discretionary deposit—that is, a medium and long-term passive investment in commercial companies—gave an annual return of 8 per cent (Goldthwaite 2009, p. 438; De Roover 1992, pp. 883–884); and the agricultural sector did not offer returns above 5 per cent. It is more useful, however, to compare returns on short-term investments, similar to those concerning the Monte officials.

The exchange market, by definition volatile and particularly insidious, between Florence and Lyon in the 1470s generated profits of 18 per cent, with marked fluctuations between a minimum of 4 up to a maximum of 33 per cent. Lorenzo Morelli, a Monte officer who performed his function in the 1480s, paid less than 14 per cent on the money borrowed through the exchange market between Florence and the fairs of Lyon (Goldthwaite 1996; Tognetti 1999, p. 283; Conti 1984, p. 77). The yield on a government loan, therefore, was to be considered satisfactory, in that the prospects to be reimbursed were much more robust than those concerning the forced loans. A point that has been stressed by scholars concerns certain political aspects connected to the magistracy of the Monte officials. According to Louis Marks (1960), the officers mirrored at the financial-institutional level the oligarchic character of Lorenzo Medici's Florence, based on a patronage network that distributed substantial benefits to its members. This perspective was subsequently revised, however, by smoothing down the highly negative aspects and at the same time highlighting a relatively large participation of Florentines in the floating debt system (Goldthwaite 1996). The catchment area of the underwriters who between November 1494 and November 1496 lent 450,000 florins at 14 per cent was quite wide (Barteleit 2004, pp. 150–160; Cambi 1786, p. 3). From the early sixteenth century, however, recourse to the Monte officers diminished in intensity, although the magistrates still represented an effective financial instrument (Barteleit 2004; Ciappelli 2006, pp. 189–234).

Duke Cosimo I (1519–1574) used traditional devices to cope with war expenses: ordinary taxes, extraordinary charges, forced loans and indebtedness on both the domestic and international market. Unlike the republican practice, however, the duke did not turn solely to the large area of lender-taxpayers, but also to merchant-bankers who belonged to the European financial aristocracy (Parigino 1999, pp. 56–74). The mechanism based on the sovereign who borrows personally from bankers, merchants, officers and courtiers is typical of the princely regimes; the urban-republican one, instead, as in the case of Florence, was based on forced loans collected on the basis of tax records in which the tax capacity of each citizen was registered. In summary: floating debt in the first case, consolidated debt in the second. This obvious difference tends to hold true until the early sixteenth century, when princely governments also resorted increasingly to issue securities on the open market, similarly to what city-republics had long been doing. Cosimo, therefore, would seem to act against the current by financing himself through merchant bankers rather than raising funds on the domestic market. The problem lay in finding liquidity quickly, so as to maintain a steady flow of money for the troops; and the only way to ensure this flow was to ask the Fuggers, Grimaldi and Negroni for money. After all, the duke had already dealt with German banking firms, so it was obvious that he borrowed from their agents in Antwerp and Venice. One wonders whether the involvement of the Fuggers was a choice to be placed in the broader context of relations between the emperor and the Florentine duke (Von Pölnitz 1942). The fact is that the state budget of 1567 records 50,000 *scuds* (with an interest of 9464 *scuds*) loaned by the Fuggers of Antwerp,

25,000 in the name of the Florentine Filippo Salviati, along with the Genoese Antonio Maria Grimaldi and Andrea Imperiali and some names that evoke the most eminent Florentine patriciate.[1] This would suggest that traditional relations with foreign financiers were maintained and that the area of possible lenders widened. We must not therefore dramatize the lack of Florentine financial capital, since other magistracies, such as the General Depositary, on the eve of the war in Siena record short-term loans at 12 per cent in favour of the duke (Menning 1993, p. 146).

2 The Monte di Pietà

It was the institution of the Monte di Pietà of Florence that represented a fundamental event in the history of indebtedness of early modern Florence. Initially established as a pawn bank, the Monte di Pietà evolved into a veritable public deposit-and-loan bank (Goldthwaite 2009, pp. 471–479). In 1582 just 280,809 *florins* were lent against pawns, while 629,882 *florins* were granted as larger loans. At the same time, the Monte di Pietà became a sort of treasury for the government, where numerous public agencies deposited money, and where the grand duke himself borrowed for himself, his family, friends and clients. The Monte, thus, served as a lender to the weaker sections of the population, a provider of larger loans to private individuals as well as to the government.

The Monte di Pietà managed the floating debt of the state by issuing deposit certificates in favour of its creditors, who could transfer them to third parties; the government recognized those certificates with paying debt power and accordingly committed itself to pay its obligation to the holder. Following this new role, the Monte di Pietà replaced the system of short-term debt centred on the Officiali del Banco and bankers. The government resorted to the Monte's money for several reasons: expenses for the plague, for the war, for subsidies to foreign powers, to buy cereals, for the construction of palaces and public works, to finance trips and gifts as well as the purchase of buildings and jewellery for the Medici family.

In addition to managing the floating debt, the pawnshop also became an element of the long-term debt system. In 1616 it launched a series of securities at 5 per cent for 2 million *scuds* divided into shares of 100 *scuds*

[1] Florence, State Archives, *Carte strozziane*, I, fasc. 22, c. 40v.

each, whose interest was to be paid by the yield of the Customs of Florence, one of the largest revenues in the state budget (Cantini 1804, pp. 28–37). At the same time, the borrowers of the Monte would have paid 5.75 per cent in order to meet the operating costs of the institute. It is interesting to note, however, that a part of the bonds was assigned to local communities and state agencies that had been obliged to transfer to the Monte their budget surplus. Actually, their credits at the Monte were transformed into bonds. In 1619 another 400,000 *scuds* were issued as annuities at 5 per cent. The war of Castro (1642–1645), which saw an alliance between Florence, Venice and Modena in support of the duke of Parma and against the Pope, provoked a further demand for money. The government launched a new series of annuities but not involving the Monte di Pietà, which was probably in financial difficulty. In fact, in 1646 the total debt of the Mount reached 7,750,000 *scuds*, while thirty years earlier it was about 2,250,000 *scuds*. From that year until 1651, the debt was converted by lowering the interest rate to 4 per cent first, then to 3 per cent and finally as low as 1.5 per cent (Pampaloni 1956).

To support the financial institution, the revenue from some taxes was earmarked to its coffers, but the efficiency of the Tuscan tax system turned out to be rather modest: of the 204,000 *scuds* earmarked to the Monte in 1646, 90 per cent (184,257 *scuds*) were made available to the Monte, not enough, considering that it was estimated that it needed 310,000 *scuds* a year. It is not surprising, therefore, that from the mid-seventeenth century any reference to the Monte di Pietà disappeared from the list of extraordinary income of the Florentine state budget. The situation of the institution had progressively deteriorated and now it was unable to provide financial resources to the ducal government. The only trace that remained in state finance was the payment of the interest of the annuities issued in the early seventeenth century, which continued to be paid until 1770, when the debt of the Monte di Pietà was incorporated into the new Monte Comune (Felloni 1971, pp. 283–289).

Between the seventeenth and eighteenth century the need to find short-term loans was met by bankers, mostly Tuscan and Genoese. In 1707, requesting financial help from the emperor, the Grand Duke Cosimo III (1642–1723) resorted to Florentine bankers and financiers in Milan, where the headquarters of the imperial army resided. While the Florentine bankers generally required an interest rate of 7 per cent, in Milan the presence of the troops had made the cost of money extremely high, so that in the years 1708–1710 the loans cost the grand duke

12 per cent, and on one occasion even 24 per cent (Waquet 1990, pp. 100–106). To quickly repay these capitals, the government sought money at medium and long-term, finding it in Genoa and issuing securities.

The limits of the financial demand of the Grand Duke did not lie so much in his credibility as a debtor, but in the scarce supply of capital that the Florentine market presented. It was therefore necessary to resort to bankers and financiers who, through their personal relationships, could raise money. These same people then found themselves in the main financial agencies of the state, in the General Depositary, in the management of public debt and in the collection of taxes (Waquet 1990, pp. 117–119). The role of bankers, however, was limited to the financial sphere and did not extend their influence to other areas of ducal politics.

3 State Bank and Finance in Venice

It is well known that Venice was one of the most important financial centres of preindustrial Europe. She probably reached her heyday in the fifteenth and sixteenth centuries, as her financial institutions provided a model to other European centres. The most important aim of the Venetian financial market was first to provide merchants, rightly considered as the protagonists of the economic success of the city, with services. A foreign merchant coming in the Rialto was immediately struck by the ease to do business without cash. From the late thirteenth century, some local bankers kept their clients' deposits and transferred money by simply writing the sum from an account to another one (Mueller 1997). This system facilitated transactions and limited considerably the use of coins. The main features of the Venetian banking system were the generally accepted use of bank money, a lesser stock of money than the volume of deposits, and the fact that bankers had accounts in the other banks. Local bankers were more interested in supporting trade than granting credit, but when they permitted depositors to overdraw they created credit for their clients, who could then even lend to other clients (Mueller 1997, pp. 16, 23).

Bankers often exceeded the limits imposed by the law, and the government itself occasionally required their credit services. Furthermore, although the government required an exact equivalence between the money deposited and the value of the transactions recorded, bankers usually took advantage of the availability of money to make investments on their own account, hoping the depositors would not have requested their money in the meantime. But as soon as it was rumoured that a banker had been struck by some unfortunate event (loss of merchandise, bankruptcy of merchants close to him, death of some protector) a multitude of creditors huddled in front of his bank claiming their money back. In most cases there was nothing but to declare bankruptcy and rely on the justice for the settlement of debts.

The relationships between banks and government were quite close. Bankers were requested by the authorities to pay a draft, advance money for grain supplies, and so on. During the fifteenth and early sixteenth century local bankers provided several short-term loans, especially in the frequent periods of war. In 1473–1475, during the Turkish war, the four banks then operating at the Rialto lent at least 300,000 ducats (Mueller 1997, p. 432). At the beginning of the sixteenth century the banks of Rialto had provided various loans to the government: between 10 July 1510 and 5 September 1510 the Pisani and Capello-Vendramin banks anticipated at least 30,000 ducats 'for the satisfaction' of Swiss mercenaries and to hire other soldiers; of the 13,500 *ducats* sent to the Venetian proveditor Cappello in March 1511, 8000 were lent by the Cappello and Vendramin bank, and 5500 from the Priuli bank. These short-term loans were usually guaranteed by tax revenues and did not undermine the banks' financial health.[2]

The frequent bank crises, however, forced the government to intervene. In 1564 the Venetian senate forbade the opening of new banks, and in 1584 the failure of the last private bank of Pisani and Tiepolo, which had a loss of 1.4 million ducats, paved the way to the first public bank (Tucci 1981, pp. 231–250). Three years later, in 1587, the Banco della Piazza di Rialto, which basically performed the same function of the former private banks, was founded. The novelty was that the government itself exerted a close control over the management of the new financial institution and was the guarantor of the deposits. The Bank received deposits and made giro transactions between current accounts. The clients' chances to be in the red faded away, for the function of the Bank was limited to controlling the monetary system by providing, at least until the end of the sixteenth century, reliable bank money.

The republic avoided exploiting the funds intrusted to its bank, sought no profit from the use of its credit and, in short, merely

[2]Venice, State Archives (henceforth ASV), Consiglio dei Dieci, Misti, reg. 33, cc. 47r-v, 66v, 107r, 124v; reg. 34; Gilbert (1980, pp. 33–34).

undertook to keep the money of depositors in safety, and to pay it out or transfer it to others at the will of the owner. At a given moment the depositors might even withdraw the whole of the cash, in full satisfaction of their claims, if they chose, and nobody could prevent them from doing it. Some functions of the private banks were thus transferred to the public bank. For some years its budget recorded a perfect balance between deposits and cash: in 1588 it amounted to 546,082 ducats, in 1592 to 705,849 ducats, in 1597 to 950,440 ducats, and in 1618 to 1.7 million ducats (Tucci 1981, pp. 240, 248). Such expansion undoubtedly reflected the prosperity of the bank. The increase in deposits was accompanied by limited withdrawals of money, so that in 1593 the sum earmarked to the daily cash service could be reduced from 30,000 to 20,000 ducats.

The new bank operated as a monopoly, for it was forbidden to open private banks that might be in competition with it. The state seldom used the Banco just for specific operations, and on these few occasions it paid back soon the sum withdrawn. In order to meet short-term financial needs, the authorities sometime established funds that allowed providers to use their credit through transfer to others with debt-paying power, until the debt would be extinguished. On 4 January 1596, for example, a giro fund was established in favour of some suppliers of precious metals to the mint. In 1607 this practice was renewed with a Banco Giro delle Biave, to be used by suppliers of huge amounts of grains. When it was closed in 1614, the government had paid back three-fourths of the original amount and the rest was spread throughout several creditors, even for as low as ten ducats. The sum was assigned to the Banco della Piazza, with coins as guarantee placed into a chest of the mint.

4 The Banco Giro

The establishment of the Banco Giro in 1619 marks a crucial event in the Venetian economic history. Although its accounting mechanisms were similar, the new Banco was quite different from the Banco della Piazza di Rialto (Tucci 1973). While the latter was a bank in which procedures implied real deposits, the former used transfers of state credits, which formed a fiduciary circulation controlled and guaranteed by the state. With respect to earlier experiences, this new bank was to lose its temporary character and become a true public bank. In 1637 the Banco della Piazza di Rialto was suppressed because of the growing importance of the Banco Giro. Initially a huge supply of silver to the mint was paid with both gold and a credit recorded in a new giro fund, so as to make the sum quickly at the disposal of the provider. Further loans and provisions of goods and services were fulfilled by crediting suppliers at the Banco. Such practice was so successful that in 1620 a new accountant was hired, and in 1626 it was said that the clerks worked all the days and even at night. The new floating debt managed by the Banco Giro was born.

In this early phase the Banco's assets were formed of its credit toward the state and a sum of money regularly assigned by the government to extinguish its debt; the liabilities were just the balance of the holders' accounts. The government, in fact, intended to exploit the new bank only briefly and wanted to redeem this kind of debt as soon as possible. Although initially the two public banks did not seem to be in competition, within a few years the Banco della Piazza di Rialto suffered consistent outflows of money. While in 1618 the amount of its deposits was 1.7 million ducats, in 1630 it dropped to as low as 56,185 ducats. No surprise, then, that in 1637 the government decided to close the Banco di Rialto. The very nature of the Banco Giro turned out to be successful: its linkages to the public finance and the mechanism of supplying precious metals to the mint implied that most of its clients were merchants, who found it extremely convenient to operate by means of transfers on the Giro's books.

Although the Banco Giro offered convenient means of payment and a stable money of account, the merchants considered it to be primarily as an instrument of public finance. Because bank money was a form of public debt, the government sought to limit the issuance of it and gradually amortize the debt. To this aim, the authorities had initially allocated a sum of 10,000 ducats monthly, but in 1625 the amount had been raised to 80,000 ducats, as a result of the expansion of debt (Fig. 1).

The first years of the Bank also saw a good assessment of its money, which enjoyed a legal premium (*aggio*) of 20 per cent (120/100) on the current money of account; in 1624, for example, the price was 121.[3] The second half of the 1620s was characterized by financial commitments that culminated in the plague of 1630–1631. In 1629 the *aggio* had fallen to

[3] ASV, Senato, Giro, fz. 2, December 26, 1624.

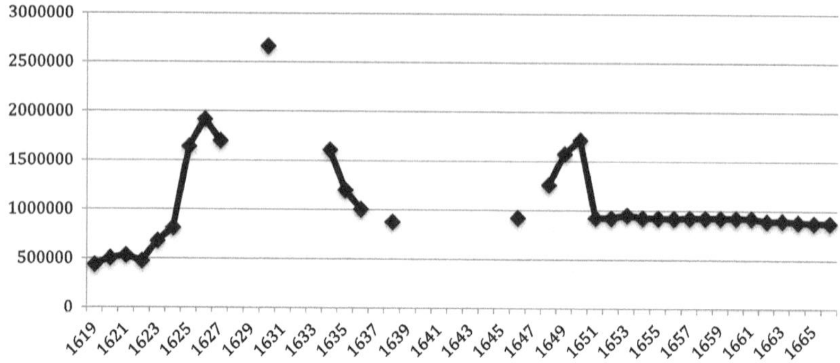

Fig. 1 Debt of the Venetian government at the Banco Giro, 1619–1666. *Source* Tucci [1973], p. 370; ASV, Senato, Giro, fz. 2, September 29, 1626

19.5 per cent, causing an alarm among both merchants and authorities; but the following year the price fell to 90, making the value of the bank money even lower than the current money of account. In the following years, however, the level of debt was significantly reduced, which allowed the Venetians to pay a portion of their taxes in bank money. The closing of the Banco della Piazza di Rialto and the policy of debt control favoured a consolidation in the confidence of Banco Giro and consequently an increase in the price of its money of account, which reached 122 in 1635 and in 1638. This obviously worried the authorities, since the merchants preferred to pay custom duties in cash with a premium of 20 per cent rather than using the bank money priced at 22. In 1643 the situation became even more complicated, as the price of the bank money reached 25 due to an unusual inflow of bills to be paid at the Banco Giro (Mandich 1957, pp. 1169–1170).

The outbreak of the war of Crete (1645–1669) naturally involved a tough strain on Venetian state finance. The government imposed new taxes, above all to support the growth of the public debt. It is likely that the major effort that the Republic produced was in the first years of the war, when both the tax burden and the demand for loans grew significantly. Tariff increases and extraordinary direct taxes characterized the fiscal policy of the government in the second half of the 1640s; in the following years some taxes were made ordinary to support the debt service. While in 1641 the long-term debt corresponded to less than 170 tons of silver, in 1670, a year after the end of the war, it had increased to about 890 tons. Table 1 shows the situation in 1670.

Table 1 Funded debt of the Republic of Venice in 1670

Ducats

Deposits in the Mint	*Capital*	%	%	*Interest*	%	%
Series						
4%	1,127,952	5.3		45,118	3.0	
5%	8,485,806	39.6		424,290	28.2	
6%	3,707,307	17.3		222,438	14.8	
7%	4,346,029	20.3		304,222	20.2	
10%	292,412	1.4		29,241	1.9	
12%	179,591	0.8		21,549	1.4	
14%	3,284,280	15.3		459,799	30.5	
Total	21,423,336	100	46.5	1,506,657	100	63.4
Interest in arrears	11,000,000		23.9			
Total	32,423,367					
Loans out of the Mint						
Venice	12,670,750	92.8		825,316	94.7	
Mainland	988,551	7.2		45,863	5.3	
Total	13,659,301	100	29.6	871,179	100	36.6
Grand Total	46,082,668		100	2,377,836		100

Source Pezzolo (2006, p. 101)

War finance characterized the central decades of the seventeenth century but, as on previous occasions, after the end of the war the government put its debt in order and began to lower the interest rate paid on its securities. In 1672 the various redeemable series between 5 and 7 per cent that had been issued during the war were unified in a single fund at the interest rate of 3 per cent. The consequences of the war do not seem, therefore, heavy for the financial health of the Republic, but what happened to the Banco Giro?

A state budget drawn up in 1670 indicates that the role of the Banco Giro as an instrument of indebtedness was rather limited: just over a million ducats at 5 and 6 per cent were recorded on the books of the bank, that is less than 3 per cent of the entire debt, not considering the interest arrears. The government debt at the Bank in fact, after an initial growth, stabilized around 900,000 ducats, a level considered customary by the financial authorities. The limited amount of capital collected is not surprising: the Venetian government had instruments far more effective than the Bank; the so-called deposits in the Mint (annuities) enjoyed a well-deserved reputation and were widespread in society. It would have been extremely dangerous for the Venetian government to exploit the Bank as a central element of the financing system, since the institute also performed delicate functions in controlling the money market. The decision to suspend the convertibility of bank money in 1648 (which was to last until 1666) lay precisely within the sphere of the money market rather than in the context of the financial needs of the state.

Although there is scanty information on the first years of the war, we know that in 1648 the bank money dropped to 113, and in 1650 the price had actually fallen to 96–97, also due to the suspension of government payments in favour of the Banco. In December of that year the senate, however, decided to increase the sum earmarked to the bank from 10,000 to 15,000 ducats per month, and the following year managed to pay off 600,000 ducats of debt, thus favouring a substantial rise in the price of bank money. The stability of debt shows that the government avoided issuing bank money.

With the end of the forced convertibility in 1666 a new phase for the Banco Giro opened, since it also assumed the function of a deposit bank available to all potential customers. Now the bank money could be transformed into cash and cash into bank money. The bank issued certificates of deposit, but they were never allowed to be transferable.

The first half of the eighteenth century was characterized by the Second War of Morea (1714–1718), which saw the Republic lose the Greek region that had been conquered after a long war in the last twenty years of the previous century. It has been estimated that the four years of war cost 15 million ducats in extraordinary expenses, which were found by first resorting to the debt. Between 1710 and 1719 the size of the state debt grew moderately from 67,578,000 ducats to 69,997,000.[4] In December 1714, the government decreed a forced conversion of the debt, making the rate of interest uniform at 2 per cent. A year later, charitable institutions and guilds of Venice were involved, more or less voluntarily, in collecting loans of which they were guarantors. These institutions operated as intermediaries between investors and state: the former remained anonymous, had the right to transfer their securities as a means of a notarial act, and the maturity of the loan was predetermined; the latter managed to obtain loans in a context where investors' confidence had diminished following the reduction in interest rates two

[4]ASV, Savio Cassier, 579, cc. 139ff; Da Ponte (1801, Table VIII).

years earlier. Furthermore, in 1716 the tariff increase of the grinding duty allowed government to launch a series of public debt at 4 per cent.

During the war, the government turned to the Banco Giro withdrawing cash and expanding the volume of bank money. Between 1710 and 1714, the government deposited gold and silver coins to pay precious metal suppliers in bank money, but within a short time it withdrew the cash without extinguishing its previous credits. In 1714 the authorities decided that the bank money was not convertible, and this regime lasted until 1739. The lack of confidence in the Bank is evident in Fig. 2, which presents the bank money prices over the seventeenth and eighteenth centuries.

In 1717 the volume of bank money in circulation exceeded 2 million ducats and consequently the merchants tended to avoid use of the Bank for their operations. The Giro advanced to the state at war 1.4 million ducats, which although it did not represent a considerable percentage of total spending, was a substantial injection of money into the market. The general economic condition was certainly not favoured by the expansion of the money supply. Because bank money inflation caused foreign exchange to rise, merchants preferred to pay for imports with good coins, thus causing the disappearance of precious currencies while the bank money depreciated. To address the problem, it was decided to offer

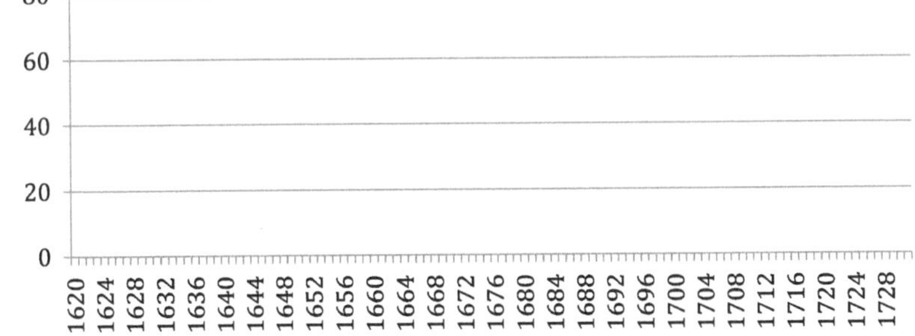

Fig. 2 Price of bank money in Venice, 1620–1731. *Source* Mandich [1957] and Tucci [1973]

Banco creditors the opportunity to bind for a period a certain sum in favour of the state; in return, the creditor received 6 per cent as interest, which was higher than 4 per cent offered by the deposits in the Mint. The implications of this mechanism are highlighted in Table 2, which shows how the rumours circulated in Venice and how the prices were influenced by the decisions of the government.

The advantage of the state, besides transforming a short-term debt into a medium long-term debt, mainly lay in increasing the price of the bank money, with which it paid for goods and services. The problem was certainly not to be overlooked. In 1716 it was estimated that the depreciation of 13 per cent of the bank money on a military expenditure of 4 million ducats had caused a loss of 520,000 ducats. The problem was exemplified by the exchange rate between bank money and the current money of account: as the cost of goods and services purchased by the state was expressed in current money of account, if current money was higher valued than bank money, more bank money was needed for

Table 2 Price of bank money and government activity in 1718. Official price 120

		Price
1718	April	Before the decree
	18	96.25
	23	97
	26	97.25
	28	97.75
	29	99.75
	30	100
	May	Before its performing
	2	103.5
	4	103.25
	7	103.62
	14	106.37
	May	After its performing
	21	107.75
	23	108.75
	27	109
	June 2	109.25
	10	112.83
	30	113
	July 18	114
	August 25	114

Source Tucci (1973, p. 384)

payment. This was in fact a tool for short-term indebtedness, as is evident in an operation carried out in 1718. A foreign merchant provided 100,000 ducats in bank money through the Giro, which 26 months later was paid back in current money by the Treasury of Verona. Since the bank money loan had been valued at 99, the repayment in cash yielded 8.3 per cent of annual interest. Moreover, this return was not much higher than the 7 per cent that in 1722 had been promised to some local merchants in order to keep 500,000 ducats for 4 years at the Banco Giro. The relatively high interest rate compared to that offered by the government deposits in the mint (4 per cent) was aimed at reducing the volume of bank money that was considered adequate to meet the demand of the market. The fact that at the beginning of the century this volume was around a million ducats, and that twenty years later 600,000 ducats were considered enough highlights the severe difficulties the Venetian economy had to cope with.

From the mid-seventeenth century the life of the Republic of Venice was characterized by three wars against the Ottomans and by numerous armed mobilizations along the eighteenth century. To cope with these commitments, the government resorted to extraordinary measures: in addition to imposing new taxes and borrowing, it had sold 90,000 hectares of common land, offices and access to the Venetian patriciate. Yet, around the mid-eighteenth century the Venetian authorities could affirm that the state enjoyed ample and deserved credibility. The basis of this trust lay in the punctuality in payments of interest on loans, the mint, and the Banco Giro. From 1739, when the convertibility regime was re-established, to the fall of the Republic in 1797 the state debt in the Bank was kept at a moderate level. Despite some crises, the fiduciary issues had never been increased so as not to cause the collapse of the banking system; and as soon as the situation permitted it, the authorities re-established the good health of the institute. This was also facilitated by the government's financial policy, which aimed to ensure the balance of the budget between revenue and expenditure. The intensive exploitation of credit by means of bank money would have brought about a crisis, with consequent devaluation of exchange rates, taxes, state payments and would have encouraged speculation. From 1739 until the end of the Republic the state debt to the Banco Giro was maintained under a million ducats, even in 1760, when the Ottoman threat had led to naval mobilization with a consequent extraordinary expense of 1,000,000 ducats, taken from the war chest.

5 Conclusion

Our overview of the relationships between banking and government in Florence and Venice shows marked differences between the two cities. First of all it is necessary to underline that the role of the state in Venice is much more evident than in Florence. In the Renaissance, the bankers are few and concentrated in the Rialto, while the Florentine banking companies are scattered; this allows the Venetian government to control operators with ease (Goldthwaite 2009, p. 457). They are also subject to strict regulations that form close links between banks and state institutions. The opening and closing of a bank in Venice was an event that involved the city. The Florentine banks operated on much wider horizons than the Venetian ones, who mostly limited themselves to transactions in the city. As far as relations with the government are concerned, in Venice the bankers were asked to provide short-term loans and to advance payments; in Florence the bankers were involved in the indebtedness system through the Officiali del Banco, although this office did not count solely on finance specialists.

With the establishment of the Banco della Piazza di Rialto the difference between the two cities became even wider. The Venetian state was the guarantor of clients' deposits and assured, at least in principle, the control of the monetary standard. In Florence there was no such institute: the Monte di Pietà probably could have performed the functions of a public bank, but the heavy influence of the ducal family and the insufficient support of state taxation caused the decline of the Monte.

The creation of the Banco Giro increased the distance between the lagoon and the Arno, not only in terms of managerial performances but also in terms of results. Despite various tensions in time of war, the Banco Giro managed to maintain a central role in the system of state financing and, above all, in providing a reliable service to the market. It seems that in Florence all this was missed. The Venetian authorities were always extremely worried about the effects of fluctuations in bank money prices, while the Florentine government was apparently less interested. It could be said that the reliability of the Venetian banking institutions relied on a higher fiscal capacity than that one could find in Florence. In the seventeenth and eighteenth centuries the series of wars that Venice fought stimulated the search for new ways of financing, while the few wars that involved Florence did not have the same outcome. This mechanism could explain the difference between the Italian financial market and the one that developed in Northern Europe in the seventeenth and eighteenth centuries. The level of intense inter-state conflict in the North encouraged the development of new financial instruments, while the Italian peninsula, at the forefront until the early seventeenth century, was unable to catch up the Dutch and the British powers.

References

Barteleit, Christian. 2004. *Die Staatsverschuldung in Florenz Ende des 15. Jahrhundert. Der Monte Comune (1494–1512)*. Berlin: Logos.

Cambi, Giovanni. 1786. Istorie. In *Delizie degli eruditi toscani*, XXIII. Firenze: Cambiagi.

Cantini, Lorenzo. 1804. *Legislazione Toscana*, vol. XV. Firenze: Stamperia Albizziana.

Conti, Elio. 1984. *L'imposta diretta a Firenze nel Quattrocento (1427–1494)*. Roma: Istituto storico italiano per il medioevo.

Ciappelli, Giovanni. 2006. *Fisco e società a Firenze nel Rinascimento*. Roma: Edizioni di storia e letteratura.

Da Ponte, Lorenzo Antonio. 1801. *Osservazioni sopra di depositi della veneta zecca*. Verona.

De Roover, F. Edler. 1992. Andrea Banchi setaiolo fiorentino del Quattrocento. *Archivio storico italiano* 150: 883–884.

Felloni, Giuseppe. 1971. *Gli investimenti finanziari genovesi in Europa tra il Seicento e la Restaurazione*. Milano: Giuffrè.

Florence. State Archives. Carte strozziane, I.

Gilbert, Felix. 1980. *The Pope, His Banker and Venice*. Cambridge, MA: Harvard University Press.

Goldthwaite, Richard. 1996. Lorenzo Morelli, Ufficiale del Monte, 1484–88: interessi privati e cariche pubbliche nella Firenze laurenziana. *Archivio storico italiano* 154: 605–633.

———. 2009. *The Economy of Renaissance Florence*. Baltimore: Johns Hopkins University Press.

Mandich, Giulio. 1957. Formule monetarie veneziane del periodo 1619–1650. *Studi in onore di Armando Sapori*, vol. II, 1145–1183. Cisalpina: Milano.

Marks, Louis F. 1960. The Financial Oligarchy in Florence Under Lorenzo. In *Italian Renaissance Studies*, ed. E.F. Jacob, 123–147. London: Faber and Faber.

Menning, Carol B. 1993. *Charity and State in Late Renaissance Italy. The Monte di Pietà of Florence*. Ithaca: Cornell University Press.

Molho, Anthony. 1971. *Florentine Public Finances in the Early Renaissance, 1400–1433*. Cambridge, MA: Harvard University Press.

Mueller, Reinhold. 1997. *Money and Banking in Medieval and Renaissance Venice*, vol. II, The Venetian Money Market: Banks, Panics, and the Public Debt, 1200–1500. Baltimore, MD: Johns Hopkins University Press.

Pampaloni, Guido. 1956. Cenni storici sul Monte di Pietà di Firenze. *Archivi storici delle aziende di credito*, vol. I, 525–560. Associazione Bancaria Italiana: Roma.

Parigino. Giuseppe V. 1999. *Il tesoro del principe. Funzione pubblica e privata del patrimonio della famiglia Medici nel Cinquecento*. Firenze: Olschki.

Pezzolo, Luciano. 2006. *Una finanza d'ancien régime. La Repubblica veneta tra XV e XVIII secolo*. Napoli: Edizioni Scientifiche Italiane.

Tognetti, Sergio. 1999. *Il Banco Cambini. Affari e mercati di una compagnia mercantile-bancaria nella Firenze del XV secolo*. Firenze: Olschki.

Tucci, Ugo. 1973. Convertibilità e copertura metallica della moneta del Banco Giro veneziano. *Studi veneziani* 15: 349–448.

———. 1981. *Mercanti, navi, monete nel Cinquecento veneziano*. Bologna: Il Mulino.

Venice. State Archives. Consiglio dei Dieci, Misti, regg. 33–34.

———. Senato, Giro, fz. 2.

———. Savio Cassier, 579.

von Pölnitz, G.F. 1942. Cosimo I Medici und die europäische Anleihenpolitik der Fugger. *Quellen und Forschungen aus italienischen Archiven und Bibliotheken* 22: 207–237.

Waquet, Jean-Claude. 1990. *Le Grand-Duché de Toscane sous les derniers Médicis: essai sur le système des finances et la stabilité des institutions dans les anciens États italiens*. Rome: École française de Rome.

CHAPTER 8

Conflicts, Financial Innovations, and Economic Trends in the Italian States during the Thirty Years' War

Giuseppe De Luca and Marcella Lorenzini

1 1550–1617: The Golden Age of Financial Innovations

The second half of the sixteenth century was a period of economic expansion that allowed the increasing financial demands on the Italian states, especially Milan and Genoa, stemming from their involvement in the geopolitical strategy of the Spanish Empire, to be met. The interplay of economics and politics fostered several financial innovations that—though at different levels—notably increased the collection of monies and tied financial capital to their processes of state-building. The innovations included the progressive substitution of bond issues for compulsory loans, the rise of a lively demand for state securities due to the earmarking of future tax income for interest payment, their easy transferability and their tax-free status. All these innovations constituted a kind

G. De Luca · M. Lorenzini (✉)
University of Milan, Milan, Italy

L. Costabile and L. Neal (eds.), *Financial Innovation and Resilience*, Palgrave Studies in the History of Finance,
https://doi.org/10.1007/978-3-319-90248-7_8

of financial proto-revolution. Eventually, the emergence of the Besançon fairs (settled in Piacenza), operating under the Genoese as an international credit market with its own currency of account according to a mechanism that avoided the charge of usury, represented the other new crucial element of the sixteenth century.

This kind of 'off shore' capital market was essential then for providing Spain with the increasing amount of financial resources raised from the savings of the urban and rural societies. In the more dynamic productive areas of Italy, public finance, private credit and economic production ended up with a meaningful complementarity based essentially on the usefulness of sovereign debt as collateral for private financial ventures. In northern Italy public debt represented also a powerful instrument to link the different social classes of the state and the subject territories to the central polities by engaging the local ruling elites and the territorial bodies in a mechanism of income redistribution.

At the turn of the seventeenth century, a general spirit aimed at making money profitable without leaving it idle was progressively spreading not only among regular practitioners but also among wealthy citizens who found the investment of money convenient, especially because it was tax-free (De Luca 2011).

2 1618–1648: The Thirty Years' War and the Changes in the Financial Architecture

The Thirty Years' War involved the Italian territories only marginally and mainly in two specific circumstances: in Valtellina and the war of succession in the Duchy of Mantua and Monferrato. Both these areas attracted the European monarchies for their strategic position.

The Valtellina, part of the Spanish Lombardy, was a fertile valley at the south of the Alps and at the border of Switzerland. It represented a key passage that—through Milan—enabled the Spanish to reach the Tyrolean regions that were part of the same Habsburg dynasty (Parker 1972). Likewise, the Duchy of Mantua and Monferrato, under the Spanish monarchy as well, was a strategic area that connected Milan to Genoa.

The conflict in Valtellina (1620–1639) broke out in the context of the Thirty Years' War. Caused initially by religious matters (between Catholics and reformed Christians), the war was in effect waged by the opposing ambitions to achieve control over that crucial stretch of territory. Spain, allied with the Holy Roman Empire, fought against the attempts of the Republic of the Three Leagues, which was later supported by the Republic of Venice, the Duke of Savoy and France, to occupy the region. For the Three Leagues, the Valtellina represented an important commercial route and a potential region for levying taxes. In the last phase of the conflict the Three Leagues, supported by the French army, finally obtained control of the Valtellina.

In the same years the War of Monferrato and Mantua (1627–1631) broke out. In this case the *casus belli* was that Vincenzo II of Gonzaga, Duke of Mantua and of Monferrato, died without leaving an heir. The natural successor would be Charles I of Gonzaga, Duke of Nevers (the closest relative of Vincenzo II), but he belonged to that branch of the Gonzaga family that had established itself at the French court. Hence the Emperor, Ferdinand II of Habsburg, fiercely opposed his nomination and imposed instead the Duke of Guastalla, Ferrante II Gonzaga. The Duke of Nevers soon reacted by asking for the help of France. On the other side, the Duke of Savoy, Charles Emmanuel, supported Spain. In 1629 the French army invaded the Italian territories and defeated the Duke of Savoy, while the Spanish troops had conquered the city of Mantua. In the meantime Germany was occupied by the Swedish troops and the Imperial army of Ferdinand II had to intervene to help the German regions, leaving Mantua and Monferrato at the mercy of the French. The Duke of Nevers, Charles I of Gonzaga, became therefore the new Duke of Mantua and Monferrato.

The war, along with the spread of the bubonic plague in 1630, surely had negative and immediate consequences on the northern Italian economy and its financial system but not as enduring or severe as much of the historical literature has stated. According to a traditional view, the changes of the seventeenth century were elements that led Italy to an irreversible crisis and stagnation from which the Peninsula would recover only at the middle of the following century. Conversely, recent studies—drawing upon new empirical evidence—have shown that the Italian economy was undergoing a transformation that implied a structural reorganization of the economic and financial system that was adjusting to the new changes and necessities (De Luca and Sabatini 2012, pp. 11–25; Lanaro 2006, pp. 19–69).

The most advanced economic areas revealed new factors such as the liveliness of rural industry, the rationalization of agricultural production, the prominence of the financial sector and, in the Spanish dominions, the positive impact of Spanish military spending (Cardim et al. 2012).

The Italian economy of the seventeenth century proved then very resilient and able to respond efficiently to the changing environment. At the macro-economic level, it has recently been estimated that real urban wages and per capita production rose after the 1629–1630 plague. Recovery was possible because the fewer surviving workers were endowed with much greater fixed capital.[1] Hence, the seventeenth century, far from being considered the age of crisis and collapse, began a favourable conversion towards a new balance based on the consolidation and industrial growth of silk production.

The financial system also readjusted, adapting to the economic conversion while no longer playing the supply-leading role that it had during the sixteenth century. This transformation did not take the shape of new tools, new operators or new credit institutions; rather it mostly produced widespread changes in the financial organization and one innovation (the *factoría*). At the domestic level these changes were represented by the emergence of new public banks, while with respect to the international financial flows they were reflected in the fragmentation of the fair networks and in the passage from the *asientos* to the *factoría*.

Almost everywhere (from Milan to Genoa and from Venice to Naples) an intensification of new public banks was taking place. This was in part the response to the crisis that affected private bankers in 1580s and 1590s, who proved unable to collect the necessary funds (De Luca 1996). In the international financial world the exchange fairs were losing their monolithic structure dominated by the Genoese, while the *asiento* was gradually being replaced by a new contract, the *factoría*, which constituted the first real innovation of the century.

In addition, meaningful transformations were occurring also in the private market. This market that had long been dominated by private bankers, who mostly knew their borrowers directly, was turning into a less personal one, based more on reputation and on selection carried out by notaries. This metamorphosis was the result of a macro impulse coming from the demand side. New actors emerged: the municipalities, the religious institutions (convents and monasteries) and *pia loca* in general, which progressively became the protagonists of the local capital market.

[1]According to the endogenous neoclassical economic model proposed by Malanima, the crisis in per capita production occurred in the following century when the population began to grow again at a greater rate than capital formation and gross production (Malanima 2006, pp. 383–404).

The municipalities in particular became more indebted as a result of the heavier taxation imposed by the state whose expenditures—coming chiefly from the need to nourish and host the troops—were steadily rising. In order to sustain their debt the municipalities turned to citizens and local charitable institutions, leading to a progressive socialization of credit.[2]

The intervention of local institutions, which could boast a large consensus due to their centrality in the social network, enabled authorities to mobilize money that otherwise would not have flowed directly into the public coffers. These institutions had abundant liquidity originating from dowries—especially for the female convents—and from large donations accumulated throughout the years for confraternities and ecclesiastical bodies. Such resources went to meet the financial needs of the rural and city communities on which the seventeenth-century fiscal pressure was concentrated. As a consequence, the considerable indebtedness of the municipalities created a thick private credit market that gradually extended throughout the seventeenth century, thanks to a relationship network centred on notaries who helped make this market progressively reliable and attractive for private lenders.

2.1 The Public Banks: Changes of the Domestic Financial Organization

With the second decade of the seventeenth century and the beginning of Mantua's first War of Succession military expenses further increased the deficit of the Milanese Hacienda, which reached in those years the sum of 1.4 million *scudi* (Muto 1995, p. 290).

The response to the conflicts and the consequent higher government indebtedness was to restructure the financial market and operators, which at the domestic level was manifested in the proliferation of public banks founded with the specific purpose of reorganizing government debt. The recourse to public banks was also the result of the failure of private bankers in the 1580s and 1590s in Milan. The intensification of public credit institutions was, on the other hand, a phenomenon that spread throughout many Italian states and that other European countries

[2]This phenomenon continued in the following century, spreading to other parts of the Italian Peninsula. See the case of Trentino, where the communities of the countryside were indebted to the nobleman Leonardo Piomarta de Langenfeld for more than 45,000 *florins* (225,000 *lire*) spread across a score of transactions (Lorenzini 2018).

like the Netherlands and the German territories soon imitated. By 1640 there were 21 public banks in the Peninsula: 8 were settled in Naples, 5 in Genoa (but they were all managed by the Casa di San Giorgio), 3 in Sicily, 2 in Venice, 3 in Milan, 1 in Rome and 1 in Siena (Felloni 1999, p. 119). While up to that moment the relationship between government and private lenders had been direct, now it became intermediated by new public financial institutions that aimed at guaranteeing and safeguarding credit, collecting capital among subscribers and lending it to the state.

The term 'public banks' refers to credit institutions that could be either public or private but needed the authorization of the government (Felloni 1999, p. 116). On the basis of their origins, they can be classified into three groups. The first type includes banks that were created by decision of the state (central offices). The most emblematic case is the Banco della Piazza di Rialto, founded in 1587 by the Republic of Venice (Muto 1983, pp. 85–102). The second type comprises those banks created per resolution of city institutions, like the Banco di Prefetiza in Trapani (1459) and Monte dei Paschi di Siena (1472). Most of them had benefited from the resources of the state. The intervention of the government in the activity of these institutions progressively increased and the banks lost much of their independence so that the state ended up in control of their resources. The third group consists of banks established by religious bodies or associations, whose activities were formally and publicly recognized by the state (Muto 1995).

In the state of Milan two new credit institutions were born in the seventeenth century: Monte di San Carlo (1637) and Monte San Francesco (1648). Beside these, the Banco di Sant'Ambrogio, that was founded in the previous century (1593) and with quite a different purpose, underwent a significant change in the seventeenth century and began interacting with them.[3]

The Monte di San Carlo was founded in 1637 with the aim of consolidating the Milanese public debt. Finding new capitals to finance the rising expenses was becoming more and more urgent. The city administration

[3]Besides these three institutions, the Monte di Pietà (Mount of Piety) also operated in the seventeenth century Milanese financial market. The Pawnshop was founded in 1497 but compared to the public banks its activity was limited. The highest sum it lent in the seventeenth century was 85,000 *lire*, and generally its loans were much smaller (Cova 1991, pp. 329–340).

appealed to other Spanish Viceroyalties and looked for receiving *asistencias* from the Kingdom of Naples, of Sicily and from the Hacienda of Madrid (Marsilio 2013). Public finance collapsed in the second decade of the century. The Duke of Feria—the governor of the Duchy of Milan—appointed Giovanni Salvaterra to raise new capitals necessary to finance the mounting expenditures of the state because the funds collected from private citizens had proved insufficient. After looking for new resources in the Milanese square without success, he turned to Genoa.[4] Here he met one of the most influential bankers of the Genoese credit market, Stefano Balbi, who agreed to lend the money to the state of Milan (Cova 1995, p. 367). The agreement implied heavy conditions for the government that had to grant high guarantees for the indebtedness, i.e. the revenues from duties on merchandise and other minor revenues, the remittances from Naples and Madrid, etc. Also, prospective losses on the exchange fairs would be charged to the state (Marsilio 2013). The Milanese Chamber borrowed from Balbi 1,470,000 *ducatoni* (8.5 millions of Imperial *lire*) at 8 per cent interest. 700,000 *ducatoni* still had to be returned. Being unable to collect that sum through traditional methods, the Chamber agreed to Balbi's project to create an institution in order to raise the funds owed to him. The Monte di San Carlo issued 7,000 *luoghi* of 100 *ducatoni*, at 5 per cent interest (Cova 1991, p. 330). New tax revenue was destined to pay the interest rates. In addition, in order to make the *luoghi* attractive they were made tax-free and could not be confiscated. The *luoghi* were nominal and transferable credits and gave rise to a secondary market, anticipating the modern state bond market (Felloni 1999, pp. 102–103). By turning debt into *luoghi*, public debt was transformed from a floating into a consolidated debt.

Balbi was appointed to the administration of the Monte and as a consequence put in control of the Milanese public debt. In the 1630s the Milanese economy was undergoing a negative economic conjuncture with worsening state indebtedness. Balbi realized the necessity to reallocate the public debt to domestic and foreign markets. Most of the capital invested in the Monte did not come from the Milanese bankers, but from the Genoese. Among the most prominent operators there was Gio. Filippo Spinola, who from 1645 to 1649 purchased 28,757 *scudi di marche*

[4] Milanese bankers with sufficient liquidity were present in the Ambrosian city, but they preferred to invest in less risky operations with high guarantees, as for instance in the Banco di Sant'Ambrogio (Cova 1995, p. 366).

(Marsilio 2008, p. 163).[5] The payments were made by way of bills of exchange issued in the fairs. These instruments enabled the state to have at its disposal large amounts of capital quickly, but the interest rates charged on debts were becoming very onerous for the government. The Monte started issuing new *luoghi*, which in turn increased the state's indebtedness that amounted to more than 1,200,000 *ducatoni*. The urgency to extinguish or at least diminish the debt led the institution to involve the Banco di Sant'Ambrogio, which—having ample liquidity—agreed to give credit to the state. Its final aim was to obtain control over the city tax revenues, including the management of the Monte di San Carlo.

Differently from the Monte di San Carlo that was mainly financed by Genoese operators, the Banco di Sant'Ambrogio founded in 1593 was a credit institution entirely constituted by Milanese and conceived to collect capital for the city and to meet the growing demand from the Milanese merchants.[6] The Banco di Sant'Ambrogio was initially a success. Also the Monte di Pietà during the metamorphosis of the Thirties—coinciding with the diffusion of the plague that had decimated a large part of the population—had begun to invest its capitals in the Banco, whose operations were considered safer as well as yielding higher profits compared to other credit institutions. In addition it was possible to withdraw the invested capital at any moment to obtain ready cash (Fraccaroli 2008, pp. 59–62). However, the growing expenditures of the Milanese Hacienda—due to the rise of taxation levied by the monarchy—made the administration rely on private bankers who lent money by means of bills of exchange. If on the one hand they were highly profitable for private lenders, on the other they proved excessively burdensome for the city. The Banco di Sant'Ambrogio hence was authorized to issue *luoghi*, which turned out to be a success for the Banco's activity.[7]

[5] 1 *scudo di marche* equalled 20 *soldi* and 1 *soldo* equalled 12 *denari*. In 1646 Spinola along with other exponents of the Airoldi and Ceva families made a loan (called 'soccorso') to the city of Milan.

[6] The Banco di Sant'Ambrogio was created with the purpose of lending money to the Milanese great merchants. However it enlarged its activities and became soon a punctual lender to the Milanese administration (Marsilio 2008, p. 154).

[7] By means of *luoghi* the institution had collected 13,5 millions of Milanese *lire*, beside 400,000 *lire* originated by non-interest-bearing deposits. In addition the Banco lent the city 7 millions of credits (through bills of exchange) and another 5 millions of loans (Cova, p. 365).

In the meantime also the Monte di San Carlo was issuing new *luoghi* but this caused a further increase in the State's indebtedness which reached the amount of 1,756,000 *ducatoni*. Stefano Balbi was at that point dismissed and in 1654 the administration, along with the management of public debt, shifted to the municipality's hands (Marsilio 2008, p. 155).

Meanwhile, the Banco di Sant'Ambrogio also revealed it was unable to pay the interest rates on *luoghi*, but it obtained from the city the control over all municipal duties, a sum of about 900,000 *lire*. This fiscal manoeuvre implied the subordination of the general interests of many to the interests of a small group.

Ten years after the Monte di San Carlo's foundation, another credit institution was created, Monte San Francesco (1648), with the purpose of collecting capitals to finance the expenses of the city. The institution issued 1000 *luoghi* of 100 *ducatoni* each at 10 per cent interest rate, so a high rate, and initially it adopted—without success—an articulate way to pay the interest rates. Interest rates that came from the revenues of the duties on oil and soap were paid in installments of one twelfth for each month. The surviving shareowners would then divide the entire revenue of the duty throughout their lives. The last survivor would receive the entire amount of the interest. However, this method of payments proved inefficient and was abandoned and the Monte di San Francesco turned to traditional methods (Cova 1991, pp. 331–338).

2.2 *The Fragmentation of the Exchange Fairs and the Emergence of a New Apex Changes at the International Level*

At the international level, the bills of exchange fairs, some of the most crucial financial innovations of the early modern age, still represented a key element in the capital market of the seventeenth century. However a transformation was occurring in the traditional structure. Since the sixteenth century the Ligurian *hombres de negocios* had dominated this market. During the fairs, periodical meetings occurring every three months and gathering bankers from all over Europe, large short-term loans and modest private transactions were negotiated, yielding high profits to traders, especially the Genoese, who had achieved a high expertise in this sector. The Spanish monarchy, more and more hungry for resources, was soon attracted by these bankers and turned to them to borrow money.

By means of *asientos*—short-term credits at high interest rates—the Ligurians became rapidly the major financiers of the *Real Hacienda* and Genoa the *metropoli financiera* of the Habsburg (Álvarez Nogal 1997, p. 51). Their role of chief creditors began to suffer, however, from the incapacity of the Spanish monarchy to repay the principal. The defaults of 1607 and 1627—that had added to the previous crises of 1557, 1575, and 1596—led the financial operators of the Genoa *Superba* to renegotiate and restructure their debts with the *Real Hacienda*. Interest rates were then reduced and the deadline for repayment extended. The debt was transformed into an irredeemable and consolidated loan. The *asientos* were turned into *juros*, which allowed the holder to receive interest perpetually but not the initial capital. Although these conditions were not as profitable as earlier for the Genoese, the renegotiation proved as suitable as in the past to resolve the immediate crisis.

After the default of 1627, however, the Genoese bankers began to diversify their risks and move their loanable funds to safer operations, especially investments in the foreign public debt of northern Italian States: the Duchy of Milan, the Duchy of Savoy and the Republic of Venice (Felloni 1971). These operations represented new profitable and secure opportunities to place revenues that originated from their extended networks of finance and from the swaps of short-term *asientos* for long-term *juros* that the Spanish Monarchy had realized at the conclusion of each default. Meanwhile the relationship with the Habsburgs was deteriorating. The real estate that the Genoese owned in Spanish dominions was confiscated; in addition they were obliged to make extraordinary donations and loans. Likewise, their relationship with the Kingdom of Naples was changing, at least in the Genoese modes of operation. Along with their activity as lenders, in the second half of the seventeenth century they shifted their interests toward holding positions as officials of the administration and purchasing feudal possessions as well as achieving noble titles that helped them to consolidate their social and economic role in the Neapolitan Kingdom.

In order to maintain or increase their control over the international fairs, the Genoese transferred the meetings from Piacenza to Novi Ligure (1621), under the Republic of Genoa. It would be a temporary solution, justified by the necessity to safeguard the Genoese from the dangers and risks caused by the war in Valtellina in 1620s. This was an occasion for other financial groups to free themselves from the Genoese hegemony. Tuscans, Venetians and Milanese wanted to separate and create their independence so they established fairs to meet in cities under their dominion. In the second decade of the seventeenth century the international financial network of the fairs, which up to then centred upon the Ligurian *hombres de negocios*, began to break up and reshape its organization (Marsilio 2007).

At the first meeting in Novi Ligure the rivalry among the bankers of the other *nationes* was emerging. In 1622 the Tuscans separated from the Genoese and along with the Venetians established one fair in Parma and two in Verona.[8] The alliance between the Tuscans and the Venetians however soon vanished. In the fair held in Marignolle—a site established by the Tuscans under the Duchy of Tuscany—the Venetian operators lost 25 per cent of their money employed in bills of exchange, which started the division of the two groups. Under the pressure of the Genoese government the fair was placed again in Piacenza in 1638, but the gathering proved to be just a momentary reunion. The conflicts among the several operators persisted and in 1641 the Genoese placed the fair in Novi Ligure once again.

The Milanese bankers, also characterized by a compact and national spirit, wanted to replace the *hombres de negocios*' primacy in the *asientos* business with the Spanish Empire, and two years before (1639) they stated that it would be desirable that His Majesty employ his efforts to attract the skilful Milanese traders to Madrid.[9] They highlighted that:

[8]For the fairs in Verona, see Lanaro (2003, pp. 21–51) and Mandich (1947, pp. 1–16).

[9]The document states: 'Sarebbe cosa buona che SM [Sua Maestà] porcurasse di far venire detti negotianti di Milano habili a tal mestiere allettandoli col ben trattarli, dandogli assegni avvantaggiati e massime nella cautione, poiché una volta incaminata la tresca con questi requisiti potrà SM accresce e continuare con maggior facilità li assenti de quali la natione Genovese non manca d'haverne gelosia e sin adesso alcuni di detta Natione hanno fatto stimolare quei pochi milanesi che in questi tre o quattro anni hanno servito a SM per dargli danari e pigliare patrecipazione nelli assenti fatto o da farsi'; Archivo General de Simancas (henceforth Ags), Estado, leg. 3352, 1639.

> The traders of the Milanese market, vassals of His Majesty (and very united) could alone, along with their capitals, talent and credit that have throughout European markets, undertake and finalize considerable *asienti* (*tirare a buon fine assenti*) in Italy, the Flanders, and Germany for His Majesty. In these three or four years—that have been years of calamity—some bankers were able in effect to succeed and could reduce the groups of Venetians and Florentines.[10]

2.3 A Real Innovation in the International Financial Market: From asiento to factoría

The system of *asientos* (short term loans at high interest rates) was gradually replaced by a new instrument, the *factoría*, a contract that did not include an interest rate (like the *asiento*), but only a percentage, a commission, because the lender (theoretically) did not take the risk of providing or managing capitals for the Royal administration on which he anticipated sizeable differences.[11]

It was with Giovanni Giacomo Durini, Marc'Antonio Stampa, Marcellino and Cesare Airoldi, and Giovanni Battista Crotta that the Milanese financiers achieved in the seventeenth century by statute the position of *factores reales*, the '*cúspide de las actividades financieras*' linked to the Spanish crown (Sanz 1989, p. 34). In those years neither the war nor the finances were going well for Spain with new revolts in Portugal and Catalonia supported by the French in addition to the ongoing revolt of the Netherlands. The Genoese lenders to Spain were gradually disappearing in favour of the Portuguese. On 2 January 1640 Giovanni Giacomo Durini drew up the first contract of *factoría* signed by a Milanese. It implied the provision of 140,000 ducats to the Real Hacienda. Differently from the *asiento* the *factoría* did not imply an interest rate but a commission that was fixed at 2 per cent, which remained unvaried for 20 years.[12]

[10] Literally the document states: 'Non ha dubio che li negotianti della Piazza di Milano Vassalli di SME (et massime uniti) potrebbero loro soli *con i loro capitali, talento e credito che hanno per le piazze d'Europa* intraprendere e tirare a buon fine assenti di qualche considerazione per Italia, Fiandra et Alemagna per il servitio di SM, come pure si è visto in prattica che alcuni pochi hanno fatto in questi tre o quattro anni, che pure sono stati tempi calamitosi, e con questo forse ridurrebbero le nationi Venetiane e Fiorentine nel negotio'; Ags, Estado, leg. 3352, 1639: 'sobre introducir el negocio de letras de cambio en Milano.'

[11] The *factor* could also receive a fixed sum 'un sueldo fijo' (Sanz 1989, pp. 36–40).

[12] Archivio di Stato di Milano (henceforth Asmi), *Registri delle Cancellerie dello Stato* (henceforth Rcs), *serie XXII*, *Mandati*, vol. 60, 221r.–222v., Vercelli, 18 May 1640.

According to the letter issued in 18 May 1640 from the Magistrato Ordinario, the *factoría* was something new: 'era cosa nuova che la Regia Camera habbi a pagare tal fattoria non essendo a nostra notizia sin hora usata cotal forma.'[13] The Magistrato manifested concern about the *factoría* because it was still an uncommon innovation. Despite the initial scepticism, however, the contract spread. The *factorista* was an operator who worked in close contact with the central administration. He worked in practice for the Royal Chamber as he managed the money on its behalf. His role was more important than the simple *asientista* and benefited from more privileges.

Along with Durini, who thanks to his performance as *factor* of the Duchy of Milan was named Earl of Monza, Marcellino Airoldi also began to operate as *factorista*.[14] In 1649 Marcellino's activity enabled his brother Cesare to obtain the office of General Treasurer of the State, which was then transferred to his grandchild. Marcellino Airoldi was undoubtedly the most influential banker of the Milanese market in that period. His commission provided to the state's coffer about a half million *lire* (De Luca 1997, p. 75). His first contract of *factoría* was drawn up in 1643. Others then followed in 1644, where he anticipated the sum of 300,000 *lire* for the payment of bills of Naples; another one in 1645 in which he lent 445,000 *lire* 'per servizio urgenti di sua Maesta' (for urgent needs of His Majesty). In the contract signed in 1645 he provided Vienna with 200,000 *lire* 'per soccorrere il Sacro Romano Impero' (for supporting the Holy Roman Empire), along with another sum of 216,500 *lire*.

Marco Antonio Stampa was another notable Milanese financier. In 1640 he signed up the second (in chronological terms) contract of *factoría*, in which he anticipated 86,000 *lire*, from which he received 10 per cent from exchanges and *factoria* and 1 per cent for the risk of collecting cash in Genoa. The following year, by means of *factoría* he gave credit for 128,400 *lire* to Antonio Cermilli (the collector of the bread tax) at 2 per cent.

[13] Asmi, Rcs, series XXII, Mandati, vol. 60, ff. 221–222, Vercelli, 18 May 1640.

[14] For the many *asientos* and *factorías* drawn up by the Airoldi, from 1635 to 1688, see Archivo General de Simancas (henceforth Ags), Contaduría Mayor de Cuentas, 3ª Época, leg. 2169, n. 64; leg. 2319, n. 4; leg. 2558, n. 3; Ags, Estado, Milán, leg. 3353, f. 6; leg. 3366, ff. 132–140; Asmi, Rcs, series XXII, Mandati, vol. 60, f. 198r. For the role of General Treasurer held by Cesare from 1649, see Ags, Secretarías Provinciales (henceforth Sp), book 1367, ff. 173–180.

Though the Genoese primacy as chief lenders of the Spanish crown was declining in those years compared to the Milanese, there were agents operating in the market that were descendants of some of the most influential Genoese families of the time, i.e. the Spinola, Balbi and Pallavicino. Bartolomeo Spinola in particular was the biggest banker of the Republic of Genoa during the Reign of Philip IV. Thanks to the services that he had provided to the Crown, he was awarded with noble titles and in 1627 he was nominated *factor general* of the king, becoming soon after the *Consejo de Hacienda* and of the War. Bartolomeo died in 1644 and by that date he had provided the king with over 50,000,000 *scudi*. In 1643–1645 other *factores* operated in the state of Milan, in particular Gio. Francesco Spinola and Cristoforo Spinola. The first one provided to the Royal Chamber 525,000 *lire* by means of *factoría*.[15] Cristoforo Spinola, however, was the chief lender to the Monarchy, reaching a total sum of 950,000 *lire*, at the usual percentage. Other prominent *factoristas* came from the family of Pallavicino. Gio. Luca's activity for the crown, for instance, focused on the transfer of funds from Seville to Madrid. In 1637 by means of *factoria* he lent 200,000 *scudi* that the President of the Council (Don Antonio de Camporredondo) employed to pay to Madrid the consignations owed to several bankers. At his death, Gio. Luca's estate had credits to the Spanish crown amounting to 9 million ducats.

2.4 The Emergence of a Vast and Reliable Private Credit Market

Along with the emergence of new financial instruments, the seventeenth century is characterized by the increasing importance of a profession that, though not specialized in financial activities, played a key role in the local credit market: the public notary. Economic historians have long neglected this profession by considering him only in terms of his function of drawing up a myriad of deeds. His relevance has been attributed mainly to the wealth of data and information recorded in his registers. In the last 20 years, however, a new stream of research has shed new light on the role of the notary and on his effective importance in the credit markets of the *ancien régime* (Hoffman et al. 2000). Large strata of the population used to go to notaries to sign up contracts regarding a will, a

[15] ASMI, Rcs, series XXII, Mandati, vol. 62, Tortona, 23 May 1643.

dowry, a rent, a sale and also a debt/credit contract. Most of the citizens, especially aristocratic families, had their own '*notaio di fiducia*' (trusty notary), who managed all the business and patrimony of the family. As a consequence, notaries collected a large amount of information about their clients, their social positions, relations and patrimonies and reputation. They also knew who was looking for loanable funds (debtors) and who had liquidity to invest (creditors). The notary was able to use this information appropriately to match borrowers and lenders. By easing the circulation of information he helped reduce the information asymmetries and transaction costs and made the credit market work more efficiently. By matching demand and supply of money he operated as an informal financial intermediary. Unlike specialized operators (i.e. cambists, money changers, *sensali*, etc.) the notary was not allowed to collect commissions on transactions. His profits came from his own reputation and the ability to satisfy his clients that would increase his fame and client networks. Deeds had a price (established by the government) that varied according their typology and length. Hence the more contracts a notary signed, the higher his profits (Lorenzini 2016). Compared to the evolution of modern banks, which are able to bring together liquidity and risk pooling, notaries who dealt only in information were in effect making the best of an old job.

The financial instrument drawn up by notaries that related to credit was the *census consignativus*, a kind of mortgage loan, used in the Italian States and European catholic countries since the second half of the sixteenth century but one that spread widely throughout the seventeenth. The *census consignativus* was based on the structure of the *emptio cum locatione* (literally a sale followed by a rent), a contract already present in the Middle Ages and probably devised to bypass the usury laws imposed by the Church. The *c. consignativus* was definitively regulated in 1569 with the bull *Cum Onus* issued by the Pope Pius V. This instrument granted the owner the *dominium directum* (right to direct), while the *dominium utile* (right to use) was ceded to the tenant (De Luca and Lorenzini 2018). The *c. consignativus* had to be drawn up before a notary. The borrower had to give as collateral the entire or part of his/her real estate, normally a plot of land, a house or a shop which could produce an annual rent, that constituted the yearly interest rate. The restyled form of *c. consignativus*, introduced by the papal bull, implied the rebalance of the pull between the debtor and the creditor in favour of the debtor. These mortgage contracts made up 90 per cent of all loans transacted by notaries (De Luca and Lorenzini 2018). The debt had to be guaranteed by a rent-bearing property. As a consequence, the borrower kept paying taxes on the portion of patrimony used as collateral. Historically, real estate had been the most common and most favoured collateral for these loans. In the more economically active regions, however, real estate gave way to other forms of collateral that were less linked to farmland and much more linked to moveable assets such as public bonds, tax and farming revenues, tithes, etc. Thus this innovation contributed to making the credit market more liquid and resilient and enabled the more responsive areas of the Italian economic system to expand during the long sixteenth century.

While the private capital market was undergoing a general shift from short-term loans to long and medium-term ones, in business financing an instrument was rapidly spreading, the limited partnership (*società in accomandita*). It was a kind of partnership more fitting to the new economic structure of northern Italy, in which the exports of semi-finished products prevailed. Indeed, compared to the long waiting intervals, especially in the sector of silk manufacturing oriented to volatile export markets, the previous short term loans, ratified with *polizze*, proved more and more inadequate to meet the unpredictable swings in foreign demand. In Milan, even without a precise juridical recognition, the limited partnership had been used in the wool manufacturing system since 1575.[16] While it was emerging in the leading sector of urban economy, however, only at the end of the sixteenth century did the silent partnership receive its regulatory institutionalization from the bankers themselves—pushed by the state.

By means of this contract the merchant had more possibility to plan his activity, while he found himself managing a larger operating capital (represented in this case by 'risk capital') that was available without sudden interruptions for the entire life of the partnership, initially five or seven years and renewable. Moreover, the not negligible cost of defaulting on loans, which risk had to be borne also in times of bad business, were now on the contrary charged proportionally on the distribution of profits. These profits, coming from the extraordinary prosperity of the

[16]See Bortolotti (1985, pp. 118–119). The limited or silent partnership was a medieval institution initially used only for risky operations, although it had been present in Florentine legislation since 1408. It spread from the mid-seventeenth century especially in Tuscany (Melis 1981, pp. 448–449).

Milanese golden silk sector (manufactures) constituted the distinctive factors encouraging the participation of the financial operators of the city in these organization forms. Sharing (in majority percentage) the profits of merchandise that produced 15 and 20 per cent of profits, meant a fundamental incentive (for those who paid attention to silk trade) in the higher profits yielded by the capital compared to the collateralized short-term loans that generally yielded only 10 per cent.[17]

It is not possible to calculate the weight of this form of agreement out of the total types of partnerships of that period or to evaluate with certainty whether the bankers provided new money and whether a large part of these firms ceased automatically at the end of the initial contract. However, as proved by deeds of these financiers, the importance of the silent partnership for the Milanese silk industry at the end of the seventeenth century was not inferior to that of silk, gold and silver in the Florentine industry for instance, both for capitals and subscribers (Malanima 1982, pp. 131–143). In Milan, their diffusion was not caused by a flight to safe havens for those who had capitals that they would otherwise transfer towards the purchase of real estate, but rather to the fact that limited partnerships represented a more functional meeting point between the necessities of the most expanding economic sector and the availability of the financial operators (Malanima 1982, pp. 131–132).

3 Conclusions

During the Thirty Years' War a true socialization of finance was going on in the main economic centres of Northern Italy. In Milan an increasing array of people became involved in payment affairs, public banks, and mortgage loans. Rather than real innovations, a general restructuring of the system's organization was taking place, both at the domestic level and at the international level. The financial fabric of the Italian territorial states underwent adverse selection and private merchant bankers,

[17]Quotation from Vigo (1977, p. 92). As stated by a witness of the time, bankers did not ignore that the golden-silk merchants (auroserici), "divengono ricchi presto, e molto bene si sa, che diversi Abbati et Mercanti nel corso di dieci anni in circa si sono fatti ricchi chi di mille, chi di dua milla, et chi di tre milla scuti d'entrata." One of his examples, a dead merchant Giovanni Battista Surano, began with a capital of 2000 *scudi* and in fifteen years had a capital stock of 3000 *scudi*. In addition his two daughters had married wealthy citizens with a dowries of 5/6000 *scudi* each. Ags, *Visitas de Italia*, libro 403 (23), ff. 73–74: document of 10 December 1608.

who constituted one of the pivotal elements of the late sixteenth century financial network, fell into a crisis. As a reaction to their failure, public banks were founded with the purpose of reorganizing permanently government debt, which was steadily increasing as a result of the growing expenditures brought about by military needs. The relationship between state and lenders shifted progressively from direct and personal ties to indirect and distant contacts. Public banks operated as the exclusively financial intermediaries between the government and its financiers.

At the level of the international movement of money the Thirty Years' War brought about the loss of the hegemony of the Genoese as the leading bankers of the Spanish Empire. After all, the huge interest rates that the Spanish Crown had to pay to the Ligurian *hombres de negocios* for the realization of the *asientos* was one of the reasons for the cyclic crisis that led the Spanish Monarchy towards the *factoría*. This new contract constituted the real innovation—in the strict sense of the word—of the seventeenth century and it began to spread especially from 1640s. Differently from the *asiento* that implied high interest rates (which were becoming unbearable for the Crown), the *factoría* required only the payment of a commission as the banker did not take any risk in managing a large amount of capital for the monarchy.

Also the dominant position of the Genoese bankers in the international fairs was changing and at the same time the international fair network was restructuring. The Besançon fairs were not settled in Piacenza any longer but were transferred to other cities. The Genoese established Novi Ligure, in order to have higher control, but other groups of bankers were emerging: the Tuscans, Venetians and Milanese. They wanted to get free from the Ligurian hegemony and looked for their independence. These new forces led to a polarization of the international capital market and to its reshaping.

At local level, the private credit market was growing, thanks to the emergence of notaries as informal financial intermediaries. Though they were not specialized in financial activities they proved able to channel appropriately the information they collected in the capital market, matching demand and supply of funds. The rising role of notaries in debt/credit transactions reflected in the market that expanded, attracting larger strata of the population, not only aristocrats, wealthy citizens or big merchants but also artisans, widows and all who were generally not familiar with the financial world.

Another significant change was the function of urban organizations like guilds, trusts, charitable institutions and local communities, which began to play a role as financial intermediaries. In some cases, the governments resorted to forced loans from these bodies through direct taxes or developed the sale of annuities to be assigned directly to them. The mediation of local institutions, which could boast a large consensus due to their centrality in the social network, enabled governments to mobilize money that otherwise would not have flowed directly into the public coffers. The considerable indebtedness of the municipalities in order to meet the rising financial requests of the governments created a thick private credit market, which was supplied by well-off citizens and above all ecclesiastical bodies (monasteries, convents and other *pia loca*), which had accumulated huge patrimonies through time thanks to dowries and donations.

References

Álvarez Nogal, C. 1997. *Los banqueros de felipe iv y los metales preciosos americanos (1621–1665)*. Banco de España, Servicio de Estudios de Historia Económica, n. 36.

Archivio di Stato di Milano (Asmi).

Archivo General de Simancas (Ags).

Bortolotti, M.P. 1985. Uomini, capitali e mercanzie: le società commerciali a Milano nel secolo XVII. In *Aspetti della società lombarda in età spagnola*, I, 118–119. Como: New Press.

Cardim P., T. Herzog, J. Javier R. Ibáñez, and G. Sabatini (eds.). 2012. *Polycentric Monarchies. How did Early Modern Spain and Portugal Achieve and Maintain a Global Hegemony?* Sussex Academy Press-Red Columnaria.

Cova, A. 1991. Banchi e Monti pubblici a Milano nei secoli XVI e XVII. In *Banchi pubblici, banchi privati e monti di pietà nell'Europa preindustriale*, Atti della Società Ligure di Storia Patria, 31/1, 329–340.

———. 1995. Banchi e Monti pubblici a Milano tra interessi privati e pubbliche necessità. In *Lombardia borromaica, Lombardia spagnola 1554–1659*, ed. P. Passivino and G. Signorotto, 363–383. Bulzoni: Roma.

De Luca, G. 1996. *Commercio del denaro e crescita economica a Milano tra Cinque e Seicento*. Milano: II. Polifilo.

———. 1997. Struttura e dinamiche della attività finanziarie milanesi tra Cinquecento e Seicento. In *La lombardia spagnola. Nuovi indirizzi di ricerca*, ed. E. Brambilla and G. Muto, 37–75. Milano: Unicopli.

———. 2011. Come i fiumi che entrano nel mare e che poi escono e ad esso ritornano. II pensiero sul commercio del denaro nella Milano borromaica.

In *II Seicento allo specchio. Le forme del potere nell'Italia spagnola: uomini, libri strutture*, ed. C. Cremonini e E. Riva, 319–340. Roma: Bulzoni Editore.

De Luca, G., and G. Sabatini (eds.). 2012. *Growing in the Shadow of an Empire. How Spanish Colonialism Affected Economic Development in Europe and in the World (XVth–XVIIIth cc.)*. Milano: Francoangeli.

De Luca, G., and M. Lorenzini. 2018. Not Only Land: Mortgage Credit in Central-Northern Italy in the Sixteenth and Seventeenth Centuries. In *Land and Credit. Mortgages in the Medieval and Early Modern European Countryside*, ed. C.J. Briggs and J. Zuijderduijn. New York: Palgrave Macmillan.

Felloni, G. 1971. *Gli investimenti finanziari genovesi tra il Seicento e la Restaurazione*. Milano: Giuffré.

———. ed. 1999. *Moneta, credito e banche in Europa: un millennio di storia. Dispense per il corso di Storia della moneta e della banca*. Genoa: University of Genoa.

Fraccaroli, E. 2008. *Fra pubblico bene e privata utilità. II Monte di pietà di Milano dagli ordini del 1635 all'età napoleonica*. Bologna: Il Mulino.

Hoffman, P.T., G. Postel-Vinay, and J.L. Rosenthal. 2000. *Priceless Markets: the Political Economy of Credit in Paris, 1660–1870*. Chicago: University of Chicago Press.

Lanaro, P. 2003. Periferie senza centro. Reti fieristiche nello spazio geografico della Terraferma veneta in età moderna in *La pratica dello scambio. Sistemi di fiere, mercanti e città. In Europa e in Italia, 1400–1700*, ed. P. Lanaro. Venezia: Marsilio.

———. 2006. *At the Centre of the Old World: Trade and Manufacturing in Venice and the Venetian Mainland (1400–1800)*. Toronto: Centre for Reformation and Renaissance Studies.

Lorenzini, M. 2016. *Credito e notai. Capitali per l'economia veronese del secondo Seicento*. Bologna: II Mulino.

———. 2018. Borrowing and Lending Money in Alpine Areas During the Eighteenth Century: Trento and Rovereto Compared. In *Financing in Europe: Evolution, Coexistence and Complementarity of Lending Practices from the Middle Ages to Modern Times*, ed. M. Lorenzini, C. Lorandini, and D'M. Coffman. New York: Palgrave Macmillan.

Malanima, P. 1982. *L'economia italiana nell'età moderna*. Roma: Editori Riuniti.

———. 2006. A Declining Economy: Central and Northern Italy in the Sixteenth and Seventeenth Centuries. In *Spain in Italy. Politics, Society and Religion 1500–1700*, ed. T.J. Dandelet and J. Marino, 383–404. Leiden and Boston: Brill Publishers.

Mandich, G. 1947. Istituzione delle fiere veronesi (1631–1635) e riorganizzazione delle fiere bolzanine (1633–1635). In *Cultura atesina*, 2–3, 1–16.

Marsilio, C. 2007. La frammentazione del network finanziario delle fiere di cambio genovesi (1621–1640 circa). In *Debito pubblico e mercati finanziari in Italia. Secoli XIII–XX*, ed. G. De Luca and A. Moioli, 103–118. Milano: FrancoAngeli.

———. 2008. Debito pubblico milanese e operatori finanziari genovesi (1644–1656). *Mediterranea. Ricerche storiche*, V: 149–172.

———. 2013. Genoese Finance, 1348-1700. In *Handbook of Key Global Financial Markets, Institutions, and Infrastructure*, ed. G. Caprio, 123–132. Oxford: Elsevier Science Publishing.

Melis, F. 1981. Tecniche degli affari e produttività nei documenti commerciali e nei manuali aziendali (secc. XIII–XVI). In *Produttività e tecnologia nei secoli XII–XVII*, ed. S. Mariotti, 447–456. Firenze: Le Monnier.

Muto, G. 1983. Tra 'Hombre de Negocios' e banchi pubblici: progetti di autonomia finanziaria nello Stato napoletano (secoli XVI–XVII). In *Studi storici Luigi Simeoni*, XXXIII, 85–102.

———. 1995. The Spanish System: Centre and Periphery. In *Economic Systems and State Finance: The Origins of the Modern State in Europe 13th to 18th Centuries*, ed. R. Bonney, 231–259. Oxford: Oxford University Press.

Parker, G. 1972. *The Army of the Flanders and the Spanish Road, 1567–1659.* Cambridge: Cambridge University Press.

Sanz, Ayán. 1989. *Los banqueros de Carlos II.* Valladolid: Biblioteca de Castilla y León.

Vigo, G. 1977. *Finanza pubblica e pressione fiscale nello Stato di Milano durante il XVI secolo.* Milano: Banca Commerciale Italiana.

CHAPTER 9

Experimenting with Paper Money during the English Civil Wars and Interregnum: Monetisation Versus Securitisation, 1643–1663

D'Maris Coffman

1 Introduction

Writing in 1695, Davenant observed in *An Essay Upon Ways and Means of Supplying the War*:

> War is quite changed from what it was in the time of our Forefathers; when in a hasty Expedition, and a pitch'd Field, the Matter was decided by Courage...now the whole Art of War is in a manner reduced to Money... that Prince, who can best find Money to feed, cloath, and pay his Army, not he that has the most Valiant Troops, is surest of Success and Conquest. (Davenant 1695, pp. 26–27; Murphy 2013, p. 178)

The Thirty Years' War fuelled this process in continental Europe, with the widespread use of mercenary armies and their military entrepreneurs,

D. Coffman (✉)
University College London, London, UK

L. Costabile and L. Neal (eds.), *Financial Innovation and Resilience*, Palgrave Studies in the History of Finance,
https://doi.org/10.1007/978-3-319-90248-7_9

but the changing scope and scale of warfare also imposed serious financial demands on both the Parliamentary and Royalist factions during the English Civil War. In turn, the demands of war finance catalysed financial and fiscal innovations (Scott 2003; Coffman 2013; Pierpoint 2017; Horsefield 1960). The Civil War, essentially a confessional conflict between various factions of English Protestants (the more Calvinist Roundhead Puritans and the more Arminian Royalist Cavaliers), bore such similarities to religious divisions on the continent that John Morrill famously declared: 'the English civil war not the first European revolution: it was the last of the Wars of Religion' (Morrill 1984, p. 178, 1993).

The central claim of this chapter is that these mid-century experiments in Britain could have culminated in a genuinely public land bank. Instead, because the combined political and financial pressures on the Commonwealth regime required immediate cash to relieve them, large-scale land sales dissipated their capital assets. Although the array of excise-backed credit instruments, all of which had been tried during the Interregnum, eventually become important tools of British state finance (Dickson 1967), monetisation of the rents of seized lands never found broad support despite the potential of such schemes.

2 Monetisation Versus Securitisation

Modern financial economics makes a distinction between 'securitisation' and 'monetisation'. This distinction is useful to the discussion of mid-seventeenth-century experiments with paper money, despite the fact that neither term entered the English lexicon until the late twentieth century. 'Securitisation' is a form of financial engineering involving the issuance of tradable securities, backed by an underlying asset (in this case a revenue ordinance) which serves as collateral and the income from which pays debt service. The growth of excise-backed securities during the English Civil Wars and Interregnum prefigured the use of such instruments during the Financial Revolution of the 1690s. These included callable life annuities, numbered warrants struck off an array of funds that became assignable (negotiable) after 1646, and also included a wide variety of loans and advances collateralised by individual revenue ordinances and then syndicated through the money markets. A large number of these instruments were short term (no more than twenty-four months), but longer-term debt instruments did exist and were still circulating after the Restoration (Coffman 2013).

Anne Murphy has noted the role of creditor action in compelling the eighteenth-century British state to make a 'credible commitment' to service the public debt (Murphy 2013). Similar demands were made and honoured, subject to the exigencies of regime change, during the 1640s and 1650s. The disappearance of such instruments after 1649 was largely the product of the shift to farming the collection of the excise. Tax farmers gave the regime access to advances from the farmers of their rents, but that made it impossible for the regime to further encumber the excise ordinances as backing for additional loans. The tax farmers, of course, could and did re-hypothecate in effect their assigned privilege to collect specific taxes, but they did this for their own financial benefit.

When financial economists use the term 'monetisation', it is taken to mean the establishment of legal tender. This can take the form of coins, bank notes, etc. and can take the form of either fiat or promissory currency. This is not what is meant, for instance, by monetisation of feudal obligations, which is a different usage of the term, i.e. monetising obligations by agreeing to accept a fee in lieu of performing military service or manual labour. This distinction is particularly important in the context of monetary experiments of the 1640s, because the monetisation of feudal obligations was a fiscal strategy of the early Stuart monarchs, namely James I and Charles I, in the collection of everything from knighthood fines and forest fines, to the aggressive use of the Court of Wards and the revival of Ship Money and other archaic feudal obligations.

By the outbreak of the English Civil Wars, Charles I and his advisors had run out of feudal dues to 'monetise' (i.e. through conversion into a financial obligation). In this chapter, 'monetisation' refers to the decision to make a tradable interest-bearing security, such as a 'public faith bill', into a negotiable instrument to be used to settle debts. Another important caveat in the discussion of monetisation in the 1640s is the extent to which paper money could or could not be used to settle tax debts. In my study of the excise, I found no evidence in their declared accounts that the receivers of the excise accepted paper instruments to satisfy such debts. Pierpoint (2018) finds limited evidence in the records of the assessors that they might have done so in his study of the assessments and subsequent land taxes. This may be a feature of the sources used. In the declared accounts that I used, the excise commissioners do not attempt to claim for defalcations for negotiable paper, but they do so for 'bad' foreign money and clipped coin. It is quite likely they bore the risk for any promissory notes they accepted. By contrast, Pierpoint's records are not declared accounts, but rather receipt books, which were constructed for different purposes. Even so, he acknowledges it is very difficult to say for certain the basis for claims, and if the claims were against promissory notes these would have represented a very small fraction of the total transactions. This is line with the general maxim that taxes in the early modern period had to be paid with metallic coin, whereas the state issued credit instruments to pay its own debts and private parties used paper instruments amongst themselves (Muldrew 1998; Wennerlind 2011).

3 Management of the Public Finances During the Civil Wars and Interregnum[1]

In earlier work, I documented the extent to which the management of the public finances during the English Civil Wars and Interregnum was fundamentally informed by an unprecedented constitutional crisis for the English monarchy. Between 1643 and 1653, England and Wales functioned without a formal Exchequer or treasury to administer the revenues. Instead, Parliament engaged in 'administration by legislation', a process by which the Long and Rump Parliaments handled treasury functions through ordinances and parliamentary orders that governed the excise, the assessments and the minor branches of the revenue (Coffman 2013). To administer their legislation, they set up parliamentary committees, which included the Committee for Compounding, the Committee for Assessments, the Committee for Sequestrations and the Committee for Regulating the Excise, to name but a few. Some of the standing committees were revenue committees, others were judicial committees and yet others were concerned with the prosecution of the war. The only practical solution to the absence of a Treasury was for the committees themselves to issue warrants for payment of the regime's debts. These warrants were sequentially numbered and struck off of parliamentary funds as they could be redeemed by available tax revenues.

Alternatively, debts could be collateralised by specific revenue ordinances. As the regime's financial needs grew, Parliament issued 'public-faith bills' which were not secured by any ordinance at all, but rather backed by the 'public faith'. The orderly and continuous operation of

[1]This and the next section draw heavily from Coffman (2013), Chapters 3 and 4, which was also published by Palgrave Macmillan and is available on SpringerLink.

money markets in London meant that all of these instruments were traded, often at varying rates of discount. As a result of the active secondary market, speculators whose proximity to the regime helped them resolve information problems about when funds would be available to satisfy creditors could enrich themselves. Not surprisingly, in 1646, Parliament enacted legislation that enabled the negotiability and assignability of these debts, though there is evidence that had been the practice long before it became the letter of the law.

Such a system was cumbersome, costly and rife for criticism, and there is evidence that the regime took complaints seriously and was at pains to answer them in print (Coffman 2013). The Army, in particular, felt aggrieved, because the revenue collected from the excise duties appeared to enrich financiers, bankers and receivers of the revenue with much less available to pay the troops. This was one of the major reasons the Army demanded the abolition of the excises in its *Head of Proposals*, though the rhetoric was couched in terms of relieving the common people. Although the Committee for Regulating the Excise had issued a handful of callable life annuities against the excise, these instruments were rare; the majority of excise-backed securities were of short-term duration and paid high interest (Coffman et al. 2013).

4 The Debt Crisis of 1647/1648

By early January 1647, Parliament had accumulated nearly £400,000 in unpaid charges (exclusive of interest) against the main excise ordinance (the Grand Ordinance of Excise), which meant that further short-term debt against the excise was regarded to be unrealistic. Debts owed to the London Common Council totalled an additional £400,000 to satisfy the Scots Army. These loans had also been charged against the excise, although the intended sale of the episcopal lands was supposed to redeem them.

One interpretation of this arrangement is that it demonstrated the perceived lack of creditworthiness of the regime. The London Common Council wanted to be repaid immediately, lest they find themselves at the back of the queue in the face of religious differences with the Army (Brenner 1993). No doubt that was a pressing concern, as the confessional conflict (between the largely Presbyterian aldermen and the fiercely independent leadership of the Army) was rife. Mistrust was so great that after the establishment of the Protectorate, Cromwell did his best to distance himself from traditional London financial interests by re-establishing the Exchequer, purging the revenue commissioners and even moving to readmit the Jews to obtain access to other sources of credit.

One thing, however, that Presbyterians and Independents could agree upon was the virtue of abolishing the episcopacy, and divesting the regime of the seized bishops lands would make it difficult to re-establish the bishops. Although the sale of the episcopal lands represented a lost opportunity to restructure the regime's finances (as the rents from these lands were reliably paid by tenants, and could have been securitised, as Lord Fairfax had suggested, to pay off the army), the decision was not altogether surprising. Likewise, the decision to sell off the Crown lands to holders of army pay warrants was also politically expedient. Otherwise, disbanding the English Army would have been beyond the immediate means of the regime given the attitude of the London Common Council.

Unfortunately, the manner in which the land sales were conducted was further destabilising, arguably fatally so, for the Commonwealth regime. The enticement for raising the £200,000 necessary to pay off the Scots was to enact 'doubling' legislation, which allowed holders of 'public faith bills' to 'double down' by making an additional loan to the regime, at eight percent interest, equivalent to the value of the bill they held. The 'doubled bill' then enabled them to bid even more for the episcopal lands. This expedient had quickly raised the funds necessary to pay off the Scots, but had also saddled the Grand Ordinance of the Excise with the interest owing on an additional £660,000. The additional interest, paid until the land sales were finalised, ultimately cost the regime another £193,017.

By October 1649, this financial engineering had caused debts collateralised against the excise to rise to over £1.5 million. Only a tiny fraction of the land sales, less than five percent in the case of the episcopal lands, royalist lands and crown lands, were settled in coin. The degree of rent seeking was such that similar proposals to dispose of seized Scottish and Irish lands failed to find support. No wonder, then, that the land sales failed to solve the regime's financial woes. But what other possibilities might have been available had the Commonwealth regime been on a sounder financial footing, or had factional rivalries between the London Common Council and the Army been less profound? One interesting proposal, long neglected in the literature, was to make use of the lands seized from the Crown and Royalist supporters in quite a different way, one that combined elements of both securitisation and monetisation.

5 Land Sales and Land Banks

If the disposal of episcopal lands was all but a foregone conclusion, the fate of the crown lands and seized royalist lands was far less a matter of political necessity, and more of rent seeking by wealthy army officers (Habakkuk 1963; Gentles 1980, 1981). As noted above, Sir Thomas, Lord Fairfax had advocated securitisation instead of outright sales (Coffman 2013). His plan was to use the rents from the crown lands to retire the army pay warrants, either over time or preferably through the issuance of debt instruments backed by those rents which could be used to retire the pay warrants. Taken together, royal and royalist lands were worth well over £2.5 million, the rents from which had been well-established by the imposition of the Assessments. Assessments were a form of direct taxation on land which, though chargeable against the freeholder, had for convenience sake been collected from the tenants (Pierpoint 2017). The lands had to be surveyed before their sale, which is one reason why sales took as long as they did (at a rate of eight percent interest *per annum*), but the regime knew the amounts of rents owed.

Perhaps one of the most interesting proposals to appear during the Debt Crisis of 1647–1649 came from Dr. Peter Chamberlen, who is better known for his unsuccessful attempt to establish a Corporation of Midwives in 1643 and his successful effort in 1648 to obtain a parliamentary monopoly on public baths. On the basis of the Paracelsian medical training he obtained at the University of Padua in 1619, he practised obstetrics as a man-midwife. He held unorthodox religious views, having been associated with the Fifth Monarchists (Chamberlen 1659). His biographer notes in passing that Peter Chamberlen took after his famous son Dr. Hugh Chamberlen (Chamberlen 1690; Horsefield 1960), who 'like his father in 1649, and his brother Paul in 1705–1706, was continually bombarding parliament with banking proposals' (King 2004).

Peter Chamberlen's proposal, *The Poore Mans Advocate or Englands Samaritan*, deserves careful consideration, as he presents a scathing critique of the sequence of events noted above and tries to prevent further land sales with the maxim: 'Keep your lands and keep your credit. Sell your lands and sell your credit' (Chamberlen 1649, p. iii). In this thirty-page proposal, Chamberlen argued for the establishment of a joint-stock bank secured by the remaining seized lands with the bank acting as a cashier for Parliament. Although Chamberlen's proposals are somewhat exaggerated, in that he appeared to believe that the rents from the lands would be sufficient, over time, to abolish all taxes, the scheme itself was ingenious. Further, it had the merit of possibly establishing the political legitimacy of the new parliamentary government by returning to the Tudor constitution where the monarch was expected to function from revenues from royal domains.

Chamberlen argued forcefully that a 'joint stocke' land bank is the 'most firm and viable basis for a banck in Europe, &c' and will 'cause a great quickenesse of trade' (Chamberlen 1649, p. 6). More to the point, perhaps, in terms of the preoccupations of this volume, Chamberlen believed his bank would make it possible to reduce the interest rate from eight percent to three or four percent and would 'invite forrain Nations to secure their money here, rather then Amsterdam or Venice' (Chamberlen 1649, p. 7). He also believed it would help settle domestic peace by paying off the debts of the army. Another element of his proposal was to improve the quality of the coinage, much as the public banks on the European continent were doing.

A conservative reading of Chamberlen's proposal suggested that he envisioned the bank receiving approximately £1 million per annum in rental income, which it could use to service public debts, though he proposed a number of other schemes for raising revenues. The capital value of the lands was much higher, certainly in excess of the approximately £5.5 million represented by the nominal value of the actual land sales.

Chamberlen's proposal did not find a sympathetic audience in 1649, in large part because participants in the land sales had found them to be personally enriching. Chamberlen recognised that as well and interpreted that as the habit of 'some men can eat their cake and have their cake' (Chamberlen 1649, p. iv). Whether or not the Commonwealth regime was stable enough to implement the proposal had Chamberlen found support for it remains a matter of some doubt, but the important thing to recognise at this juncture is that such proposals existed in the late 1640s and were widely circulated. Chamberlen's proposal ended up as part of the Thomason Tracts in the British Library. Chamberlen's schemes and those of Lord Fairfax and his allies deserve further study, in light of the number of similar proposals made in the 1690s, when the reputed 'financial revolution' took place in England (Landale 2012).

6 Conclusions

The aim of this chapter was to give some sense for the degree of experimentation with various forms of excise-backed paper during the English Civil Wars and Interregnum. Compared to the regime's exercises in securitisation and the desires of Lord Fairfax for the disposition of the crown lands, proposals for monetisation were relatively rare, but the most developed of which anticipated the eighteenth-century land banks. More importantly, the partial monetisation of public faith bills proved disastrous for the Commonwealth regime in late 1640s and played a part in ushering in Cromwell's coup (Coffman 2013). What is often forgotten is that these public faith bills were the most straightforward antecedents of the French Revolutionary *assignats*, essentially interest-bearing public faith bills, similar to those circulating during the American Revolution, which were subsequently monetised in 1790. John Law's Mississippi Scheme and his earlier proposal for a Land Bank (Murphy 1994) were not yet in view.

One ironic by-product of the extent to which the British financial and monetary historians have largely ignored the late 1640s is that financial experiments of the English Civil Wars appear to have held greater interest for Adolphe Thiers and François Guizot in their attempts to make sense of the National Assembly's adoption of the *assignats*, than they have for modern historians attempting to understand the origins of the Bank of England (Thiers 1834). John Morrill may well be correct that in terms of its origins, the English Civil Wars were the last of the Wars of Religions, but in financial, fiscal and monetary terms, they also represented the first modern revolution.

References

Anonymous. 1652. *A New Way, to Pay Old Debts.*

Brenner, R. 1993. *Merchants and Revolution: Commercial Change, Political Conflict, and London's Overseas Traders, 1550–1653.* Princeton: Princeton University Press.

Chamberlen, H. 1690. *Dr. Hugh Chamberlen's Proposal to Make England Rich and Happy*.

Chamberlen, P. 1649. *The Poore Mans Advocate or Englands Samaritan*.

———. 1659. *The Declaration and Proclamation of the Army of God*.

Coffman, D.D. 2013. *Excise Taxation and the Origins of Public Debt*. Basingstoke: Palgrave Macmillan.

Coffman, D.D., A.B. Leonard, and L.D. Neal (eds.). 2013. *Questioning Credible Commitment: New Perspectives on the Rise of Financial Capitalism*. Cambridge: Cambridge University Press.

Davenant, C. 1695. *An Essay Upon Ways and Means of Supplying the War*.

Dickson, P.G.M. 1967. *The Financial Revolution in England: A Study in the Development of Public Credit, 1688–1756*. New York: Macmillan.

Gentles, I. 1980. The Sales of Bishops' Lands in the English Revolution, 1646–1660. *The English Historical Review* 95 (376): 573–596.

———. 1981. Confiscation and Restoration: The Archbishopric Estates and the Civil War. *Borthwick Papers* 59, pp. 1–53.

Habakkuk, H.J. 1963. Public Finance and the Sale of Confiscated Property During the Interregnum. *The Economic History Review* 15 (1): 70–88.

Horsefield, J.K. 1960. *British Monetary Experiments, 1650–1710*. Harvard: Cambridge University Press.

King, H. 2004. Chamberlen Family. *Oxford Dictionary of National Biography*, Online ed. Oxford: Oxford University Press. https://doi.org/10.1093/ref:odnb/58754.

Landale, C. 2012. Land Bank Proposals 1650–1705. *The Student Economic Review*, vol. XXVI. Dublin: Trinity College Dublin Press.

Morrill, J. 1984. The Religious Context of the English Civil War. *Transactions of the Royal Historical Society* 34: 155–178.

———. 1993. *The Nature of the English Revolution: Essays by John Morrill*. Abingdon: Routledge.

Muldrew, C. 1998. *The Economy of Obligation: The Culture of Credit and Social Realtions in Early Modern England*. Basingstoke: Palgrave Macmillan.

Murphy, A.E. (ed.). 1994. *John Law's 'Essay on a Land Bank''*. Dublin: Aeon Publishing.

Murphy, A.L. 2013. Demanding 'Credible Commitment': Public Reactions to the Failures of the Early Financial Revolution. *The Economic History Review* 66 (1): 178–197.

Pierpoint, S.J. 2017. The Importance of Direct Taxation to the Fiscal-Military State in Early Modern Britain. *Structural Change and Economic Dynamics* 41: 13–28.

———. 2018. *The Administration of the Land Tax, 1643–1733*. Basingstoke: Palgrave Macmillan.

Scott, J. 2003. 'Good Night Amsterdam.' Sir George Downing and Anglo-Dutch Statebuilding. *English Historical Review* 118 (476): 334–357.

Thiers, A. 1834. *Histoire de la Révolution française*. Paris, France: Lecointe.

Wennerlind, C. 2011. *Casualties of Credit: The English Financial Revolution, 1620–1720*. Cambridge: Harvard University Press.

Whitworth, C. (ed.). 1771. *The Political and Commercial Works of That Celebrated Writer Charles Davenant*, 5 vols. London.

PART III

Comparative Perspectives on the Spread of Public Banks

CHAPTER 10

Neapolitan Banks in the Context of Early Modern Public Banks

François R. Velde

1 Introduction

The purpose of this essay is to place the public banks (*banchi pubblici*) of Naples (sixteenth–eighteenth century) in the broader context of the public banks of early modern Europe and highlight their specificity.

If we go back far enough in time—say, to the twelfth or thirteenth century—what banking activities we find are performed by the private sector. But as we return back to the present we quickly see the public sector scrutinizing, regulating and intervening. Today, the banking sector remains more regulated than most. Indeed, a special form of banking, called "central", is (but hasn't always been) performed by special institutions, which are (but haven't always been) at some arms' length from political authorities. One might read this history as a gradual understanding, driven by experience and necessity, that some functions of banking require a public actor, but of a rather special kind.

F. R. Velde (✉)
Federal Reserve Bank of Chicago, Chicago, IL, USA

L. Costabile and L. Neal (eds.), *Financial Innovation and Resilience*, Palgrave Studies in the History of Finance,
https://doi.org/10.1007/978-3-319-90248-7_10

The content and accuracy of this accumulated knowledge are what a history of central banking might attempt to recover, by trying to map over time the shifting boundaries between private and public banking. In such an enterprise, the Neapolitan public banks deserve a special place.

The origins of central banking in Europe are to be found in a large array of publicly sponsored institutions that first appeared in the early fifteenth century. Broadly speaking, one can distinguish two "generations" on the basis of both chronology and the nature of their liabilities. The first generation arose in merchant cities such as Barcelona and Genoa (fifteenth century), Venice (sixteenth–seventeenth century), Amsterdam and Hamburg (seventeenth century) and provided means of payment on their ledgers. The second generation arose in the late seventeenth century in monarchical states, first Sweden and England, and later Austria, France and Prussia, and was characterized by liabilities circulating hand to hand (notes). All were "public" in the sense that they were either chartered (privileged) or owned outright by the local public authority, but their ownership could be private or public, their purpose could be profit-making or only providing a public service, and their assets consisted of a varying mix of public and private debt as well as coin or bullion. The reasons for establishing them varied, but a theme recurs, particularly for the first generation: providing a reliable means of payment, in the sense of being safe, liquid and stable in value. The fortunes of these institutions varied: the two main sources of difficulties or outright failures were monetary disturbances (fluctuations in the prices of various coins) and demands from fiscally pressed governments.

The public banks of Naples are chronologically between the two generations. They emerged in an important economic centre but also in a monarchical state; they were also unique in being a collection of independent entities rather than a single bank and in being owned by charitable corporations rather than by a government or by shareholders maximizing private gains. The Neapolitan banks thrived within a context arguably more difficult than those of their peers, buffeted by revolutions and plagues, held back by long periods of stagnation and subject to both monetary disturbances and heavy fiscal demands from the crown. Yet, they were also successful relative to their peers. They experienced suspensions of payments, but no worse than others, and only one was shut down.

Their total liabilities surpassed those of the Amsterdam Wisselbank and compared favourably with those of the Bank of England, the two giants of seventeenth- and eighteenth-century Europe. They were also remarkably innovative, for example circulating paper liabilities long before the better-known examples in Stockholm and London.

In this essay, I will first summarily review the European public banks of the time.[1] I will then present the Neapolitan banks, detailing their origin and summarizing their aggregate history. The next section details the specificities of the banks, focusing on their resilience in the face of multiple idiosyncratic as well as aggregate shocks, investigating their governance and relation with political histories, and detailing some of their more remarkable financial innovations.

2 The Public Banks of Early Modern Europe

Private banking emerged early on in the Middle Ages out of money-changing and deposit-taking. The use of the *depositum irregulare* wherein the exact objects deposited were not returned, but ones of similar quality, led to fractional reserve banking and financing of both private and public debt. Developments in accounting led to the use of payment by transfer on the books of bankers. None of this required the emergence of public banks—yet, but in the early fifteenth century, the need for stable, long-lived and privileged institutions manifested itself. In addition, neither private bankers nor government authorities had yet found a lasting solution to the provision of a stable unit of account in a world of multiple coins (Sargent and Velde 2002). For the most part these institutions emerged in city states (Venice, Genoa) or commercial cities with strong autonomy (Catalonia) and merchant oligarchies (Amsterdam, Hamburg).[2] Naples was a large city (Table 1) but not a city state or merchant city; yet it witnessed the creation of a system of banks that was both unique and functionally similar to the other public banks.

[1] I draw largely on previous work (Roberds and Velde 2016a, b, c) and refer the interested reader to the works cited therein, as well as to the surveys of Van Dillen (1934) and Ugolini (2017).

[2] Less prominent institutions nevertheless arose elsewhere, such as in Palermo (in 1552), Milan (in 1599) and Rome (see the contributions in this volume by Luigi Balletta, Francesco Balletta and Eduardo Nappi; Giuseppe De Luca and Marcella Lorenzini; and Luciano Pezzolo).

Table 1 Population of European cities with public banks, in thousands

	1500	*1600*	*1650*	*1700*	*1750*	*1800*
Amsterdam	–	54		200	210	217
Genoa	58	63		65	87	90
Barcelona	–	32		–	50	100
Venice	100	150		138	150	138
London	50	200		575	675	950
Naples	125	275		300	340	430
Naples (alt)	48	230	400	210	320	420

Sources Bairoch and Pierre Chèvre (1988), Fusco (2009) and Muto (2013) for the alternate Naples estimates

2.1 Genoa

Genoa's public bank, the *Banco di San Giorgio*, started as a side business of another remarkable institution, the *Casa di San Giorgio*, essentially a syndicate of government creditors that in time took over direct management of the collateral behind its assets, namely tax revenues. There are two banks under that name, one running from 1408 to 1444 and the second from 1530 to the end of the Republic in 1805, although it seems that the Casa continued to provide payment services on its books in the interim.

The explicit purpose of the first bank was to assist the government to enforcing legal tender laws. As elsewhere in Europe, the multiplicity of media of exchange (gold coins, large and small silver coins) entailed a multiplicity of relative prices, or exchange rates between coins, and governments often resorted (ineffectually) to fixing the rates by law. In 1444, the city government gave it the choice between enforcing a fixed rate for the appreciating gold coin and giving up the banking license, and the Casa chose the former. For the next century, there was no "public" bank (open to anyone) but the Casa, by its very nature, did business with tax farmers and the city, extending trade credit to the former or short-term loans to the latter, as well as bondholders to whom it made interest payments. The habit of keeping credit on the books of the Casa rather than demanding cash payment led to giro transfers between bondholders, and claims on the Casa (the *lire de paghe*) became a ledger money.

From 1530, the Casa ran again a deposit bank, but (rather than confronting exchange rate risk directly) it segregated deposits by coin: first gold coins and then silver coins. Only in 1675 was a general deposit bank opened, the key provision being that the bank had a choice of which coins to pay out. The bank also had a number of features common to early public banks, such as a requirement that bills of exchange be settled on its books, protection from judicial seizure. But it was not allowed to open a Lombard bank, nor was it granted the monopoly on foreign exchange it requested. It was only allowed to lend to the city, with approval from the Casa. Finally, the 1675 reform of the bank included an explicit import from Naples (Sieveking 1899, 2:216–217, 259): the *biglietti di cartulario* were imitated from the Neapolitan banks' *fede* (see below).

The general deposit bank's opening coincided with a monetary reform (broadly similar to the one that Naples implemented in the 1680s) that temporarily put an end to the rise in the price of large silver coins. When the rise resumed in 1709, the bank's unit of account did not follow and an exchange rate between bank balances and current money developed, the so-called *agio*.

The bank was generally successful, just as Genoa successfully navigated the complicated international politics of the time. But when the city was subjected to a large war indemnity in 1746, the bank experienced a run and all accounts were frozen and converted into bonds, repaid over several decades. The bank disappeared when the old order was turned over by the occupying French in 1797 and the Casa itself disappeared.

2.2 *Venice*

Venice had two public banks, the *Banco della Piazza di Rialto* (1587–1638) and the Banco Giro (from 1619) of quite different structures and purpose, although both were ledger money banks.

The first was created in response to repeated failures of the private sector, and its purpose was to provide a secure payment system. The Venetian Senate approved its founding after years of contentious debates that revealed its reluctance to get involved in banking. Consequently, the bank was organized as a "narrow bank", with 100 per cent reserves: although private, it was tightly supervised, with the charter up for renewal every three years and forced liquidation as a form of extreme auditing. Among its notable features, in common with other early public banks, was a requirement by the state to enforce legal coin parities, a monopoly on foreign exchange clearing, an immunity of balances from judicial seizure. As we will see in the Neapolitan case, Venice in the late sixteenth century also struggled with a poor coinage and alternated between forcing the bank to deal only in full-weight coins and allowing it to accept bad coins by weight.

The Banco Giro was quite different and arose separately (and initially alongside) its predecessor. A large government creditor (supplier of silver to the mint) offered to not request payment in cash but instead be allowed to use his claims, in the form of book entries in a bank, to pay others. The bank, run out of the mint, was from the start not a narrow bank, and the Senate explicitly allowed it to create new entries to pay creditors of the state: but it initially appropriated enough monthly sums to maintain convertibility on demand. It seems that the bank had freedom to choose in which coins to pay, and an *agio* over current money soon developed. The Banco Giro, however, only became a deposit bank (i.e. sold bank balances for cash) in 1645.

While the Banco Giro was successful enough that it put the older bank out of business, its fortunes were closely tied to those of the Most Serene Republic and its numerous wars. The government did not hesitate to use it as a source of wartime financing, and the bank underwent several suspension of payments and partial defaults: suspension from 1648 to 1666, with resumption of nominal payments indexed to a debased coin, and from 1714 to 1739.

2.3 Aragon

The municipalities of the crown of Aragon (comprising Catalonia as well as Valencia and Majorca) enjoyed a high degree of financial autonomy, and as many as a dozen opened public banks at some time between 1400 and 1650. The best known is the one located in Barcelona.[3]

There were two official motivations for the creation of Barcelona's *Taula de Canvi* (1401): one was a response to failures of private banks and the city's need for a reliable bank, and the second was to help financing the city debt more cheaply than with annuities.

The bank had no capital and was wholly owned by the city: it was run by city-appointed officials and the deposits were guaranteed by city. However, unlike the Venetian and Dutch models, the bank not only accepted deposits, but also issued annuities, hence was not 100 per cent reserves. It was also in principle only allowed to lend to the city, but in practice private loans and overdrafts were made. One of the big sources of funding was judicial or conditioned deposits, on which it

[3]See Hernández Esteve (2002) for a summary of the literature and a comparison with Naples.

had a monopoly. Deposits were made safe from judicial seizure in 1468. Although not an initial motivation, dealing with coin valuations and enforcing legal tender laws soon became part of the Taula's obligations, as with public banks elsewhere. Eventually, Barcelona created another municipal bank, the Banch de la Ciutat, in 1609 to deal with copper coinage.

Ostensibly created to remedy the failures of the private sector, its relations with the latter were contentious. At various times, the city used its regulatory powers to restrain competition from private bankers or prevent them from using the municipal bank as a clearing institution. The back and forth between restriction and tolerance continued until 1615, when private banking disappeared in Barcelona.

In spite of being wholly owned by the city, the relations between city and bank were subtle. Early on it was apparently used as a delegating device: when municipal finances were reformed in 1412, monitoring the city's accounts was delegated to the Taula. In practice, however, the Taula became a financing arm of the city under exceptional circumstances. There were three major episodes when the Taula provided wartime financing (1463–1468, 1640–1653, 1706–1713), with all resulting in a suspension of payments and conversion of deposits into bonds with haircuts. The second episode, which coincided with the war of independence against the Castilian crown and a massive over-issue of copper coinage, inflicted lasting damage to Barcelona's Taula and to similar banks elsewhere in Catalonia. The third episode, in which Catalonia sided with a rival claimant to the throne of Spain, ended in disaster for the banks as for Catalonian institutions as a whole.

2.4 Northern Europe: Amsterdam and Hamburg

Amsterdam's *Wisselbank* was founded in 1609 on the model of the first bank of Venice, the *Banco della Piazza di Rialto*, although it was wholly owned and managed by the city. The context was once again one of monetary instability, with competing coinage of unstable relative values. The purpose of the bank was to take the business of settling foreign bills of exchange from the private bankers and enforce the legal parities. As in other instances, several measures were enacted to make the bank's balances a desirable instrument, notably immunity from seizure by creditors, and a requirement to clear bills above a certain size through the bank. On the other hand, hefty fees were charged for withdrawing coins.

Over time several innovations allowed the bank better to manage the relation between its balances and the circulating currency. One was the emergence of a discount on current money, the *agio*, which had also emerged in Genoa and in Venice as a consequence of debasements. The other, in 1683, was to create a negotiable receipt for new deposits of coins, which allowed the bearer to withdraw coins for a smaller fee. In effect, the receipt system disconnected bank balances from redeemability: only balances coupled with a receipt were entitled to withdraw cash. Eventually, the bank learned to manage the *agio*, or relative price between (effectively fiat) balances and current money, through the forerunner of open-market operations, buying and selling current money on a discretionary basis. Later, in the eighteenth century, the bank engaged in several instances of crisis management, lending against collateral during financial crises in 1763 and 1773 (see Chapter 13 by Quinn and Roberds in this volume).

The bank was initially supposed to be a narrow bank like its Venetian model, but soon it started lending to the city and later to the Dutch Indies Company and other privileged entities. These pressures increased greatly at the end of the eighteenth century, during the Anglo-Dutch war and the early stages of the war against France in 1792.

The Hamburg bank was founded in 1619, during the period of copper debasement in Germany known as the *Kipper- und Wipperzeit*. It was closely modelled on the successful bank of Amsterdam, although it also operated a lending facility, mostly geared towards providing loans to the municipality. As elsewhere an *agio* developed on bank balances relative to current money, which the bank managed through discretion in the coins it paid out for deposits. Contrary to Amsterdam, it encountered several periods of suspension (1672, 1755–1761, 1766–1768). A reform of 1770 led it to establish a silver-bullion standard, which proved successful and lasted until 1875 in spite of crises in 1848 and 1857.

2.5 *The Second Generation*

The second generation of public banks begins in the mid-seventeenth century and is marked by two changes: a shift from city states and merchant republics to large monarchies (Sweden, England, Austria, France, Prussia, Denmark, Spain), and the use of a different financial instrument, the circulating note.

There is no simple pattern of public or private ownership, although the forerunners (Stockholm, England, France) were private ventures and later ones tended to be publicly owned. The circulating note, in spite of its usually large value, expanded the customer base beyond the wealthy merchants typical of Amsterdam or Venice: after the failure of John Law's bank in 1720 claimants (largely note-holders) numbered a half million. Although some continued to provide deposit and giro services, this was a minor line of business. The Bank of England and its French counterparts (Law's short-lived bank and the more successful *Caisse d'Escompte* eventually reincarnated as the *Banque de France*) became bankers' banks and governments' banks in varying proportions. As problems with coinage had been largely solved the payments function was not a motivation. Government financing, on the other hand, was an explicit selling point. The Bank of England (like Law's bank) was essentially a potentially lucrative banking license stapled to a debt issue as inducement for investors. Keeping at bay the fiscal pressures that had threatened the first-generation banks at various times was an even greater challenge for the second-generation banks, as governments saw the user-friendly paper note as an efficient way to mobilize savings during wartime.

The cataclysm of wars that engulfed Europe from 1792 to 1815 was the ultimate test, which two banks in particular managed to pass for very different reasons: the Bank of England and the Banque de France, which provided templates for nineteenth-century central banking. Of the first generation only Hamburg's bank survived until 1875 largely intact. The Neapolitan banks, also pressured into wartime service, were ultimately merged into the central bank of the Kingdom of Two Sicilies.

2.6 Common Themes

Several common themes emerge from this survey that are pertinent to the Neapolitan experience.

There were two types of motivation for creating these public entities. One was to provide a payments function, and stemmed from perceived failures of the private sector to supply a stable means of payment along two dimensions.

The first, more obvious, dimension was the fragility of fractional reserve banking and its susceptibility to runs, best described in the debates in Venice over the creation of the Rialto bank. A long-lived institution, more or less backed by the state, closely supervised and often required to maintain 100 per cent reserves (though rarely held to that strict standard) was seen as a solution. This usually did not prove sufficient, and various benefits or privileges had to be granted on the banks' balances to enhance demand: recurrent features are immunity from seizure, obligation to use them for conditional deposits and for settlement of large payments or bills of exchange. Once in place, the banks were often very successful in providing an efficient means of payment, in the form of ledger money, although such centralized systems were mainly useful in small communities. Hence, the early public banks remained for the most part merchants' banks, with a narrow clientele.

The other, more complex, failure to provide stable money stemmed from the nature of the monetary system of the time. The advantage of a commodity money system is, in principle, the anchoring of the price system to a real value, but the complexities of a commodity money using several metals and denominations, coupled with the depreciation of coins through wear, debasements and currency competition from foreign coins, resulted in unstable units of account. Regulations of relative prices by governments were understandably ineffective, and private bankers were often castigated for their unwillingness to enforce them. The hope, often expressed, that a public-minded institution would abide by the laws proved unfounded, but over time public banks groped towards a solution, best exemplified by Amsterdam's fiat money whose value was actively managed through open-market operations. A key element in management was granting the bank discretion over the coins it paid out. A partial substitute could be found in the ability to buy and sell coin or bullion, and especially to engage in repurchase transactions. By the eighteenth century, however, improvements in technology and coin management made these problems obsolete, and the second-generation banks did not have to deal with them.

The second type of motivation appears more intermittently, but is never far from the scene: namely, government financing. In the case of the second Venetian bank, it was front and centre: the bank was created to make liquid a form of government debt. In other cases, government finance came in from the wings: once a bank was up and running, and providing an easily produced but trusted medium of exchange, it was tempting to resort to it for financing emergencies. None of the public banks entirely escaped this pressure, and some (Venice, Barcelona) suffered acute reverses on this account. The second-generation banks were, by the circumstances of their origins in monarchical polities, even more exposed to this pressure. Their model, nevertheless, proved the dominant one after the upheavals of the wars of 1792–1815.

2.7 *Naples in the European Context*

Tables 2, 3 and Fig. 1 provide a quantitative comparison of the Neapolitan banks with the public banks discussed above. The tables provide cross-section comparisons of size at various points in time (the points chosen as a function of data availability), using current exchange rates.

The figure is limited to those first-generation banks for which we have time series. In spite of the periodic reversals that will be detailed later, the Neapolitan banks in the aggregate held their own: they were considerably larger than Hamburg or Venice, and larger than Amsterdam for sustained periods of time. A comparison with the Bank of England, the most prominent second-generation bank (Roberds and Velde 2016b, Figs. 22.1–22.2), would show that it surpassed the Neapolitan banks in size fairly quickly, just as it overtook the Amsterdam Wisselbank by 1720. Yet, as Table 3 shows, even as late

Table 2 Total assets/liabilities of various public banks, converted to Venetian ducats (a gold coin containing about 3.5 g)

	Year	*Thousand ducats*	*Ducats/capita*
Barcelona	1433	477	13
Naples	1597	611	2
Venice	1597	950	6
Genoa, c. oro	1586	179	3
Hamburg	1621	339	8
Amsterdam	1631	1,646	30
Nuremberg	1631	462	11
Venice	1631	1,462	15
Naples	1631	1,450	5
Venice	1666	876	6
Genoa, c. moneta corrente	1675	967	15
Amsterdam	1675	2,731	13
Naples	1675	5,147	17
Venice	1721	1,722	12
Genoa, c. banco	1721	7,531	116
Amsterdam	1721	13,610	68
Naples	1721	4,298	14
London	1719	46,545	72

Source Roberds and Velde (2016b, Table 22.1)

Table 3 Deposits and note issue of various banks in 1788. The amounts are converted to marcs banco of Hamburg at current exchange rates using Denzel (2010)

	Deposits	*Notes*
	'000M banco	
Caisse d'Escompte, Paris	3,435	52,703
Bank of England	30,649	128,869
Wisselbank, Amsterdam	21,166	–
Wisselbank, Hamburg	6,716	–
Banco del Giro, Venice	5,535	–
Wiener Stadtbank, Vienna	–	27,605
Bank of Stockholm	4,926	18,748
Banco de San Carlos, Madrid	2,260	791
Neapolitan Banks	49,967	–

Sources Roberds and Velde (2016b, Table 22.2), Tedde de Lorca (1988, 186) (Spain), and Balletta (2008) (Naples)

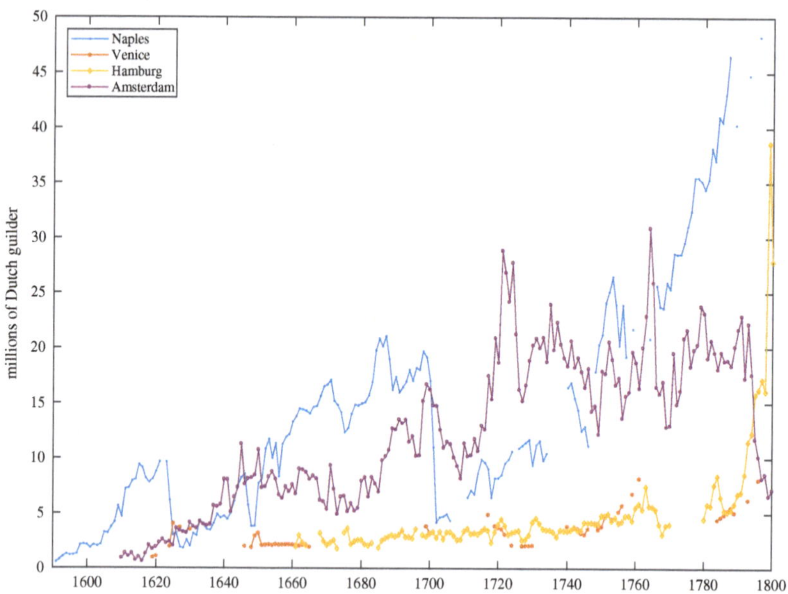

Fig. 1 Quantitative comparison of the Neapolitan banks with the public banks

as 1788 the Neapolitan banks were one third as large as the Bank of England. This alone justifies a study of the Neapolitan banks. As we will see, the services they provided were very similar to those of the other early public banks, and their financial engineering was in some cases superior.

In the remaining sections, I delve into the history and specificities of the Neapolitan public banks.[4]

3 Naples: Context and Beginnings

3.1 *Overview*

The kingdom of Naples, and independent kingdom (split from Sicily in 1282), was the object of a long contest between Aragon and France, until finally conquered by king Ferdinand of Castile in 1503. It became thereafter a dominion of the crown of Spain, ruled by the Habsburg descendants of Ferdinand's daughter Juana. As such, it maintained most of its institutions but the executive powers were in the hands of a Spanish viceroy answerable to the king of Spain. This situation of rule from abroad lasted until 1734 (with an Austrian episode from 1707 to 1734), when the younger son of the king of Spain, Carlo VII, conquered the kingdom and ruled from home.[5]

[4]On the history of the banks, in addition to the contributions in this volume by Costabile and Nappi, Balletta, Balletta and Nappi, and Avallone and Salvemini, see Somma (1860), Nisco (1866), Petroni (1871), Filangieri (1940), and Balletta (2008) and the overviews in Di Somma (1960) and De Rosa (2001, 2002). The documents in Tortora (1890) are particularly rich. On the securities (*fedi*) issued by the banks, see Ajello (1882) and Demarco (1985) as well as Palmieri (1905) and L. De Simone (1922) for later aspects; on the banks' internal structure and accounting, see Rocco (1785), Di Somma (1960), Avallone (1991) and Demarco (1996). Studies of specific banks include De Rosa (1955), Di Somma (1960), E. De Simone (1974) and Avallone (1995). On public finance see Bianchini (1859), Calabria (1991), Bulgarelli Lukacs (1993) and De Rosa (1997, 1998). Published statutes are in Vario (1772) and Giustiniani (1803–1804); see especially the titles *De Bancis, De Literis Cambii, De Monetis, De Nummularis.*

[5]When Carlo VII succeeded his brother as King Carlos III of Spain, he left the kingdom to his younger son Ferdinando I, who ruled until 1825 except during the French occupations of 1799 and 1806–1815. The Kingdom of the Two Sicilies (Naples and Sicily) was annexed by Italy in 1860.

Thus, the general context in which the public banks emerged and first developed was one characterized by a monarchical system, increasingly absolutist but nevertheless bounded by the compromises needed to keep Naples as "fedelissima" as it ought to be. Throughout Spanish rule, Naples was at the periphery of a large empire and increasingly burdened by the costs of its maintenance. Naples itself ceased to be on the front lines of the Spanish empire, once France abandoned its Italian ambitions and the Turkish threat receded after the battle of Lepanto; but it remained an occasional source of military costs, for example the revolt of Naples in 1647 and the ensuing French invasion, or the revolt of Messina in 1674–1678 again supported by France. Moreover, Lombardy, to the north, remained a battlefield during the Thirty Years' War, and the long conflict with the Netherlands (ended in 1648) and with France (ended in 1659) imposed fiscal pressure on Naples as on other realms.

3.2 Banking: The Private Sector Before the Public Banks

First, a question of vocabulary. The term *banco pubblico*, in Neapolitan texts, appears long before the *banchi pubblici* that are the subject of this volume, and appears to denote a banker accepting deposits from the public. For simplicity, however, I will use the term to refer to the seven banks created in the late sixteenth century by charitable institutions, as described below.

Second, the term "non-profit" is ambiguous. I use it to distinguish the eight public banks from private bankers, which operated as partnerships. It does not imply that the public banks were not seeking to maximize profits: in fact, one of their motivations for providing banking services was precisely to generate additional revenues for their charitable activities.

Private bankers existed in Naples since medieval times (Silvestri 1950, 1951a, b, and the contribution of Avallone and Salvemini, this volume), mostly Aragonese in the fifteenth and Genoese in the sixteenth century. Concerns about bank failures led to various regulations, imposing from 1549 deposits of increasing sizes and, as in Venice and Amsterdam at the time, concerns about chain endorsements and the difficulty of being paid in cash led to restrictions on endorsements in 1579 (Tortora 1890, 113–117; De Rosa 2002). By 1604, however, private bankers (at least of the deposit-taking kind) had disappeared.

Whereas in Barcelona and Amsterdam it had taken active prohibitions of private bankers, this disappearance seems to have been a natural displacement by the emerging public banks.

3.3 *The Beginnings of Non-profit Banking*

Naples in the sixteenth century had a large network of nearly a hundred confraternities providing welfare services in Naples, largely managed by members of the middle class such as lawyers, merchants and craftsmen (Muto 2013, 48; Campanelli 2002, and the contribution by Rosalba di Meglio in this volume). Some provided only to a limited set of recipients, such as members of a specific guild, but others had a broader constituency. Of the eight historic public banks, seven were founded by such charitable institutions (I will come to the eighth one later). Five of these: the *Casa dell'Annunziata* (fourteenth century), the hospital of *Sant'Eligio* (1270), *San Giacomo* (circa 1540), the hospital of the *Incurabili* (1519) and *Spirito Santo* (1555) provided shelter, medical assistance and education. Two others provided from the start financial assistance as part of their mission: the *Monte di Pietà*, founded in 1539 to combat usury by providing small interest-free loans collateralized by personal property,[6] and the *Monte dei Poveri*, founded in 1563 to help imprisoned debtors.

When these institutions went into the business of deposit banking is less clear because the surviving account books do not go back earlier than 1573. But recent research (Silvestri 1953; Demarco and Nappi 1985) finds the oldest traces of such activity with the Annunziata, with examples of deposits as far back as 1463, as well as loans (1466), interest on deposits (1482) and the earliest known *fede di deposio* (1564). The activity appears to be uninterrupted and fairly well established, clearly confirming the representation made by the Annunziata in 1580 to the Viceroy that it "has and has always had the ability to receive deposits, issue certificates therefor and present those in the royal courts and they have always been accepted like those of public banks" (Tortora 1890, 122). By the mid-sixteenth century, other institutions also received deposits and

[6]Many early authors thought that its foundation was a consequence of the expulsion of the Jews from Naples by Charles V, but this has been disproved (Tortora 1890, 3–11). Similar institutions had been created throughout Italy in the fifteenth and sixteenth centuries (see Barile 2012 for a recent survey).

made payments on written orders (the Incurabili in 1560, Sant'Eligio in 1570). It seems, therefore, that charitable institutions had begun early on to provide the same kind of safe-keeping and escrow services as private bankers, on the margin of their other activities.

Perhaps, the Monte di Pietà (which was housed in the building of the Annunziata) took matters a step further. Tortora (1890, 25) cites a document of 1578 stating that the Monte had been operating a distinct *cassa dei depositi* since before 1574, and in fact, Demarco and Nappi (1985, doc. 89–93) document the earliest known certificates issued by it: a *fede di deposito giudiziario*, or escrow certificate in 1569, a certificate of conditional deposit in 1573, a *fede di credito* in 1573, a *madrefede* in 1573 and a *fede di credito* payable to order in 1574.

The same Monte di Pietà was the first to receive a formal banking license, in 1584.[7] It was followed in rapid sequence by the Annunziata,[8] which opened a bank under the name of *Ave Gratia Plena* or AGP in 1587, San Giacomo sometime before 1589, the Incurabili under the name of *Santa Maria del Popolo* in 1589, Spirito Santo in 1590, Sant'Eligio around 1591 and finally Monte dei Poveri in 1599 (Tortora 1890, 49, 50, 61, 65, 83, 93, 94).

There are two possible reasons for this rush. One is an attempt by four private bankers to create a monopoly on deposit banking in 1580. It failed in the face of spirited resistance by the charitable institutions (Pietà and Annunziata) and after an appeal to Madrid (Tortora 1890, 118–123). The Annunziata was able to secure a statement from the Viceroy protecting its right to "receive money from those who wish to deposit it and spend it by means of your *cassa* and issue certificates of deposit at the request of others" (Tortora 1890, 122), and this recognition may have prompted the Pietà formally to seek a banking license. But soon after, the Pietà sought an injunction against the Poveri's deposit business (Tortora 1890, 49). This points to the second possible reason: just as private bankers had presented a threat, the Pietà's formal recognition now created the threat of another monopoly and induced the other institutions to secure their customary rights, beginning with the oldest, the Annunziata.

[7]Filangieri (1940, 14) and Demarco and Nappi (1985) say that the original document is not known and the motivations unclear.

[8]Some documents (Tortora 1890, 64–65) suggest that Annunziata did not operate its own bank at the time but used a private banker and even agreed in 1580 to use only the bank of the Pietà for a period of three years.

The eighth and last bank was of a very different nature. Salvatore was founded in 1640, not by a charitable institution but by the farmers of an indirect tax on flour, who not only had to manage their inflows and outflows, but also pay interest on debt backed by the revenues of the tax. Claiming to be ill-served in their operations by existing banks, they asked for permission to establish a *cassa di credito*, which immediately engaged in pawn lending although the license was silent on this activity. Because of its origin it eventually did much of the business associated with tax farms, although its history was perhaps more chequered than others (Tortora 1890, 97–106). Salvatore, while different in origin from the other banks, is highly reminiscent of the second Venetian bank of 1619, the *Banco Giro*, which may have inspired it.

3.4 *Overview of the Banks' History*

Figure 2 will serve as a rough overview of the Neapolitan banks' history.[9]

Over two hundred years, the story of the banks is one of strong and persistent growth punctuated by a few very sharp crises (1622, 1647, 1701, 1798) and less dramatic but still significant fluctuations. This growth is not purely due to inflation: even in real terms, the annual growth rate is 7.2 per cent between 1590 and 1620, 2.9 per cent between 1625 and 1695, 2.4 per cent between 1705 and 1785. In per capita terms,[10] one's view might depend on whether one focuses on the peaks or the slopes. The peak of the late 1690s is similar to, in fact higher than, the peak of the late 1780s, and the whole eighteenth century might seem to be just a long recovery from the shock of 1701–1702. Still, from 1705 to 1785 the growth rate of per capita balances was a respectable 1.6 per cent, during a period of essentially no economic growth (Malanima 2011).

Strikingly, from this long-term perspective a number of crises do not register significantly or persistently. For example, Sicily's revolt in 1674 and the ensuing Messina War lead to a sharp contraction of about 1/4 but growth resumes rapidly. The start of the War of Polish Succession in 1733 (which led to the conquest of Naples by Carlo VII) also leads

[9] I use each bank's "circolazione" series (Balletta 2008) and interpolate missing observations.

[10] There is a curious amount of variability in published estimates of the population of Naples. I have followed Muto (2013, 43); to his figures, I added an estimate of 400,000 right before the plague of 1656 and 200,000 right after (Fusco 2009) and interpolated to get annual estimates.

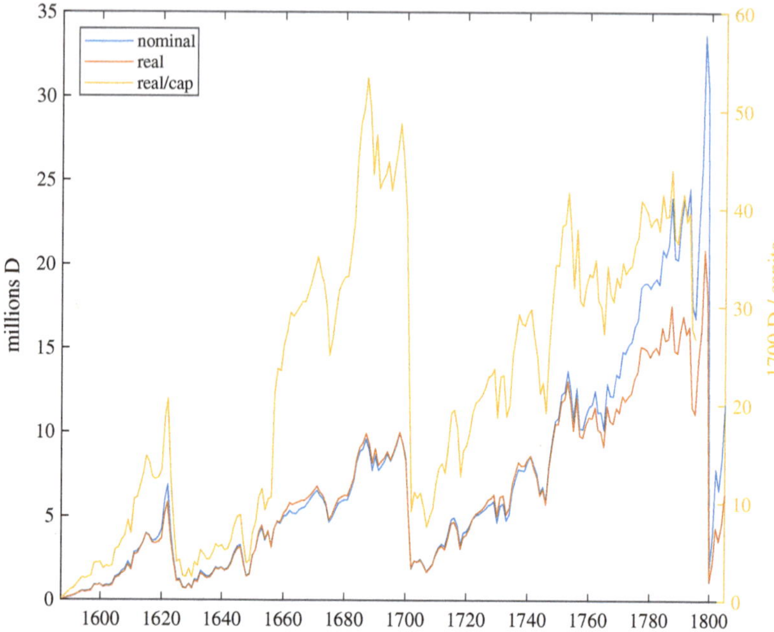

Fig. 2 Rough overview of the Neapolitan banks' history

to an 18 per cent contraction but it is quickly reversed. The War of Austrian Succession contracts balances by a third, but they rebound very quickly. The Seven Years War (in which Naples remained neutral) leaves balances stagnant. Even the effect of Masaniello's revolt, which cuts balances in half, is reversed within two years.

This resilience (in the aggregate) is all the more striking since it does not correspond in any obvious way to the cycles of growth and decline identified by the historiography: the second half of the seventeenth century is no different than other periods, and the solid growth in the second half of the eighteenth century stands in contrast to the lacklustre performance usually associated with the Italian Mezzogiorno in that period.

This only leaves two catastrophic events, both of which reduced balances by around 80 per cent: the crises of 1622 and 1701. They are, however, very different in nature: the first was an aggregate shock induced by (failed) monetary policy, leading to a bailout of the eight banks and profound changes in their business, while the crisis of 1701 was a run-induced systemic financial crisis. I will discuss both in the following section.

4 Specificities of the Public Banks

4.1 *Diversity and Resilience*

Some banks specialized in serving specific customer bases. As mentioned above, Poveri was founded by lawyers and located near the courts (Tribunali). San Giacomo, linked to Spanish institutions and located near the seat of the Spanish Viceroy, was the "bank of the court", as was to a lesser extent Spirito Santo, located on the elegant via Toledo. Salvatore had been founded by financiers and was closely linked to government finances. Popolo was seen as the city administration's bank (Tortora 1890, 80). Peri (1672, 2:126) notes that the Annunziata was (in his time) seen as the best, and that foreign merchants preferred Sant'Eligio and Popolo which gave the best services (*che danno maggior facilità*). In addition, coincidentally or not the eight banks were spread almost uniformly across the city, suggesting a degree of geographical specialization suited to the "highly fragmented urban space" of Naples (Sabatini 2013, 93).

The geographical and customer diversity seems complemented with diversity in culture. Some banks definitely seemed better managed than others. Poveri, one of the strongest, also had a strong independent streak, perhaps due to the dominance of lawyers and jurists on its board. Others displayed repeated weaknesses, as will be discussed below.

Figure 3 shows the market shares of the public banks between 1611 and 1800. No one bank dominates the others for any sustained amount of time, although at times one bank or the other reaches a third of total circulation: the Pietà between 1650 and 1670, the Annunziata briefly in the 1640s and again in the 1690s (shortly before its failure), Spirito Santo in the 1730s. Only at the end of the eighteenth century does San Giacomo maintain a pre-eminence relative to the other banks for several decades. Moreover, there is no stable ranking of the banks in terms of size, as we see them rising and falling over time.

Did this diversity make the system of banks more resilient? Deposits were demandable, and bank runs are part of the history of Neapolitan banks.[11] They could be caused by aggregate as well as idiosyncratic shocks.

[11] The Neapolitan term is *correria* (Tortora 1890, 169; D'Ambra 1873, 145).

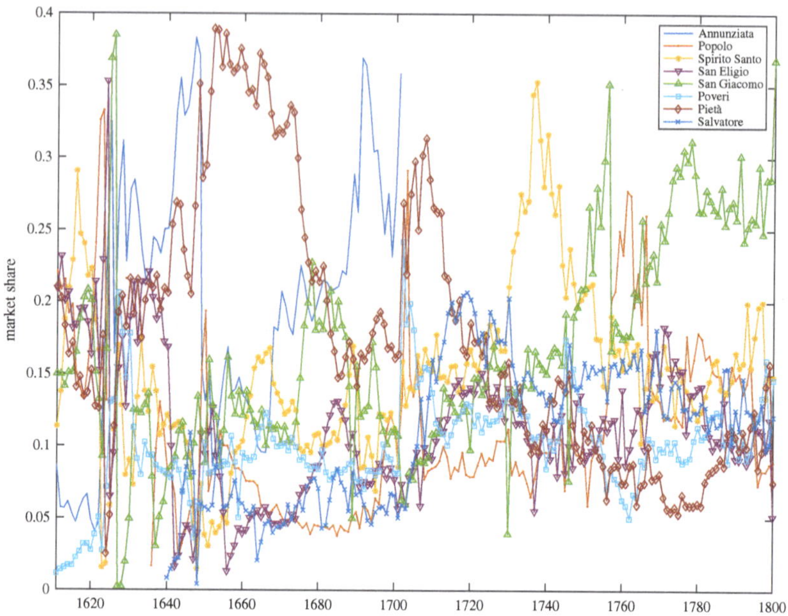

Fig. 3 Market shares of the public banks between 1611 and 1800

4.1.1 Aggregate Shocks

When faced with aggregate shocks, we see that the banks were variously affected, some coming out better than others, but the system as a whole surviving.

Aside from the crisis of 1622 discussed previously, Naples endured numerous shocks: earthquakes (1694, 1702), eruptions of the Vesuvius (1631, 1698, 1727, 1794) which had been quiet for half a millennium, revolution (1647), foreign invasions (1648, 1707, 1734, 1798) and the devastating plague of 1656 (Fusco 2009). The latter shock was not wholly adverse for the banks, as it gave rise to unclaimed deposits (*denaro de mortuo*) over which the government and the banks fought (Balletta 2008, 71; Tortora 1890, 153–154, 203–215). But the main crises, after 1622, were 1647 and 1701 (Fig. 2).

The revolution of 1647 (the Masaniello revolt) affected the banks severely, partly because some of their assets were pillaged either by the mobs (Pietà and Poveri) or by the Viceroy (San Giacomo and Spirito Santo).

In the aftermath, Poveri had to suspend its payments in 1648; San Giacomo failed and repaid its creditors 26 per cent on the *ducat*, while Salvatore paid 60 per cent and Spirito Santo repaid its creditors in full by ceding bonds in its portfolio and opened a new set of books (Di Somma 1960, 73); Pietà managed to continue payments throughout (Tortora 1890, 200–202).

The crisis of 1701 was a pure crisis of confidence, although triggered by an international crisis. The death of the king of Spain without an immediate heir in November 1700 set into motion a European conflict over the division of his domains, but full-scale war did not break out until March 1702, and the fighting in Italy remained limited to northern Italy until 1707. It is true that a conspiracy favouring the Austrian rival of the new king of Spain Philip V was uncovered in September 1701 (*congiura di Macchia*), but it was quickly suppressed.

It remains that in this tense climate banks evidently faced increasing withdrawals. In March 1701, the Viceroy asked the banks to increase their cash reserves by calling in loans and also to accept each other's notes. The stronger banks resisted this last request and repeatedly showed the Viceroy how the weak banks' debt to them kept increasing. Finally, on December 2 the Viceroy prohibited reciprocal acceptance of notes and ordered the banks to settle their accounts half in cash and half in other assets. At this point, the difficulties of the weaker banks increased considerably, and the Viceroy partially suspended payments on deposits, precipitating a run on the weak banks.

The Viceroy tried to coordinate a bailout, leaning on the strong banks to lend to the weak ones, particularly Annunziata. Poveri was asked to lend 50,000 ducats against collateral of its choosing on Annunziata's books, but the managers knew better and dragged their feet long enough for the inevitable to happen: Annunziata's creditors sued, and Poveri could then argue that the collateral was not free of lien (Tortora 1890, 244–253).

Several banks, like Poveri, emerged relatively unscathed. Others (Annunziata, Salvatore and San Giacomo) had to suspend payments. Salvatore succeeded in securing an official moratorium on payments and was able to resume payments soon after. San Giacomo had to liquidate assets and convert part of the deposits into bonds repaid over 22 years. The worst hit was Annunziata, which had to be liquidated and most of its deposit business transferred to Poveri (Ferrandino 2009, fn174).

4.1.2 *The Crisis of 1622*

The crisis of 1622 was an important and complex event. Suffice it to say that it resulted from the government's inability properly to manage the currency system, especially in providing small coins. Responses to shortages left smaller coins overvalued, leading to arbitrage (large coins were melted and sold to the mint for small coins) and to occasional surges of prices and exchange rates above the normal level corresponding to large coins. In addition, increasing clipping left the currency stock in poor condition and widened to range for possible price variations. A crisis point was reached in 1621–1622 which bears remarkable similarities with the years preceding the Great Recoinage of 1695 in England (Sargent and Velde 2002, Chapter 16). To reform the coinage required, as it did in England, a complete recoinage. The key question was, whether to debase the standard of coinage so as to leave prices unchanged and minimize the costs of reform. If a return to the old standard was demanded, as it was by the Spanish authorities, the question became: who would bear the cost of converting nominally overvalued coins into new coins? The Viceroyalty government apparently intended to bear the cost, but was either unwilling or unable to do so, and expectations of the reform drove money demand down and prices up to an intolerable level, forcing the government to rush the reform and abruptly demonetize the small coins.

The crisis of 1622 had important consequences for the banks. The impact of the monetary reform on their balance sheets immediately threatened their survival, and the government had to take a number of measures to save them. In the long term, the business model of the banks was altered.

4.1.3 *The Bailout*

As Fig. 2 shows, the aggregate balances of the banks had grown rapidly, doubling from 1609 to 1615, then fallen back around 15 per cent in 1616 and stabilized. From the end of 1620 to the end of 1621, they went up by 40 per cent, as depositors exchanged currency for deposits. Some banks, such as Poveri, had started building up reserves by calling in loans (De Rosa 1987, 140). The banks' reserves, which had averaged 15 per cent in the 1610s, reached a low of 10 per cent at end of 1620 but rose to 28 per cent at end of 1621. But the cash reserves resembled the money stock and consisted almost entirely of the small coins that were demonetized on 2 March 1622 (Di Somma 1960, 57); hence, the banks were unable to maintain convertibility and had to close their doors for two days.

The first measure taken by the Viceroy was a "bank holiday" of eight days, followed by a limit of withdrawals to 5 ducats per day and to a maximum of two thirds of the deposit (De Rosa 1987, 141); the remaining third's fate left unspoken. In addition, payments above 30 ducats were required to be made through the banks and a 1 per cent fee on all transactions was granted to the banks (Di Somma 1960, 51), but the protests of the community quickly forced the repeal of the fee (Palermo 1846, 240).

To accelerate the recoinage, the government forced the banks to turn over their cash reserves to the mint in the summer 1622, over the banks' strenuous objections. The accounts of Spirito Santo show why: the total loss on their cash holdings was 69 per cent, of which 14 per cent was a nominal loss (the change in the legal value of the coins) and the rest due to the silver deficiency of the small coins.[12] Ultimately, the government bailed out the banks in several ways. First, all deposits as of March 1622 were frozen and written down by a third.[13] Second, the government levied taxes: one was a 25 per cent tax on interest payments to foreigners for 4 years[14] to compensate the banks for the loss they suffered when they financed the import of silver in 1621. The other was a tax on wine to back bonds issued to recapitalize the banks. Small depositors were given the option to receive the bonds themselves in redemption of their claims. Finally, a clean break was made and new books were opened to receive deposits in the new money. The liquidation in cash of the pre-1622 balances, kept on separate books, was initially capped at 2 per cent of balances per week; the task took a number of years but was ultimately completed (De Rosa 1987, 150–152).

[12] The small coins, which were slightly overvalued were demonetized and bought by the mint at the new standard net of minting costs, so that a 10 per cent loss would be expected if they had been of full weight. Incredibly, their silver content fell short by two thirds, either because of extreme (!) clipping or else counterfeiting.

[13] It seems that this was later modified by the next Viceroy (Tortora 1890, 187–190) to 40 per cent for deposits made between July 1622 and February 1623. There were additional claw-back provisions for deposits and transfers made in January and February 1622, widely believed to have been made in anticipation of the imminent reform, and there were suspicions that the banks accepted deposits of small coins even after the reform.

[14] This measure seemed to open a twenty-year-long debt default (Calabria 1991, 128–129). The principal sums were not reduced, but interest payments were withheld frequently (continuously from 1630 to 1642) by a third or two thirds (Foscari 2006, 264–268).

In the end, the losses suffered by the banks were relatively limited because their cash reserves were relatively low, and the nominal depreciation was modest. In the case of Spirito Santo, an account by the Viceroy's commissioner shows that the write-down of deposits and taxes were sufficient to make the bank whole (Di Somma 1960, 58).

4.1.4 A Changed Business Model

Were the banks innocent victims of circumstances, or did they play a role in the crisis? As early as 1604 the government accused their cashiers of removing the heavier coins from circulation and later of trafficking in coins (Pr. 7 and 14 De Monetis, Giustiniani 1803–1804, 7:257, 270). By 1621, Madrid had reached the conclusion that, since all payments were made through the banks, they handled all the cash of the realm and must be responsible for clipping and price increases. The regulation of banks sent from Madrid also hinted at another theory, since they restricted lending and non-cash payments. This theory, attributed by Biblia (1621, 20) to "certain Spaniards", blamed the high price of large coins on exchange rates and the latter on traders borrowing from banks. The jurist Tassone (1632, 363) was more blunt when he asserted that "all evils came from the banks because of the loans they made to private individuals to attract their business".[15] This theory has been defended since by De Stefano (1940) and De Rosa (1987, 128), who both blame the banks for increasing the money supply, fuelling speculation and prices. Di Somma (1960, 45) disagrees: growing balance sheets were a consequence rather than a cause of the monetary situation, which he blames on the inadequate provision of small change and on recurrent current account deficits.

Rightly or wrongly, the government tried to rein in the banks' activities, both in terms of their role in the payments system and in terms of their balance sheets. The restrictions on their payments activities probably did not last. By May 1622, the requirement that bills of exchange be settled only in coin was relaxed and allowed in bank, as long as post-reform

[15] "Omniaque mala ex Bancheriis provenere, ex causa mutui, quod particularibus faciebant, pro concursu negotiantium in eis." Nihil novi sub sole…

balances were used; in 1632, settlement of domestic and foreign bills with bank balances was made mandatory (Pr. 7 and 8 De Literis, Giustiniani 1803–1804, 101–102). But the government also tried to bring the banks back to their charters, limit their investments to government bonds and reduce them so as to earn just enough to cover their expenses (which were also cut by reducing payroll); it even entertained the idea of prohibiting all loans to private individuals (De Rosa 1987, 142).

Figure 4, which plots the reserves ratio of the individual banks, shows that 1622 was indeed a turning point.

Henceforth, their assets were much more conservatively managed. Although they did not stop lending to individuals (De Rosa 1955), their reserves remained at high levels, as was noted by Avallone (1991, 377–378). By the 1660s, Spirito Santo had become, in the opinion of Di Somma (1960, 85), a "simple deposit and transfer bank", a perhaps excessive simplification.

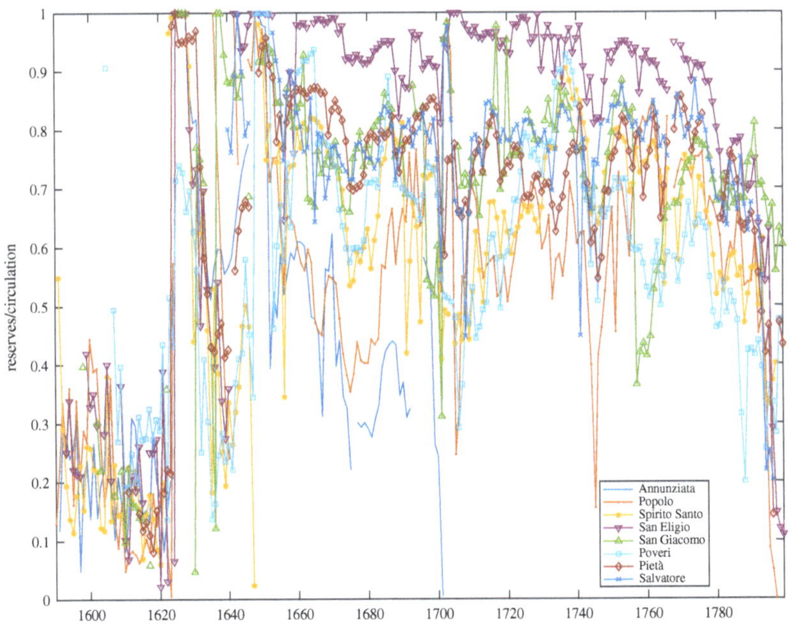

Fig. 4 Reserves ratio of the individual banks

In order to provide the banks with more sources of income, and also because of the economic depression that seemed to follow the reform (De Rosa 2002, 455), the government allowed the banks in 1628 to lend against personal collateral (pawns) at interest. The fact that the collateral could be gold or silver, in bullion, wrought or coined form, led to interesting innovations discussed below.

4.1.5 Idiosyncratic Shocks

The banks also suffered idiosyncratic shocks, many due to fraud and mismanagement, or we would say today weak internal controls (Avallone 2017). News, or rumours, of malfeasance could prompt a run against one bank.

Popolo was placed under city administration from 1623 to 1636 and suffered a bank run in 1639 (Tortora 1890, 74–76). Spirito Santo was victim of serious embezzlement by the head cashier in 1691.[16] San Giacomo was victim of fraud in 1744 (its pawns were secretly "re-hypothecated" by unscrupulous employees) and had to suspend payments in 1758 because of a run. Salvatore had a particularly troubled history, with a lengthy suspension from 1647 to 1650 after the Masaniello revolt, and again in 1664 because of embezzlement (Tortora 1890, 95–106).

In cases of idiosyncratic shocks, there are a number of examples of forbearance by other banks, either at the request of the Viceroy or spontaneously. San Giacomo was saved in 1758 when the other banks held back 400,000 ducats in notes (Tortora 1890, 95, 301–302). During Spirito Santo's difficulties in 1691, Pietà stepped in and bought some of its assets to provide cash (Balletta 2008, 95). In 1769, one finds again the banks lending 200,000 ducats to Spirito Santo in difficulty.

The bank runs arguably placed a form of discipline on the banks, since they sometimes prompted examination of the banks' books. This is also true of the 1701 systemic run, whose severe effect is partly blamed on prior mismanagement.

[16] The fraud may have involved more than him; the fact that he died in prison two weeks after his arrest "trying to escape" suggests that he may have known too much (Tortora 1890, 88).

4.1.6 Risk-Sharing

How well did the banks share risk? According to Tortora (1890, 302), "their entire history displays an admirable spirit of harmony, indeed solidarity", and Ferrandino (2009, 89) sees "an efficient and well-coordinated banking system, in which each bank, rather than competing against the other in search of supremacy, seemed to aim for unity and complementarity in the development of banking". This judgement appears on the whole warranted, although the case of 1701 displays the limits to that self-preservation placed on solidarity.

There was also some degree of risk-sharing with the government. The bailout of 1622 shows how co-dependent the banks and the Viceroyalty government had become. The resources that the government should have marshalled ex ante to fund the reform were provided ex post to the banks, in the form of dedicated tax revenues, a "bail-in" of depositors (partly justified by speculative deposits in the weeks before the reform began) and a remarkable tax on foreign creditors. In contrast, the 1689–1691 reform was much better managed (Filangieri 1940, 98–108; Balletta 2008, 90–94), and on that occasion risk-sharing played in the other direction: the nominal capital gains made by the banks on the revaluation of their cash reserves were appropriated by the government (Tortora 1890, 227).

4.2 *Governance*

In contrast to the other public banks of Europe, the Neapolitan banks emerged organically out of civil society. Non-profit institutions, independent of government, requested banking licenses from the government. They did so at a time when private banks existed, and were apparently only asking formal authorization to provide, as they had been doing informally for a while, some of same services as private bankers.

4.2.1 Charter and Corporate Structure

What did a banking license mean in late sixteenth-century Naples?

The license granted to the hospital of the Incurabili to open the bank of Santa Maria di Popolo in 1590 (Tortora 1890, 69–71) did three things: it ratified a set of regulations for the banking business drawn by the hospital's officials, it gave them permission to receive of deposits of money, jewels and fabrics, and it instructed all courts to accept as valid the certificates of deposits issued by the bank. In doing so, it made explicit reference to the licenses previously granted to Annunziata and San Giacomo, and placed the new bank on an equal footing with them, suggesting that these two held similar licenses.

From a modern perspective, one would want to know if the banks were corporations distinct from the founding institutions, who owned them, and what the liability structure was. This is perhaps too much of an anachronism, but there are indications that some at least were seen as distinct entities: the banks operated by the Annunziata and the Incurabili had distinct names and Popolo was formally separated from the hospital in 1645 (Tortora 1890, 76). In terms of ownership, the regulations approved by the Viceroy specified that the hospital received the profits from the bank but could not use the money deposited (i.e. could not borrow from it) even in extreme circumstances. In terms of liability, the bank's senior employees were liable for any losses arising from mistakes in the books, counterfeit order payments and counterfeit coins or changes in valuation of coins.[17] There is evidence that the institution put up capital specifically to secure the banking business: 18,000 ducats in the case of Spirito Santo (Tortora 1890, 82). When banks extended into Lombard lending, specific capital was assigned for that branch of business (Di Somma 1960, 65).

More broadly, the institutions, if not the banks, were subject of canon law. Most, if not all, had at various times received recognition, protection and privileges from both ecclesiastical and civil authorities: for example, the statutes of the Pietà were approved by the Pope in 1559 and those of the Poveri were approved by the Pope in 1572 and by the Viceroy in 1585 (Tortora 1890, 22, 45). This gave the institutions some measure of autonomy with respect to government authorities, particularly with respect to Spanish Viceroys and the Catholic Majesty they represented. Nor should one underestimate the prestige and holiness associated with the charitable activities. Significantly, in 1582 two private bankers asked the hospital of the Incurabili for the right to open a bank under its name, in exchange for an annual rent, although this may have been in part a manoeuvre to defeat a planned private banking monopoly (Tortora 1890, 125–126).

[17] Senior employees were required to put up bond money; in addition, they were personally liable up to the values of their estates (Avallone 2017).

Protection from judicial seizure was a common benefit attached to early public banks elsewhere in Europe. Although I have not found evidence of similar privileges for the Neapolitan banks,[18] the use of the phrase "deposits in sacred places" (depositi poenes [sic; paene?] aedes sacras) by Poveri (Tortora 1890, 120) suggests an implicit reference to the papal bull "Clericis laicos" of 1296, which became part of canon law (De immunitate c. clericis, VI 3.23.3) and protected ecclesiastical property, but also deposits in sacred places, from secular taxation and confiscation. This, in addition to the goodwill generated by the sponsoring institutions' charitable purposes and the sense of contributing however indirectly to the relief of the poor, may have proven attractive to depositors.

Ecclesiastical privilege manifested itself in at least two occasions. The first was in cases of malfeasance by employees: whether bank premises that were adjacent to consecrated buildings were entitled to immunity from lay prosecution was not resolved until a concordat between Naples and the Holy See in 1741 (Avallone 2017, 12). The second, more pertinent (and somewhat less pleasant for depositors), was the failure of the Annunziata's bank in 1702, which immediately raised the question whether the Annunziata's assets could be used to compensate depositors and bondholders of the bank (Avallone 2013, 103). The Annunziata argued for the immunity of all its assets; the arbitrators appointed by the Viceroy rejected this but admitted that the assets that predated the opening of the bank were immune, to which the creditors responded that the bank had been created for the Annunziata's benefit, and therefore, it should bear any loss, and that the very existence of these pre-existing assets had impelled the public to trust the bank. In the end, depositors received 46 *grani* on the *ducat* and secured bondholders reached a settlement with the Annunziata in 1714, approved by the Emperor (as sovereign of Naples), the Viceroy, the archbishop of Naples and the Pope (Tortora 1890, 263–289). The institution as owner of the bank was thus held liable.[19]

[18] Rocco (1785, 2:23) explains the manner in which sequesters were placed on deposits when ordered by a judge.

[19] Final discharge took another two centuries, and the association of the creditors of A.G.P. was only dissolved in 1880.

4.2.2 Internal Governance

The banks had similar internal organizations. The major decisions and oversight were entrusted to a board of governors (*governatori*), one of whom, the *mensario*, was delegated and on active duty for one month. The day-to-day operations were directed by a manager, the *razionale*, to whom the various cashiers reported (Rocco 1785; Demarco 1996, 17–36).

The board of the banks comprised between four and seven members. The details varied from one bank to another. The board of the Pietà's bank had three noblemen, two advocates and one merchant. After a two-year term, the outgoing member presented a list of six names to the Viceroy, who in practice always chose the first. The board of the bank of Spirito Santo, after it was formally separated from the *conservatorio* in 1629, comprised one nobleman, one advocate and five commoners including a foreign merchant. Replacements were chosen by the incumbents and representatives of the city administration. The Popolo's board included two high magistrates, two untitled noblemen of the city, one advocate and two merchants (one a foreigner). At Sant'Eligio, four members were chosen by the city administration and three by the Viceroy: a magistrate, a gentleman and a representative of the cobblers' guild. At San Giacomo, the governors supposed to turn over every two years as in other banks, but often didn't; only when difficulties arose did the Viceroy intervene to enforce the term limit. At Salvatore there were six members (later four) chosen by the farmers of the flour tax, and subjected in 1758 to the two-year term limit like the other banks (Tortora 1890, 38–40, 53–58, 68, 84–85, 93, 94, 98). Of course, the banks were not entirely free of government oversight or interference.

First, they held their charters from the Viceroy and were subject to his laws (*prammatiche*, *bandi*) and other commands. Second, from the mid-seventeenth century or earlier the Viceroy appointed a delegate,[20] who served two functions: one was to relay instructions from the Viceroy and monitor the banks' conditions and the other was to serve as judge over litigation involving the banks, with appeal only to the highest court,

[20]There is some disagreement over the exact date: Filangieri (1940, 93–94) places it in 1654, Di Somma (1960, 4, 71) in the mid-seventeenth century and no later than 1650, Avallone (1995, 14) in the 1630s at the latest, Sabatini (2013, 96) in 1606. After the 1622 crisis, a banking committee (*Giunta dei Banchi*) was formed by the Viceroy to oversee the ensuing liquidation, initially composed of six magistrates and six merchants, then six magistrates only (De Rosa 1987, 151), but it seems that this committee was ad hoc.

the *Sacro Regio Consiglio* (Tortora 1890, 299–300). In practice, it seems that the second function was the predominant one. It's worth noting that the Poveri's Viceroyalty delegate was in practice a member of the confraternity, even after it was required in the 1730s that the delegates be magistrates (Avallone 1995, 16, 38). Finally, by the eighteenth century the choice of governors had passed into the hands of the government, albeit from a list of names provided by the outgoing governor, which excluded relatives of any governor, debtors of the bank and anyone subject to a serious conflict of interest (Tortora 1890, 300).

Whether this supervision was a good thing or not is unclear. Avallone (2017) takes a dim view of the banks' internal controls, while Tortora (1890, 246) blames the government for having "placed the lawyerly sophistry of its delegates and the aristocratic indolence of the governors it approved in the stead of the vigilance, common sense, and benevolence" of the earlier governors. It may not be a coincidence that Poveri, run by lawyers, was considered to have the best track record.

4.2.3 Relations with Government

The relations between the banks and government are particularly interesting in the European context, because the banks were not created by government, and because government was less likely to have the same interests, in comparison with the banks of the city-republics of Genoa, Venice and Amsterdam.

It's somewhat harder to discern the government's intentions or goals when granting the banking licenses than in the latter cases. But there was, early on, a recognition by Viceroys that the banks provided a useful payments function. Even before the first licenses were granted, some legislation suggested a preference for deposits held in "banks without profit" (Pr. 3 De Numm., 1553, Giustiniani 1803–1804, 8:130). As mentioned above, the publication of the early licenses required all the courts of the kingdom to "hold for true and real" the certificates of the banks. Di Somma (1960, 13) and De Rosa (2002, 477) interpret this as making the banks' certificates legal tender. The state administration also quickly manifested its preference for handling debt payments through the banks because they were deemed "most secure and pious places" (Silvestri 1951a, 2). As in other public banks (like Genoa), the government also hoped that its currency laws could be better enforced, hence the placement of coin weighers in the banks.

Yet, in the late sixteenth century Viceroys seemed uncertain whether to back the emerging public banks or to turn to another arrangement. Spanish authorities were at the time entertaining plans for privileged private banks in Spain (Hamilton 1949; Cano Borrego 2014). Two attempts at setting up a private monopoly on banking in Naples are known, in 1580 at the behest of a consortium of Genoese bankers (Tortora 1890, 118–119, 127–131) and in 1598 possibly fuelled by the viceroy's desire to curb bank lending (Tassone 1632, 363), but both were fought off by the banks and their supporters throughout the city. Indeed, the second attempt led to a recall of the Viceroy, hinting at the degree of political support that the banks already garnered. As mentioned above, the banks' governors judiciously included representatives of the most powerful groups in the city, notably the urban nobility and the *togati*, magistrates and lawyers of the courts.[21]

In the late eighteenth century, the government's views of the banks may have evolved. They came under repeated criticism from various quarters (Tortora 1890, 297–306), and in 1772, the government set up a commission (the *Giunta suprema degli abusi dei banchi*) in 1772 (Tortora 1882, ccxl). When the emergencies of the 1790s came, the government rapidly took control of the banks.

4.2.4 Government Debt

Were the banks licensed to fund the public debt? Their charters might suggest so.

There is some ambiguity in the literature on whether the banks were restricted to invest in public debt, issued by either the *Corte* (the Viceroy's court) or the city. Di Somma (1960, 13) argues that Spirito Santo, like San Giacomo, Popolo and Annunziata, was restricted to purchasing publicly issued annuities (see also De Rosa 1955, 96 fn1), which seems confirmed by the text of the 1589 charter of Popolo cited in Tortora (1890, 69), whereby the governors of the bank "cannot dispose of the money received except to purchase annuities either with the Royal Fisc or the city of Naples". But the following year the Viceroy required

[21] A third threat fought off by the city came in the 1720s, under Austrian administration, when a Banco di San Carlo was opened somewhat on the model of the Viennese bank (see the contribution by Clemens Jobst in this volume), though its main purpose seems to have been as a vehicle for a leveraged buyout of the state's mortgaged assets (Di Vittorio 2009).

Popolo to use the income from these annuities to "make other purchases of annuities from those individuals that you know to be most secure" (Tortora 1890, 73; see an identical clause in the 1590 charter of Spirito Santo, Demarco 2000, 72 fn2). In any event, Pietà did not seem to be under such restrictions, since Tortora (1890, 137) cites rules endorsed by the Viceroy in 1612 for the "accommodations made for the convenience of merchants" (the term *accomodi* became standard to describe loans to merchants). From the start, banks lent to private individuals and continued to do so even after the crisis of 1622 (De Rosa 1955, 96–98).

Di Somma (1960, 13) says that "without the presence and the organization of the banks, government bonds would have had difficulty finding buyers rapidly" but the assertion is difficult to reconcile with the facts. In the 1640s, Poveri's holdings of government debt were 120,000 D, and it represented 8 per cent of the banks' aggregate balances (De Rosa 1955, 97). If Poveri's holdings were representative, then the banks together held 1.5 million ducats of government debt, which stood at 40 million ducats in 1636 (Foscari 2006, 56). Simply put, the volume of public debt vastly exceeds that of the banks' balance sheet.

This does not mean that the banks were not subject to demands. In the 1630s and 1640s, when government borrowing was frequent, the banks were apparently taking fixed shares of each new issue (Di Somma 1960). Even in the late seventeenth century, they were repeatedly asked for loans (1676–1683, 1695; Filangieri 1940, 92–93, 109).

4.3 Financial Innovation

4.3.1 Assets

Compared with most European public banks of the time, the assets and liabilities of the Neapolitan banks were quite diverse (Demarco 2000, Chapter 2). On the liability side, they issued deposits but also sold debt instruments bearing interest. On the asset side, they held a variety of government debt, mostly debt assigned on direct taxes (the *fiscali*) or indirect taxes (the *arrendamenti*), both fairly liquid instruments (Calabria 1991, Chapter 5) or shares in tax farming partnerships (*partite di arrendamenti*). They also lent to the city of Naples or to other municipalities of the kingdom, transacted with the mint and with foreign exchange dealers.

Finally, they lent to individuals, either by buying life annuities, long-term loans collateralized or not, small short-term loans collateralized by personal estate (pawns), lines of credit and overdrafts. Loans to merchants and other individuals were called *accomodi* and seemed to have been commonplace. Costabile and Nappi (this volume) document precisely the mechanisms by which banks did in fact engage to a significant extent in "money creation" at least prior to 1622, in the form of *vuoti introiti*, i.e. deposit creation with no cash counterpart.

4.3.2 The Fede

The singular innovation of Neapolitan banks was undoubtedly the *fede di credito*. It arose from the *fede di deposito*, originally a certificate issued by the deposit-taker that a certain deposit had been made, for example for legal purposes: in effect, an escrow certificate. The certificate served a legal function: it could be exhibited in court to prove that certain requirements of a contract had been met, for example a marriage contract stipulating that a dowry be set aside. Deposits that could only be released when certain conditions were met were called *vincolati*; free deposits were *sciolti*. As mentioned above, certificates of free deposits appeared early on among public banks, probably in imitation of practices among private bankers.

As Ajello (1882) argues, the true innovation in the *fede di credito* is that it is a liability of the bank itself, not of the depositor. This liability was demandable: the bank was obliged to pay it in cash on demand to the presenter. The creditor was usually named, although they could be made blank, and could also be endorsed. These circulated and functioned as bank notes.[22] The sums could be relatively small, down to 4 ducats, although in the eighteenth century they tended to be larger. Printed *fede* appear in 1749, but they apparently never took the form of notes with round numbers, as later with the *Banco di Napoli*, the successor institution to the public banks in the nineteenth century. The *poliza* was a different instrument, simply a payment order or check, endorsable but still a liability of the individual issuer, although it could become the equivalent of a banker's acceptance or certified check when endorsed by the bank's cashier (*polize notate*). There was no time limit to their validity and they could remain outstanding for months or years and still be honoured (Tortora 1890, 147).

[22] Demarco (1996, 47) argues that only a licensed bank could issue a *fede di credito*, although the early examples seem to run counter to that claim.

4.3.3 Riscontrati

Long before the London Clearinghouse of 1775, the Neapolitan banks had established procedures for accepting and clearing each other's circulating liabilities. The system was called *riscontrati*, and although they were forbidden on 22 June 1635, the prohibition was largely ignored (Tortora 1890, 197, 241). Every week banks cleared with each other, and the remaining balance was carried forward in a *fede di resto* (Rocco 1785, 1:27–28).

4.3.4 Pawns and Repos

Although Pietà and Poveri began as a pawn operation, this was not initially a common characteristic of the banks. San Giacomo began a pawn operation in 1606, Spirito Santo in 1629 and Popolo in 1648 (Tortora 1890, 80, 84, 94). As noted above, the ability to lend at interest on pawns in 1628 induced all banks to enter the business. The pawn business was run on a distinct set of books and with its own rules.

Pawnbroking (Lombard lending) might seem like an anecdotal activity, but one finds it in certain German municipal banks, in particular the Bank of Hamburg, and it is notable that the Banco di San Giorgio requested (but was denied) the authority to engage in it in 1675. As Costabile and Nappi (this volume) note, from the beginning ambiguities in Poveri's license allowed it to lend against large pawns. For the Neapolitan banks, it was a sizeable activity, and pawns represented liquid assets that could be sold off during runs (Tortora 1890, 246–249). Conversely, lending against collateral (like bullion or foreign coins) that was safe in having high intrinsic value, but illiquid in not being legal tender, was an important crisis management tool (Quinn and Roberds 2015).

Rocco (1785, 19–22) describes in detail one particularly striking use of pawns at the bank in case of foreign coins. These coins were accepted as regular deposits (i.e. the exact same coins had to be returned), like pawns, subject to a haircut to protect the bank from exchange rate variations. But, unlike pawns, no receipt was issued and their deposit was considered a favour. Hence, the custom was that the bank was free to dispose of the deposit after a year, but could sell it off earlier, after notice, whereas the term for pawns was scrupulously respected. Conversely, money-changers were sometimes able to take advantage of the bank when the haircut had not been judiciously chosen:

"Money-changers deposit foreign coins and wait for the time when the agio moves to their advantage; and it often happened that the deposits fell in value below the sum lent, to the loss of the Banks".[23]

4.3.5 The Missing Agio

In the light of the experiences in Amsterdam, Genoa and Venice, one wonders why no *agio* (or *alaggio* in Neapolitan) ever developed on the banks' balances. The reform of 1622, had it been carried out like the similar monetary reforms in Genoa and Amsterdam, might have led to the same result. But returning to the old standard prevented the emergence of a distinction between bank balances and current money.[24] It may also be that the existence of multiple banks by itself would have precluded such a development.

5 Conclusion

The Neapolitan banks were, as a group, a sizeable banking system, on a par with the largest public banks of the time and served many of the purposes that were sought by the creators of other public banks. Collectively, I see them as a special case of early public banks, all the more interesting because they arose organically rather than by design, and because compared to their peers they were successful and innovative, in spite of a difficult environment. Contrary to many others, they were never intended to adhere to a "narrow banking" view of banking and invested in a variety of private and public securities. They nevertheless proved robust to a variety of adverse events, in part due to a conservative approach to their balance sheet, learned the hard way during the crisis of 1622.

Several factors were likely behind this success: the religious or charitable purpose of their owners, their governance structure, their informal risk-sharing arrangements or policies of judicious forbearance towards

[23]"I cambiamonete impegnano ne' Banchi le monete forestierie, ed aspettano il tempo, onde si avanzi l'alaggio a loro profitto; e sovente è accaduto, che tali pegni per esser bassato l'alaggio, o altro, si sono trovati di minor valore della somma prestatavi, a danno de' Banchi." He further cites the case of one Leonardo Perillo who left Popolo with a large quantity of *thalers*.

[24]There is the possibility that the balances frozen on the *libri dei due terzi* were discounted, but they were eventually redeemed.

each other and their independence with respect to the representatives of a distant monarch. They also proved themselves useful, if not indispensable, to the economic life of Naples and as such came to be (after some initial misgivings) respected and protected by the viceroys, who nevertheless used them as source of funds, albeit not a large one compared to the overall size of the debt. As such, they found the "gentlemanly distance" between state and bank that often proves elusive.

One can still ask: does it matter? A resilient banking system, an efficient retail-oriented payments system with circulating notes and interbank clearing, a relatively stable price level, did not put Naples at the vanguard of economic development. The successful early banks were Amsterdam in the seventeenth century and England in the eighteenth century, but those were also the most successful economies, and which way causality runs is unclear. At a minimum, the Neapolitan experience sheds light on the preconditions for successful banking and suggests that financial development is not a sufficient condition for economic success.

References

Ajello, Pietro. 1882. I depositi, le fedi di credito e le polize dei banchi di Napoli. *Il Filangieri* 7: 641–665, 713–755.

Avallone, Paola. 1991. L'organizzazione contabile dei banchi pubblici napoletani tra XVI e XVIII secolo. In *L'Impresa: Industria Commercio Banca Secc. XIII–XVIII*, ed. Simonetta Cavaciocchi, 371–383. Atti delle "Settimane di Studi" e altri Convegni 22. Florence: Istituto Internazionale di Storia Economica "F. Datini", F. Le Monnier.

———. 1995. *Stato e Banchi Pubblici a Napoli a metà del '700*. Naples: Edizioni scientifiche Italiane.

———. 2013. Bankruptcy in the Kingdom of Naples: The Case of the Public Banks (17th to 18th Centuries). In *The History of Bankruptcy: Economic, Social and Cultural Implications in Early Modern Europe*, ed. Thomas Max Safley, 97–107. London and New York: Routledge.

———. 2017. Accounting Crimes: The Case of the Neapolitan Public Banks (17th–18th Centuries). *Accounting Historians Journal* 44 (1) (June): 5–16.

Bairoch, Paul, and Jean Batou et Pierre Chèvre. 1988. *La population des villes européennes, 800-1850: banque de données et analyse sommaire des résultats.* Geneva: Droz.

Balletta, Francesco. 2008. *La circolazione della moneta fiduciaria a Napoli nel Seicento e nel Settecento (1587–1805)*. Napoli: Edizioni Scientifiche Italiane.

Barile, Nicola Lorenzo. 2012. Renaissance Monti di Pietà in Modern Scholarship: Themes, Studies, and Historiographic Trends. *Renaissance and Reformation* 35 (3): 85–114.

Bianchini, Lodovico. 1859. *Storia delle finanze del Regno di Napoli*. Naples: Stamperia Reale.

Biblia, Fabrizio. 1621. *Discorso sopra l'aggiustamento della moneta e cambii del Regno di Napoli*.

Bulgarelli Lukacs, Alessandra. 1993. *L'imposta diretta nel regno di Napoli in età moderna*. Milan: Franco Angeli.

Calabria, Antonio. 1991. *The Cost of Empire: The Finances of the Kingdom of Naples in the Time of Spanish Rule*. Cambridge: Cambridge University Press.

Campanelli, Marcella. 2002. Chiesa ed assistenza pubblica a Napoli nel Cinquecento. In *Gli Inizi della circolazione della cartamoneta e i banchi pubblici napoletani nella società del loro tempo*, ed. Luigi De Rosa, 146–168. Naples: Istituto Banco di Napoli Fondazione.

Cano Borrego, Pedro Damián. 2014. Una aproximación al estudio de los proyectos de creación de un banco nacional en España durante la edad moderna. *Pecvnia* 19: 157–179.

Da Silva, José-Gentil. 1969. *Banque et Crédit en Italie au XVIIe siècle*. Paris: Klincksieck.

D'Ambra, Raffaele. 1873. *Vocabolario napolitano-toscano domestico di arti e mestieri*.

De Rosa, Luigi. 1955. Una struttura bancaria napoletana alla vigilia dell'insurrezione di Masaniello: Il Banco dei Poveri dal 1641 al 1646. *Bollettino dell'Archivio storico del Banco di Napoli* 9: 93–120.

———. 1987. *Il Mezzogiorno spagnolo tra crescita e decadenza*. Milan: Arnoldo Mondadori.

———. 1997. L'Aziende e le Finanze. In *Spagna e Mezzogiorno d'Italia nell'eta della transizione: Stato, finanza ed economia (1650–1760)*, ed. Luigi De Rosa and Luis Miguel Enciso Recio, 127–148. Napoli: Edizioni Scientifiche Italiane.

———. 1998. Immobility and Change in Public Finance in the Kingdom of Naples, 1649–1806. *Journal of European Economic History* 27 (Spring): 9–28.

———. 2001. The Beginnings of Paper-Money Circulation: The Neapolitan Public Banks (1540–1650). *The Journal of European Economic History* 30 (3): 497–532.

———. 2002. Gli Inizi della circolazione della cartamoneta e i banchi pubblici Napoletani. In *Gli Inizi della circolazione della cartamoneta e i banchi pubblici napoletani nella società del loro tempo*, ed. Luigi De Rosa, 437–461. Naples: Istituto Banco di Napoli Fondazione.

De Simone, Ennio. 1974. *Il Banco della Pietà di Napoli, 1734–1806*. Arte Tipografica.

De Simone, Luigi. 1922. *La Fede di credito*. Naples: Borrelli.

De Stefano, Mario. 1940. *Banchi e vicende monetarie nel Regno di Napoli: 1600–1625*. Livorno: Il Tirreno.

Demarco, Domenico. 1996. *Il banco di Napoli: Dalle Casse di deposito alla fioritura settecentesca*. Napoli: Edizioni Scientifiche Italiane.

———. 2000. *Il banco di Napoli: L'Archivio storico: La Grammatica delle scritture*. Napoli: Edizioni Scientifiche Italiane.

Demarco, Domenico, and Eduardo Nappi. 1985. Nuovi documenti sulle origini e sui titoli del Banco di Napoli. *Revue internationale d'histoire de la banque* 30–31: 1–78.

Denzel, Markus A. 2010. *Handbook of World Exchange Rates, 1590–1914*. Farnham: Ashgate Publishing Group.

Di Somma, Carlo. 1960. *Il Banco dello Spirito Santo dalle origini al 1664*. Naples: Arte Tipografica.

Di Vittorio, Antonio. 2009. Il Banco di S. Carlo in Napoli ed il riformismo asburgico. In *Wirtschaftlische habsburgische Themen und Probleme zwischen Wien und Neapel, 18. Jahrhundert*, 15–39. Innsbruck: Athesia.

Ferrandino, Vittoria. 2009. La clientela dei banchi pubblici napoletani al tempo di Carlo di Borbone (1734–1759). *Rivista di storia finanziaria* 22 (1): 57–94.

Filangieri, Riccardo. 1940. *I Banchi di Napoli dalle origini alla costituzione del Banco delle Due Sicilie*. Naples: Tipografia degli Artigianelli.

Foscari, Giuseppe. 2006. *Stato, politica fiscale e contribuenti nel Regno di Napoli, 1610–1648*. Rubbettino: Soveria Mannelli.

Fusco, Idamaria. 2009. La peste del 1656–58 nel Regno di Napoli: diffusione e mortalità. *Popolazione e Storia* 10 (1): 115–138.

Giustiniani, Lorenzo. 1803–1804. *Nuova collezione delle prammatiche del regno di Napoli*. Naples: Stamperia Simoniana.

Hamilton, Earl J. 1949. Spanish Banking Schemes before 1700. *Journal of Political Economy* 57 (2) (April): 134–156.

Hernández Esteve, Esteban. 2002. I Banchi pubblici napoletani a confronto con la banca pubblica della corona d'Aragona. In *Gli Inizi della circolazione della cartamoneta e i banchi pubblici napoletani nella società del loro tempo*, ed. Luigi De Rosa, 462–507. Naples: Istituto Banco di Napoli Fondazione.

Malanima, Paolo. 2011. The Long Decline of a Leading Economy: GDP in Central and Northern Italy, 1300–1913. *European Review of Economic History* 15 (2) (August): 169–219.

Muto, Giovanni. 2013. Urban Structures and Population. In *A Companion to Early Modern Naples*, ed. Brill, 35–62. Leiden, Boston.

Nisco, Niccola. 1866. *Il Banco di Napoli*. Napoli: Tipografia del Giornale di Napoli.

Palermo, Francesco. 1846. *Narrazioni e documenti sulla storia del regno di Napoli dall'anno 1522 al 1667*. Florence: Gio. Pietro Vieusseux.

Palmieri, Nicola. 1905. *La fede di credito del Banco di Napoli*. Roma: Officina poligrafica italiana.

Parrino, Domenico Antonio. 1770. *Teatro eroico e politico de' governi de' Vicere del regno di Napoli*. Giovanni Gravier.

Peri, Giovanni Domenico. 1672. *Il Negotiante*. Venice: G. G. Herz.

Petroni, Giulio. 1871. *De' banchi di Napoli*. Naples: Raimondi.

Quinn, Stephen, and William Roberds. 2015. Responding to a Shadow Banking Crisis: The Lessons of 1763. *Journal of Money, Credit and Banking* 47 (6) (September): 1149–1176.

Roberds, William, and François R. Velde. 2016a. Early Public Banks I: Ledger-Money Banks. In *Money in the Legal Western Tradition: Middle Ages to Bretton Woods*, ed. David Fox and Wolfgang Ernst, 321–355. Oxford: Oxford University Press.

———. 2016b. Early Public Banks II: Banks of Issue. In *Money in the Legal Western Tradition: Middle Ages to Bretton Woods*, ed. David Fox and Wolfgang Ernst, 465–488. Oxford: Oxford University Press.

———. 2016c. The Descent of Central Banks. In *Central Banks at a Crossroads: What Can We Learn from History?* ed. Michael D. Bordo, Øyvind Eitrheim, Marc Flandreau, and Jan F. Qvigstad, 18–61. New York: Cambridge University Press.

Rocco, Michele. 1785. *De' Banchi di Napoli e della lor ragione*. Naples: Fratelli Raimondi.

Sabatini, Gaetano. 2013. Economy and Finance in Early Modern Naples. In *A Companion to Early Modern Naples*, ed. Tommaso Astarita, 89–108. Leiden: Brill.

Sargent, Thomas J., and François R. Velde. 2002. *The Big Problem of Small Change*. Princeton, NJ: Princeton University Press.

Sieveking, Heinrich Johhann. 1899. *Genueser Finanzwesen mit besonderer Berücksichtigung der Casa di S. Giorgio*. Freiburg in Brisgau: J. C. B. Mohr.

Silvestri, Alfonso. 1950. Sui banchieri pubblici napoletani nella prima metà del cinquecento. *Bollettino dell'Archivio storico del Banco di Napoli* 2: 22–34.

———. 1951a. Sui banchieri pubblici napoletani dall'avvento di Filippo II al trono alla costituzione del monopolio. *Bollettino dell'Archivio storico del Banco di Napoli* 3: 1–35.

———. 1951b. Sui banchieri pubblici nella città di Napoli dalla costituzione del monopolio alla fine dei banchi dei mercanti. *Bollettino dell'Archivio storico del Banco di Napoli* 4: 1–24.

———. 1953. Sull'attività bancaria napoletana durante il periodo aragonese. *Bollettino dell'Archivio storico del Banco di Napoli* 6: 80–120.

Somma, Aniello. 1860. *Trattato de' banchi nazionali del Regno delle Due Sicilie*. Antonio Cons.

Tassone, Gian Domenico. 1632. *Observationes jurisdictionales politicae, ac practicae ad regiam pragmaticam sanctionem editam de anno 1617, quae dicitur de antefato*. Napoli: Secondini Roncalioli.

Tedde de Lorca, Pedro. 1988. *El Banco de San Carlos (1782–1829)*. Madrid: Alianza Editorial.

Tortora, Eugenio. 1882. *Raccolta di documenti storici e delle leggi e regole concernenti il Banco di Napoli*. Naples: F. Giannini.

———. 1890. *Nuovi documenti per la storia del Banco di Napoli*. Naples: A. Bellisario.

Ugolini, Stefano. 2017. *The Evolution of Central Banking: Theory and History*. London: Palgrave Macmillan.

Van Dillen, Johannes Gerard (ed.). 1934. *History of the Principal Public Banks*. The Hague: Martinus Nijhoff.

Vario, Domenico Alfeno. 1772. *Pragmaticae, Edicta, Decreta, Interdicta Regiaeque Sanctiones Regni Neapolitani*. Naples: Antonio Cervone.

CHAPTER 11

The Institutional Foundations of Successful Public Borrowing—Models of Public Banks in Habsburg Austria and Habsburg Naples 1700–1800

Clemens Jobst

1 Introduction

Between the two functions performed by public banks in the seventeenth and eighteenth centuries—the provision of payment services and the management of government debt (Ugolini 2017)—the latter was clearly the main purpose of all banking projects initiated in the eighteenth-century Habsburg Monarchy. If in addition the banks provided useful services to holders of obligations, depositors and users of banknotes, then it was to make their liabilities more attractive and thereby support government borrowing. Habsburg Austria did not experience the reverse story of banks created to provide a reliable means of payment and which were later used to help government financing (Velde 2018, Chapter 10).

The origin and fate of public banks in Habsburg Austria during the seventeenth and eighteenth centuries have thus to be read within the

C. Jobst (✉)
Oesterreichische Nationalbank (OeNB), Vienna, Austria

L. Costabile and L. Neal (eds.), *Financial Innovation and Resilience*, Palgrave Studies in the History of Finance,
https://doi.org/10.1007/978-3-319-90248-7_11

broader history of Habsburg public finances, which in turn was deeply entwined with the rising needs for military spending. Given the limits to increasing taxation, the linchpin of Habsburg finance was borrowing. After a default at the beginning of the eighteenth century, government credit was at a low point. To obtain new funding at a reasonable cost, the crown had to establish robust and enduring mechanisms that would assure creditors that loans would be repaid on time.

This chapter provides a history of public banks in the Habsburg Monarchy through the lens of their role as a commitment device in the issuance of public debt (Stasavage 2011). In principle, various mechanisms are possible. The concept featuring most prominently in the literature on public credit and property rights is a strong representative assembly that would discipline government policies. Such an assembly, however, was established in Habsburg Austria in the 1860s only. In the eighteenth century, the crown instead built on the pre-existing forms of autonomy enjoyed by cities and the provincial Estates. As the examples of the banking projects surveyed here show, the viability, let alone the success, of these arrangements depended crucially on the careful balancing between granting a sufficient degree of autonomy while keeping the institution close enough to the crown to ensure it provided the services it was set up for. Banks that were founded but failed to take off typically suffered from a government influence deemed excessive. This was the case for the Vienna-based Banco del Giro (1703) and Universalbankalität (1714) as well as for the Banco di San Carlo (1726/1729) created during the brief Austrian Habsburg rule in Naples between 1707 and 1735. The projects not realized, on the other hand, were typically rejected by the central administration for a fear of loss of control over government revenues. Examples here include notably the early designs by Schröder (1680s) and Starhemberg (1700s) as well as a number of projects under the reign of Maria Theresia.

The only design that successfully operated for the entire eighteenth century was the Wiener Stadtbanco (Vienna City Bank), founded in 1706. As I will argue below, the link of the Stadtbanco to the autonomous municipality of Vienna provided for the right mix of autonomy and control. It was probably also helpful that the bank met a general need for the safe depositing of money and that previously no comparable institution had been present in Vienna. This is in contrast to the Banco di San Carlo in Naples, which had to compete with a well-developed banking system and ultimately foundered not only due to its close link to the crown but also because of the resistance of the City of Naples and the established banks.

The further history of the Stadtbanco along the eighteenth century suggests that institutional underpinnings of credibility can evolve. While in its first years the close association with the City of Vienna allowed the bank to borrow from the City's credibility and establish itself as a valuable help to the government, it was soon the bank's success in raising funds that became its best protector against government encroachment. Over time, the government increasingly curtailed the role of the municipality in the management of the bank and replaced it with autonomous structures within the central administration, which were further guaranteed by the appointment of strong and influential personalities at the head of the bank. But even when the bank was gradually incorporated into the Aulic Chamber (Hofkammer, originally the body administrating the revenues of the crown, then the nucleus of the evolving Ministry of Finance), from the 1760s onwards, the name of the bank was retained and the obligations issued by the Stadtbanco continued to fetch higher prices in the market than other types of government debt. The Stadtbanco also lent its name to the first experiment in the issuance of paper money in 1762. It was only in the financial catastrophe brought about by the Napoleonic Wars that the specific model of autonomy of the Stadtbanco finally became obsolete. In 1816, the Stadtbanco was dissolved—a fate it shared with most of Europe's other public banks—and replaced by the Oesterreichische Nationalbank.

2 The Exigencies of War and the 'Austrian Financial Revolution'

In the two centuries before 1700, the way war was waged in Europe had undergone a fundamental transformation (Storrs 2009). Armies had become more permanent, much larger and more complex in structure. They had also become much more expensive to maintain. During the Thirty Years' War (1618–1648), European governments pioneered a number of financial innovations (Neal 2018, Chapter 6), which they improved upon in the century that followed (Neal 2000). This was also true of the Habsburg Monarchy.

In 1700, the Habsburgs in Vienna ruled over a conglomerate of kingdoms, duchies and provinces, which included, among others, Lower and

Upper Austria, Styria, Carniola, Carinthia, Tyrol, the Littoral as well as the Lands of the Bohemian Crown, then still together with Silesia. A couple of years before, the Habsburgs had also reconquered much of the Lands of the Hungarian Crown from Ottoman rule. Thanks to territorial expansion, the Habsburgs could now claim great power status, which they fought hard to maintain for the rest of the eighteenth century. In terms of the internal organization of their possessions, over the course of the seventeenth and eighteenth centuries, the Habsburgs increasingly concentrated on transforming their hereditary lands into a more consolidated entity, which by 1700 came to be called *monarchia austriaca*. In the Austrian and Bohemian lands, their efforts were relatively successful, while Hungary, though an integral part of the monarchy, retained a significant degree of autonomy despite attempts during the reigns of Leopold I (1654-1705) and later Joseph II (1765/1780-1790). In addition, the Habsburgs' realm also comprised territories in the Low Countries and Italy, including between 1707 and 1735 the Kingdom of Naples.

Austria was at war for sixty of the hundred years between 1695 and 1794 (Hochedlinger 2003). Among these wars, the most expensive were the War of the Spanish Succession (1701–1714), the War of the Austrian Succession (1740–1748) and the Seven Years War (1756–1763). Due to the only gradual establishment of centralized accounting, fiscal data for the period are not fully reliable and often missing, in particular for the years of war (Winkelbauer 2006). The available estimates for expenditures shown in Fig. 1 still illustrate the exigencies of wars as well as the general upward trend over the course of the eighteenth century, which can only in part be explained by a rising price level. Expenditures doubled at the beginning of the century. While declining somewhat after the end of the War of the Spanish Succession, peacetime expenditures climbed up in the following decades, and after the mid-eighteenth century, expenditures never again fell below the levels attained during the War of the Spanish Succession, even despite the loss of the wealthy province of Silesia in 1742.

Despite their notoriety for always being close to bankruptcy—'ohne Geld, ohne Credit, ohne Armee' in Maria Theresia's own terms (Dickson 1987)—the sustained increase in expenditures testifies to the Habsburgs' success in raising funds, which even allowed Austria to reduce the gap relative to archenemy France (Winkelbauer 2006). To do so, Austria developed its own mix of reforms in taxation and borrowing (Godsey 2018). Within this process, much emphasis has been put traditionally on Maria Theresia's reforms around 1750, but significant changes in the

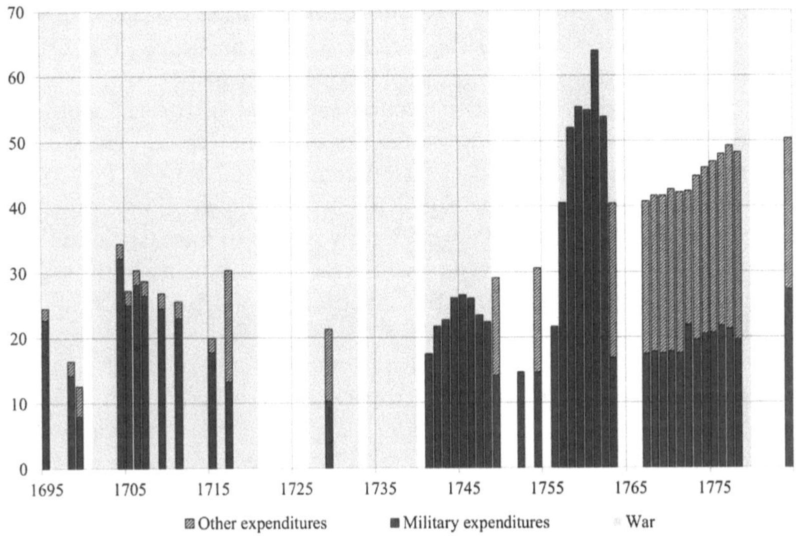

Fig. 1 Military and total government expenditures in million *florins*. *Note* Civilian expenditures are only available for selected years. *Sources* 1695–1740: Winkelbauer [2006] and 1740–1785: Dickson [1987]

domain of tax collection and debt finance already took place at the turn of the century, which Winkelbauer (2006) has recently labelled the 'first Austrian financial revolution'.

Throughout the eighteenth century, government revenue was fed from two main sources. The so-called Camerale stemmed from the ruler's domain lands and royal prerogatives, like monopolies, returns from mining and the rights to levy tariffs, customs and excise duties. The Contributionale, on the other hand, referred to grants by the provincial Estates (Landstände), which were composed of representatives from the landed nobility, the clergy and the cities. These contributions go back to the Middle Ages, even though the name 'contribution' seems to date from the Thirty Years' War. The contribution became a significant source of revenue for the first time in response to Ottoman attack in the 1680s and 1690s. Constitutionally, the contribution was considered a free gift of the Estates but evolved into a permanent source to finance the standing army when by the late 1680s the Estates of Lower Austria assented, by way of a formal accord with the ruler known as a 'recess', to a fixed annual grant over several years. From now on, the contribution was a sort of tax on landed revenue (Godsey 2018). While in principle recognizing the need to support the crown financially, the Estates used the ruler's dependence on their cooperation in both the negotiation of the contribution and the actual collection of the tax as a lever in the negotiation of financial matters. As such, the Estates remained an important player throughout the eighteenth century. Over the course of the century, the crown managed to increase the receipts from both Contributionale and Camerale significantly thanks to increases in indirect taxation—notably on tobacco and salt—and improvements in the assessment of the contribution and the inclusion of the previously exempt nobility and clergy (Dickson 1987).

During wars, however, ordinary revenues fell far short of required expenditures. While subsidies from foreign allies—notably England during the War of the Austrian Succession—somewhat helped to fill the gap, Austria relied to a considerable extent on loans. As can be seen in Fig. 2, total debt increased from 49 million *florins* in 1711 to 99 million *florins* in 1739 and 290 million *florins* in 1781. To ensure the success of new loans and to keep funding costs low, the government had to take

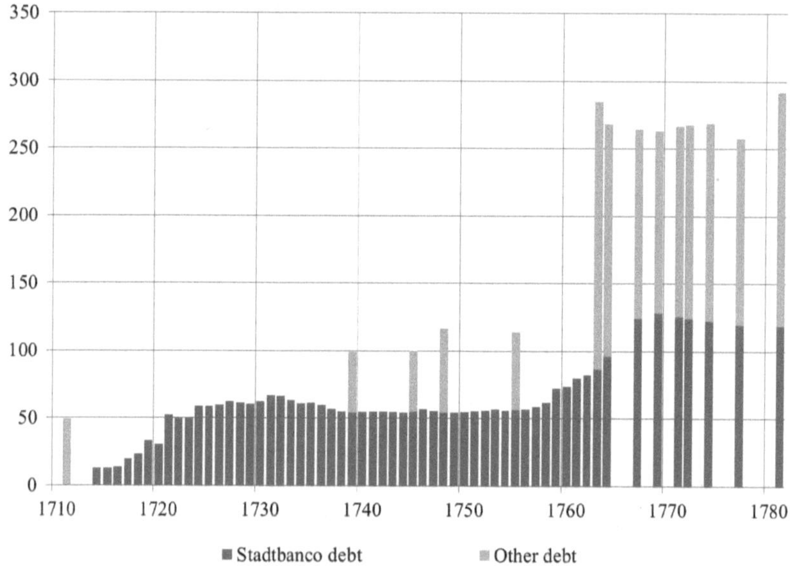

Fig. 2 Austrian government debt in million *florins*, selected years. *Sources* 1714–1749: Mensi [1890] and 1750–1781: Dickson [1987]

measures to keep its debt at least reasonably attractive. The traditional mechanism to provide some assurance to creditors was to pledge the receipts of specific taxes or other revenue streams as well as to have the Estates or corporations to provide additional guarantees (Mensi 1897). Such a pledge was however only as good as long as the crown kept to the deal and did not divert revenues to other uses and/or attach additional debts to them. Key was thus the development of specific institutional arrangements to credibly safeguard the quality and integrity of the revenue streams used as guarantees. Over the course of the eighteenth century, several designs were proposed or tested. All involved the imposition of some intermediary institution between the government and the ultimate creditors. The following sections compare the designs that failed with the designs that worked.

3 Unrealized Projects and Projects that Failed

By the time of the foundation of the first public bank in Vienna in 1703, projects for banks had been discussed already for almost a century and decision-makers were well aware of the merits of public banks for a well-functioning economy and for improving public credit. Indeed, based on Italian models, a number of blueprints had been developed, without any of them having ever been implemented. The focus of these plans was on improving the payment system, mobilizing private credit and supporting trade (Sommer 1925). In 1620, Baron Seyfried von Breuner, then president of the Aulic Chamber, recommended the creation of Italian style montes pietatis as well as of a giro bank that should organize the trade in bills of exchange and encourage cashless transactions by imposing a 2 per cent tax on cash withdrawals. During the second half of the seventeenth century, public banks became a topic of public debate. Most authors were sceptical of involving the state in their project, arguing as did Wilhelm Schröder, that in order to obtain public confidence in a monarchy, any bank had to be necessarily set up as private institution and independent of the government. Only after having earned the public's confidence, such a bank could be used to support government objectives (Hönig 1922; Mensi 1890). Schröder presented his plans, which included the issuance of dry bills with specified maturity dates and backed by merchandise or real estate collateral, a sort of paper money—to the Aulic Chamber and—shortly before the Second Siege of Vienna in 1683—to the Estates of Lower Austria, but without success (Holl 1976).

3.1 *Banco del Giro (Vienna, 1703)*

Ultimately, it needed an acute fiscal and financial crisis before a first public bank would be founded. In May 1703, Samuel Oppenheimer died. Oppenheimer had from the 1690s onwards assumed an increasingly central position in the provision of the army as well as of short-term loans to the crown (Grunwald 1913). After his death and at the very moment when the War of the Spanish Succession created new demands for finance, Oppenheimer's creditors turned to the crown for payment. They argued that Oppenheimer had merely brokered their business and that their claims on Oppenheimer ultimately represented claims on the government. As the government did not have the funds to service its debts with Oppenheimer, it imposed a moratorium, precipitating a general financial crisis. The government lost all access to further financing. In response, the old plans for a bank came back on the table, now however clearly with the aim of supporting government credit.

The project that was finally agreed upon was called Banco del Giro. The key idea was to convert claims on the state, notably those from the Oppenheimer bankruptcy, into deposits that were transferable and could be used as a means of payment (Mensi 1890; Holl 1976). The deposits received a number of privileges, including freedom from taxation and protection from attachment. In addition, there were also a number of coercive measures aimed at increasing demand for Banco deposits, as Vienna merchants were required to settle bills through the Banco and money orders on the Banco were declared legal tender. Thereby the authors of the plan hoped that the claims against the government transferred to the Banco could be kept in circulation as book money. In the medium term and if accountholders found that Banco money was useful in facilitating payments, the government even stood the chance of attracting additional deposits from individuals—provided the liabilities of the Banco del Giro were credibly backed. That was to be achieved by assigning selected state revenues as collateral. At this very point, the project failed.

While the Banco found itself quickly burdened with significant amounts of government debt, the corresponding revenues failed to arrive or were already pledged for other purposes. As a result, the public soon suspected that the scheme mainly served to buy time while favouring some of the Oppenheimer creditors, without however being sustainable in the longer run. The declaration of bank liabilities as legal tender did not inspire confidence either; neither did the fact that the management of the bank depended directly on the crown. Even though some improvements were made in 1704—most notably funding was improved and some of the coercive clauses withdrawn—the Banco found itself unable to fulfil the role it had been assigned (Holl 1976). The Banco was closed for new business in 1705, and its liabilities later transferred to the Wiener Stadtbanco, founded in 1706 and discussed in detail below (Mensi 1890).

3.2 *Universalbankalität (Vienna, 1715)*

The next attempt at a government-controlled bank came after the end of the War of the Spanish Succession (1701–1714). Charles VI, who had succeeded Joseph I in 1711, strove for a systematic overhaul of the financial administration (Mensi 1890; Holl 1976). By that time, the Stadtbanco had operated successfully for eight years, and it therefore seemed reasonable to place a bank at the centre of the new design. Like the Stadtbanco, the Universalbankalität, finally founded in 1715, was to accept deposits and grant loans to the government, guaranteed by revenues transferred to the Bankalität. The crucial difference was that the Bankalität was directly answerable to the Emperor. The exercise of direct control by Charles VI has often been interpreted as sign of his hostility to the independent Stadtbanco (Walter 1937). As Godsey (2018) notes, however, the Stadtbanco must have enjoyed Charles VI's support, as it would otherwise not have survived given 'the cupidity that the bank's assets aroused among competing ministers'. So for a couple of years, the two institutions operated side by side. In the end, the Universalbankalität did not live up to the expectations of its proponents, who had hoped that the possibility to draw notes on deposits and circulate them as means of payment would make deposits at the Bankalität very attractive. Public scepticism about the Bankalität's close relationship to the crown did not help either. By 1721, the Bankalität found it impossible to service the debts that had been piled upon it. The only solution left was the transfer of the debts to the Stadtbanco.

3.3 *Banco di San Carlo (Naples, 1726/1729)*

The reign of Charles VI also provides for a direct link with the history of banking in Naples. Charles VI had assumed the Neapolitan crown as Carlo VI in 1713. In the following years, the Austrian Viceroys pushed for reforms to increase the tax-paying capacity of the newly acquired territory, including a project for the foundation of a public bank to support government credit (Di Vittorio 1969). The plan bears some similarities to the Stadtbanco and Charles' project for the Universalbankalität.

At that time and unlike Vienna, Naples looked back at a long history of public banks, having originated with the foundation of the Monte di Pietà in 1539 (Di Meglio 2018, Chapter 3; Avallone and Salvemini 2018, Chapter 4). Initially set up as charitable institutions, the banks attracted deposits and provided payment services, which saw their use significantly boosted by the government accepting certificates of deposit in the payment of taxes. Over time, the money deposited with the banks was also invested in public debt (Balletta et al. 2018, Chapter 5) so that the banks became doubly tied to the state financial administration (Sabatini 2013).

The project for a new bank carrying the name of the Emperor's patron—Banco di San Carlo—was envisioned by Cardinal Michael Friedrich Althann, serving as Viceroy in the years 1722–1728, and further pursued by his successor Count Aloys Harrach, Viceroy from 1728–1733. Incidentally, Harrach had first-hand knowledge of public banks in Vienna, having formerly served as Landmarschall (president) of the Estates of Lower Austria as well as a member of several government commissions, in which role he appears to have belonged to a group hostile to the autonomy of the Stadtbanco (Godsey 2018). The main purpose of the Neapolitan bank was to redeem alienated revenues that had previously been sold at yields between 7 and 11 per cent (Benedikt 1927). To do so, the bank should receive an annual endowment of 100,000 ducats. More importantly, the Viceroys hoped to attract private deposits at an interest rate of 4 per cent, allowing the government to refinance its debt at about half the interest rate paid before. The savings thus made would be used to liberate further alienated taxes. The administration of the bank was entrusted to a *Giunta* appointed by the King and chaired by the Viceroy but which included a member of the Collateral Council (the kingdom's highest administrative organ formed by nobles and *Togati*), a councillor of Santa Chiara (the highest court of the kingdom), the president of the Royal Chamber as well as two doctors, a knight and a banker (Di Vittorio 1969).

The *Giunta* was appointed in 1726, and the Banco seems to have received its first endowment in 1729 (Benedikt 1927). Using an account at the Banco della Pietà, the Banco di San Carlo also started to redeem some of the alienated taxes as it had been set up to do (Di Vittorio 1969). In principle, the repurchase of royal taxes from dedicated funds and their refinancing through the issuance of new liabilities at lower interest rates was similar to activities pursued by the Stadtbanco. If the Banco di San Carlo had succeeded in attracting more deposits, it would probably also have started to lend to the government, as did the Stadtbanco. Yet the project never took off in Naples. From the beginning, the plan faced the dogged resistance of the Seggi, the municipal government of the City of Naples that by that time was dominated by the nobility and magistrates (Musi 2013). In a petition to the Emperor in 1726, the Seggi argued that the payment of interest by the Banco would divert deposits from the existing banks, which paid lower or zero interest, leading to their default. They also complained that holders of the annuities would lose income. Benedikt (1927) argues that the failure of the Vienna Girobank and the crises of the Stadtbanco in 1723 and 1727 further undermined the confidence in an institution under control of the crown. Conscious that 'the Banco was hated in Naples', Charles VI instructed Harrach in 1730 to slow down his building up of the institution and to wait for better times (Benedikt 1927). The better times never came.[1]

3.4 *Projects for a Bank of the Estates (Vienna, 1760s)*

But bank projects could also founder on the government's fear of losing control over an institution designed to be autonomous. Such a perspective on the feasibility of public banks and the organization of government debt is afforded by the discussions around the

[1] In this context, it is interesting to note that already before the Austrian reign the Spanish crown had repeatedly attempted to establish in Naples a single larger bank under the direct influence of the crown. Similar to Charles VI's project, all had foundered on local resistance. In 1573, Philip II had instructed the Viceroyalty to project a general deposit bank in Naples with branches in provincial capitals and linked to the public banks, thus facilitating public payments while allowing the government to obtain long-term loans at favourable conditions. The project was however turned down by Naples' private bankers, before being revived in 1594 as part of larger programme of administrative reform. To obtain the support of local interests and both local and Genoese private banks, the Council of Italy then envisaged the bank's management to include three royal ministers, two representatives of the city as well as two Neapolitan and two Genoese bankers. When the offer by a Genoese to purchase the secretaryship of the projected bank threatened to shift the balance of power towards the Genoese bankers and may have even undermined the activities of the existing public banks, the municipal government attacked the plan until it was abandoned in 1607 (Sabatini 2013).

reorganization of the public administration following the unsuccessful and expensive Seven Years War. Chancellor Wenzel Anton Kaunitz criticized the lack of state control over the tax revenues earmarked for the Stadtbanco and designed a scheme for a state bank that would have fully integrated the Stadtbanco as well as the Bancodeputation into the treasury (Walter 1937), even though a link to Vienna would have been preserved by inviting the burgomaster of the city to sit on the bank's board (Dickson 1987). An alternative plan by Count Karl Zinzendorf envisaged a uniform state debt overseen by a new Estates Credit Deputation (Ständische Credit Deputation), representing all provinces in a 'Corps de Nations'. The uniform state debt would be matched by a new Banco di Deposito, again guaranteed by the Estates Credit Deputation, with branches in all provinces of the German Hereditary Lands. The bank would issue notes against cash, discount foreign bills and negotiate foreign loans (Dickson 1987; Beer 1894). While the Stadtbanco would be merged into the new bank, it was thought to lose its previous role as intermediary in the issuance of government debt; Zinzendorf's intention being that government funding needs would no longer be met by the Stadtbanco but directly by investors, who would trade the debt on a stock exchange to be newly established (Baltzarek 1973). The idea of an Austrian bank was hardly new and harked back to the earlier projects of Becher, Schröder, Starhemberg as well as others ventilated from the seventeenth century onwards (Dickson 1987). As back then, the implied shift of power to the Estates made the plan unfeasible, and the Stadtbanco was retained.

4 Commitment Mechanisms that Worked

Before turning to the history of the Stadtbanco as the principal example of a credible intermediary it is useful to consider again the two main sources of tax revenue of the Habsburg Monarchy. As argued above, the key element of successful government borrowing was the credible protection of the revenue streams dedicated to the reimbursement of the debt from government encroachment. The possibilities for such a design differed depending on the type of the revenues considered. While many different arrangements for the guaranteeing of debt titles can be observed along the eighteenth century—not least due to the sometimes desperate situation of the public household—it seems possible to identify three basic set-ups that each replied to a specific combination of type of revenue and identity of creditors.

In the first case of foreign loans, in particular the loans issued in Amsterdam, the guarantee was often provided in the form of a physical transfer of mercury or copper produced in Austrian mines and to be sold in international markets by the same merchant bank that had also served as underwriter in the issuance of the loan. As an agent on behalf of the ultimate creditors, the merchant bank had an interest to protect the proceeds of the sale of mercury to service the debt, increasing in turn the confidence of local creditors (Mensi 1890).

4.1 *The Estates as Intermediaries*

In the second case of domestic creditors, a useful distinction can be made according to whether the debt was secured on the Camerale or the Contributionale (Mensi 1897). Contributions were typically used in debts issued through the intermediation of the Estates. In this set-up, the Estates lent money to the central government (or took over the servicing of debts previously contracted by the central government) and refinanced the loan by issuing obligations in their own name. Typically, a significant share of these debts was held by the landed nobility, the clergy as well as other foundations and cities, all groups directly or indirectly represented in the Estates. Following the argument by Stasavage (2011), the identity (or at least the close link) between creditors and the body managing the specific taxes pledged for the loan significantly increased the likelihood of payment and lowered the yield required to raise funds (Godsey 2018).

The same can even be argued—with some restrictions –for forced loans, which played some role during the War of the Spanish Succession (Mensi 1890), but were of crucial importance during the Seven Years War, when a sum of more than 90 million out of an estimated total of 390 million *florins* was financed through forced loans levied in the Austrian and Bohemian lands (Dickson 1987; Mensi 1897). In the earlier years forced loans were typically assessed on select small and wealthy groups, were negotiated rather than imposed and de facto substituted for taxation that was not feasible due to political or administrative constraints. The forced loans during the Seven Years War were mainly raised through the intermediation of the Estates and to be paid out of the Estates' future contributions. Again, the fact that those who lent were also those who paid the contribution supported the political viability of the arrangement in the same way as for voluntary loans issued through the Estates. The fuzzy boundary between forced and voluntary loans can also be seen in the special privileges, including the exemption from tax and freedom from attachment at law, that—depending on necessity—the government was willing to offer for both forced and voluntary loans (Dickson 1987).

Given the value of the Estates as intermediaries, the central government had an interest in keeping in place those elements of provincial autonomy that underpinned their credibility. Such an interpretation of the continuing role of the Estates is in line with recent scholarship that has downplayed the traditional interpretation of Habsburg state-building as a struggle between the (modernizing) centrally controlled administrative power, notably in the Austrian and Bohemian lands, and (backward) forms of provincial autonomy as embodied by the Estates. Instead, dynasty and aristocracy appear to have formed an alliance founded on common mentality as well as an alignment in economic interests. In this reading, the Court served as place bringing ruler and elites together: landed magnates serving both at the Court and in the territorial Estates made their local authority available to the central government while pursuing their own family interests. As a result, the Estates of the central lands, rather than being a historic relic, 'were transformed into leading financiers of the Habsburg dynastic state', as Godsey has recently argued (2018).

4.2 *Establishing the Stadtbanco 1706–1740*

While the Estates' control over the Contributionale provided a natural candidate for a check on monarchical power, the situation was different for the Camerale or crown revenues. Here the central government enjoyed much more freedom; at the same time, however, it lacked any inbuilt constraints that could assure creditors that dedicated revenues would remain attached to the debt title as promised. In this third case, rather than relying directly on existing autonomous bodies, a possible solution was to create new institutional safeguards within the central administration, even if existing and trustworthy autonomous bodies could be integrated to enhance the credibility of the set-up. It is here that the story of the Stadtbanco comes in.

In 1703, at the moment when the recently founded Banco del Giro tried to sort out the mess of the Oppenheimer bankruptcy, Count Gundaker Thomas Starhemberg served as president of the Aulic

Chamber. From the very beginning, he had been hostile to the Banco del Giro and promoted his own competing projects. While Starhemberg did not make any attempt to deny that his banking project would essentially serve government financing just like the Banco del Giro, he was well aware of the Achilles heel of any public bank in a monarchical regime: the need to obtain the trust of the public. Accordingly, he identified the close association of the Banco del Giro to the government as the fundamental flaw in its design. To resolve the credibility problem of a government bank, Starhemberg suggested relying on the Estates of the hereditary lands, which at the time enjoyed a better credit standing than the central government (Holl 1976). In 1702, Starhemberg suggested to raise over six years an annual sum of fifteen million *florins* against 9 per cent interest, secured on the joint guarantee of the Estates of the Austrian and Bohemian hereditary lands and backed by new taxes yielding five million a year (Holl 1976). The project appeared at the same time overly ambitious and very expensive and was rejected by Leopold I. But Starhemberg's efforts were finally crowned with success when Joseph I ascended to the throne in 1705.

The scheme that was actually implemented in 1706 accorded the role of guarantor not to the Estates but to the City of Vienna. In his proposal, Starhemberg cited the example of the City of Paris (Holl 1976), which served as an intermediary for the issuance of French public debt (Stasavage 2011). The City of Vienna formed together with eighteen princely cities and market towns (landesfürstliche Städte und Märkte) the Fourth Estate of Lower Austria, and in this respect, the new and the old proposals were related. But suffering from a decline in trade and commerce that had begun in the late sixteenth century, Vienna was economically weak in comparison with the three other Estates and was thus presumably a less credible guarantor for a bank (Godsey 2018). The existing literature is silent on why Starhemberg switched plans from linking the bank to all Estates to the much narrower concept of a municipal bank. We can only speculate on the reasons; a likely candidate being that the central administration wanted to avoid the involvement of the still very powerful Estates in the management of the bank. Linking the bank to the City of Vienna could have been the compromise that guaranteed a sufficient degree of credibility vis-à-vis creditors while keeping the institution as much as possible within the influence of the central administration, even more so as Vienna due to its status as princely town was subject to the financial oversight of the crown in a way that the noble

Estates were not. That Starhemberg did not want to give the municipality more than a limited say in the operation of the bank anyway soon became evident.

The Stadtbanco started to operate on 1 April 1706 (Mensi 1890). The basic purpose of the new bank—taking over government debt and servicing it out of dedicated tax revenues—was similar to the Banco del Giro's. The set-up however differed in several important respects. A central element was the so-called proportionality; that is that for every hundred *florins* of debt transferred the bank would receive tax revenues equal to ten *florins*. Out of these revenues, which were managed by the bank, the bank would pay 5 per cent interest and amortize the principal amount over a fifteen-year period. The revenues provided were typically Camerale, including tolls, taxes on wine, meat and salt, often of varying quality and yielding less than promised or being partly pledged already for other purposes. Nevertheless and unlike in the case of the Banco del Giro, here the municipality, whose finances were in relatively good shape, was responsible for payment and therefore had a great interest to prevent any assumption of debt without proper funding, thus helping to enforce the statutes which explicitly forbade the bank from doing so. Moreover, the Stadtbanco was given jurisdiction for managing the revenues (Fuchs 1998). In return, the bank had to cede to the state any excess profits from its more efficient administration of the pledged taxes or from lower interest on debt.

In other words, like the Banco del Giro, the Stadtbanco was not a bank in the modern sense, but a special agency administering parts of the public debt. Key purpose was the amortization of debt and the collection of fresh funds. Other banking businesses were only performed to the extent that they were necessary for fulfilling the role as government financing institution, namely the acceptance of remunerated deposits, their transfer and the issuance of debt. With very few exceptions the bank only granted loans to the central government while even advances on government debt were not permitted. The discounting of bills or the operation of current accounts did not play any role at all (Mensi 1890).

In addition to the City's guarantee, several other measures were taken to increase public confidence and to make claims on the Stadtbanco more attractive. Depositors were promised exemption from taxation and protection against seizure of property. The bank was run by municipal government officials and, as a further signal of independence, was housed in the city hall. In reality, however, the officers nominated by the municipality were subordinated to the Ministerial-Bancodeputation—initially a supervisory body consisting of a representative from the government of Lower Austria and the Aulic Chamber that however soon started to interfere in the daily operations of the bank (Mensi 1890). Furthermore, in its administration of the transferred taxes, the municipality required the agreement of the Aulic Chamber. In 1716, the municipality lost its right to appoint the bank's officials. In reaction, the municipal authorities announced in 1717 that they would be liable for the Stadtbanco's debt only to the extent of the anticipated income on the revenues assigned to the bank, thereby effectively withdrawing the City's guarantee for the bank's liabilities (Bidermann 1858). Over time, the separation between the bank and the treasury thus became more and more blurred.

Despite the close association between the Stadtbanco and the treasury, the new institution succeeded in gaining the trust of the public. In its first years, the bank was mainly engaged in unwinding the liabilities it had inherited from the failed Banco del Giro and in rolling them over into longer-term obligations issued by it. It achieved also some successes in increasing income by a more efficient management of the taxes and duties transferred to it. Even though the first years were not easy—at times and in violation of its charter the bank had to offer interest rates as high as 9 per cent and organized a forced rescheduling of its debts in 1708—private depositors came to increasingly trust the bank and from 1712 onwards, growing volumes of new funds flowed to the bank. In the following decades the bank managed to maintain its good standing, even though at times the takeover of large amounts of government debt without a concomitant transfer of corresponding revenues as stipulated in the charter brought the bank to the brink of collapse, most notably following the takeover of the debts of the failed Universalbankalität as mentioned above. Unfavourable rumours led to deposit outflows in 1723, 1727 and 1733, but all episodes were weathered well.

Part of the Stadtbanco's success was its appeal to small investors. By 1724, some 90,000 investors had made deposits with the Stadtbanco (Fuchs 1998). No small part of the Stadtbanco's success was due to the scarcity of interest-bearing, liquid investment alternatives in the early eighteenth century. The Estates of deceased craftsmen, for instance, frequently contained deposits of 100 to 1000 *florins*, sometimes also more (Eigner et al. 1991). The circle of government creditors expanded, marking a key step towards broadening the investor base for government debt (Winkelbauer 2003).

The great appeal to investors as well as a general improvement in public credit was also reflected in the drop in the yield on government debt from between 9 and 20 per cent at the start of the century to just 5–6 per cent in the late 1720s. Consequently, all 6 per cent bonds were converted into 5 per cent bonds in 1732 (Beer 1894; Mensi 1890). At the same time, the Stadtbanco's credibility made it possible to raise large volumes of funds for the state at short notice if required (Fuchs 1998).

From the finance administration's perspective, the Stadtbanco was thus a tremendous success. In addition to the evolution of total debt, Fig. 2 above gives the share issued through the intermediation of the Stadtbanco. A comparison of the public debt at the beginning and at the end of Charles VI's reign illustrates the Stadtbanco's importance: While the government debt held by the Stadtbanco rose from 12 million to nearly 55 million *florins* from 1711 to 1740, the volume of other government debt barely changed and came to just under 50 million *florins*, meaning that in net terms all new government borrowing during Charles VI's thirty-year reign was handled by the Stadtbanco.

4.3 The Stadtbanco 1740–1816

Maria Theresa's accession to the throne in 1740 did not result in any immediate changes in the Stadtbanco's management. 1745 marked the death of Starhemberg, who had served as president of the Bancodeputation since 1711 and decisively contributed to the good standing of the bank. In 1748 the War of the Austrian Succession ended with the painful loss of Habsburg Austria's most valuable province Silesia. The following years of the long reign of Maria Theresa as well as of her son Joseph II saw repeated reforms aiming at increasing the military and political clout of Austria and fostering the cohesion of the Austrian and Bohemian lands (Vocelka 2001). Efforts targeted the military, educational and legal systems and especially public administration and finances, including the Stadtbanco. Every time, the Stadtbanco was a point of contention due to its administration of significant parts of indirect taxes. Radical proposals in 1748, 1761 and again 1763 aimed at ending its privileged and semi-independent position (Dickson 1987). From 1749, the influence of the Vienna municipal authorities was limited to appointing the chief tax collector and cashier, whereas the bank was run exclusively by civil servants seconded from the central administration. A Prussian diplomat in Vienna aptly described this change when remarking that the Bancodeputation, originally simply charged with supervising the management appointed by the municipal authority, had 'gradually taken full management control of the Stadtbanco, reducing the role of the municipal administration to that of lending its name' (Bidermann 1858). However, against alternative projects, which would have abolished most of the Camerale revenues supporting the Stadtbanco while transferring others to the Estates thereby destroying the Stadtbanco, the reform agenda finally adopted in 1749 left the statutory organization of the Stadtbanco and of the Bancodeputation unchanged as the bank found a strong supporter in the person of the financially able Emperor Francis Stephen, husband of Maria Theresia (Walter 1937; Dickson 1987). In the end, nobody dared to damage the bank's creditworthiness by moving it too close to government control.

After the *de facto* exclusion of the City of Vienna from the bank's management, the president of the Bancodeputation now personified the guarantee that the bank would retain a certain degree of independence from the treasury. The strategy worked for the time being when Count Rudolf Chotek was selected president of the Bancodeputation in 1749 (Walter 1937). Dickson (1987) concludes that 'while the "state" character of the Bank from 1749, usually insisted upon in the literature, cannot be denied, it in some ways acquired at the same time a renewal and confirmation of its special status, which was to last at least until 1762 and in many respects longer'. In 1764, the Bancodeputation was officially incorporated into the Aulic Chamber. But the appearance of independence was kept up, and even Joseph II was aware that the autonomy of public debt management, for the very purpose of which the Stadtbanco had been launched in 1706, had to be preserved on paper so as not to compromise the attractiveness of the Stadtbanco's obligations (Beer 1894). As a result, the Bancodeputation continued to exist and was finally dissolved in 1816 only (Walter 1956).

Turning to the business done by the Stadtbanco during the second half of the eighteenth century, its main purpose continued to be the provision of cash advances to the government and the issuance of debt certificates that the government used in payments or as collateral (Fuchs 1998). As can be seen in Fig. 2, new lending was balanced by the amortization of older debts and the total level of Stadtbanco debts remained broadly unchanged until the mid-1750s. During the War of the Austrian Succession (1740–1748) other debts increased somewhat, while Stadtbanco debts remained constant, not least because the Stadtbanco was financially exhausted as Starhemberg had repeatedly protested already before 1740 (Dickson 1987). Overall, debts played a limited role in the financing of the war.

The picture is very different for the Seven Years War, which saw total government debts more than double. This time and unlike in earlier years, the brunt of the effort was borne by the Estates, not by the bank, which nevertheless contributed substantially to the war effort. Government debt to the bank increased from 56.7 million in 1756 to 90 million in 1763. In return, the government again transferred additional revenues. As a result, bank revenues doubled to 9 million by 1763 (Dickson 1987). The significant endowment of the bank helps to explain both the continued good standing of bank obligations in the markets and the temptation it represented for rival political factions at the Vienna court. During the Seven Years War, only part of the new lending was provided in cash. While the bank succeeded in maintaining a healthy cash position and in attracting net deposits, at least until 1762, cash inflows did not suffice to satisfy the government's need. Instead, lending was in the form of bank obligations, which the government used in transactions (Dickson 1987). The resulting decline in bond prices rendered the issuing of new debt increasingly unattractive, giving rise to new innovations in government financing.

The first one was the already mentioned Estates Credit Deputation. Representing the combined Estates of Austria and Bohemia, the debt titles issued by the Deputation mark according to some authors the beginning of a 'national' debt of the Austrian monarchy (Mensi 1897). The initial plan provided for a mix of a long-term subscription loan and the direct issuance of short-term payment bonds that could be used as medium of exchange, initially by the government, subsequently by individuals as well, notably in the payment of taxes. However, the subscription loan failed to meet expectations. As a result, the government turned to the Stadtbanco, instructing it to issue twelve million *florins* of paper money, called Bancozettel. The Bancozettel carried neither interest nor could anybody be forced to accept them. But they came with the convenience of being legal tender at par for up to half of tax payments due. They could also be redeemed for coins at the Stadtbanco (Raudnitz 1917). To further make the Bancozettel attractive for use in payments, they were issued in fairly small denominations: Some four and a half million of the twelve million *florins* had a face value of five *florins* only. The issue was intended as a temporary measure to tide over the government until it could return to floating longer-term bonds. Therefore, holders of at least 200 paper *florins* were entitled to exchange these for Stadtbanco obligations bearing 5 per cent interest (Raudnitz 1917), and the law called for the destruction of redeemed Bankozettel. 7.8 million *florin* Bankozettel were returned until 1766 and were burned publicly just outside the city walls (Pressburger 1959; Raudnitz 1917).

After the end of the Seven Years War, public credit was re-established rather quickly. Bond prices recovered and in 1766 large parts of the government debt were successfully converted from 5 to 4 per cent (Dickson 1987). In this process, about 16 million *florin* of bonds issued by the Estates Credit Deputation were converted in Banco Obligationen, leading to the post-war increase in Stadtbanco debts visible in Fig. 2. In 1767 the Stadtbanco was closed to new depositors to direct investors towards alternative—and cheaper—ways of placing funds, notably at the Kupferamt, which had begun accepting deposits in 1760 (Dickson 1987). In the following years, the Stadtbanco gradually amortized parts of its debt, but contributed indirectly to government financing by issuing so-called anticipation obligations, which were used to guarantee sizeable loans issued in Amsterdam and Genoa amounting to almost twenty million *florins* between 1764 and 1771 (Fuchs 1998).

The bank also returned to issuing Bancozettel. The experience of the war had shown that there was a demand for paper money. Bancozettel had remained in circulation for a notable period and their appeal showed among other things in a premium of 1 to 2 per cent in the market (Mensi 1895). Their success made Bankozettel a keystone of government strategies for future wars, and small scale issues even during peacetime were heralded as a way to economize on coin and to accustom the public to paper notes (Mensi 1895, Raudnitz 1917). When the bulk of the paper *florins* launched originally had been redeemed by 1770, a second tranche of 12 million paper *florins* was issued in 1771. This time, some privileges of the notes were cancelled—they could no longer be exchanged for interest-bearing bonds—while half of all tax debts over 10 *florins* had now to be settled in paper money. This forced the general public to use paper money, resulting in the spread of paper *florins* to more peripheral areas previously unfamiliar with the Bancozettel. When more paper money was issued in 1785, geographical coverage was extended to Galicia, Hungary and Transylvania (Raudnitz 1917). By that time the value of the paper money issued reached twenty million *florins* throughout the Habsburg Monarchy. The value of the Bancozettel remained stable for three decades, testifying to a prudent management by the treasury and the public confidence in what remained of the Stadtbanco.

5 Conclusions

While historical happenstance surely had played a role, the success and failure of the various projects advanced in eighteenth-century Habsburg Austria and Naples testify to the fundamental difficulties of running public banks in a territorial monarchy. In principle, the institutional set-up of the banks that operated successfully in Vienna and in Naples was similar: the banks' management was entrusted to an independent public agency designed to defend creditors' interests, which happened to be the City of Vienna for the Stadtbank and charities with a strong link to the local community in Naples (Avallone and Salvemini 2018, Chapter 4). On the other hand, attempts to establish banks under the more or less direct control of the crown failed to take off. This was the case of the Banco del Giro and the Universalbankalität in Vienna as well as the Banco di San Carlo in Naples, even though the Giunta had provided for a broader participation of interests than the board of the Bankalität.

At the same time, successful public banks also needed to satisfy the needs of the crown, which had a strong interest in avoiding the devolution of too much control to autonomous and thus potentially competing political players. The particular institutional solution that worked in Naples could thus be explained by the Viceroyalty trying to legitimize its monetary and fiscal actions while keeping out politically unreliable partners like the Seggi or the Collateral Council, both composed of powerful local elites, and limiting the influence of the Genoese bankers (Sodano 2013; Ugolini 2017). Charities provided an attractive alternative, being popular among all classes of the Neapolitan society, while their large number and relatively small size limited their potential power against the Viceroyalty. The result was a stable equilibrium that allowed for an extraordinary development in the circulation of certificates, both in Naples and in the provinces (Roberds and Velde 2016). In Vienna, a similar solution was found with tying the bank to the well-respected yet comparatively weak City of Vienna rather than to the unwieldy Estates.

After having formed an integral part of Austrian public finance for nearly a century, the Stadtbanco did not survive the onslaught of the Napoleonic Wars; a fate it shared with most of Europe's other public banks (Roberds and Velde 2016). Due to the length of the conflict and its—at least for a long time—unfavourable development for Austria, Bancozettel soon became the principal source of finance. From twenty million *florins* in 1788, note issuance exploded to more than three billion in 1815, leading to a government default and two currency reforms in 1811 and 1816 (Jobst and Kernbauer 2016).

In 1816, the privilegirte Oesterreichische Nationalbank was set up to bring back stability to the monetary system. The same year the last remainders of the Stadtbanco were finally dissolved (Walter 1956). Historians of the Nationalbank have emphasized its novelty: the organization as a quoted company, the election of its directors by the shareholders, the giro business, the discount and lombard facilities providing credit to the private rather than the government sector (Pressburger 1959). But in important respects the new bank continued practices from the eighteenth century. For several decades its asset side consisted mainly of claims on the government that resulted from the conversion of the inflationary paper money into banknotes. The second governor of the bank, Count Joseph Dietrichstein served at the same time as president of the Estates of Lower Austria, also in this respect providing continuity to the demised Stadtbanco and attesting to the continued importance of the Estates for public credit (Godsey 2018). Not surprisingly, the bank operated in close partnership with the government, an arrangement that was to the benefit of both government and the bank's owners (Jobst and Kernbauer 2016). Ultimately, it was only in a long process that the Nationalbank slowly evolved from a government bank to becoming the central institution of the banking system, thus finally emancipating itself from the model the Stadtbanco had pioneered in 1706.

References

Avallone, Paola, and Raffaella Salvemini. 2018. Between Charity and Credit: The Evolution of the Neapolitan Banking System (Sixteenth–Seventeenth Century). In *Financial Innovation and Resiliency*, ed. L. Costabile and L. Neal, 71–93. Cham: Palgrave Macmillan (in this volume).

Balletta, Francesco, Luigi Balletta, and Eduardo Nappi. 2018. The Investments of the Neapolitan Public Banks: A Long Run View (1587–1806). In *Financial*

Innovation and Resiliency, ed. L. Costabile and L. Neal, 95–123. Cham: Palgrave Macmillan (in this volume).

Baltzarek, Franz. 1973. *Die Geschichte der Wiener Börse*. Vienna: Verlag der Österreichischen Akademie der Wissenschaften.

Beer, Adolf. 1894. Die Finanzverwaltung Oesterreichs 1749–1816. *Mitteilungen des Instituts für Österreichische Geschichtsforschung* 15 (2): 237–366.

Benedikt, Heinrich. 1927. *Das Königreich Neapel unter Kaiser Karl VI.: eine Darstellung auf Grund bisher unbekannter Dokumente aus den österreichischen Archiven*. Vienna: Manz.

Bidermann, Ignaz. 1858. Die Wiener Stadt-Bank. In *Archiv für Kunde österreichischer Geschichtsquellen*, 341–446.

Dickson, P.G.M. 1987. *Finance and Government Under Maria Theresia, 1740–1780*, vol. 2. Oxford: Clarendon Press.

Di Meglio, Rosalba. 2018. Before the Public Banks: Innovation and Resilience by Charities in Fifteenth-Century Naples. In *Financial Innovation and Resiliency*, ed. L. Costabile and L. Neal, 55–70. Cham: Palgrave Macmillan (in this volume).

Di Vittorio, Antonio. 1969. Il Banco di S. Carlo e il riformismo asburgico. In *Rassegna economica* 1969(2), 235–263. Reprinted in ed. Antonio Di Vittorio 2009. *Wirtshaftliche* [sic] *habsburgische themen und probleme* [sic] *zwischen Wien und Neapel 18. Jahrhundert*. Innsbruck: Athesia.

Eigner, Peter, Michael Wagner, and Andreas Weigl. 1991. Finanzplatz: Wien als Geld- und Kapitalmarkt. In *Wien Wirtschaftsgeschichte 1740–1938*, vol. 2, ed. Günther Chaloupek, Peter Eigner, and Michael Wagner, 909–997. Vienna: Jugend & Volk.

Fuchs, Rudolf. 1998. *Die Wiener Stadtbank. Ein Beitrag zur österreichischen Finanzgeschichte des 18. Jahrhunderts*. Frankfurt: Peter Lang.

Godsey, William. 2018. *The Sinews of Habsburg Power. Lower Austria in a Fiscal-Military State 1650–1820*. Oxford: Oxford University Press.

Grunwald, Max. 1913. *Samuel Oppenheimer und sein Kreis*. Vienna: Braumüller.

Hochedlinger, Michael. 2003. *Austria's Wars of Emergence, 1683–1797*. Edinburgh: Routledge.

Holl, Brigitte. 1976. *Hofkammerpräsident Gundacker Thomas Graf Starhemberg und die österreichische Finanzpolitik der Barockzeit (1703–1715)*. Vienna: Verlag der Österreichischen Akademie der Wissenschaften.

Hönig, Fritz. 1922. Schröders Bankprojekt. In *Zeitschrift für Volkswirtschaft und Sozialpolitik* N.F. 2, 489–533.

Jobst, Clemens and Hans Kernbauer. 2016. *The Quest for Stable Money. Central Banking in Austria, 1816–2016*. Frankfurt: Campus.

Mensi, Franz. 1890. *Die Finanzen Oesterreichs von 1700 bis 1740*. Vienna: Manz.

Mensi, Franz. 1895. Geld: C. Papiergeld. In *Österreichisches Staatswörterbuch*, vol. 1, ed. Ernst Mischler and Josef Ulbrich, 672–686. Vienna: Hölder.

Mensi, Franz. 1897. Staatsschuld. In *Österreichisches Staatswörterbuch*, vol. 2.2, ed. Ernst Mischler and Josef Ulbrich, 1080–1120. Vienna: Hölder.

Musi, Aurelio. 2013. Political History. In *A Companion to Early Modern Naples*, ed. Tommaso Astarita, 131–151. Leiden, Boston: Brill.

Neal, Larry. 2000. How It All Began: The Monetary and Financial Architecture of Europe During the First Global Capital Markets, 1648–1815. *Financial History Review* 7 (2): 117–140.

Neal, Larry. 2018. The Variety of Financial Innovations in European War Finance during the Thirty Years' War (1618–1648). In *Financial Innovation and Resiliency*, ed. L. Costabile and L. Neal, 127–145. Cham: Palgrave Macmillan (in this volume).

Pressburger, Siegfried. 1959. *Das österreichische Noteninstitut*, vol. 1. Vienna: Oesterreichische Nationalbank.

Raudnitz, Josef. 1917. *Das österreichische Staatspapiergeld und die privilegierte Nationalbank. Erster Teil: 1762 bis 1820.* Vienna: k. k. Hof- und Staatsdruckerei.

Roberds, William, and François Velde. 2016. Early Public Banks II: Banks of Issue. In *Money in the Western Legal Tradition*, ed. David Fox and Wolfgang Ernst, 465–488. Oxford: Oxford University Press.

Sabatini, Gaetano. 2013. Economy and Finance in Early Modern Naples. In *A Companion to Early Modern Naples*, ed. Tommaso Astarita, 89–107. Leiden, Boston: Brill.

Sodano, Giulio. 2013. Governing the City. In *A Companion to Early Modern Naples*, ed. Tommaso Astarita, 109–129. Leiden and Boston: Brill.

Sommer, Louise. 1925. *Die österreichischen Kameralisten in dogmengeschichtlicher Darstellung*, vol. II. Vienna: Konegen.

Stasavage, David. 2011. *States of Credit: Size, Power, and the Development of European Polities.* Princeton, NJ: Princeton University Press.

Storrs, Christopher. 2009. Introduction: The Fiscal-Military State in the 'Long' Eighteenth Century. In *The Fiscal-Military State in Eighteenth Century Europe: Essays in Honour of P.G.M. Dickson*, ed. Christopher Storrs, 1–22. Farnham: Ashgate.

Velde, François. 2018. Neapolitan Banks in the Context of Early Modern Public Banks. In *Financial Innovation and Resiliency*, ed. L. Costabile and L. Neal, 201–241. Cham: Palgrave Macmillan (in this volume).

Vocelka, Karl. 2001. *Glanz und Untergang der höfischen Welt: Repräsentation, Reform und Reaktion im Habsburgischen Vielvölkerstaat.* Wien: Ueberreuter.

Walter, Friedrich. 1937. Die Wiener Stadtbank und das Staatsbankprojekt des Grafen Kaunitz aus dem Jahre 1761. *Zeitschrift für Nationalökonomie* 8 (4): 444–460.

Walter, Friedrich. 1956. *Die Geschichte der österreichischen Zentralverwaltung 1780–1848. Teil 2: Die Zeit Franz II. (I.) und Ferdinands I.* Vienna: Böhlau.

Winkelbauer, Thomas. 2003. *Ständefreiheit und Fürstenmacht: Länder und Untertanen des Hauses Habsburg im konfessionellen Zeitalter*, 2 vols. Vienna: Ueberreuter.

Winkelbauer, Thomas. 2006. Nervus rerum Austriacarum: Zur Finanzgeschichte der Habsburgermonarchie um 1700. In *Die Habsburgermonarchie 1620 bis 1740: Leistungen und Grenzen des Absolutismusparadigmas*, ed. Petr Maťa and Thomas Winkelbauer, 179–215. Stuttgart: Steiner.
Ugolini, Stefano. 2017. *The Evolution of Central Banking: Theory and History.* Basingstoke: Palgrave Macmillan.

CHAPTER 12

John Law: A Twenty-First Century Banker in the Eighteenth Century?

Antoin E. Murphy

1 Introduction

In ascribing to John Law (1671–1724) certain characteristics of the twenty-first-century 'banker', it is necessary to understand that the representation of the twenty-first-century banker has undergone, and is continuing to undergo, an important transformation in the first two decades of the new century. At the start of this century, bankers, whether private (commercial or investment bankers) or public (central bankers/regulators), were regarded as people of power and substance. Banking people occupied a status at the top of the financial tree. As creators of new types of credit, they were lauded for the innovations that they had introduced to enable the global exchange of money and credit which in turn facilitated trade and investment. As central bankers/regulators, they had apparently devised a light touch regulatory system capable of tweaking the financial system into the golden age of macroeconomic moderation through a policy of low interest rates that benefitted capital markets. Bankers were paid extraordinarily well benefitting from stratospheric

A. E. Murphy (✉)
Trinity College Dublin, Dublin, Ireland

L. Costabile and L. Neal (eds.), *Financial Innovation and Resilience*, Palgrave Studies in the History of Finance,
https://doi.org/10.1007/978-3-319-90248-7_12

salaries and option benefits that separated them from other mere mortals working in the real economy. Central bankers, such as the then Chairman of the Federal Reserve System, Alan Greenspan, were regarded as equal to presidents and, at times, were lauded as even more important than politicians.[1]

Alas, these perceptions quickly changed with the financial crash of 2008. Bankers, both private and public, were quickly blamed for the events that almost caused the Western financial system to implode. They became much-denigrated figures and were mocked across society. Matthew Parris, writing in the London Times summed up the anti-finance, anti-banking mood with some Swiftian barbs in December 2008:

> To the tumbrils I say. I want show trials...I want to see hedge-fund managers tipped into cage fights with naked gypsies; bank managers wrestle with lions in the O2 arena; failed regulators thrown to alligators in the Royal Docks; short sellers in pits of snakes.[2]

Parris would continue on this front by adding economists to his hit list:

> ...and distinguished City economists try their luck with sharks. They've had their heyday, their bonuses, their Porsches, their fine wines and oafish ostentation – they've had their fun. Now for ours. To the guillotine![3]

It was the period in which the term 'banksters' was coined. Films such as the Wolf of Wall Street parodied bankers as cocaine snorting Lotharios concerned with ripping off the man in the street to pay for their wild excesses. At the public level, banking regulators were criticised for opening the doors to banking excess while Alan Greenspan, the Chairman of the Federal Reserve System from 1987 to 2006, was quickly transformed from hero to zero by a vengeful media. The age of the vilification of bankers had arrived. However, such vilification is not unique to the twenty-first century.

This vilification of the modern banker has many parallels with the treatment of John Law and the Mississippi System. Law was a

[1] For a recent assessment of Alan Greenspan as Chairman of the Federal Reserve System, see Mallaby (2016).

[2] Matthew Parris, *The Times*, 18 December 2008.

[3] Ibid.

remarkable banker who attempted to revolutionise the French financial system between 1716 and 1720—for recent assessments of Law and the System, see Faure (1977), Murphy (1997), and Velde (2003). When the Mississippi System collapsed in 1720, Law had to make a hasty departure from France, eventually dying in Venice in 1729. Contemporary assessments of John Law, as presented in engravings, were quite scathing. The famous Dutch *Het Groote Tafereel der Dwasheid* (Mirror of Folly), first published in 1720, ridiculed Law as a man of air, a man of bubbles, a clown, a knave and so on. One of the most famous contemporary engravings, the frontispiece of *Arlequin Actionist* (Harlequin Stockholder) shows Law consuming gold and silver coins and transforming them through his body—here politeness dictates—so that they exited as paper shares and banknotes.[4] Satirists across Europe caricatured Law and the System in much the same way that journalists caricatured twenty-first-century bankers.

Economists were no less scathing in their disapproval of Law castigating him for not understanding that the basis of the monetary system was metallic money. The list of disapproving economists is a long one starting with Richard Cantillon and then moving on to David Hume, Adam Smith, Karl Marx and Alfred Marshall amongst others—Murphy (1997).[5] Even Keynes, though aware of Law's work, could not even mention him in his notes on mercantilism in Chapter 23 of the *General Theory*—a huge missed opportunity by Keynes to acknowledge how closely Law may have anticipated so many of the ideas of the General Theory.

So which twenty-first-century banking *personae* can be associated with John Law? At the private banker level was he a banking charlatan and a dangerous financial innovator? At the public level was he, like a later Alan Greenspan, attempting to manipulate excessively financial markets? In this paper, it will be argued that, at one level, it may be shown that Law had many of the characteristics of the twenty-first-century banker in the form of a self-interested drive to enrich himself and spend the proceeds of this personal enrichment in equities, real estate, futures bets and art. It can also be argued that Law, like his twenty-first-century counterparts, was heavily involved in financial innovation the excesses of which

[4]Frontispiece from Arlequin Actionist, a short play by Pieter Lagendyk (Amsterdam, 1720).

[5]Murphy (1997, pp. 4–7).

produced the Mississippi boom and collapse, excesses that were mirrored in the rise and fall of the South Sea Bubble in Great Britain in that same year of 1720. However, it will also be argued that from the ashes of the 2008 financial debacle a new type of banker, the interventionist 'quantitative easing' central banker emerged. This new type of post-financial crisis twenty-first-century central banker was ready, through a policy of significant monetary expansion, to address the problems of an imploded financial system that had pushed economies into negative economic growth. The adoption of such a policy heralded a dismissal of the near consensus view that money did not matter in the economy—a consensus implicit in Alan Greenspan's emphasis on price stability rather than financial stability and in the European Central Bank's continued obsessive pursuit of inflationary control at a time when the global banking system was collapsing. This new type of central banker led by Ben Bernanke, the chairman of the Federal Reserve System, and Mario Draghi, the President of the European Central Bank, understood that money matters and that money has a real effect on the economy. From this perspective, it will be contended there are many parallels between these central bankers and John Law.

2 John Law and Wealth

First of all, it is necessary to examine some apparently self-evident parallels between Law and the twenty-first-century private bankers. The latter have been frequently condemned for their self-interested pursuit of wealth at the expense of the social good which some have termed their greediness. In this pursuit of wealth, they have also been indicted for their financial innovation that led to the creation and development of sub-prime loans, which in turn spawned a burgeoning range of financial derivatives later to be classified by Warren Buffet as 'weapons of mass destruction'. Sub-primes and their financial derivatives enabled the US banking system to tap the international capital markets for vast sums of money that enabled credit to be expanded at a very fast pace not just in the USA, but, also, in certain European economies, most notably Italy, Spain, Greece, Portugal and Ireland, countries which would be branded under the unfortunate acronym of PIIGS. How does Law stand up to these accusations of excessive self-interested pursuit of wealth and excessive financial innovation?

Like many of his twenty-first-century equivalents, John Law had a strong element of self-interest in his pursuit of wealth and was not averse to making money with the profits accruing from his banking operations. The wealth that he accumulated comprised shares, real estate, futures contracts and art. Law would later remark that such was his wealth at the height of the Mississippi System that he was 'the richest individual who ever lived'.[6] In fairness to him, the basis for his wealth was derived initially from his success at the gaming tables, the proceeds of which he invested in shares of the newly founded Compagnie d'Occident in 1717. At the start of the Company's operations, there were few investors prepared to risk their fortunes in this venture and Law's willingness to use his own wealth showed a courageous belief in the potential viability of his enterprises. He was prepared to put his money where his mouth was. On 22 October 1717, the *Gazette de la Régence* warned of the imminent demise of the Mississippi Company:

> It is said that the Mississippi affair will fall; it was not obvious to create and maintain this type of establishment through an individual working with such weak measures and mediocre funds.[7]

Consistent with this initial weakness, it must be remembered that the shares of the *Compagnie d'Occident* sold at a discount from its founding in 1717 to the early summer of 1719. However, once the shares reached a premium and Law made further issues (the *filles*, *petites filles* and *cinq cents*), he was, as one of the largest shareholders, able to leverage his wealth a great deal more as further issues of shares were linked to initial holdings of the *mères* issued in 1717.

Law also borrowed money and shares from the Royal Bank and the Mississippi Company as is evident from the later Commission established 'pour juger les affaires de la Compagnie des Indes'. In their report, the Commissioners judged on 27 August 1720 that John Law owed the Compagnie des Indes 16.3 million *livres* and his brother, William, owed 3.5 million *livres* giving a total of 19.7 million *livres* of debts between the two of them. At the time Law's assets in shares, bank deposits and

[6] Bibliothèque Méjanes, Aix-en-Provence, Ms. 614. John Law's Letter Book. Letter from Law in Venice to the Marquis de Lassay, 14 June 1721, f. 71 r.

[7] Gazette de la Régence, Janvier 1715–Juin 1719, ed. Le Comte de Barthélemy, Paris, 1887, translation.

Table 1 John Law's French real estate

Properties	*Sellers to John Law*	*Auction price*
Toucy	Madame de Vantadour	100,000
La Marche	Desmaretz	90,000
La Mare du Parc	D'Houdeton de Somery	46,000
Emplacement rue de Varenne	Madame d'Estampes	82,000
Arcades (4) Place Vendôme	Seronville	160,600
Maisons (10) Faubourg St Honoré	Miscellaneous	230,600
Charleville & Baqueuille	De Ris	279,000
Yville	Madame d'Estampes	158,000
Orcher	De Novion	301,000
Berreville	De Tavannes	122,000
La Fontaine Romé	De Vernouillet	39,000
L'Hôtel Mazarin	Compagnie des Indes	630,000
Maison rue des Petits Champs		61,000

banknotes amounted to 15.3 million *livres*, leaving a shortfall of over 4 million *livres.*[8]

As his wealth accumulated, a rise mirroring the increase in the Mississippi Company's share price from an initial price of 170–200 *livres* in 1717 to over 10,000 *livres* in the autumn of 1720, Law diversified some of his assets into land and real estate. These acquisitions became part of the common Parisian gossip between 1718 and 1720. On 23 April 1718, the Marquis de Dangeau reported that Law had been busy in the property market and had bought from Desmaretz 'la maison de la Marche' for 110,000 *livres.*[9] In late July, Dangeau reported that the Comte d'Evreux had sold his property at Tancarville for 650,000 *livres* and an annual life pension of 6000 *livres.* The same writer further reported in May 1719 that Law had purchased 'the palais Mazarin', an immense city centre property, later to be transformed into the Bibliothèque Nationale. Dangeau confirmed this in November 1719 reporting that Law had paid a million *livres* for the Hôtel Mazarin, alongside a two-year interest-free loan to Monsieur Mazarin so that the seller could construct an alternative property for his needs. Alongside this purchase, Dangeau reported that Law had purchased Count Tessi's

[8]Archives Nationales Paris, V7 255. Extrait des registres du Conseil d'Etat, 15 September 1722.

[9]Journal du Marquis de Dangeau, Paris, 1859, XVII, pp. 295–296.

property for 550,000 *livres*. Sometime earlier that month of November 1719, Law had bought an estate at Roissy, four leagues from Paris, for 1,250,000 *livres*.[10]

Using manuscripts in the Archives Nationales, Paris, along with Law's letter book for the years 1720–1722, located in the Bibliothèque Méjanes in Aix-en Provence, it is possible to reconstitute the extent of Law's real estate acquisitions. Table 1 details the country estates and Parisian properties that Law acquired between 1718 and 1720. It lists the names of the sellers of these properties to Law along with the subsequent prices of these properties when they were sold at public auctions after Law's bankruptcy between 1722 and 1729. The totality of these properties sold for 3,629,000 *livres* at auction. The list is not exhaustive because it does not include properties over which there were ownership disputes with respect to title, most notably the huge estate at Guermantes.

Law's edifice complex appears to have started with the purchase of the estate of the former Controller General of Finances, Nicolas Desmaretz (1648–1721) at La Marche, situated between St Cloud and Versailles in 1718. Desmaretz had occupied the key role of Controller General of Finances from 1708 to 1715. After Louis XIV's death, Desmaretz had been sacked by the Regent. Law was the newly emerging man of power and would in time also become Controller General of Finances. In purchasing Desmaretz's estate, he laid down a marker as to his emerging status. The estate would also have provided him with a country home close to Paris and within a short ride to Versailles.

From 1719 onwards, he appears to have had a dual strategy of acquiring both large rural estates as well as properties inside Paris. Amongst the estates that he purchased were those at Roissy (which presumably would have incorporated the land that is now Charles de Gaulle Airport at Roissy), a wide range of estates in Normandy (Charleval, Effiat, Gerponville, La Fontaine Romé, etc.). The acquisitions of two other sizeable estates, those of Toucy and Guermantes, may be highlighted to give some flavour to Law's real estate purchases.

On 26 August 1719, Law acquired the estate of Toucy, close to Auxerre, from Madame la Duchesse de Vantedour. This acquisition was important because Madame de Vantedour was the guardian of the

[10] Ibid., pp. 150, 163.

Dauphin, the future Louis XV. Such a purchase implied that Law was close to the centre of the monarchical system and that he wished to facilitate Madame de Vantedour with the purchase of Toucy so that she could use the proceeds to acquire Mississippi shares.

Guermantes has now acquired a mythical status due to its central role in the works of Marcel Proust. It was sold to Law by Paulin Prondre, the receveur général des finances de Lyon. Proust would have been fascinated by the murky world of financial and property dealing of this particular transaction. Law later wrote that he had paid Paulin Prondre a sum of between 1.3 and 1.4 million *livres* for it. However, Prondre, obviously wishing to evade the taxes on such a transaction, only wanted the price of 600,000 *livres* recorded in the sale contract. Law, writing to De Bully noted 'There were sums of money paid to those from whom I bought which were not registered in the sale contracts. When M. Prondre sold me Guermande [the contemporary spelling for the estate at the time] he arranged to sell it to me for 600,000 *livres tournois*, but as the price of the lands rose, I gave him 1,300,000 or 1,400,000 *livres*'.[11] In addition to the initial 600,000 *livres* which was paid in shares, Law indicated that he had paid a 'pot de vin' of 100,000 *livres* in banknotes to Prondre's wife and a further 30,000 in banknotes to Prondre's secretary. Prondre would later maintain, despite Law's strong protestations, that he had received nothing from the sale of Guermande [there are multiple spellings of this name]. Law contended that he had paid for Guermande with Mississippi paper and that his secretary, Bellanger, would confirm this.[12] If credibility is given to Law's account, then it appears that Prondre was rapacious at both the beginning and the end of the contract, attempting to minimise the recorded sale price to avoid taxation and then contending that Law had not paid him for the estate.

Besides the acquisition of country estates, Law bought up sizeable properties in Paris itself. His most noteworthy Parisian acquisition was that of the Hôtel Mazarin—mentioned above—which he purchased from Paul-Jules Mazarin Ruzé, Duc de Mazarin, on 12 February 1720. This huge building was described in a later auction document as 'Grand

[11] Bibliothèque Méjanes, Aix-en-Provence, Ms. 614. Law to M de Bully, 26 February 1722, letter 135.

[12] Ibid.

Hotel rue Neuve des Petits Champs et Maisons en Dependantes'. It was used by Law as the headquarters for the Banque Royale and the Mississippi Company. It would be later sold to the Compagnie des Indes at auction in 1723 for 630,000 *livres*. Law's desire for property stretched into the beaux quartiers in Paris. As Table 1 shows, he acquired five houses in the Place Louis-le-Grand, which had been renamed as the Place Vendôme by the time of their subsequent sale at auction.[13] Additionally, he had plans to build further houses in this square. He acquired ten houses in the very chic Faubourg St Honoré as well as further acquisitions in the rue de Varenne, the rue Neuve des Petits Champs, properties at l'Hôtel de l'Anglée, la Grange Batelière and so on.

The question may be asked as to why Law committed himself to these real estate purchases. Did he fear the System would collapse and that it was important to have a diversified wealth portfolio to guard against such a risk? Did he plan to embark on massive construction projects in Paris and across the French countryside as a further way of advancing his fortune? Or was he in many cases enabling the French aristocracy to purchase Mississippi shares by providing them with cash in return for the sale of their estates and town houses to him? Leading aristocrats of the period such as the Comte d'Evreux, who sold Law his estate at Effiat along with twelve other estates; Madame de Ventadour who sold him her estate at Toucy; Madame d'Estampes who sold her estate at Yville; Madame de la Carte who sold her estate at Roissy; and so on were probably keen sellers in order to obtain in return Mississippi shares.[14] Indeed, it is noticeable that some of the biggest property sellers to Law were aristocratic widows, namely Madame de Ventadour, Madame d'Estampes and Madame de la Carte. All of these aristocratic ladies were enthusiastic speculators in Mississippi paper, and all lost huge estates and other personal property in their Mississippi-related transactions.

Law was prepared to invest overseas also. He established companies to develop lands in French Louisiana. He set up one of these companies with the English investor Joseph Edward Gage and the Irish banker, Richard Cantillon. In 1719, Cantillon's brother, Bernard, led a

[13] See also 'John Law, Jacques Gabriel et la place Vendôme' in Pons (1986).

[14] Archives Nationales Paris V7 254–258.

group of colonists from La Rochelle to Louisiana to develop the Law–Gage–Cantillon concession.[15]

One of Law's biggest financial commitments did not involve shares or real estate in France. It was a futures contract that he contracted with Thomas Pitt, Jr, Lord Londonderry, on the price of East India stock. Larry Neal has shown that 'Law was personally responsible for paying out £541,043 and 6 shillings to Londonderry by the end of 1720' as a result of the East India wagers between Law and Londonderry.[16] This was a huge financial contract and given the problems that Law later experienced in meeting it, the question arises as to why he made it. It was probably a combination of hubris and his gambler's belief that it was a good bet. Hubris because he believed that his System was so vastly superior to anything that the British could conceive that the money would flow from London to Paris and so cause the price of East India stock to fall. Furthermore, as I have said elsewhere, it represented a good marketing exercise with Law proclaiming through the gossip channels of Paris and London that the Mississippi was a great bet and the East India Company a bad one.[17] Once again Law had put his money on the table. The Londonderry futures contract was not unique. On 14 March 1720, when the Mississippi System was under stress, Law entered into a 30,000 *livres* futures contract on the French exchange rate between London and Amsterdam with the Marechal d'Estrées, with Law betting that the French exchange rate would rise relative to both the British and Dutch rates.[18]

Like twenty-first-century bankers, Law patronised the art world. He invited the Italian artist Giovanni Antonio Pellegrini (1675–1741) to Paris to paint the ceiling of the 'grande salle' of the Royal Bank in the Palais Mazarin. The art historian, Bernardina Sani, has described Pellegrini's work for Law as creating 'an elaborate allegory celebrating the success of the bank and the glory of the King'.[19] Though the *grande salle* of the Palais Mazarin was later destroyed, some of the paintings that were to serve as the models for the panels in the ceiling have

[15] Murphy (1986, pp. 88–104).

[16] Neal (2012, p. 53).

[17] Murphy (1997).

[18] Archives Nationales Paris, V7 254.

[19] Sani (1988).

survived—two are in Venice and one is currently on show in the Petit Palais in Paris.

For this work, Law agreed to pay Pellegrini a considerable sum of money, £5000 sterling, with an initial down payment of £1000 plus 9000 French *livres*.[20]

At the time that Pellegrini was fulfilling his contract for Law, his sister-in-law, Rosalba Carriera, arrived in Paris in the spring of 1720. A famous portrait painter of the period, she was contracted by Law to paint a portrait of him, his common-law wife, Katherine, and his son William. In fact, Carriera, as was her usual practice, painted two pastels of Law and each member of his family. The smaller of these pastel portraits of Law, and therefore the copy of the main portrait, is now located in the Altemeister Gallery in Dresden (portrait 1763). The larger portrait has been recently located in a private collection in Paris by the art historian, Valentine Toutain-Quittelier (2017). This magnificent portrait, most probably painted and finished in September 1720, displays a somewhat wry looking Law, quite a different portrait to that attributed to Alexis Simon Belle in the National Portrait Gallery in London. Law's hiring of artists of the quality of both Pelligrini and Carriera are just two examples of his interest in fine art. We know from his later correspondence that he had acquired many other paintings during his period of office in France. He would later, in Venice, build an impressive collection of paintings the details of which are now being unveiled by art historians. Jolyn Edwards who has examined Law's art collection has noted:

[20]Bibliothèque Méjanes, Aix-en-Provence. Ms. 614. Letter from John Law to the Duc de Bourbon Venise le 1 Juin 1721:

Monseigneur. Le Sr Pelegrini qui a peint la galerie de la banque est presentement a Venise et s'adresse a moy pour regler ce que luy est due pour cette ouvrage.

Lorsque je l'employa il me demanda cent mille livres, je ne fis aucun marché par ecrit, mais je luy promis que si l'ouvrage etoit bien fait, il seroit content du payement.

Il a recue de moy mille livres sterlin, et neuf mille livres de France lors qu'il s'est engage avec moy, les cent mille livres valoient entre trois et quatre qu'il sera paye avec mille livres sterline de plus de ce qu'il a deja recue, et il me paroit qu'il en sera content.

Comme je ne doute pas que Mgr le Regent n'agree la proposition que j'ai eu l'honneur de luy faire touchant mes biens; par cette offre la nouvelle Compagnie des Indes deviendra proprietaire des hotels de Mazarin et de la banque; et ce sera a cette compagnie a payer au Sr Pelegrini les mille livres sterline qui luy seront dues. Cela repond meme aux intentions du Regent, qui avoit envoyé son placet aux directeurs, comme il paroit par ce placet qui est joint a ma lettre.

> The Law inventory typifies its owner, a truly urbane and international figure involved with new capitalism, who aspired to wealth, power and status through his personal accomplishments and taste in music and pictures.[21]

3 Law and Financial Innovations

Despite the recent bad press relating to financial innovations such as sub-primes and the financial derivatives that were spawned from them, it is appropriate to observe the necessity for financial innovation in the progression of the modern financial economy. The Naples conference celebrated a city that was at the very heart of global financial innovation in the sixteenth and seventeenth centuries. It was here that paper money circulated for one of the first times in Europe. It was here that the Neapolitan bankers first discovered the merits of bank overdrafts, a couple of hundred years before their Scottish counterparts who have traditionally been credited with the discovery. Without this type of financial innovation, we could still be operating a specie-based financial system.

There has always been a continuous tension between financial innovation and financial prudence. The financial innovation that has been incorporated into banking systems thereby enabling them to progress has in many cases gone unnoticed. On the other hand, excessive financial innovation with its costly consequences has in the harsh headlights of hindsight vision been very quickly criticised and condemned. The difficulty of course is in identifying *ex ante* progressive from excessive financial innovation. The great financial innovations that have been at the core of the evolution of banking have typified a Schumpeterian progression of creative destruction that has enabled previously blocked borrowers to access a wide range of new credit facilities. This has enabled consumers to purchase household durables, automobiles and real estate and new investors to acquire different types of capital. While today's subprimes have been the whipping boy for the media, it must be remembered that their initial objective of providing credit for low-income borrowers thereby enabling them to access the property market was a laudatory one.

So *a priori*, it is important to have a balanced perspective on the merits and de-merits of financial innovation. Law's main financial

[21] Jolyn Edwards 'John Law and his Painting Collection: Conoisseur or Dupe?' (Goodman 2001).

innovations were (1) the substitution of paper money for specie and (2) the conversion of fixed interest-bearing government debt (mainly annuities) into the shares of the Mississippi Company. There was an inherent logic to both operations in his desire to increase the circulation of money in France and to lower the interest costs on government debt. By increasing the money supply, Law believed that he could drive the French economy towards greater prosperity. By reducing the interest rate on government debt, he believed that he could greatly reduce the burden of Louis XIV's legacy of a sizeable national debt. Law's macroeconomic vision was correct on both of these fronts. Law was able to envisage a monetary system freed from the shackles of gold and silver a long time before mainline economists realised the possibilities of such a monetary habitat. His plan to reduce the burden of the national debt was extremely innovative. There was an inherent logic in Law's System. But if this is the case, why did Law fail?

Ultimately, Law failed because he pushed the System too fast and too hard. Initially, for a brief period, Law was able to change the mindset of the French public. This opportunity arose when the financiers were forced to adopt a low profile during the Chamber of Justice's pursuit of the financiers in 1716–1717. Law stepped into the vacuum created by the absence of the financiers. He initially showed how the General Bank, later to become the Royal Bank, could successfully operate by creating a new type of paper money. Then, once he acquired the trading rights to French Louisiana he was able to start his debt management operations through the *Compagnie d'Occident's* acquisition of French short-term debt in the form of *billets d'état*. Then in a series of deft moves, he positioned the popularly known Mississippi Company to take over the totality of the French debt. Law was able to change the French mindset on these operations by seemingly offering vast opportunities for profit making to the traders who bought Mississippi Company shares. However, once fissures appeared in the System from February 1720 onwards the French mindset changed once again. As the share price rose, Law had many followers. But when it started to fall, these followers quickly deserted him. The financiers re-grouped, and benefitting from Law's initial fall from power in late May 1720, ultimately ensured the restoration of the old system of finances with the return of the Paris brothers to power at the end of 1720.

4 Law the Modern Central Banker

However, prior to this fall Law had become immensely powerful. In the second week of January 1720, he had been appointed Controller General of Finances, the equivalent of Prime Minister of France. As such, he became a type of central banker attempting to stabilise a financial system that had overheated and was in danger of imploding. He had been responsible for a great deal of this overheating in that he had used the Royal Bank to make further banknote issues that had helped drive the price of Mississippi shares to over 9000 *livres* a share. Law realised that he needed to exercise control over a financial sector that had gone seriously out of line with the real economic sector. As a precursor to modern central bankers, he needed (1) to manage expectations and (2) to control the money supply.

His initial efforts to manage expectations involved an attempt to set a ceiling price for Mississippi shares through the introduction of an options scheme (*les primes*). Law believed that by issuing options for 1000 *livres* which guaranteed holders the right to buy Mississippi shares at 10,000 *livres* a share he would wipe out an incipient futures market for Mississippi shares and at the same time convince traders that the ceiling price for the shares would not exceed 10,000 *livres*. However, as central bankers now understand, market expectations can be highly volatile and very difficult to control at times. Transactors, instead of buying into Law's expectation as to the future Mississippi share price, perversely interpreted the *primes* scheme as a further possibility to optimise their Mississippi gains. Thus, they sold their Mississippi shares and used the proceeds to purchase multiple units of *primes* in the belief that such a policy enabled them to leverage significantly their ability to acquire more Mississippi shares at a future date. For a brief period, the expectations of such leveraged gains, aggravated by production delays in the issuance of *primes*, created a second bubble in Mississippi paper. Within days, the *primes* going to a premium of over 170 per cent, Montesquieu later explained how certain insiders, most notably aristocratic ladies, were able to exploit the market opportunities offered in the primes market:

> During the *primes* episode one saw the Court's first ladies enter the Bank, purchase primes for a thousand *livres* and then lower them through a window in a small bag to one of their servants who quickly went to the rue Quincampoix and sold them at 1700 *livres* and then returned and placed

the proceeds in banknotes in the same bag making five or six such similar journeys in the morning.[22]

Ultimately, Law, realising that there were supply-side constraints to the issuance of *primes* because they were handwritten by clerks at the Royal Bank, overcame these problems by printing the *primes.* This technical change quickly increased the supply of *primes* and snuffed out the *primes* bubble though the amount of transactions in *primes* was really quite remarkable with Law indicating that over 300 million *primes* were sold to the public.[23] Such sales could have enabled the owners of the primes to acquire 3 billion *livres* of shares! As I have shown elsewhere if these *primes* had been used to purchase fully priced Mississippi shares at 10,000 *livres* each, this would have increased the Mississippi Company's market capitalisation by close to 50 per cent.[24]

Law also attempted to control expectations on the value of gold and silver. Law believed that the financial system could exist without the use of gold and silver specie or bullion. To operationalise such a policy, he needed to dramatically change the public's expectations on this front, to persuade the French public that the future was in banknotes and shares rather than specie and bullion. He initially changed expectations by making shares apparently more attractive assets than gold and silver. Side by side with this development, he introduced measures stipulating that taxes would be paid in banknotes. From May 1719, he had introduced legislation stipulating the phased devaluation of gold with the ultimate objective of the demonetisation of gold. This policy gathered pace in March of 1720 when he introduced an *arrêt* stipulating that gold would be demonetised by May 1 and that silver would be progressively reduced in value by monthly reductions relative to the value of banknotes until the near virtual demonetisation of silver on 1 August 1720. This legislation was accompanied by further measures that criminalised the holding of more than a certain quantity of gold or gold objects—this promoted a secondary market in the creation of gold crucifixes which appeared initially to be outside the scope of this legislation!

For a period, Law's policy of changing expectations away from metallic money and wealth to this new world of banknotes and shares

[22] Montesquieu (1950, vol. 2, p. 776). My translation.

[23] Law, *Oeuvres*, III: 371.

[24] Murphy (1997, p. 216).

actually worked. One of his assistants in the Royal Bank, Nicolas Du Tot, would later write that posterity would not actually believe that for a period the French economy operated without gold and silver.

Law's policy of substituting bank money in the form of banknotes and credit for specie was not just a technical substitution of one means of payment for another. Behind this technical substitution, Law believed that the expansion of the new money could be used to pursue macroeconomic objectives. Here, there are two important lines linking Law with modern central bankers: (1) his belief that money had a real effect on economic activity and (2) consistent with this belief, the need for monetary expansion—quantitative easing—to push the economy towards economic growth and full employment.

The debate on the role of money in the economy has featured prominently in economic discourse over the centuries. In recent decades, up to 2008, it appeared that the new classical approach that money did not matter held sway. Various aphorisms such as money does not matter, money is a veil, money is neutral, and money is super neutral dominated the macroeconomic literature. However, when the 2008 financial implosion came and financial markets froze as a result of banks' reluctance to lend to one another it quickly became apparent that money played a real role in the economy.

When the Queen of England posed the question on the failure of economists to foresee the events of 2008, the answer, as Felix Martin in *Money* reported, may have been that 'their main framework for understanding the economy didn't include money'.[25] Martin went on to add that '... by the same token, the question that many were keen to put to the bankers and their regulators—Why didn't they realise what they were doing was so risky?—also turned out to be simple. – Their framework of understanding finance did not include the macroeconomy'.[26]

The reality of 2008 for the economics profession was one of near-total unpreparedness. The near dominance of new classical macroeconomics had dismissed money off stage and presented the view that financial bubbles did not exist because transactors were blessed by rational expectations. Consistent with the belief in rational expectations were the views

[25] Martin (2013, p. 225).

[26] Ibid., pp. 225–226.

that markets could self-regulate and that official regulation was costly and unnecessary. As for money, it was believed to respond endogenously to the needs of the economy. Essentially, the prevailing view was that the monetary/financial economy would take care of itself.

This of course did not happen. The collapse of Lehman Brothers in September 2008, along with the near collapse of insurers AIG, generated a frozen monetary landscape with banks reluctant to lend not only to traditional borrowers but also to inter-lend. These events caused central bankers to change their approach. This change was initially heralded by Ben Bernanke, chairman of the US Federal Reserve System. As an academic Bernanke had studied the Friedman/Schwartz message about the Great Depression, namely that the Fed had to counter major monetary failures by an expansionary monetary policy – see Friedman and Schwartz (1963). The initial fire-fighting involved the provision of large amounts of liquidity to the financial system to help de-freeze it. This policy was followed by a systematic policy of quantitative easing with the objective of expanding the money supply and keeping interest rates low. This policy was adopted, somewhat belatedly, by the European Central Bank on the arrival of its new president, Mario Draghi. This was a sea change in policy for the ECB which, under its previous president, Jean Claude Trichet, had been unidimensional with its policy of controlling inflation while all around the financial system was in a state of near collapse.

The essential core belief of the quantitative easing approach is that money matters and that expansions in the money supply can drive economic activity. This core belief was at the heart of John Law's approach. His book, *Money and Trade with a Proposal for Supplying the Nation with Money* (1705), said it all. It expressed his belief that money drives trade and that when trade (economic activity) is depressed there is a need to ensure that the banking system adopts new approaches to increase the money supply. From this perspective, it may be argued that, notwithstanding the failure of the Mississippi System, Law's banking successors have been Ben Bernanke, Janet Yellen and Mario Draghi. As such, it may be argued that he provided intimations on the future vital role of the twenty-first-century central banker, a role that has counterbalanced the excesses and froth of many of the other bankers/banksters of the period.

Despite the collapse of the System, not everyone turned against Law. There were some notable contemporary exceptions. First and foremost, there was the Regent, Philip, Duc d'Orléans. Notwithstanding the crash of the Mississippi System, the Regent never stopped believing in Law. Indeed, once Cardinal Dubois, the Minister of Foreign Affairs and a strong enemy of Law, died in 1723, the Regent invited Law to return to France to re-introduce some variant of his System. Unfortunately, for Law, the Regent died very soon after issuing this invitation and Law was unable to return to France—the new Regent, the Duke of Bourbon, though a huge beneficiary of the System and a former friend of Law did not wish to see the Scotsman returning to France.

While in exile from France, Law did receive a strong invitation from the Czar, Peter the Great, to come to Russia to help re-structure its financial system. On 10 November 1721, Law wrote to the Czar thanking him for his invitation to come to Russia noting that as he was still in discussions with the Regent—presumably as to Law's return to France—he was not in a position to reply positively to the Czar's invitation.[27] Additionally, Count Rosemberg, President of Finances in Serbia, was keen to have Law come to establish a bank in Serbia.[28]

So there appears to have been a perception amongst certain eighteenth-century European leaders that Law was not a charlatan but rather a man of intellectual rigour who had the ability to analyse and solve financial problems. Even on his deathbed, Law continued to believe in his ideas. The French ambassador Vincent Languet de Gergy wrote of him just before Law's death in Venice in 1729:

> I have never seen a man more stubborn than him about his cursed System, and in such a way that it is probable that from the start of its operations he really believed his projects to be infallible and as a result never thought about his own affairs.[29]

Montesquieu who visited Law in Venice, a year before his death in 1728, wrote in a similar vein:

[27] Bibliothèque Méjanes, Aix-en-Provence, Ms. 614. ff.99 v and r.

[28] Ibid. Letter from Law to Rosemberg, 15 May, 1722, letter 163.

[29] Paris, AAE CP Venise 183, fos. 90–92.

> He is a specious man who can reason and who devotes all his energy in trying to turn your argument against you by finding something inconvenient in it; moreover he is more interested in his ideas than in his money.[30]

Perhaps it is best that we leave the last words to Law himself when he came to summarise his approach and the difficulties that he experienced in his attempt to revolutionise the French financial system. Addressing Count Rosemberg, in the last letter of his 1720–1722 letter book, Law wrote:

> Princes, for the most part, are badly advised and pursue false objectives. They seek to spread their domination while they should be working to make their people happy. It is a type of miracle if the honest man, who wishes to work for the public good and faces such great opposition, manages to succeed....
>
> I had a plan to restore France which had been destroyed by long wars; and even more so by a sequence of poor administration. I wanted to make this state powerful and its people happy. Beyond all hope I succeeded in this plan. I worked with an enlightened Prince who was capable of listening to me and who was well disposed. I surmounted huge difficulties both within and outside the Kingdom...
>
> The Prince was the head of a rich people, his revenues increased and the burdens on his people reduced. There were no longer uncultivated lands or workers without work. Peasants were fed and clothed and owed nothing to either King or master. Manufactures, navigation and trade increased and were valued...I am not talking here of the period when paper fell. I am talking about the time when credit was preferred and gained relative to specie.[31]

If only. Law's plan failed, but he left the blueprints with us through the *Essay on a Land Bank* and *Money and Trade*. Rather than remembering his foibles—and he had many—it is still worthwhile to observe that he believed that money had a real role to play in the economy. In today's world of quantitative easing, this may, perhaps, qualify him as a real twenty-first-century banker.

[30] Montesquieu (1950, vol. 2, p. 1007).

[31] Bibliothèque Méjanes, Aix-en-Provence, Ms. 614. Letter to M de Rosemberg, 15 May 1722, Letter 163.

References

Faure, Edgar. 1977. *La Banqueroute de Law*. Paris: Gallimard.

Friedman, Milton, and Anna Jacobson Schwartz. 1963. *A Monetary History of the United States 1867–1960*. Princeton: Princeton University Press.

Goodman, Elise, ed. 2001. *Art and Culture in the Eighteenth Century: New Dimensions*. Newark: University of Delaware Press.

Law, John. 1705. *Money and Trade Considered*. Edinburgh, the heirs and successors of A. Anderson.

———. 1934. *Oeuvres Complètes*, ed. Paul Harsin. Paris: Sirey.

———. 1994. *John Law's Essay on a Land Bank*, ed. Antoin E. Murphy. Dublin: Aeon Publishing.

Mallaby, Sebastian. 2016. *The Man Who Knew: The Life and Times of Alan Greenspan*. New York: Penguin Press.

Martin, Felix. 2013. *Money*. London: Bodley Head.

Montesquieu, Charles de Secondat. 1950. *Oeuvres Complètes de Montesquieu*, ed. André Masson. Paris: Nagel.

Murphy, Antoin. 1986. *Richard Cantillon Entrepreneur and Economist*. Oxford: Oxford University Press.

———. 1997. *John Law Economic Theorist and Policy-Maker*. Oxford: Oxford University Press.

Neal, Larry. 2012. *'I Am Not Master of Events': The Speculations of John Law and Lord Londonderry in the Mississippi and South Sea Bubbles*. New Haven: Yale University Press.

Pons, Bruno. 1986. *De Paris à Versailles 1699–1736, Les Sculpteurs ornemanistes parisiens et l'art décoratif des bâtiments du Roi*. Strasbourg: Universités de Strasbourg.

Sani, Bernardina. 1988. *Rosalba Carriera*. Turin: Umberto Allemadi.

Toutain-Quittelier, Valentine. 2017. *Le Carnaval, la Fortune et la Folie. La rencontre de Paris et Venise à l'aube des Lumières*. Rennes: Presses Universitaires de Rennes.

Velde, François. 2003. Government Equity and Money: John Law's System in 1720 France. Federal Reserve Bank of Chicago Working Paper, 2003–31.

CHAPTER 13

The Bank of Amsterdam's Search for Success and Stability

Stephen Quinn and William Roberds

1 Introduction

Monetary and financial markets are built on safe assets. These are assets that markets accept as is and trade at a stable value (Gorton 2017). Put differently, individuals do not use superior knowledge of these assets to take advantage of others. In contrast, the valuation of other types of financial assets very much relies on information, and the investment industry puts considerable effort into producing private information. So the equilibrium of mutual confidence in symmetrical ignorance that defines a safe asset liberates people to use them as media of exchange, as

Views expressed are those of the authors and not those of the Federal Reserve Bank of Atlanta or the Federal Reserve System. The authors are grateful to Lilia Costabile, Larry Neal, and participants in the Banco di Napoli's conference The Rise of Modern Banking in Naples.

S. Quinn (✉)
Texas Christian University, Fort Worth, TX, USA

W. Roberds
Federal Reserve Bank of Atlanta, Atlanta, GA, USA

L. Costabile and L. Neal (eds.), *Financial Innovation and Resilience*, Palgrave Studies in the History of Finance,
https://doi.org/10.1007/978-3-319-90248-7_13

stores of value, as collateral for loans and as means of settling obligations. In the Early Modern era, an important example was the Spanish dollar coin. Spanish coins travelled from Peru and Mexico to Europe and Asia with everyone accepting them as presented.

Creating and maintaining this status is no simple thing. The Spanish empire, continuing the example, learned from hard lessons to maintain mint standards. After the reforms of Isaac Newton (1696–1717), the English also offered to produce high-quality silver coins, but England did not control silver mines as Spain did. Instead England, like most European mints, had to attract the silver. Newton, however, set the price of the pound sterling higher in gold than in silver, so London's reliable mint attracted little of the world's silver. In a different twist, numerous other states debased coins to exploit perceptions of coin safety. Taken together, the production of coins in Europe before 1800 was a mixed bag of a few successes, many failures and intermittent abuses.

To escape the confusion created by multiple coinages with different metals, the financial systems of Europe attempted to create safe assets based on paper. These included trade fairs, bills of exchange and deposit banks. A successful paper asset could mimic the liquidity of coins but at lower costs. The challenges, however, remained of how to get people to accept paper debt without extensive examination. Merchants learned to use endorsement on bills of exchange (Santarosa 2015). Banks, such as the eight public banks of Naples, learned to use coin reserves (Balletta et al. 2018). Most successes struck a balance: paper substituted for coin in payments yet relied on coin as a backing asset (Roberds and Velde 2016b). When these innovations were successful, trade grew, markets deepened and networks expanded (Neal 1991; Gelderblom 2013). Only slowly and in pockets did systems like Naples' public banks (Costabile and Nappi 2018), Genoa's Banco di San Giorgio or England's Treasury (Coffman 2018) learn to use government debt as a backing asset. When financial innovations were unsuccessful, development languished. When the equilibrium collapsed, panic followed. Taken together, efforts to substitute paper for coin was another collection of successes, failures and abuses.

2 The Bank of Amsterdam

In the midst of this era, the Bank of Amsterdam (the Bank) began in 1609 as yet another effort to substitute paper for coins. In this case, ledger balances replaced coins as the means of payment in Amsterdam's bill market. The Bank offered a traditional arrangement: deposited coins created account balances with a right of withdrawal, but the Bank controlled which coins it handed back. If merchants put Spanish dollars into the Bank, then they would receive some combination of Dutch coins at withdrawal. The arrangement was successful enough to survive several decades, but few outside the bill market preferred bank accounts to coins (Quinn and Roberds 2014).

That changed when the Bank reformulated its process of safe asset production. The Bank invented a process similar to modern repurchase agreements that increased customer control over coins. The Bank did this by unbundling the control of coins from the control of bank money. Starting in 1683, when people brought coin to the Bank, they received account balances and a separate receipt for the coins. The customer controlled the new balances in the Bank and could use them to settle debts and make large-value payments. Accounts, however, no longer imposed an obligation on the Bank to convert them into coin. Accounts became a type of fiat money. Instead, the power to compel the Bank to convert accounts into coin resided in the receipt. The receipt controlled who got to reclaim the coins and when. As a result, when merchants put Spanish dollars into the Bank and received receipts, they retained control over the ultimate dispersion of the Spanish coins. The merchants also had full use of the bank's ledger money credited to them while the coins remained unclaimed. The new product was very popular in both bullion and bill markets.

For the next century, the Bank of Amsterdam's challenge was how to sustain this new process. The system required large flows of coins into and out of the Bank. The system also required that bank money have a stable value. The Bank sought to calm both the amount and the value of bank money despite the volatility of deposits and withdrawals.

The Bank's solution was to manipulate its assets that were not encumbered by a receipt. For example, when the Bank purchased coins in the open market, it paid the seller in newly created bank money. The seller did not receive a receipt. The Bank owned the coins outright. Later, if a merchant deposited Spanish silver under receipt, the Bank could sterilize that inflow by selling some of the coins the Bank had purchased earlier. In this way, the Bank altered the amount of bank money without altering the Spanish coin that customers controlled.

This chapter argues that the system worked remarkably well for decades. People considered bank money perhaps the safest asset in Europe. "Europe's merchants and bankers chose the bank guilder as their currency of choice almost as a matter of course" (Gillard 2009, 108).

Yet, customers moved large volumes of coin into and out of the Bank. To offset these swings in market pressures, the Bank used open market operations. The Bank used vigorous yet reactionary monetary policy to stabilize the amount of bank money and to stabilize the value of bank money.

The regime proved vulnerable to at least two kinds of shocks. At the end of the Seven Years War (1756–1763), people deposited more coin than the Bank could sterilize. The Bank lost control until demand returned to normal. In contrast, at the end of the Fourth Anglo-Dutch War (1780–1784), customers abandoned the Bank. The collapse of the Dutch East India Company caused people to fear for the company's creditors, and the Bank of Amsterdam was one of the largest. Bank money suddenly became an "unsafe" asset, and people withdrew their coins. The Bank was never able to recover its status.

3 Bank Money, 1609–1683

The Bank of Amsterdam was a public bank owned and operated by the City of Amsterdam from 1609 to 1820 ('t Hart 2009). It was centrally located on the first floor of city hall on Dam Square. The Bank's money was in the form of accounts on the Bank's ledgers. People transferred balances to make payments, and the Bank used a comprehensive system of double entry to record each payment as one account's credit and another's offsetting debit. Such payments were giro in that they occurred within the Bank's ledgers and were initiated by the payer.

The Bank measured accounts in florins/guilders. The terms were interchangeable, and, until the adoption of the euro, *fl* was the abbreviation for the guilder. Adding to the confusion, when the Bank was founded there existed a *florijn* coin worth 1.4 florins, and it was not until 1680 that Holland introduced a *gulden* coin (Polak 1998, 76–78). It was worth one guilder. The Dutch also distinguished between accounts at the Bank and accounts outside the Bank. Inside was "bank" money and outside was "current" money. And the Dutch sometimes used the Flemish system of pounds and shillings. For example, the London-Amsterdam exchange rate was measured in bank shillings per pound sterling. Because 20 shillings equalled one Flemish pound, and one Flemish pound equalled six florins, a bill of 200 bank shillings became 60 florins at the Bank. To promote clarity, this chapter reports all monetary units in the florin system, translates units of account into

English, leaves coin names in Dutch, labels accounts inside the Bank as bank florins and measures outside accounts in current guilders.

The primary purpose of bank florins was to settle bills of exchange. When a bill was due in Amsterdam, the city required the debtor to pay the creditor with the Bank's money. By the 1700s, only bills under 300 bank florin or bills wherein both parties agreed to settle outside the Bank were exempt. The transfer of Bank money both paid the bill with finality and recorded its retirement. Settlement mattered because bills of exchange were the era's dominant form of international credit. Traditionally, bills were drawn as an advance on merchandise in transit. Collateral, however, was not explicitly stated on a bill, so bills were also instruments of unsecured short-term borrowing. Rolling over maturing bills with new bills extended the length of funding. Bill brokers deepened the market, and, at the apex of intermediation, merchant banks specialized in both drawing and discounting bills. Similar to the way modern match-book dealers use repurchase agreements as both liabilities and assets, the merchant banks of Amsterdam gained a spread by selling bills at a lower rate to fund the purchase of bills at a higher rate (Kirk et al. 2014). Bank money was the instrument used to settle all this business, so it was a valued asset in Amsterdam and in cities doing business with Amsterdam. That list came to include most every mercantile city in Europe. Dehing (2012, 364) finds that by 1650 the number of cities with regular bill business with Amsterdam (measured as quotations in the financial press) had caught up with Europe's leaders, Venice and Antwerp. By this measure, Amsterdam was the dominant bill market after 1650 until at least 1750 (Dehing 2012, 364). The success of the Bank of Amsterdam in supplying stable money contributed to the centralization of the international bill business in the city.

At its founding in 1609, however, the success of bank money was not assured. The initial vision was for the stability of bank money to follow from its convertibility into high-quality silver coins. This followed the design of the Banco di Rialto in Venice (Van Dillen 1934, 79–80). The city obliged the Bank of Amsterdam to create accounts in exchange for coins of large-denomination and high-fineness (called trade coins). At withdrawal, customers surrendered accounts and received back trade coins. Also, the Bank was not to lend, so bank money would be fully backed by trade coins.

In the early decades of the Bank, these mechanisms were compromised. Debasement meant that the Bank of Amsterdam could not maintain the quality of coins. Also, the Bank lent funds. By 1629, loans had grown to over half of the Bank's balance sheet (Van Dillen 1925, 715–716). But then policy changes reversed the situation. In the 1630s, the city learned to constrain bank lending (Uittenbogaard 2009). Then, in 1659, the Republic set and successfully maintained a new coinage standard so that the Dutch guilder became a reliable unit of silver (Dehing and 't Hart 1977, 41). The new discipline regarding lending and minting stabilized the Bank's liabilities by assuring the quality of backing assets.

A credible balance sheet, however, did not cause bank money to flourish. The Bank of Amsterdam had limited appeal beyond the people required to use its money to settle bills of exchange. The root problem was that the Bank offered little incentive to deposit coins at the Bank. First, people other than wholesale merchants with large payments to make were not obliged to put coin into the Bank. That was in keeping with the Dutch Republic's particularly accommodating policies regarding precious metal. The Dutch Republic did not restrict the free flow of gold and silver nor did it exclude foreign coins from use in domestic payments. It even assigned some foreign coin values in local payments. This environment encouraged the international silver and gold markets to locate in Amsterdam, but left it to the Bank to find ways to entice the metal into its vaults.

Second, the benefits of deposit were unclear for those who were not bill debtors. For example, at withdrawal, the Bank chose which type of coin it would disperse from a set of Dutch trade coins. This policy meant that the Bank had the incentive to deliver out coins with the most current guilders per mark (a unit of weight) of metal. That ratio is called the mint equivalent, and the higher its value, the less metal there is per guilder, making those coins overvalued relative to coins with lower ratios. For example, in 1620 *rijksdaalder* coins had a mint equivalent of 23.9 current guilders per mark and *leeuwendaalder* coins had a mint equivalent of 23.7 (Polak 1998, 70–71). The depositor of low mint equivalent coins (i.e. *leeuwendaalder*) would expect a small loss in quality at withdrawal as the Bank would disperse overvalued *rijksdaalder* coins instead of the originals. Alternatively, someone could negotiate with the Bank to withdraw a low mint equivalent coin, but the Bank would charge a fee if it agreed. Table 1 organizes the categories of silver mentioned in this chapter and how the Bank of Amsterdam handled each form by era.

Table 1 How the bank handled silver

	Before 1683	*After 1683*
Domestic trade coins e.g. *rijksdaalders* and *leeuwendaalders*	Deposit and withdrawal	Receipt
Foreign trade coins e.g. Spanish dollars	Deposit and sale	Receipt
Other forms e.g. *gulden* coins and ingots	Purchase and sale	Purchase and sale

Another asymmetry was that the Bank accepted at deposit a larger set of coins than it was obliged to relinquish at withdrawal. The larger set reflected the variety of foreign coins the Dutch Republic recognized as valid means of payment. If Dutch ordinances said you could pay debts with Spanish dollars, then the Bank accepted that coin. Again, if Spanish coins had a higher mint equivalent than Dutch coins, then each deposit-withdrawal cycle would allow some customers to gain silver at the Bank's expense by demanding Dutch coins with lower mint equivalents. Moreover, the Bank would have to pay a local mint to convert foreign coins into Dutch coins. To prevent this process, the Bank charged all withdrawals a base fee. The Bank could vary this base fee, and the fee for the withdrawal of low mint equivalent coins (above) was added to this base fee if applicable. As a result, withdrawals typically paid fees in the range of 1.5 to 2.5 per cent. The fees discouraged deposits because (1) they applied regardless of what type of coin was deposited and (2) regardless of when the deposit occurred. The shorter the expected time before withdrawal of the deposit, the higher the annualized rate created by the fees. For example, a six-month deposit might pay 4 per cent per annum. The system made the Bank an expensive place for people to "park" gold and silver.

Fees also discouraged deposits by creating space for a substitute process. Instead of bringing coin to the bank, a debtor could buy the needed bank money from an existing account holder. The seller of bank money would transfer the balances inside the Bank while the buyer would give coin outside the Bank. Because this swap avoided withdrawal fees, the seller of bank money shared a portion of the savings to attract a buyer. This inducement, measured as a per cent, was called the agio, and it was calculated as the ratio of the value of coins paid outside the Bank over the value of balances transferred inside the Bank: $Agio = \left(\frac{\text{Value of coins given outside the Bank}}{\text{Value of balances transferred inside the Bank}} - 1\right) * 100$. The ubiquity of such trades led to a daily agio market with brokers and dealers. Amsterdam's financial press regularly published agio prices, and dealer spreads were typically 1/8 per cent or less.

The Bank might have ameliorated these disincentives by paying interest on deposits, but it never did. Conceptually, an exchange bank did not lend, so the initial design did not expect interest income with which to pay depositors. Later, when the Bank lent anyway, the interest revenue was surrendered to the city as a form of seigniorage. Even when not lending, profits from fees were paid to the city. The Bank was a reliable revenue source (Dehing and 't Hart 1997, 50). Finally, paying interest on deposits would have undermined the goal of the fees: to prevent people from using the Bank for inter-coin arbitrage.

By the 1660s and 1670s, the combination of an expensive primary market for bank money and a cheap secondary market for the same meant that people who needed to pay a bill of exchange often bought the necessary bank money on the agio market. People with coin seemed to have largely kept it out of the Bank. As a result, withdrawal rates regularly exceeded deposit rates. Figure 1 shows that as negative cumulative net deposits starting in February 1666. To make up the incremental shortfall of inflows, the Bank occasionally engaged in large-scale open market purchases. Figure 1 shows that as the positive accumulation of purchases beginning in 1666. These operations restored the volume of bank money but left unchanged the dynamic of decline. To be clear, the Bank was not a failure. Bills of exchange were routinely settled. The Bank even withstood a severe run at the start of the Third Anglo-Dutch War in 1672. Dehing (2012, 163) finds that the use of bank money, measured as the volume of giro payments per year, averaged 180 million bank florins from 1654 to 1686. The Bank, however, was not a money much favoured for purposes other than the settlement of bills of exchange due in Amsterdam.

Yet another form of potential arbitrage was between gold and silver. The Dutch Republic recognized coins in both metals as legal money. A bimetallic system is particularly complicated because the relative mint equivalents of the two types of coins are a function of the gold-to-silver price ratio set by bullion markets. If the price of gold is low relative to silver, then people will want to deposit gold and withdraw silver. If the

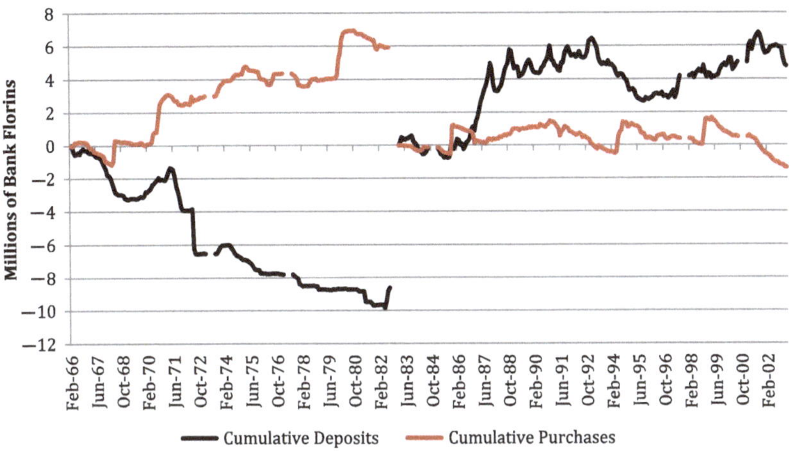

Fig. 1 Deposits and purchases before and after 1683

Bank responds by handing out gold, then people who deposited silver feel cheated because they now receive a less valuable metal. This problem affected the entirety of the Dutch economy. The wider solution in the Dutch Republic was to set official coin prices in favour of silver and then let the market set a price for gold coins above the official rate. The Bank adopted this structure, but without the higher floating price for gold. As a result, gold was a minor part of the Bank's balance sheet except in moments when the price of gold was remarkably low.

4 The Transformation, 1683

The extraordinary era of the Bank of Amsterdam begins with a change in approach. In 1683, the city authorized the Bank to return the same types of coins that someone had deposited. This new process would stop people from using Bank accounts to arbitrage between types of coin because customers got back what they put in. In turn, the Bank would no longer have to use fees to prevent arbitrage. The key innovation, however, was in implementation. Around 1600, the Casa di San Giorgio in Genoa created separate account systems for each type of coin (Roberds and Velde 2016a, b). This prevented arbitrage, but it also fractured ledger money by types of coin. The Bank of Amsterdam avoided this loss of standardization by instead unbundling accounts from coin. It did this by recording the type of coin deposited on a separate piece of paper called a receipt that was retained by the depositor (Mees 1838, 95–110). At withdrawal, a depositor surrendered both the receipt and the bank money to regain that type of coin. In the meantime, the customer could spend the Bank money. The customer just had to re-acquire the funds by the time of withdrawal. Bank money remained fungible but the type of coin was not. Accounts recorded value while receipts recorded the specific type of collateral.

A consequence was that the Bank greatly reduced fees. The new withdrawal fees were ¼ per cent fee for most silver coins. Gold coins paid a ½ per cent fee. The fee was paid when someone surrendered a receipt and sufficient bank money to repurchase the coin. This had to happen within six months or else the receipt became invalid and the coin became owned outright by the Bank. For example, on 25 February 1737, Jan Albert Vos brought 800 silver *rijksdaalder* coins to the Bank. His account was credited for 1,920 bank florins. He was given a receipt that optioned the repurchase of 800 *rijksdaalder* coins within 6 months at the cost of 1,920 bank florin plus a ¼ per cent fee of 4.8 bank florins. Alternatively, he could pay just the fee to extend the receipt for another half year. That would mean paying 4.8 bank florins to renew the receipt to February 1738. For Mr. Vos, parking coin at the Bank of Amsterdam cost a ½ per cent annual rate. The receipt also brought certainty regarding the type of coin awaiting repossession.

During the half year following his deposit, Mr. Vos could use the 1,920 bank florins to pay bills, invest, purchase commodities, etc. For those payments, it mattered not how Mr. Vos acquired the bank money. The coins only came back into consideration when someone wanted to use or roll over the receipt. Retaining standardization of accounts also meant that when the Bank of Amsterdam engaged in loans or open market purchases, the bank money created was the same as all the existing bank money.

Finally, the receipt was transferable. If someone wanted *rijksdaalder* coins, they could buy the receipt from Jan Albert Vos for a price typically around one to 2 per cent of the principal (≈20–40 bank florins). In this way, bank money travelled different routes and created different markets than did claims on coins. As Adam Smith summarized, "The receipt and the bank credit seldom keep long together, and there is no occasion that they should (Smith 1981 [1776], 483)".

For all these reasons, the new policy increased the popularity of putting coin into the Bank. To see the change in behaviour, return to Fig. 1. After 1683, deposits exceeded withdrawals, so the cumulative net deposits became positive. As a result, the Bank no longer had to offset withdrawals with purchases. After 1683, the cumulative purchases line fluctuated close to zero.

The new customers were not bill debtors obliged to use the Bank. Instead, the new funds were free to pursue investment opportunities. Receipts expanded the supply of loanable funds, and indicators point to a contemporaneous increase in the quantity of loans in Amsterdam. For example, Dehing (2012, 163) finds that giro payments within the Bank increased by 50 per cent from 1686 to 1706. The situation also suggests a reinforcing process: both borrowers and lenders increasingly favoured the Amsterdam market because it was growing and deepening. In this way, the bank money became the dominant international currency: what Gillard (2004) calls the European florin.

Receipts were the catalyst because they changed the relationship between bank accounts and coins. Before receipts, bank money was a somewhat imperfect substitute for coin because balances had no certain path back to the type of coins deposited. In contrast, a receipt was an explicit and fixed path back, so a depositor relinquished possession of the coin but not eventual use of the coin (Van Dillen 1934, 102). Bank money now acted as a complement to coin in that a depositor could be considered as having both the Bank balance and the coin.

To see this by analogy, consider the modern repurchase agreement (repo): two parties agree that Person A will sell government bonds to Person B and tomorrow B will repurchase the bonds from A at a slightly higher price. Strictly speaking, the agreement is a sale and repurchase wherein A gives up possession of the bonds. In accounting terms, the asset side of Person A's balance sheet should add the money and subtract the bonds. In practice, however, the agreement sets a clear path back to repossession of the bonds, so people consider themselves in control of both the bonds and the money. Modern accounting standards recognize this perspective. In repo accounting, Person A's balance sheet records: (1) the government bonds as an asset, (2) the money as an asset and (3) the repurchase agreement as a liability. By treating the agreement as a loan, financial accounting confirms that Person A gets both the money and the bonds. The result is powerful. Modern brokers and dealers use this perspective to maintain a book of securities and simultaneously use those securities as collateral to fund operations.

Bank of Amsterdam depositors made this change in perspective after 1683. Conceptually, customers borrowed bank money instead of lent coins. The effect in Amsterdam was also powerful. Merchant bankers could simultaneously hold a position in the silver market and hold balances at the Bank. The cost was to owe the Bank of Amsterdam at ½ per cent per year. More, the Bank offered this through an open facility. The Bank did not change the amount of bank money it paid for each coin, it did not limit the amount of coins that could be presented and it did not adjust the rate it charged. Customers knew that they could rollover this funding at constant terms for as long and for as much as they wanted.

For the Bank of Amsterdam, how receipts increased the amount of bank money was different than traditional methods. For example, when the Bank created money through unsecured loans, the credibility of the Bank suffered. The early Bank had trouble with excessive lending in the 1630s, and the mature Bank had loan troubles in the 1780s. Receipts avoided this credibility problem because the coin was collateral in possession (if not control) of the Bank.

Alternatively, the Bank could create money by purchasing silver on the open market. As with quantitative easing today, large purchases would remove silver from the Amsterdam market. Altering the balance between silver and bank money would increase the price of silver relative to bank money. That made the operation increasingly expensive with scale, and it undermined the value of bank money. At some point, the agio (the value ratio of outside coins to inside balances) would fall low enough to encourage people to withdraw coin and undo the Bank's effort to increase the overall level of bank money. Receipts avoided this problem because depositors still thought of themselves as controlling the silver. The Amsterdam bullion market did not perceive silver parked under receipt as having left the market. It was just warehoused at the Bank instead of in someone's strong room, and the negotiability of receipts made it easy to sell control of metal without it leaving the Bank. Receipts made coins and accounts complements.

It is less clear, however, that receipts increased the stability of the amount of bank money. The low fees attracted deposits in part because it was now inexpensive to remove the coin. What came in quickly could leave quickly. Moreover, account holders could still pay the higher fees to withdraw from the traditional set of coins. If receipts ran out or were priced too high, people might exercise the old conversion rights embedded in their accounts. For example, in a crisis like 1672, the Bank of Amsterdam could suffer a run, and, if demand for redemption exceeded the supply of receipts, the Bank might fail.

Perhaps with this in mind, the Bank took advantage of the popularity of the new facility to quietly discontinue the old facility. By 1685, without any extant authorization from the city, the Bank made receipts the only way to reclaim coin from the Bank (Van Dillen 1934, 101). Put differently, the Bank suspended the old withdrawal rights inherent to each balance. Given (1) that the Bank's directors were experienced city leaders and (2) the number of firms engaged in the routine deposit and withdrawal of coin was at most a few dozen, the prominent stakeholders seem likely to have known of the change in policy. The lack of outcry suggests acquiescence.

From the city's perspective, the suspension stabilized bank money in extreme circumstances. Now, a run on the Bank could only extend to the stock of coins held under receipts. This was a maximum amount that the volume of bank money could suddenly shrink. Account holders could not drive the Bank into illiquidity. The suspension also freed the Bank's management of metal it owned outright, i.e., silver and gold not under a receipt obligation. For example, the bank no longer had to convert metal into Dutch trade coins. This was helpful because the domestic Dutch economy was transitioning to the silver *gulden* coin. The Bank might yet again switch standards and adopt the new coin. Or, the Bank might have reminted *gulden* coins, at some expense, into old-fashioned trade coins. With suspension, however, the Bank could choose to buy and sell *gulden* coins, but customers could not oblige the Bank to accept or remint them.

Instead, the Bank learned to use *gulden* coins to manage the amount and value of bank money. When the Bank bought and sold *gulden* coins, the price was negotiated and no receipt was created. These open market operations altered the amount of bank money in existence, the amount of *gulden* coins in circulation and the market's agio rate to exchange bank money for what came to be called current money.

Furthermore, the suspension policy gave the Bank wide latitude regarding how large or small a stock of *gulden* coins it wanted to hold.

Again, coins held under receipt were scrupulously warehoused, but the coins owned outright by the Bank were no longer required to cover traditional withdrawals. As a result, the Bank could, and occasionally did, sell off its entire stock of metallic reserves. Suspension both freed the Bank from precautionary reserves and created a convenient instrument to manage the quantity of bank money.

But why did the Bank's customers seemingly go along with the suspension of inherent withdrawal rights? A partial answer is that the suspension had no immediate effect on daily transactions. The routine conversion of coins and bank money now used the receipt (primary) market or the agio (secondary) market. Customers would only miss traditional withdrawal rights in a crisis, so the issue turns on expectations. With receipts, a liquidity crisis would channel demand for coin through rising receipt prices, and a small group of brokers and dealers held most of the receipts. Perhaps the concentrated benefits for insiders trumped the diffuse loss to account holders. Also, knowing that customers could not force the Bank into closure reduced the powerful first-come-first-served incentive that energizes a bank run; so perhaps individual claims were surrendered for a collective benefit. Or perhaps people were misguided. Smith, for one, thought the Bank would reinstate traditional withdrawal should a crisis consume all receipts (Smith 1981 [1776], 485). When such a crisis did arrive in 1782, the Bank did not return to general convertibility.

This system contrasts with the Anglo-American tradition of suspension. In 1797, for example, Bank of England deposits were convertible into coin until pressure forced the suspension. That suspension lasted 24 years. In contrast, the Bank of Amsterdam never suspended convertibility via receipts because it had already suspended the convertibility of accounts. In London, people sorted out who would convert paper into a limited amount of coin by queuing until the door was closed. In Amsterdam, people traded receipts until the limited amount of access was depleted. In this way, Bank of Amsterdam accounts became a kind of fiat money in that the balances had no inherent conversion rights. Receipts were tradable conversion rights, but receipts were not money. Receipts were an options contract. By disentangling ledger money from its convertibility, the Bank of Amsterdam transformed its money from a substitute to coin to a complement.

5 Stability, 1683–1783

For a century after 1683, the Bank of Amsterdam became the focus of Europe's bullion market (via receipts) and Europe's bill market (via balances). The vitality, however, created potential instability. The amount of bank money created by receipts changed easily. Similarly, the price of bank money now had wide potential variance because comprehensive conversion rights no longer anchored the value of bank money. In this environment of quasi-fiat money, the Bank of Amsterdam learned to sterilize receipt flows to maintain the overall quantity of bank money. These open market operations also helped maintain the value of bank money relative to the current money (*gulden* coins) circulating in the wider Dutch economy. For decades, the Bank of Amsterdam successfully managed the potential volatility of its Bank money.

To see the variation in market funding, Fig. 2 plots the amount of bank money backed by receipt deposits each year from 1736 to 1791 along the horizontal axis. The level ranges from less than 1 million to almost 31 million. The average level of total bank money over this sample was 19 million, so the swings in market funding were substantial. To offset these flows, the Bank purchased or sold coins it owned outright, usually *gulden* coins. To a lesser extent, the Bank also adjusted how much it lent to the Dutch East India Company. Figure 2 plots the

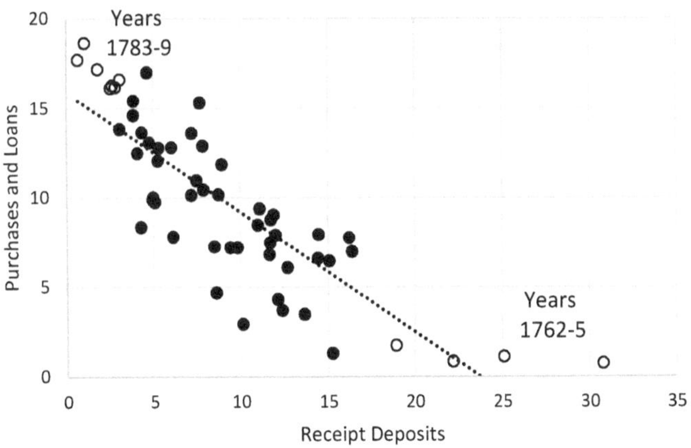

Fig. 2 Bank money by backing asset, annually from 1736 to 1791, in millions of bank Florins

amount of bank money created through the combination of open market purchases and lending on the vertical axis. This series ranges from near zero to 19 million.

Because balances were the Bank's only liabilities, the sum of an observation's vertical and horizontal value is the total amount of bank money at that time. To make the equivalence precise, the purchases and loans series deduct the slight amount of Bank equity. A correlation of -1 would mean the Bank, on average, fully maintained the total amount of bank money as the level of receipt deposits changed. In practice, the Bank managed a correlation coefficient of −0.84 (drawn as a fitted line in Fig. 2). For most years, the Bank was successful at maintaining the overall level of bank money.

The other measure of the Bank's success was stability in the market agio, the price of bank money in terms of current *gulden* coins. Again, instead of moving coin into or out of the Bank, the agio market moved coin outside the bank to offset a movement of balances inside the Bank. In the 1700s, the agio was between 4 and 5 per cent because Dutch trade coins had a current money price reflecting their price in *gulden* coins and their price in bank money. Those differed because the Bank kept using the old values for old types of coins. One effect was to highlight the difference between bank money and current money. Not only were they different ways to pay (coins versus paper), but also they were also different units of account (bank florin versus current guilder). The ratios were 1.042 for the silver *rijksdaalder* and 1.05 for the silver *dukaat* (Polak 1998, 73–74). The trade coins were rarely used for domestic payments, but one could buy them with current *gulden* coins and then deposit them at the Bank, so the ratios acted as an anchor.

Figure 3 plots the agio in Amsterdam by month from 1711 through 1792. For decades in the 1700s, the market agio stayed between 4 and 5 per cent or quickly returned to it. People could purchase bank money with silver *gulden* coins and expect to later purchase *gulden* coins with little change in price. Also, the agio was public and well known. It was reported in the financial press and circulated around the ports of Europe. In contrast, the amount of bank money was private information known only to the Bank. When the Bank purchased or sold current coins, the effect was to pressure the agio. Bank purchases of current money pushed down the agio. Sales pushed it up. The result was agio stability.

The agio was so stable that authors have asserted that the Bank had a facility to create an explicit ceiling and floor. For example, "the bank

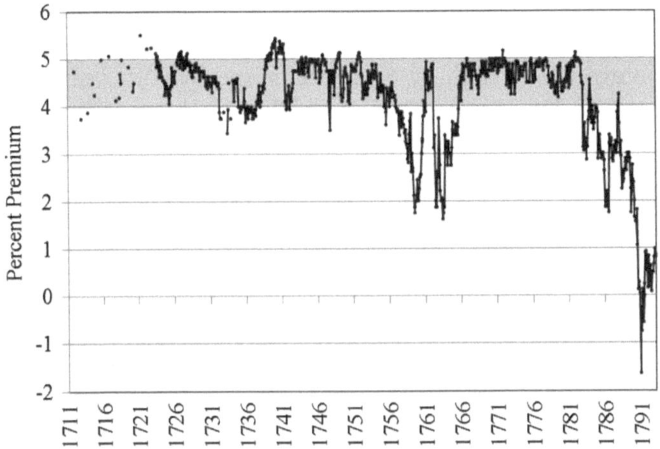

Fig. 3 The agio. *Sources* Gillard (2004) and Schneider et al. (1991)

has of late years come to the resolution to sell at all times bank money for currency, at 5 per cent agio, and to buy it in again at 4 per cent agio (Smith 1981 [1776], 486)". Or, "For many years they bought in bank money when the agio fell to 4 ¼ per cent and sold whenever it rose to 4 7/8 per cent (Van Dillen 1934, 102)". No evidence of such a mechanism appears in the Bank's accounts. Instead, the Bank would suddenly begin to buy or sell in large increments from select counterparties over the course of months. Purchase and sale prices varied. No statement has been found regarding who authorized or dictated the terms of the operations. Such operations were responsive to the agio, but they were even more responsive to the quantity of bank money (Quinn and Roberds 2017). It remains unclear if the Bank's goal was a steady quantity, a steady price or some blend. What is clear, however, is that the Bank's adjustments to the free flow of receipts resulted in decades of stability.

6 Instability

It is also clear from the series in Fig. 3 that the agio fell well below 4 per cent for two extended periods. The first era was a double dip during and just after the Seven Years War (1756–1763). The second and more serious era was after the Fourth Anglo-Dutch War (1780–1784).

Importantly, both periods of price instability correspond with extremes in the amount of receipt funding at the Bank. Returning to Fig. 2, consider the two sets of outliers. From the perspective of receipts (the horizontal axis in Fig. 2), the extreme high-end observations are for the years 1762 through 1765. The extreme low-end observations are from the years 1783 through 1789. In short, extreme agios correspond with extreme receipt behaviour. The surprise, however, is that both very low and very high receipt levels corresponded with low agios. The difference seems to be whether the shock stressed the complementarity or the substitutability of coins and bank money.

During the Seven Years War, trade coins accumulated in the Bank of Amsterdam. Perhaps coins were fleeing combatant nations. Perhaps coins were attracted to the market by silver's strong price. The result was that the rush to put trade coins under receipt simultaneously acted as a surge in the supply of bank money. The price of bank money, the agio, was suppressed below 4 per cent from 1757 to 1760. See the first major dip in Fig. 3. The supply of trade coins also helped inflate a credit bubble in the bill market (De Jong-Keesing 1939).

At the end of the war, however, causation switched direction. A sudden demand for bank money pulled trade coins into the Bank because in August 1763 the failure of the merchant bank Gebroeders de Neufville popped the credit bubble. Debtors desperately needed bank money to pay bills, but no one was lending (Schnabel and Shin 2004). To gain balances, people deposited ever more trade coins, and the total volume of bank money reached an all-time high of 31.5 million in January 1764 (Quinn and Roberds 2015). This flood of deposited silver overwhelmed the Bank's ability to sterilize it. The Bank could only sell coins it owned outright, and it simply ran out of those coins to sell. That is why the 1762–1765 outliers in Fig. 2 approach the vertical axis of purchases and loans equal to zero.

But why did such demand for bank money not drive up the agio? The answer seems to be that the demand for money outside the Bank was even greater. The Crisis of 1763 ruined many of the proto-bankers dealing in current money in the domestic economy (De Jong-Keesing 1939). Payments outside the Bank shifted to *gulden* coins, but the supply was limited. Mint production of *gulden* coins surged from 1763 through 1765 (Polak 1998, 105–63). Only when coin production caught up with demand did the agio strengthen back to 4 per cent. See the second major dip at mid-century in Fig. 3.

The Seven Year's War and the subsequent crisis demonstrate how the Bank's stabilization policy was vulnerable to extreme shocks to coins. To maintain the agio, the Bank would have needed to sell substantially larger holdings of owned coins. To already have those coins would have required the Bank to increase the total amount of bank money at some earlier date. The Bank had no easy remedy if markets wanted to create more money than the long-term level of around 20 million florins.

If the 1760s saw an excess of market funding via receipts, then the 1780s saw a collapse in the same. In 1782, the Dutch Republic was losing a war with Britain, and the Dutch East India Company was losing its holdings in Asia. The Dutch East India Company fell into default, and the Bank of Amsterdam was a major creditor. The Bank's balance sheet collapsed into insolvency (Quinn and Roberds 2016). Customers responded to the compromised Bank by withdrawing what they could. People redeemed nearly every receipt and stopped bringing in new coin. The Bank honoured all receipts, but people must have feared someday soon it might not. The outcome was the outlier years to the upper left in Fig. 2. The Bank used loans and purchases to maintain the total amount of bank money, but nearly all of it was now fiat money that could not be redeemed for coin.

After the run, the agio market responded with a long process of marking down the value of bank money. See the last, great decline in Fig. 3. The Bank lost its hold on the nexus of coins and credit. Much of the bullion and bill markets migrated to London (Carlos and Neal 2011). By the time the French invaded in 1795, the Bank had only 2.5 million florins in coin of any kind. Finally, the Bank's remnant was dissolved in 1820 as De Nederlandsche Bank, founded in 1814, had superseded its role.

7 Conclusion

The long arc of the Bank of Amsterdam can be summarized as a monetary experiment. The Bank began with the City of Amsterdam following the example of Venice. Then, after learning to control lending and debasement, the Dutch bank settled into an unglamorous stagnation. It functioned satisfactorily for those obliged to use it, but bank money was an unpopular substitute for trade coins. Then, the receipt system of 1683 and the suspension of traditional convertibility transformed Bank money into a vibrant unit of account and medium of exchange.

Popularity brought potential instability, but the Bank learned to use open market operations to sterilize changes in market funding. People could not see the steady amount of bank money in Fig. 2, but everyone knew that the agio traded between 4 and 5 per cent for decades in Fig. 3. Even when the agio weakened during the Seven Years War, people knew that the Bank was more in demand than ever. It was not until calamity undid the Dutch empire in Asia that both the bullion market and the bill of exchange market abandoned the Bank.

What replaced exchange banks like the Bank of Amsterdam were public banks that issued bank notes backed by government debt (Roberds and Velde 2016b). An early example was the public banks of Naples whose *fedi de credito* were increasingly backed by government debt (Costabile and Nappi 2018). The canonical example was the Bank of England. The Dutch example was De Nederlandsche Bank. Over time, government debt replaced coin as the underlying safe asset, and bank notes displaced trade coins in large-value payments. In the form of the modern fiat system, the combination completely displaced trade coins.

Looking back, the Bank of Amsterdam appears to have experimented with a financial innovation that led to an evolutionary dead end. Yet since the start of the fiat money era in the 1970s, central banks have been shifting their monetary liabilities back towards accounts. The recent, worldwide experiments in quantitative easing all focused on creating central bank reserves through open market purchases of various long-term securities, typically sovereign debt. Moreover, modern central banks rely on repurchase agreements for the short-term stabilization of policy rates. While repo and receipts are not the same, they both allow counterparties to control their bank money and the safe assets that act as collateral. Perhaps the Bank of Amsterdam was just centuries ahead of its time.

References

Balletta, Francesco, Luigi Ballettta, and Eduardo Nappi. 2018. The Investments of the Neapolitan Public Banks: A Long Run View (1587–1806). In *Financial Innovation and Resiliency*, ed. L. Costabile and L. Neal. Cham: Palgrave Macmillan.

Carlos, A.M., and L. Neal. 2011. Amsterdam and London as Financial Centers in the Eighteenth Century. *Financial History Review* 18 (1): 21–46.

Costabile, Lilia, and Eduardo Nappi. 2018. The Public Banks of Naples Between Financial Innovation and Crisis. In *Financial Innovation and Resiliency*, ed. L. Costabile and L. Neal. Cham: Palgrave Macmillan.

Coffman, D'Maris. 2018. Experimenting with Paper Money during the English Civil Wars and the Interregnum. In *Financial Innovation and Resiliency*, ed. L. Costabile and L. Neal. Cham: Palgrave Macmillan.

Dehing, P. 2012. *Geld in Amsterdam: Wisselbank en wisselkoersen, 1650–1725*. Hilversum: Uitgeverij Verloren.

Dehing, P., and M. t'Hart. 1997. Linking the Fortunes, Currency and Banking, 1550–1800. In *A Financial History of the Netherlands*, ed. M. t'Hart, J. Jonker, and J.L. van Zanden, 37–63. Cambridge: Cambridge University Press.

De Jong-Keesing, E.E. 1939. *De Economische Crisis van 1763 te Amsterdam*. Amsterdam: N.V. Intern. Uitgevers en h. Mij.

Gelderblom, O. 2013. *Cities of Commerce: The Institutional Foundations of International Trade in the Low Countries, 1250–1650*. Princeton: Princeton University Press.

Gillard, L. 2004. *La Banque d'Amsterdam et le florin européen au temps del la République Néerlandaise (1610–1820)*. Paris: École des hautes-études en sciences sociales.

———. 2009. The International Role of the Bank of Amsterdam. In *The Bank of Amsterdam*, ed. M. van Nieuwkerk, 108–131. Amsterdam: Sonsbeek.

Gorton, G. 2017. The History and Economics of Safe Assets. *Annual Review of Economics* 9: 547–586.

Kirk, A., J. McAndrews, S. Parinintha, and P. Weed. 2014. Matching Collateral Supply and Financing Demands in Dealer Banks. *Economic Policy Review Federal Reserve Bank of New York* 20 (2): 1–26.

Mees, W.C. 1838. *Proeve eener Geschiedenis van het Bankwezen in Nederland geduerende den Tijd der Republiek*. Rotterdam: W. Messcuert.

Neal, L. 1991. *The Rise of Financial Capitalism: International Capital Markets in the Age of Reason*. Cambridge: Cambridge University Press.

Pezzolo, Luciano. 2018. A Tale of Three Banking Systems: Florence, Genoa and Venice in the Renaissance. In *Financial Innovation and Resiliency*, ed. L. Costabile and L. Neal. Cham: Palgrave Macmillan.

Polak, Menno. 1998. *Historiografie en Economie van de "Muntchaos,"* Deel II. Amsterdam: NEHA.

Quinn, S., and W. Roberds. 2014. How Amsterdam Got Fiat Money. *Journal of Monetary Economics* 66 (1): 1–12.

———. 2015. Responding to a Shadow Banking Crisis: The Lessons of 1763. *Journal of Money, Credit, and Banking* 47 (6): 1149–1176.

———. 2016. Death of a Reserve Currency. *International Journal of Central Banking* (December): 63–103.

———. 2017. An Early Experiment with 'Permazero'. Federal Reserve Bank of Atlanta Working Paper 2017-5.

Roberds, W., and F.R. Velde. 2016a. Early Public Banks I: Ledger-Money Banks. In *Money in the Western Legal Tradition*, ed. D. Fox and W. Ernst. Oxford: Oxford University Press.

———. 2016b. Early Public Banks II: Banks of Issue. In *Money in the Western Legal Tradition*, ed. D. Fox and W. Ernst. Oxford: Oxford University Press.

Santarosa, V. 2015. Financing Long-Distance Trade: The Joint Liability Rule and Bills of Exchange in Eighteenth-Century France. *Journal of Economic History* 75 (3): 690–719.

Schnabel, I., and H.S. Shin. 2004. Liquidity and Contagion: The Crisis of 1763. *Journal of the European Economic Association* 2 (6): 929–968.

Schneider, J., O. Schwarzer, and P. Schnelzer. 1991. *Historische Statistik von Deutschland. Band XII: Statistik der Geld-und Wechselkurse in Deutschland und im Ostseeraum* (18. Und 19. Jahrhundert). St. Katharinen: Scripta-Mercuratae-Verlag.

Smith, A. 1981 [1776]. *The Wealth of Nations.* Indianapolis: Liberty Fund.

't Hart, M. 2009. Corporate Governance. In *The Bank of Amsterdam*, ed. M. van Nieuwkerk, 144–155. Amsterdam: Sonsbeek.

Uittenbogaard, R. 2009. Lending by the Bank of Amsterdam (1609–1802). In *the Bank of Amsterdam*, ed. M. van Nieuwkerk, 120–131. Amsterdam: Sonsbeek.

Van Dillen, J.G. 1925. *Bronnen Tot de Geschiedenis der Wisselbanken.* The Hague: Martinus Nijhoff.

———. 1934. The Bank of Amsterdam. In *History of the Principal Public Banks*, ed. J. G. van Dillen, 79–124. The Hague: Martinus Nijhoff.

PART IV

Lessons from the Past for the Future?

CHAPTER 14

Banks, Financial Markets and the Development of International Currencies

Barry Eichengreen

1 Introduction

A conference hosted by the Foundation of Banco di Napoli is an occasion to step back in time—in my case, in order to consider the long-term history of international currencies. Specifically, it is an occasion to focus on that portion of the history that predates the period of sterling dominance (the nineteenth century) and dollar dominance (the twentieth) that has been so heavily studied. This in turn affords an opportunity to ask whether that longer-term history has implications for the future and to investigate how it alters one's outlook on possible futures for the international monetary and financial system.

Starting with definitions: What do we mean by an international currency? The conventional answer is a currency that is widely used as a unit of account, means of payment and store of value by individuals, enterprises, banks and governments engaged in cross-border transactions

B. Eichengreen (✉)
University of California, Berkeley, CA, USA

L. Costabile and L. Neal (eds.), *Financial Innovation and Resilience*, Palgrave Studies in the History of Finance,
https://doi.org/10.1007/978-3-319-90248-7_14

(Eichengreen et al. 2017). In conventional usage, further, cross-border means across *national* borders, and hence inter*nationally*. But in the era before the modern nation state, precisely whose borders matter, in this context, is less obvious. Perhaps the best response to this ambiguity is to say: an "international" currency is one that is widely used in transactions by agents doing business or residing outside the territory of the prince, king, emperor or other similar political ruler who commands or controls issuance of that monetary unit.

If definitions are hard, hypotheses are easier. They start with the question of what makes for an international currency. What explains the predominant use of one or more national units by individuals, firms and governments undertaking cross-border transactions? What explains their rise and fall—that is to say, changes in their popularity in absolute terms and relative to rivals? And how many are there likely to be?

In the second half of the twentieth century, when the US dollar was the world's international currency par excellence, these questions appeared to have obvious answers.

- The USA was far and away the *largest* economy in the world, and it engaged in the largest volume of international transactions. It was logical and convenient for American banks, firms and individuals, when engaged in cross-border transactions, to expect payment to be made in dollars. And what made sense for them made sense equally for the banks, firms and individuals of other countries.
- Doing international business in dollars was logical and attractive, moreover, insofar as the dollar was *stable*. Under the Bretton Woods System of the 1950s and 1960s, the dollar was pegged to gold at a fixed price of $35 an ounce, and other currencies were effectively pegged to the dollar. Subsequently, the dollar fluctuated more widely on foreign exchange markets, but without obvious trend. Aside from a brief period in the late 1970s, the USA did not experience the kind of chronic high inflation that tends to undermine confidence in a currency.
- Using dollars in international transactions was also attractive because the USA had the most *liquid* financial markets in the world. Dollars could be bought and sold at low cost, subject to minimal spreads. US banks with extensive foreign operations could make payments and extend loans to counterparties in virtually every corner of the globe.

- A fourth and final prerequisite for international currency status is the capacity to project military and diplomatic *power*. A country with a strong military will be less vulnerable to attack from abroad of a sort that can destabilize its finances and economy and undermine confidence in its currency. And other countries will want to hold its currency as reserves as a way of signalling their allegiance.

These answers to the question of what makes for an international currency—*size*, *stability*, *liquidity* and *power*—seemed obvious in the second half of the twentieth century, when the dollar dominated international transactions and only the USA possessed these attributes in abundance, and in some cases at all. Moreover, that the dollar far-and-away dominated in international transactions, in virtually all parts of the world, strongly pointed to the conclusion that international currency status is a natural monopoly, that only one national unit will play a consequential international role at a point in time.

Today in the twenty-first century, the answers to these questions are less obvious. America no longer accounts for as large a share of global GDP. The USA has been overtaken by China as the world's largest exporter. China has negotiated currency swap arrangements with foreign central banks and designated official *renminbi* clearing banks for financial centres around the world. It is prepared to challenge the USA in the geopolitical sphere. The global crisis of 2007–2008 that centred on the USA understandably raised questions about the stability and liquidity of US financial markets. And now, last but not least, there is Mr. Trump (Eichengreen 2017).

For the moment, the dollar still remains the dominant currency in the international monetary and financial sphere. Perhaps this is an indication that the network effects supporting dollar dominance in the past are not just powerful but also persistent. Perhaps it means that large shocks, like the two world wars that caused the dollar to finally supplant the pound sterling as the leading international currency, half a century and more after the USA became a leading exporter and overtook Britain as the world's largest economy, will be required for the baton to be passed again. Alternatively, perhaps as we navigate the transition to a more multipolar world we will experience a similar transition to a more multipolar monetary and financial world where several national currencies play consequential international roles.

These are hypotheses and questions on which history can shed light. The rise first of sterling and then of the dollar and the transition between them is the most immediate such history. But there is also a longer prehistory of international currencies, prior to the period of sterling and dollar dominance, on which informed observers might usefully draw.

2 Perspectives from Ancient Times

The silver *drachma* coined in Athens in the fifth century BC is sometimes referred to as the first international currency, since it circulated beyond the borders of the Athenian Empire. Its successors, the Roman gold *aureus* and silver *denarius*, circulated more widely, reflecting the greater geographical scope and greater military and administrative capacity of the Roman Empire. In practice, the silver *drachma* continued to circulate alongside these Roman units for an extended period, an observation consistent with the "new view" of international currency status, according to which it is argued that multiple international currencies can coexist.

These gold and silver coins were used by the Romans to pay their legions. Their soldiers of course had to transform those high-value gold and silver coins into smaller units for use in everyday transactions. It followed that the gold and silver coins passed into other hands and were used in a range of transactions in a range of places.

Acceptance of these Roman coins declined from the first through fourth centuries AD with the mounting financial challenges and declining power of the Empire. These problems were met in part by the imperial authorities through traditional methods, namely currency debasement and inflation. The *aureus* was then supplanted by the Byzantine *solidus* introduced by Constantine the Great as part of his administrative, financial and economic reforms starting in 306 AD.

The *solidus*, like the *aureus* and *denarius* before it, was used to pay imperial soldiers. Indeed, the word "soldier" derives from *solidus*, referring to the *solidi* with which soldiers were paid. *Solidi* were the heaviest gold coins circulating anywhere in the world, despite the fact that they were only the size of a modern American dime or a 20 euro cent coin. As with the *aureus* and *denarius* before it, soldiers paid in *solidi* exchanged them for smaller monetary units, food and other goods. In practice, this meant that the coin was used mainly by merchants and aristocrats. The *solidus* circulated through much Europe and Asia for the better part of a millennium. Hoards have been found in Central Europe, Russia, Georgia,

Syria and other Arabic countries. Robert Lopez (my teacher at Yale and himself a native of Genoa, more on which below) invoked archaeological and numismatic evidence to conclude that the *solidus* was used in transactions everywhere from England to India (Lopez 1951). More recently, in 2016 (half a century after Lopez wrote), a hoard of Roman coins was unearthed in a castle in Okinawa, Japan (Blakemore 2016).

These observations are consistent with the framework above for what makes for an international currency. First, international use of the *solidus* was encouraged by the relatively large economic size of the Byzantine Empire and the substantial volume of its international transactions.

Second, the stability of the unit is key to its attractiveness as an international currency. The gold content of the *solidus* remained the same from its introduction in the fourth century until well into the tenth, a strikingly long period.

Third, that the *solidus* circulated widely meant that it was readily accepted—that it was relatively liquid compared to local competitors.

Last but not least, international use of the *solidus* was supported by Byzantium's strong military. The *solidus* was the currency of an Empire that for centuries after Constantine succeeded in controlling large swathes of territory and repelling invaders.

But the *solidus*, like the *drachma*, had rivals, again consistent with the new view of international currency competition. From the late seventh century, cross-border transactions were also undertaken using the *dinar*, a *solidus*-like gold coin introduced by Abd al-Malek of the Syrian Umayyad dynasty, who sought to unify the Moslem lands. Al-Malek's motivation was to put an end to monetary disorder, where different coins of different weights and fineness circulated, causing confusion and complicating economic development. In modern terminology, he sought to create a uniform currency. In addition, this was a period of discord between Islam and Christianity (for neither the first nor the last time it is tempting to say). The Syrians were less than pleased by the circulation of coins bearing Christian religious symbols. Where the Byzantine cross appeared on the front of the *solidus*, al-Malek substituted a column placed on three steps topped by a sphere on the *dinar* and the phrase "In the name of God, there is no deity but God; He is One; Muhammad is the messenger of God". Justinian II did not take this provocation lying down. His response was to strike a new *solidus* with the head of Christ on the front and himself, robed and holding a cross, on the back.

Eventually, this "currency war" spilled over into outright war between the Byzantine and Umayyad Empires. Ultimately, al-Malek defeated Byzantine forces at the Battle of Sebastopolis in 692, and the *dinar* became the sole circulating medium in the Moslem world. This was a clear example of the association of international currency status with military prowess if there ever was one. It circulated not just in Syrian lands but also in North Africa and Spain. Al-Malik issued a decree requiring that all Byzantine coins circulating in Umayyad territory be handed over to the treasury, which would melt them down and restrike them. Anyone failing to comply was subject to the death penalty. This, evidently, is one way that an existing international currency can be rapidly replaced by another. The *dinar's* gold content remained unchanged for fully two centuries following its introduction, again underscoring the association between currency stability and international use.

The subsequent period provided proof by counterexample, as both Byzantium and the Umayyads encountered problems of imperial overstretch, like the Greeks and Romans before them. Fiscal strains led to money creation and inflation achieved through debasement. "Byzantium's prestige plummeted as international merchants abandoned the worthless coins" (Brownworth 2009, p. 221). For the Byzantine Empire, the arrival of the Fourth Crusade at the beginning of the thirteenth century (organized by the Republic of Venice, more on which below) was then a political and economic disaster. The Empire was dismembered and forced to pay a costly tribute to the victorious Crusaders.

3 International Currencies in the Renaissance

The principal coins to circulate internationally in the subsequent period were the Genoese *genoin*, the Florentine *florin* and the Venetian *ducat*. The three Italian city states had important mercantile connections; Genoa and Venice were entrepôt centres between the Levant and Western Europe. Florence had links with the Champagne fairs and traded with the east using ships leased from the Genoese and Venetians. Genoa and Venice had significant military prowess and were able to maintain enclaves abroad useful for their mercantile activities. They possessed a degree of natural protection by virtue of their geography, which made for security and political stability. They had relatively advanced fiscal administrations capable of raising the revenues required to finance the military operations needed to defend the state. They were technologically advanced: Venetian merchant ships could carry as much as 700 tons of cargo already in the twelfth century, helping to explain the Venetians' prominence not only in commerce but also in the Crusades.

But what mattered most for the three Italian currencies' international roles was their development of large and liquid financial sectors. Venice and Genoa developed elaborate contracts, supported by a body of contract law, to facilitate collective finance of expensive commercial voyages. Venice invented double-entry bookkeeping. Florence and Venice were the inventors of deposit banking. The state required bankers to obtain a license, and required as a condition for a license that the banker deposit with the state a sum of money that would be used to pay off depositors if the bank failed. These, then, were the early modern equivalent of capital requirements. They were an indication that for a financial system to acquire the depth and liquidity needed to support an international currency required more than the spontaneous stimulus of commerce. It depended in addition on the existence of a strong state capable of adequate regulation.

In time, these bankers became major providers and brokers of bills of exchange, letters of credit that were in practice denominated in and convertible into gold *ducats*, *florin* and *genoin*. In time, bills on Venice, Genoa and Florence substituted for and supplemented gold coin issued by these city states. Effectively, Venice, Genoa and Florence met the needs of international trade and finance with more than just coin, just as the USA today meets those needs with more than physical dollar bills. Because Florentine banks had branches and did business throughout Europe, the *florin* in particular became the predominant means of payment and unit of denomination for large-scale transactions across the western part of the continent.

Interesting for present purposes is the question of why the Neapolitan silver *ducato* was not used as widely in transactions between the Italian peninsula and the Levant, at the Champagne fairs and more generally across Europe. One hypothesis would focus on the retail basis of banking in Naples: large-denomination coin and bills are needed by merchants engaged in long-distance transactions, and the Neapolitan banks focused on smaller-scale retail transactions, which occurred disproportionately locally. Another answer is that those utilizing the coins and bills of another political jurisdiction as a unit of account, a means of payment and especially a store of value were more comfortable holding claims issued by the authorities of a political republic—think republican city states—where merchants and bankers were represented in decision-making and whose authorities were subject to checks and balances than they were holding the liabilities of a monarchy with autocratic powers. The Kingdom of Naples never had political independence: it was under first the Angevins and then the Aragonese. It became part of the Spanish Empire at the beginning of the sixteenth century. Subsequently, Naples and its Kingdom served the Spanish kings as a large reservoir of money and men to be used in wars all over Europe—but not to advance its own interests. Power, one of the key requisites for a currency to become widely accepted internationally, was missing because political independence was missing.

4 Rise of the Dutch Guilder

Widespread international use of the three Italian currencies rested on a high level of mercantile activity—in modern terms, on the complementarity between trade and finance. It followed that as commercial leadership shifted from the Mediterranean to the Low Countries, Italian monies were replaced by the Dutch *guilder* as the leading international currency. Starting in the early seventeenth century, the Dutch Republic became not just the leading commercial power but also the leading source of credit and international finance for trade-related activity. Once it acquired this role, the *guilder* remained the leading currency used in cross-border transactions for the balance of the seventeenth and eighteenth centuries, reflecting the substantial value of Dutch trade and financial transactions and the Dutch Republic's retention of this commercial predominance (Neal 1991).

The Bank of Amsterdam, established in 1609 by the governing council of the city, was a key piece of financial infrastructure. It provided clearing and settlement services. It accepted and converted foreign as well as domestic coin, thereby supporting the growth of Amsterdam's international financial connections. It paid bills drawn on Amsterdam through the transfer of bank deposits denominated in bank *florin* (Quinn and Roberds, Chapter 13). It came to dominate the market, both in Amsterdam where city council regulation required all large bills of exchange to be settled through transfers of Bank of Amsterdam balances, and elsewhere on the basis of reputation.

In the prior period, a variety of coins, foreign as well as domestic, clipped and worn as well as full-bodied, had circulated in the Dutch Republic. This created reluctance on the part of foreigners to settle transactions in Amsterdam, since they were uncertain in which coin they would be paid. With the substitution of bank money for this heterogeneous circulation, the confidence problem was solved. Merchants and bankers throughout the Baltic region and in Russia now accepted bills on Amsterdam. In the same way it has been argued that the establishment of the Federal Reserve System in 1913 and its subsequent support for the development of a market in trade credits was a key condition for the emergence of the US dollar as an international currency, it can be argued that the establishment of the Bank of Amsterdam was critical for wide international acceptance of the *guilder*.

This emphasis on the importance of finance for the acquisition of international currency status is not to deny the importance of trade. The Dutch Republic was the commercial superpower of the time. Technological advances in shipbuilding—design of the "*fluyt*" as a dedicated cargo vessel and new industrial methods for its construction—supported the growth of the Dutch merchant marine, which accounted for fully half of European shipping tonnage by the middle of the seventeenth century. The lion's share of the merchandise they carried passed through Dutch ports, encouraging use of the *guilder*.

In addition, the stability of the *guilder*, like the stability of the Italian currencies before it, raises interesting questions of political economy with relevance to modern experience. In Byzantium, as noted, the stability of the unit and avoidance of debasement were rooted in the support that the emperor derived from large landowners, who as creditors dependent on rents and dues fixed in nominal terms had a natural aversion to inflation. Support for the institutions of the Dutch Republic derived not so much from landed interests as from bankers and merchants. For those bankers and merchants, what was important was not so much avoiding modest inflation as avoiding serious volatility, which might be a source of high uncertainty that disrupted trade and finance. In fact, the *guilder* was allowed to depreciate modestly, notably in the period before 1750. What were successfully avoided were major outbreaks of volatility (with the exceptions noted by Quinn and Roberds in Chapter 13) that would be bad for banking and trade. There is an obvious parallel with the dollar in the second half of the twentieth century: the currency could decline modestly on the foreign exchange market without eroding its international currency status, but only so long as serious spikes in volatility were avoided.

5 The Rise of Sterling

Sterling's emergence as the leading international currency can similarly be dated from the establishment of the Bank of England in 1694. The existence of a central bank to provide liquidity to the market was necessary but not sufficient for sterling's rise to international prominence. "Necessary but not sufficient" because, historical experience suggests, other elements, plausibly four in number, had to fall into place to cement sterling's international role.

First, the financial system had to develop further to enhance the stability and liquidity of the market. The middle decades of the nineteenth century, in particular, were a period of rapid growth and structural change in the banking system, as a formerly fragmented financial sector underwent significant consolidation.

Second, the economy had to develop so as to stimulate the volume of cross-border transactions. Britain was the first industrial nation and leading exporter throughout the nineteenth century. It had the world's largest merchant fleet, a status it maintained well into the twentieth century.

Third, there had to be a consensus favouring currency stability. Bankers saw it as central to London's status as an international financial centre, while merchants and industrialists saw it as critical to Britain's success as an exporter.

Fourth and finally, the country had to be militarily secure. Not only did Britain enjoy the natural protection of the channel ("Fog in Channel, Continent cut off"), but Britannia ruled the waves: an equally extensive naval fleet complemented its extensive merchant marine. Eventually, its naval pre-eminence, like its economic pre-eminence, would be challenged by other rising powers, notably Germany. This in turn raised questions in the minds of contemporaries about Britain's capacity to anchor the international gold standard (De Cecco 1975). But for much of the nineteenth century, sterling's heyday, these questions were remote.

The preceding makes it seem all but inevitable that sterling should have been the leading international currency in the second half of the nineteenth century. It is important therefore to emphasize that it did not monopolize this function. Both the French franc and German mark were consequential rivals, especially towards the end of the period. Data gathered by Marc Flandreau and Clement Jobst (2009) show that while sterling was quoted and actively traded on every foreign exchange market worldwide circa 1900, the French franc was also traded on 80 per cent of those markets, the German mark on 60 per cent. While sterling accounted for half of global foreign exchange reserves at the turn of the century, the French franc accounted for fully 30 per cent, the German mark 15 per cent. The franc was backed by the Bank of France, established in 1800, and by the creation of important new deposit banks starting in the 1860s, including big banks that engaged in a considerable volume of foreign lending. The international role of the mark was supported by the Reichsbank, founded in 1876, five years after the creation of Imperial Germany.

6 The Arrival of the US Dollar

The currency that is prominent by its absence from this list is, of course, the US dollar. The USA had already overtaken the UK as the single largest economy by the 1870s. It overtook the UK as the single largest exporter on the eve of World War I. And as the war made clear, it now had the most powerful military, backed by the largest industrial sector, of any country.

At first sight, it thus seems paradoxical that the dollar played essentially no role as a currency in which to invoice and settle export and import transactions, as a unit for denominating international bonds, and as a form in which central banks and governments held their foreign reserves. On closer examination, however, the paradox dissolves. The USA lacked a central bank to act as lender and liquidity provider of last resort prior to the establishment of the Federal Reserve System in 1913. US banks were prohibited from branching abroad under the National Banking Act. And the country's commitment to the gold standard was a perennial question, at least prior to 1900.

As in the case of the Bank of England before it, the creation of a central bank was a necessary condition for altering these conditions; that happened in 1914. An important motive for doing so, as I have argued elsewhere, was precisely to internationalize the dollar: to create an institutional framework in which America's currency could play a larger international role. And that goal was successfully achieved, albeit in stages: first between 1914 and 1924, when the dollar became coequal with sterling, and then after World War II when it surpassed it. This history being familiar, I won't repeat it here.

An important point, however, is that the dollar's dominance was never absolute. When currency holdings are valued at current exchange rates, the dollar's share peaked at the end of the 1970s at around 80 per cent of the global total. There was then an undulating decline in that share towards a relatively stable 60 per cent. Thus, the dollar's share of identified foreign exchange reserves at the beginning of the twenty-first century was roughly the same as sterling's share at the beginning of the twentieth. Like sterling a century before, the dollar now accounted for the largest single fraction of official foreign currency holdings, but not the entirety, not even in the Bretton Woods period.

The Bretton Woods System collapsed in 1971–1973, when first the dollar was devalued and then other currencies were floated. But there was no sharp reduction in the demand for international reserves, as some experts had predicted, and no sharp shift away from the dollar as a form in which to hold them. From the time of the Roman *aureus* through the post-World War II dollar, international currencies had been minted from or otherwise linked to precious metal. The architects of the Bretton Woods System carried on in this tradition when they obliged IMF member countries to declare par values for their currencies "in dollars of constant gold content" and singled out the dollar because it alone was convertible into gold at a fixed price by official foreign holders. Many observers therefore concluded that with the end of the dollar's fixed link to gold, the currency's international role would be significantly attenuated if not eliminated.

In the event, this was not the case. As had been true for two millennia, the acceptability of a national currency in international transactions still depended on the size, stability and security of the issuer and the liquidity of its financial markets. But now stability was gauged by more than simply the stability of its value in terms of gold. It was gauged rather by the stability of its finances, its policies and, ultimately, its economy.

7 What Next?

Thus, many historical periods have seen a dominant unit, where a significant fraction of cross-border transactions was conducted in a particular national currency, network increasing returns serving as a powerful attractor. But any such dominance has regularly fallen short of absolute. Working in the other direction is the desire of central banks, governments and other investors not to put all their eggs in one basket. That said, accumulating and utilizing a limited number of currencies could in general achieve the desired degree of portfolio diversification. Nor is there reason to expect the international currencies in question to be held in equal amounts.

The long sweep of history suggests, in my view, that the balance is tipping away from network effects and towards portfolio diversification. With the development of modern financial markets and instruments, it becomes less advantageous to utilize the same national unit as one's trading partners when engaging in international transactions and easier to exchange one currency for another. With advances in information technology, it becomes easier to compare prices denominated in different currencies. With the development of national financial markets, it becomes more attractive to diversify portfolios—to hold and transact in a variety of different currencies. This trend, if it continues, suggests that the dollar will have more rivals, and perhaps more consequential rivals, in the future than the past.

References

Blakemore, Erin. 2016. Archaeologist Finds Ancient Roman Coins in 12th-Century Japanese Castle. *Smithsonian.com*, 29 September.

Brownworth, Lars. 2009. *Lost to the West: The Forgotten Byzantine Empire that Rescued Western Civilization*. New York: Crown Publishers.

De Cecco, Marcello. 1975. *Money and Empire: The International Gold Standard, 1890–1914*. Totowa, NJ: Rowman and Littlefield.

Eichengreen, Barry. 2017. The Decline of Dollar Diplomacy? *Project Syndicate*, 11 October.

Eichengreen, Barry, Arnaud Mehl, and Livia Chitu. 2017. *How Global Currencies Work: Past, Present and Future*. Princeton: Princeton University Press.

Flandreau, Marc, and Clemens Jobst. 2009. The Empirics of International Currencies: Network Externalities, History and Persistence. *Economic Journal* 119: 643–664.

Lopez, Robert. 1951. The Dollar of the Middle Ages. *Journal of Economic History* 11: 209–234.

Neal, Larry. 1991. *The Rise of Financial Capitalism: International Capital Markets in the Age of Reason*. Cambridge: Cambridge University Press.

CHAPTER 15

Public Banks, Public Orientation and the Great Financial Crisis of 2007–2008

Gerald Epstein and Devika Dutt

1 Introduction

The Great Financial Crisis (GFC) of 2007–2008 was a watershed moment in multiple ways. Among other important matters, it called into question dominant views of the stability of private financial markets, the appropriate role of financial regulation and the appropriate understanding of macroeconomic theory and policy, including the proper role of central banks. Prior to the crisis, so-called Washington Consensus views tended to favour private over public finance, self-regulation by private financial institutions and regulation-lite by governments, open international capital markets, and inflation-targeting regimes by central banks, all under the theoretical view that capitalist economies dominated by 'modern financial markets' are inherently stable around an equilibrium of full employment (Wolfson and Epstein 2013, Chapter 1; Blanchard et al. 2010). Reality bit, leading to a reassessment of these assumptions, and some moves

G. Epstein (✉) · D. Dutt
University of Massachusetts, Amherst, MA, USA

L. Costabile and L. Neal (eds.), *Financial Innovation and Resilience*, Palgrave Studies in the History of Finance,
https://doi.org/10.1007/978-3-319-90248-7_15

towards adopting new practices in financial structure, financial regulation and in macroeconomic thinking and policy. Much of this experimentation and reassessment resulted from dire necessities being 'thrust upon' policymakers and the profession by the crisis itself (Grabel, 2018). The nationalization of large swaths of the financial system in the USA and several other countries, the abandonment of simple inflation targeting, the adoption of quantitative easing, the push towards much stricter financial regulation and the acceptance of capital controls after years of rigid opposition—these are all examples of the radical financial changes that were thrust upon policymakers, and they were ones that economists had to digest as necessity challenged their previous conventional understandings of theory and policy.

As the immediate threat has passed—or so it seems—there has been a strong tendency in many circles to try to return closer to the institutional structures and doctrinal views that were prevalent *ex ante*. This is evident in the USA where the push by the Trump Administration is towards dismantling the Dodd–Frank financial regulations passed in the aftermath of the GFC. Brexit might promote deregulatory competition from London- to European-situated financial centres to gain advantage in the fight over the locational financial spoils associated with Brexit. The macroeconomic branch of the mainstream economics profession never did much of a serious soul-searching or rethinking, Olivier Blanchard's famous paper notwithstanding (Blanchard et al. 2010). So macroeconomists do not have to travel far to return to where they started. Still, one can hope that some rethinking and experimentation will survive this current worldwide tendency of reversion towards the regulatory regime *ex ante*.

One of the areas where there has been some interesting rethinking is on the question of the role of public-oriented financial institutions in improving the cyclical and secular performance of the economy. In the aftermath of the crisis, Epstein et al. (2009) called for an increase in the role of 'finance without financiers' to help stabilize our economies and promote socially desirable economic development. A strong and growing literature, surveyed below, has engaged in careful theoretical and empirical work to enrich our understanding of the positive and negative roles that publicly oriented financial institutions can play in our economies. Of course, this is not a new topic or perspective. Alexander Gerschenkron (1962) famously showed the role of public financial institutions in the development of 'late industrializers'; Barry Eichengreen surveyed their importance in the recovery of Europe in the aftermath of the Second World War (Eichengreen 2007); and Alice Amsden described the key role such institutions played in the success of the newly industrializing countries—the 'late, late developers' (Amsden 2001). More to the point, the papers contained in this volume focus our attention once again on the often positive roles played by public banking in earlier times. Here, the public banks of Naples, as shown in this volume, played an innovative and outstanding role.

In this chapter, we look at a specific question: are publicly oriented financial institutions stabilizing forces in the modern financial world, and if so, at what cost? From the perspective of the US discussion of the causes of the financial crisis, this might seem a puzzling question: the supporters of financial deregulation argued that it was the 'public banks', Fannie Mae and Ginnie Mae, that were the main culprits in the financial crisis. According to this view, these 'quasi-public' banks underwrote the toxic mortgages and securities that became the fuel for the collapse. But as many analysts have shown, these 'public' financial institutions were largely privately oriented and, moreover, they came 'late to the party', following the leads of the private banks that drove the crisis (Financial Crisis Inquiry Commission 2011; Crotty 2009). Thus, while in the USA, quasi-public institutions might have played a role in some ways, the driving forces were the private financial institutions and the moral hazard associated with 'too big to fail status' of many of these banks. The same can be said of most other countries that helped to feed the global crisis (Haldane 2009).

In answering this question on the cyclicality of public financial institutions, we show that there is quite a bit of literature supporting the idea that, in recent decades, publicly oriented banks contribute to financial stability by lending less pro-cyclically and even, in some cases, counter-cyclically, than did their private banking counterparts.

We then ask whether this benefit comes at a great cost, namely the longer-term inefficiency of public banking relative to private banking. We show that, while earlier studies of public banking tended to show that they were inferior to private banks in terms of resource allocation, more recent literature finds that this is not generally the case.

We are left in the end with a more interesting question: given both the cyclical and secular net benefits of publicly oriented banking, should we encourage more publicly oriented financial institutions in our economies? Our answer: probably, but it's complicated.

2 Do Public Banks Promote Financial Stability?

2.1 Introduction

How do we define 'publicly oriented banks'? One distinction is between 'government owned' financial institutions and privately owned financial institutions. Much of the literature studies this world, utilizing data on government-owned banks and defining government ownership as an ownership threshold above a certain level, for example, 50 per cent.

But 'government ownership' does not exhaust the definition of 'publicly oriented financial institutions'. In particular, some financial institutions are not owned by the government, but are not purely profit-oriented either. We can think here of non-profit (or 'not for profit' financial institutions) or cooperative financial institutions that are designed to serve the interests of the members of the cooperative. An interesting literature has arisen that draws the distinction among non-government-owned institutions between 'shareholder banks' and 'stakeholder banks' (see, for example, Ferri et al. 2014; Ostergaard et al. 2016; Ayadi et al. 2010). Shareholder banks are what we think of as private financial institutions: they are profit oriented and economists usually model them as profit maximizing.[1]

In the USA, and especially in Europe, stakeholder financial institutions are common. Two of the main types of stakeholder firms are 'cooperative banks' and 'savings banks'. As explained in Ferri et al. (2014, p. 196):

> A key difference with respect to ownership structure is that cooperative banks are owned by their members, whereas savings banks either have no owners (i.e., they are non-profit organizations) or are owned by the public sector. In the case of cooperatives, the distribution of profits is limited, shares are typically not tradable, and members have only one vote, regardless of the number of shares they own. In savings banks, profit distribution and tradable ownership rights are absent altogether. Moreover, management compensation in stakeholder banks is typically not tied to profitability. For these reasons, there is no party in these banks who would benefit from profit maximization.[2]

[1] But see the fascinating paper by James Crotty, 'The Rainmaker Financial Firm' in Crotty (2016) which analyses private financial firms where the goal is not the profit maximizing for shareholders, but for the top traders ('rainmakers') and CEOs of these large financial firms.

[2] Ferri et al. (2014) conjecture that these institutions therefore try to maximize consumer surplus. As we understand from Keynes' ideas on fundamental uncertainty, and behavioural economics/ social psychology, the operators of these institutions might have more complex decision processes than can be explained by simple optimisation rules.

In the rest of this paper, we will mostly use the term 'publicly oriented banks' to refer to financial institutions that are either owned by the government and/or are 'stakeholder' financial institutions. The key idea is that they are not driven by law of the market to try to maximize profits. This absence of profit-driven imperatives, in principle, creates space for the financial institution to strive for other goals.[3]

The literature on publicly oriented banks displays an interesting trend. Older studies tend to portray public banks in a negative light. In the literature, several authors argue that state-owned banks are characterized by lower profitability, political interference, lack of transparency, low accountability to stakeholders, misallocation of resources and inadequate prudential regulation and supervision (Rudolph 2010). The literature typically describes public banks as being less efficient than privately owned banks (Andrianova 2012; Andrianova et al. 2008). This assessment is often based on the standard measure of profit-maximizing efficiency. Judging performance of public banks based on profitability or efficiency measures is problematic as, in many instances, public banks have broader goals that preclude a purely profit-maximizing objective. Attempts by public banks to maximize profits would be in contradiction with their public mandate, as public banks often make loans for activities that are higher risk and low private return activities, their social return notwithstanding.

However, more recent studies, some of them based on micro-level studies, find results more favourable to public banks relative to private ones. Perhaps the Great Financial Crisis, which demonstrated an egregious failure of resource allocation by major private banks, led some economists to look again at the efficiency and resource question with fresh eyes. They were recognizing something that James Tobin noted years ago: 'It takes a heap of Harberger triangles to fill an Okun gap' (Tobin 1977).

In this section, we describe the substantial evidence that public banks' lending behaviour is less pro-cyclical than private banks. We find a great deal of empirical evidence that suggests that public banks do in fact behave less pro-cyclically than private banks and, in the case of more developed countries, actually behave *counter-cyclically.*

[3] In a later section, we will briefly discuss the relationship between our concept of 'publicly oriented banks' and our understanding of the meaning of the 'public banks' of Naples.

In the following section, we present the evidence on the resource allocation and efficiency characteristics of public banks compared with private banks. We show that more recent studies present strong support for the argument that, when measured properly, publicly oriented banks are not less efficient and do not lead to worse resource allocation than private banks, generally speaking. In fact, under circumstances that are not fully understood, public-oriented banks achieve better longer-term outcomes than do private banks.

2.2 *Do Public Banks Behave Less Pro-cyclically Than Private Banks?*

In recent years, economists have spent significant effort to investigate the degree to which public banks can provide a stabilizing macroeconomic impact. This issue has become of great interest, understandably, in the aftermath of the GFC in which it was increasingly recognized that a highly pro-cyclical financial system played a significant role in creating the crisis (Crotty 2009; Borio 2012). More specifically, a number of studies have examined whether public banks' lending behaviour is less pro-cyclical than that of private banks, or even counter-cyclical.

This less pro-cyclical response could result from several factors (see, for example, Andrianova 2012, for a discussion of some of these factors). On the asset side, public banks might have less pressure to maximize profits and, as a result, are less likely to respond to internal or external pressures to ride the pro-cyclical financial wave and engage in excessive lending in the upswing. More positively, such financial institutions might have public mandates that orient their managers towards being more likely to take into account the social risks of over-investing in the upswing so that they are less subject to issues of moral hazard. Also on the asset side, public banks may have localized clients that are less subject to sectors with booms and busts, such as real estate. On the liability side, public-oriented financial institutions might have a more stable source of funding than the wholesale type funding that banks contributing to the financial crisis relied on. This more stable funding base might reduce the need for public banks to cut back on lending in the downturn. These factors, especially in combination, would make it more likely that public financial institutions would operate in a less pro-cyclical or even counter-cyclical fashion.

Less purely positive motives and structures could also be at work. Some have suggested that public bank managers are simply 'lazy' and don't bother to lend up in a boom so they don't have to lend down so much in the bust (see Micco and Panizza 2006, for an assessment). On the downside of the cycle, public banks, because of inappropriate political pressure, might be pressured to lend to failing companies because of inappropriate political pressure. Some studies try to disentangle these factors, but it is not always easy to do.

The recent empirical work on the cyclicality of public lending is impressive in scope. In an early study, Yeyati et al. (2004) find that public banks can play a positive role in mobilizing savings or providing consumption smoothing at times of crisis. Micco and Panizza (2006) used bank balance sheet data to show that lending by state-owned banks decreases less during recessions and increases less during expansions than private banks, thereby playing a useful counter-cyclical role. They surmise that this could be due to a range of reasons such as the government internalizing the benefits of a more stable macroeconomic environment, a stable deposit base due to perception of lower likelihood of failure of state-owned banks during recessions, or, from a more negative perspective, possibly due to the lack of proper incentive for so-called lazy bureaucrats that run these state-owned banks.

In a more recent study, using balance sheet data from 800 German Banks between 1987 and 2007, Behr et al. (2017) find that lending by public savings banks to small and medium enterprises (SMEs) in Germany was 25 per cent less sensitive to the business cycle than private cooperative banks from the same area. This is despite both types of banks being local banks that focus on basic financial services. Additionally, they argue that this large and statistically significant difference in lending behaviour cannot be attributed to political interference, especially since political interference cannot explain why public savings banks increase their lending less than private credit banks in expansions. They argue that the difference in behaviour is a result of the difference in objectives of these banks. More specifically, according to Behr et al. (2017), this difference is due to the fact that the 'savings banks' have a public mandate while the private cooperative banks do not.

Bertay et al. (2015) use a broader cross-country analysis and find that while privately owned banks increase (and decrease) their lending by 1.3–1.8 per cent in response to a 1 per cent increase (and decrease) in GDP per capita, state-owned banks increase (and decrease) their lending by 0.4 per cent. Therefore, in their estimation, while lending by state-owned banks is pro-cyclical, it is significantly less so than lending by private banks. In countries with 'good governance' (as measured by standard indices), lending by state-owned banks is even less pro-cyclical. Additionally, in recessionary times, they find that lending by state-owned banks is actually counter-cyclical, and a 1 per cent decline in growth of GDP per capita is associated with an increase in credit growth of state-owned banks by 1–1.2 per cent. Similarly, using individual bank balance sheet data over 1990–2010 for 83 countries covering 366 public banks, Duprey (2015) shows that public banking is associated with less cyclical lending policies. This is especially the case in downturns. In their estimation, however, this result is reversed for public banks in less developed countries. The lower pro-cyclicality of lending by government-owned banks in more developed countries is due to these banks increasing their lending less during expansions as compared to similar banks in less developed countries.

In order to focus on lending during systemic financial crises, Brei and Schclarek (2013) examine the lending responses of 764 government-owned and privately owned banks in 50 countries of Europe and Latin America over the period 1994–2009. Consistent with the other results highlighted, they find robust evidence for a counter-cyclical role played by government-owned banks in their respective banking systems. Crucially, their study also adds to the evidence indicating that lending by government-owned banks does not explode during expansions, but counteracts the decrease in lending by private banks during downturns. In their view, this can be a result of the following reasons: first, government-owned banks have a higher risk-bearing capacity and provide higher credit growth precisely to mitigate the fallout of systemic financial crises on growth. Second, during crises, government-owned banks find it easier to raise new forms of capital at lower costs that is unlikely to be available to privately owned banks. Finally, they argue that deposit funding for government-owned banks is also likely to be more stable over the business cycle.

Ferri et al. (2014) extend their analysis to other types of banks that may have non-profit-maximization objectives. They study the lending supply policies of banks in the Euro Area during the first 13 years of the common monetary policy. Their study extends over the period of relative financial stability prior to the current crisis and the period of the current crisis. They distinguish between profit-maximizing banks, such as shareholder banks, and non-profit-maximizing banks or stakeholder banks, such as savings banks and credit cooperatives. In their entire period, banks that they characterize as stakeholder banks followed less pro-cyclical policies as compared to shareholder banks, and their loan supply responded less to the price of credit. However, they find that the effect of ownership on loan supply is less pronounced during the crisis. They argue that stakeholder banks have more long-term relationships with their borrowers and are therefore less likely to curtail lending to them during a downturn.

It is important to note that the literature shows that the growth of lending by public banks over the expansion is lower than that of private profit-maximizing banks. This suggests that public banks are playing a role in tempering the behaviour of private banks in creating credit bubbles that can lead to crises. Restrained lending during expansions assumes significance for stability since increased credit growth is linked to the increased likelihood of the occurrence of a crisis (Schularick and Taylor 2012; Minsky 1986). It is not surprising that this is the case, since public banks are likely to be engaged in lending for specific objectives. For instance, in China, there are a variety of state-owned banks (Andersson et al. 2013) that lend for the promotion of specific policy objectives, which are unlikely to change over the business cycle. Moreover, lending by these banks is also growth promoting. It is also likely that general state-owned commercial banks lend with restraint during the expansion as, more often than not, they serve a public mandate that is unlikely to be served by engaging in risky, destabilizing credit extension.

To take an example from the USA, at the heart of the global financial crisis of 2007–2009 the Bank of North Dakota (BND), which is a state-owned bank, played an important stabilizing role. The decline in bank lending in 2009 was the most severe since 1942. In particular, the number of loans and the total amount loaned out under the Small Business Administration's flagship 7(a) programme fell by about 54 per cent and 37 per cent, respectively, between 2007 and 2009 (Center for State Innovation 2011). Of the five largest banks (Bank of America, Wells Fargo, JP Morgan Chase, Citigroup and PNC, which collectively controlled 40 per cent of the total deposits and 48 per cent of the total assets in the banking system in 2010), the two which received the largest amount in public bailout money, Bank of America and Citigroup, were lending 94 per cent and 54 per cent less, respectively, to small businesses in 2011 (McGhee and Judd 2011).

However, in North Dakota, the story was different. Between 2007 and 2009, BND was a counter-cyclical force and increased lending to small businesses by 35 per cent (McGhee and Judd 2011). The primary mechanism by which BND achieves this is through participation lending, that is by participating in loans originated by local banks or credit unions by either increasing the total size of the loan, buying down the interest rate, or providing loan guarantees. This allows small community banks and community banks to provide larger and cheaper loans than they would otherwise have the capacity to provide. Additionally, bank lending rates in North Dakota remained relatively constant between 2005 and 2011 during the height of the boom in housing prices, providing some much-needed stability in the economy of North Dakota (Center for State Innovation 2011).

3 Financial Stability, But at What Cost?

It would be easy to jump to a simple conclusion from this literature: an important tool to reduce the likelihood and severity of finance-driven boom and busts cycle would be to encourage more public-oriented financial institutions. Yet some of the literature also contains a strong cautionary tale: while public-oriented financial institutions might do better over the cycle, they might also impose significant long-run costs on the economy in terms of being less efficient, less innovative and more prone to credit misallocation because of bureaucratic stasis or, worse, crony capitalist meddling. Thus, any responsible assessment of the net benefits of public financial institutions for financial stability purposes would have to be weighed against the possible longer-term net allocative costs of public banking.

The oft-stated consensus on this matter is quite clear. One extensive and clear recent statement goes as follows (Bertay et al. 2015)[4]:

> However, the track record of state banks in credit allocation remains quite poor, questioning the wisdom of using state banks as a short-term countercyclical tool. For this purpose, alternative policy tools in the form of macroprudential bank regulation, including procyclical capital requirements and monetary policy are more appropriate, as they are more flexible than state ownership of banking and would not lead to credit misallocation resulting in low economic growth...There is a substantial literature on the impact of state ownership of banks on banking performance and

[4]This article has extensive references that we have excluded here for readability and space reasons. Please consult Bertay et al. (2015, p. 327) for this useful list of references.

> economic outcomes. A large number of cross-country studies show that state ownership of banking is associated with low bank efficiency and lower levels of financial development. State bank ownership lowers banking sector outreach and leads to wider intermediation spreads and slower economic growth as well as greater financial instability. Dinc (2005) shows that state bank lending is politically motivated, since state banks in emerging markets increase their lending relative to private banks in election years. Banking outcomes also worsen with state ownership. For example...state-owned banks report higher loan loss provisioning and achieve lower profitability than private banks using data for a large set of emerging economies...state-owned banks located in developing countries tend to have lower profitability and higher costs than their private counterparts.... the "Big Four" state-owned commercial banks in China are less profitable, are less efficient, and have worse asset quality than other types of banks that involve some domestic or foreign private ownership. Importantly, country level studies also show that politicians use government bank lending to provide political patronage leading to significant credit misallocation...Not only is state bank lending more politicized and inefficient, it also generally does not serve the more credit constrained segments of the population, such as small and medium enterprises...Hence, there is an overwhelming amount of consistent literature suggesting that state ownership of banks lowers bank performance, with negative consequences for economic growth.

As impressive and apparently definitive this view seems to be, in fact, there is a significant and strong recent literature that paints a quite different picture of the allocative and economic growth impacts of public banking. Taking this literature into account suggests that this is not a closed issue and, in fact, should be the subject of significantly more research.

Andrianova et al. (2012) re-examine the evidence on the relationship between government ownership of banks and economic growth. They present cross-country evidence that shows that, even prior to the GFC, government ownership of banks has been associated with higher long-run economic growth rates. They also cast doubt on earlier studies—described above—suggesting that government ownership of banks is associated with lower long-run growth rates. They attribute these 'flawed' findings in previous studies to their inadequate controls for more 'fundamental' determinants of economic growth (Andrianova 2012, p. 449).

Similarly, Korner and Schnabel (2011) take issue with the negative conventional wisdom discussed above. Their empirical results indicate that the previously found negative relationship between public ownership and economic growth 'fades' away when country heterogeneity is properly taken into account. In particular, they show that the relationship between public ownership of banks and economic growth depends on initial conditions. They present evidence that the negative relationship holds only in countries that have 'low financial development and low institutional quality'. The negative impact of public ownership on growth fades quickly as the financial and political system develops. 'In highly developed countries (they find)…no or even positive effects'. (Korner and Schnabel 2011, pp. 407, 434–436).

In a related paper, Shen et al. (2014) disaggregate public banks into those that do not acquire any banks, acquire healthy banks and acquire distressed banks. Assessing data from 1993 to 2007, they find that only those government-owned banks that acquire distressed banks perform worse. In fact, government-owned banks that acquire distressed banks do no worse than private banks that do so. So according to this study, government banks that are not used as a bailout device by the government perform as well, on average, as do private banks (Shen et al. 2014, pp. 338–339).

There is some evidence that the positive impacts of government-owned or stakeholder-oriented banks depend on the connections of the financial institution to the local or regional community and its needs. For example, Hakenes et al. (2015) present a theoretical model and empirical evidence that indicates that small banks, operating at a regional level can spur local economic growth and development. This impact is especially strong in regions with low access to finance.

4 Conclusion: Time to Scale Up Public-Oriented Financial Institutions?

The more recent and more positive assessments of the longer-term impacts of public-oriented financial institutions discussed in the previous section suggest that there is not an ***obvious*** trade-off between the role of public-oriented banks in helping to dampen macroeconomic financial cycles and their role in achieving social goals for the medium and longer term. With positive benefits on stability and, at least, ***neutral impacts*** on longer-run growth, do we have enough evidence to recommend that we start populating our economies with a much larger share of publicly oriented financial institutions? Perhaps, but it would be disingenuous to suggest that the evidence is all in on this question.

An interesting question, worthy of further research, is why these publicly oriented financial institutions are less cyclically prone—that is they are less likely to overlend in the boom and are less likely to cut back excessively in the bust. Many of the chapters in this volume note that a key to the relative stability and success of the public banks of Naples was the trust held in them by the members of the communities in which they operated. This trust stemmed to an important degree because their founding shareholders (hospitals and charitable institutions) were involved in philanthropic activities in favour of the poor and infirm. There were, according to the studies in this volume, other important considerations, as well, including the prosperity of the charities that backed the banks and the indulgence of the court at crucial times.

All of this raises the interesting question of whether the relative success of the public and publicly oriented financial institutions discussed in this chapter also owe their success to their value orientation towards their communities and the resulting trust they engender. In some ways, the answer to this question is embedded in the very definition of some of these institutions: they are 'publicly oriented' and not driven exclusively by a profit motive. As Adriano Giannola stresses (Giannola 2018, Chapter 16 in this volume), this orientation has been central to the structure and operations of many Italian financial institutions until very recently. This orientation appears to be an important break on excessive lending in an upturn and helps sustain their lending on the way down. The role of trust here and the desire to create it on the part of the bankers is more difficult to judge. It appears that in recent years, strong financial regulations and limits on financial competition that helps publicly oriented financial institutions to survive may be more important. In the case of the Landesbank in Germany, for example, changes in laws that attempted to foster more competition facing Landesbank, and removed certain regulations on them, contributed to the speculative investments that brought them serious problems during the GFC (Hendrikse 2015).

Whatever the reasons, the evidence we have surveyed suggests that publicly oriented institutions perform best when they are not pushed by political authorities to take inappropriate actions. These results suggest that countries with a relatively high level of institutional development and high-quality governance performance are likely to be more successful in reaping the positive benefits associated with publicly oriented institutions with lower costs. The evidence also suggests that smaller, more local and more specialized institutions that have access to common infrastructure and network structures are able to best combine local relationship investment that overcomes well-known problems such as asymmetric information, with being able to reap economies of scale associated with some size in banking (see Ferri et al. 2014; Butzback and von Mettenheim 2015; Ayadi et al. 2010, for a discussion). The sustainability of these small public-oriented banks, especially in a competitive environment, is another concern. Ostergaard et al. (2016) analyse the viability of stakeholder-oriented firms in the face of economic or regulatory adversity. In a study of how Norwegian stakeholder banks fared in the aftermath of financial deregulation in Norway, the authors found that those banks that have close connections to communities that were highly socially oriented—what they refer to as having high levels of 'social capital'—were more likely to survive. In other words, it might 'take a village' to maintain a socially oriented small bank in a highly competitive environment. Absent that, the government may need to control competition or provide subsidies in exchange for the role that these banks play in overcoming externalities or providing other social or public goods.

Ayadi et al. (2010) and others emphasize the positive role that diversity plays, per se, in the financial ecology of a country or region. So even if public financial institutions are, in a one to one match up, no more efficient than private banks, over the business cycle it is better to have a diversity in one's portfolio of financial institutions. However, it will take more research and understanding before we can say whether, in any particular case, we have too few or too many public-oriented financial institutions.

We conjecture, however, that, at least in the case of the USA, and in the light of the current state of our financial system, we could use considerably more. This would help the USA move back from a system of 'Roaring Banking' to one of 'Boring Banking'. We could probably use a bit less excitement in our financial system at this point, and a bigger dose of publicly oriented financial institutions could help us achieve that, and some other useful social goals, as well.

References

Amsden, A. 2001. *The Rise of the Rest*. New York: Oxford University Press.

Andersson, F., K. Burzynska, and S. Opper. 2013. Lending for Growth? An Analysis of State-Owned Banks in China. Lund University Working Paper No. 2013: 19.

Andrianova, S. 2012. Public Banks and Financial Stability. *Economics Letters* 116 (1): 86–88.

Andrianova, S., P. Demetriades, and A. Shortland. 2008. Government Ownership of Banks, Institutions, and Financial Development. *Journal of Development Economics* 85 (1): 218–252.

———. 2012. Government of Ownership of Banks, Institutions and Economic Growth. *Economica* 79: 449–469.

Ayadi, R., D.T. Llewellyn, R.H. Schmidt, E. Arbak, and W.P. DeGroen. 2010. Investigating Diversity in the Banking Sector in Europe: Key Developments, Performance and the role of Cooperative Banks. Center for European Policy Studies Paperback.

Behr, P., D. Foos, and L. Norden. 2017. Cyclicality of SME Lending and Government Involvement in Banks. *Journal of Banking and Finance* 77: 64–77.

Bertay, A.C., A. Demirgüç-Kunt, and H. Huizinga. 2015. Bank Ownership and Credit Over the Business Cycle: Is Lending by State Banks Less Procyclical? *Journal of Banking and Finance* 50: 326–339.

Blanchard, O., G. Dell'Ariccia, and P. Mauro. 2010. Rethinking Macroeconomic Policy. *Journal of Money, Credit and Banking* 42 (6): 199–215.

Borio, C. 2012. The Financial Cycle and Macroeconomics: What Have We Learnt? BIS Working Papers No. 395.

Brei, M., and A. Schclarek. 2013. Public Bank Lending in Times of Crisis. *Journal of Financial Stability* 9 (4): 820–830.

Butzbach, O., and K. von Mettenheim. 2015. *Alternative Banking and Financial Crisis*. New York: Routledge.

Center for State Innovation. 2011. *Maine State Bank Analysis*. Available at https://d3n8a8pro7vhmx.cloudfront.net/pbi/pages/175/attachments/original/1417651542/CSI_Maine_State_Bank_Analysis.pdf?1417651542.

Crotty, J. 2009. Structural Causes of the Global Financial Crisis: A Critical Assessment of the New Financial Architecture. *Cambridge Journal of Economics* 33 (4): 563–580.

Duprey, T. 2015. Do Publicly Owned Banks Lend Against the Wind? *International Journal of Central Banking* 11 (2): 65–112.

Eichengreen, B. 2007. *The European Economy Since 1945; Coordinated Capitalism Since 1945*. Princeton: Princeton University Press.

Epstein, G., D. Plihon, A. Giannola, and C. Weller. 2009. Finance Without Financiers. *Papeles de Europa* 19: 140.

Ferri, G., P. Kalmi, and E. Kerola. 2014. Does Bank Ownership Affect Lending Behavior? Evidence from the Euro Area. *Journal of Banking and Finance* 48: 194–209.

Financial Crisis Inquiry Commission. 2011. The Financial Crisis Inquiry Report. https://fcic.law.stanford.edu/report.

Gerschenkron, A. 1962. *Economic Backwardness in Historical Perspective.* Cambridge: Cambridge University Press.

Giannola, A. 2018. Profit and Non-profit Motives in Public Banks of Naples: An Old Model in Modern Perspectives. In *Financial Innovation and Resiliency*, ed. L. Costabile and L. Neal. Cham: Palgrave Macmillan (this volume).

Grabel, I. 2018. *When Things Don't Fall Apart.* Cambridge: MIT Press.

Hakenes, H., I. Hasa, P. Molyneux, and R. Xie. 2015. Small Banks and Local Economic Development. *Review of Finance* 19: 653–683.

Haldane, A. 2009. *Banking on the State.* Bank of England.

Hendrikse, R.P. 2015. The Long Arm of Finance: Exploring the Unlikely Financialisation of Governments and Public Institutions. Dissertation, University of Amsterdam.

Korner, T., and I. Schnabel. 2011. Public Ownership of Banks and Economic Growth; The Impact of Country Heterogeneity. *Economics of Transition* 19 (3): 407–441.

McGhee, H.C., and J. Judd. 2011. Banking on America: How Main Street Partnership Banks Can Improve Local Economies. *Demos.* Available at http://www.demos.org/sites/default/files/publications/Demos_NationalBankPaper.pdf.

Micco, A., and U. Panizza. 2006. Bank Ownership and Lending Behaviour. *Economics Letters* 93 (2): 248–254.

Minsky, H.P. 1986. *Stabilizing an Unstable Economy.* New Haven and London: Yale University Press.

Ostergaard, C., I. Schindele, and B. Vale. 2016. Social Capital and The Viability of Stake-Holder Oriented Firms: Evidence from Savings Banks. *Review of Finance* 20 (5): 1673–1718.

Rudolph, H.P. 2010. State Financial Institutions: Can They Be Relied on to Kick-Start Lending? *World Bank*, Working Paper Number 10216. Available at http://siteresources.worldbank.org/EXTFINANCIALSECTOR/Resources/282884-1303327122200/Note12.pdf.

Schularick, M., and A.M. Taylor. 2012. Credit Booms Gone Bust: Monetary Policy, Leverage Cycles, and Financial Crises, 1870–2008. *The American Economic Review* 102 (2): 1029–1061.

Shen, C., I. Hasan, and C. Lin. 2014. The Government's Role in Government-Owned Banks. *Journal of Financial Services* 45: 307–340.

Tobin, J. 1977. How Dead Is Keynes? *Economic Inquiry* 15 (4): 459–468.

Wolfson, M., and G. Epstein (eds.). 2013. *The Handbook of The Political Economy of Financial Crises*. New York: Oxford University Press.

Yeyati, E.L., A. Micco, and U. Panizza. 2004. Should the Government Be in the Banking Business? The Role of State-Owned and Development Banks. *Inter-American Development Bank*, Working Paper Number 517.

CHAPTER 16

Profit and Non-profit Motives in the Public Banks of Naples: An Old Model in Modern Perspective

Adriano Giannola

1 Introduction

From 1936 to the beginning of the 1990s, the Italian banking industry was mainly managed by the state or by local public institutions. After 1990, thanks to the so-called Amato-Carli Law, in few years the entire banking sector was privatized. The privatization process occurred in parallel with an equally fast process of concentration, inspired, if not directly managed, by the Italian Central Bank (Banca d'Italia). The objective was to promote a system of large private banks in the form of limited companies. Moreover, while traditionally commercial banks had been limited to provide short-term commercial credit, in the 1990s, coherently with the general de-specialization trend, Italian banks were allowed to operate as 'universal' as well as 'mixed' banks.

The relevant literature has largely ignored that the lawmakers, by enacting Law no. 218 (the Amato-Carli Law), reintroduced after more

A. Giannola (✉)
Università di Napoli Federico II, Naples, Italy

L. Costabile and L. Neal (eds.), *Financial Innovation and Resilience*, Palgrave Studies in the History of Finance,
https://doi.org/10.1007/978-3-319-90248-7_16

than four centuries something similar to the ancient model of the public banks of Naples. As this chapter argues, they did so by resuming a distinction between, on the one hand, the 'conferring institution' (*banca conferente*), that is the Banking Foundation, a philanthropic institution, and, on the other hand, the 'underwriting institution' (*banca conferitaria*), namely the private commercial bank created by the Foundation in the form of a limited company. The Banking Foundation is now the main, or sometimes the only shareholder of the newly created private bank.

As a matter of fact, the intention of the Amato-Carli Act was not to resume the distinction between foundations and commercial banks, a distinction that had been lost over the centuries, but to use the Banking Foundations as a vehicle for privatizing the banking system. Nevertheless, it can be argued that the model of the Neapolitan public banks was, perhaps unintentionally, restored in 1990, and represents today the prevailing model. At least two of the three most important Italian bank groups (Intesa-San Paolo and Unicredito) have been, and still are, strictly controlled by the network of Banking Foundations emerging from the bank consolidation process led by the Bank of Italy.

This chapter starts with a description of the Italian banking system at the beginning of the 1990s, highlighting the role of the public sector within it. It continues with a discussion on the specific solution that was devised in order to privatize the system in the face the new competitive challenges arising from the process of integration in the European Union. It then illustrates how the new system reproduces several features of the ancient model of the public banks of Naples, and discusses the stabilizing function played—at least thus far—by this governance model.

2 From a Public to a Private Banking System

In the early 1990's, the Italian banking system was organized in a variety of institutions directly or indirectly controlled by the public sector for almost 80 per cent of its activity.

The public nature of the banking system is clearly established by the Italian Constitution that, in Article 47, states that the mission of banking is to preserve and protect national savings. Only in 1980, the High Court (*Corte di Cassazione*) accepted that banks are firms, and that their activity is business activity as that of all other firms. Also, from the early 1930s until the end of the 1970s, the general consensus was that public ownership favoured bank efficiency and guaranteed neutrality in the allocation of credit.

In fact, the efficiency principles were increasingly sacrificed after 1973, when Italian banks became crucial instruments for the management of monetary policy through the imposition of caps on lending, constraints on their portfolio composition, etc. That experience inspired the definition of the Italian banking system as a 'petrified forest'.

Up to the 1990's, the main categories of public banks, now completely disappeared, were:

1. *Istituti di Credito di Diritto Pubblico* (ICDPs, Public Law Credit Institutes). This category included the Banca Nazionale del Lavoro established in 1926 and owned by the Ministry of Treasury, and the four most ancient Italian banks, whose origins go back to the fifteenth or sixteenth century: Banco di Napoli, Banco di Sicilia, Istituto San Paolo di Torino and Monte dei Paschi di Siena. The top management of these banks was appointed by the Treasury. Although they were not state-owned banks, they were *de facto* managed by the state and by representatives of local government institutions.
2. *Banche di Interesse Nazionale* (BINs): Banca Commerciale Italiana; Credito Italiano; Banco di Roma. These were limited companies with a private origin, but whose main shareholder was the state. For this reason, they were called *banche a partecipazione statale* and considered to be 'public' banks.
   While the ICDPs were born as non-profit organizations, with strong links to their mutualistic origin, the BINs were for-profit organizations. Since they had been saved in the early 1930s by the state, they belonged to the system of *Partecipazioni Statali* (state-participated firms). This was an original formula, largely applied in Italy, through which banks and industrial firms were controlled by a public holding called IRI, the Institute for Industrial Reconstruction. IRI was active until 2002.
3. *Casse di Risparmio* were non-profit organizations born to foster local development, to support small firms and to promote and protect local savings. These eighty-nine *Casse di Risparmio* were managed by local authorities and institutions such as universities, chambers of commerce and professional associations all in the interest of local communities.

4. *Banche Popolari* (BPs) and *Banche di Credito Cooperativo* (BCCs, cooperative-credit banks) also had a mutualistic approach and promoted the interests of their members. In the 1980s and 1990s, this specific sector of the banking system, helped by the wise management of currency devaluations, was the financial 'core' behind the successful experience of the Italian Industrial Districts.

While the privatization process involved the ICDPs and the Casse di Risparmio (all transformed into private limited companies), it was not able to dissolve the cooperative structure and the mutualistic principles that still prevail in the BP and BCC system.[1]

Due to privatizations, the share of public sector in total banking assets fell from 80 per cent to around 60 per cent in 1995 and to less than 10 per cent in 1999.

Taking stock, after almost twenty years of privatizations, the following evidence emerges concerning bank performance. From 1993 onwards, the Italian banking system has registered an overall decline in cost and profit efficiency. In this general context, the mutualistic banks (BCCs and BPs) showed a much less disappointing performance. This relative advantage holds both at the national and at the regional level (Giannola 2009; Giordano and Lopes 2015; Barra et al. 2016; Stefani et al. 2016).

With regard to the present situation of financial stress, the large limited companies represent the most critical elements in the Italian banking system. And it is clear that the real safeguard of 'stable' governance for these large banking groups is the highly distinctive nature of their main shareholders, that is the network of Banking Foundations, which was brought back to life in 1990. The Italian Supreme Court (*Corte Costituzionale*) ruled that these Banking Foundations are private institutions; they are non-profit institutions; and their mission is to pursue philanthropic objectives. As 'patient shareholders', the Banking Foundations have been acting as a protective factor for the largest for-profit banks. Because of their interest in preserving their patrimonies for their statutory philanthropic objectives, they are in fact less exposed than for-profit institutions to pure market incentives. Also, importantly, the public-philanthropic orientation of these shareholders has, to some extent, contributed to insulate the large banks from speculative activities by third parties. Interestingly, banks that were not included in the protective belt

[1] In 2015, however, a new law required that eight Popular Banks (BPs), each with total assets exceeding eight billion euros, should be transformed into limited companies.

of the Banking Foundations, such as Banca Nazionale del Lavoro, are now in foreign hands.

Thus, the most important component of the Italian banking system, namely the large banks' sector, is not only owned by publicly oriented institutions but also derives at least part of its strength from this public orientation. For these reasons, it is a debatable issue whether the Italian large banking groups are really 'private and on the market'.

With increasing economic tensions lurking at the horizon, the current model is now under pressure. Nevertheless, it has functioned thus far as a stabilizing factor in the Italian banking system.

3 Where Do the Italian Banking Foundations Really Come from?

In order to gain a better understanding of the banking model characterizing the current Italian experience, it is useful to put things in historical perspective.

'Modern' banking was born in Italy, and one of its most important developments occurred in the Kingdom of Naples in the second half of the sixteenth century, when the 'banks of the charities' were licensed as 'public banks' (for developments in the fifteenth century, see Di Meglio, Chapter 3 in this volume). The innovative Neapolitan banking model has very little to do with the better-known experience of the Renaissance moneylenders. These moneylenders were not proper bankers, in the following sense. Just as merchant banks or investment banks do today, they lent capitals retrieved somehow (nowadays on the market, in the past in their own fortunes and those of wealthy people). While some kind of capital market has always existed, the credit market has instead developed slowly. It is a relatively modern invention, which 'organizes' reputation and trust in order to provide a production factor, that is credit, in addition to capital. In this scenario, banks as credit producers made the crucial difference for the development of the modern world by activating and increasing production, if not by creating new economic resources.[2]

[2] The origins and nature of banking is an issue which fuels endless debates, an 'obsession-like' theme that earned twenty years in a US mental asylum for such a poet as Ezra Pound ('*il gran fabbro*' according to T. E. Eliot). Pound described the rise of modern banking as follows: "Rise of Banking: Banks of two sort: A. Gangs of creditors, organised to squeeze the last ounce out of debtors, conquered cities, etc. B. Reconstruction banks.

As this book illustrates, an important feature of the public banks was the nature of their founders. These were the *luoghi pii* and Holy Houses, philanthropic institutions whose mission was to provide aid and health care to the weakest social groups (orphans, abandoned children, prisoners and unmarried mothers), and to grant accessible credit to the poor, as was the case with the loans upon pledge granted by the Monte dei Poveri and Monte di Pietà. These institutions accomplished their philanthropic mission in a measure depending on their original patrimonial assets and on further accumulation through bequests and donations, and, most importantly, through revenues from their banks' activities.

At the outset, these charities were still traditional moneylenders, that is intermediaries in the capital market, rather than modern banks as defined above. Nevertheless, from the very beginning, their approach was completely different from that of private moneylenders, such as the 'most glorified [...] Banca S. Giorgio, the pitiless company of Genoese creditors' (Pound 1973, p. 240). The Neapolitan charities and their banks were not allowed to charge interest on their loans. When, in 1628, the authorities eventually allowed them to charge an interest, they justified the new provision as responding to the banks' need to cover their running costs.

Loans at an interest gained an increasing favour not only among the classes benefitting from the banks' philanthropic mission, but also among the general public. Therefore, an increasing competitive pressure was imposed upon private moneylenders. Thus, the public banks' credit activity was introduced through the door of philanthropy.

The great light among which was and is the Monte dei Paschi di Siena" (Pound 1973, p. 61). Pound seems to ignore the experience of the Neapolitan public banks, parallel to Monte dei Paschi, and equally alternative to the 'Gangs of creditors.' The obsession with banks, usury and credit is rooted in Pound's analysis of the origin and the governance of money (Desai 2006). "Without history one is lost in the dark, and the essential data of modern history cannot enlighten us unless they are traced back at least to the foundation of the Senese bank, the Monte dei Paschi; in other words, to the perception of the true basis of credit, viz., 'the abundance of nature and the responsibility of the whole people'" (Pound 1973, p. 278). Pound was a follower of Silvio Gesell, the "strange, unduly neglected prophet...whose work contains flashes of deep insight" (Keynes 1936, p. 353). Gesell's ideas (Gesell 1958) inspired the sophisticated analysis of Chapter XVII, a crucial and 'unduly neglected' part of the Keynes's *General Theory*.

The Neapolitan charities became dominant in the credit market thanks to the special licenses that they were granted by the Spanish Viceroys, so that they soon defeated their competitors by virtue of a code of conduct that, given the nature of their activities, could neither allow usury nor treat customers as a mere object of speculation. This is a significant example of how an efficient non-profit policy easily wins over the for-profit logic typical of the private management of the credit relationship.

The public banks were established as outright banks, as a direct emanation of the original philanthropic institutes that became their owners. Thus, these charities became the shareholders of their respective banks and benefited from these banks' revenues, statutorily assigned to their philanthropic mission. Most importantly, thanks to the trust that they inspired, these institutions were able to introduce a system of fiduciary circulation and modern forms of credit based upon the *fedi di credito* and *polizze* issued by their banks, well in advance of similar, better-known inventions elsewhere in Europe. Trust in the public banks of Naples in turn depended on the charities' patrimonial assets, as well as on the generalized belief in a 100 per cent correspondence between their paper circulation and the amount of the precious metals deposited in their vaults.

Further insights in the nature of the system can be gained by a short theoretical *detour* on the Neapolitan banks' operating model. In their origins, they were an example of a 'reactive' banking model, comparable to the well-known Wicksellian bank.

Wicksell's banks have no reserve constraints and operate in a pure credit economy. They are 'reactive' because their task is to create credit in response to entrepreneurial demands. For this type of banks, both in expansions and in contractions the multiplicative process is only limited by the appropriate alignment between the market interest rate (which is both the cost of circulating capital for firms and the reward for savings) and the 'natural' rate, resulting from technology and investment activity. This feature makes these banks distributionally neutral in equilibrium. This model may be contrasted with Schumpeterian banks, an example of 'active' banks. Here, credit production implies the banks' active participation in, and sometimes the direct promotion of, their customers' industrial strategies. This influences the 'natural rate' of interest and inevitably implies 'non-neutrality', because the joint and interactive action of banks and firms endowed with market power contrasts with the requisites of the competitive model.

The Neapolitan public banks were 'reactive', although at an early stage what they accommodated was not the firms' demand for loans as in Wicksell, but rather the public's willingness to deposit metallic money in exchange for circulating paper certificates (*fedi di credito*). This was the beginning of a delicate process that favoured the first realization, in Naples, of a regime of fiduciary circulation, thus laying the foundations of a modern banking system.

This way of creating paper money was the initial step in a system of money creation that became increasingly independent from the constraint of a 100 per cent metallic coverage and eventually gave raise to money creation via the granting of loans (Costabile and Nappi, Chapter 2 in this volume). Nevertheless, the public banks' remained 'reactive', rather than 'active' in the Schumpeterian sense, because now they accommodated the demand for loans of their customers.

4 The Public Banks' Accounting Procedures and the Size of the System

In this book, the chapter by Costabile and Nappi provides quantitative evidence on the public banks' monetary circulation, the amount of their metal reserves, deposits and investments. These data illustrate the early evolution of the Neapolitan banking system and trace the roots and effects of the 1622 monetary reform and bank crisis. Chapter 5, by Balletta, Balletta and Nappi presents further interesting data on the Neapolitan public banks' activities in a long-term perspective.

Building on these contributions, this section offers some simple calculations intended to study the size of the Neapolitan banking system in the seventeenth and eighteenth century and its quantitative role in the local economy. Moreover, using an old accounting document, it provides a simple framework for the analysis of the Neapolitan public banks' balance sheets.

Let us start with the latter exercise. The classic reference for the public banks' accounting procedures is the so-called *Scheda Galanti*, a document produced by Tortora (1882, p. 245) on the basis of a study by the economist Giuseppe Maria Galanti (1789, pp. 347–354; see also Filangieri 1940, pp. 131–132).[3] This document presents a cumulative

[3]Giuseppe Maria Galanti (1743–1806) was an economist of the Genovesi School. On behalf of the Bourbon Court, he was in charge of a general study of the economic

Table 1 Banchi pubblici napoletani: Balance Sheet 1788

Liabilities	ducats	Assets	ducats
deposits	21.421.195	**investments with interest**	8.995.375
		reserves (*)	12.425.820
		total investment	21.421.195
equity	13.000.000	**fixed assets (patrimony)**	13.000.000
net profit (accruing to equity)	92.750	**net profit** (accruing to capital)	92.750
TOTAL LIABILITIES	**34.513.945**	**TOTAL ASSETS**	**34.513.945**

* *cassa piccola + cassa grande*

balance sheet for all the public banks active in 1788, as well as a stylized profit and loss (income) account.

In the balance sheet, the main assets are loans, loans upon pledge with and without interest, reserves and fixed assets owned by the charities, while the main item on the liability side is deposits (Table 1).

As for the Income Account (Table 2), the *Scheda Galanti* reports Interest Income as the only item in the Total Earnings (*Totale Attivo*). Since deposits did not earn interest, and there were no charges for the services provided to the banks' customers, the 'interest margin' and the intermediation margin coincide with Total Earnings.

The average rate of interest on investments (loans) is 6.2 per cent.

Total Earnings less Operating Costs gives Total Profits, which amount to 16.4 per cent of these earnings. Total Profits are allocated for about 60 per cent to the expenses for charitable purposes of the mother

conditions of the whole Kingdom of Naples. He published the result of his inquiry in his *Nuova descrizione geografica e politica delle Due Sicilie*, 1782–1791. For the accounting procedures of the Neapolitan public banks, see also Michele Rocco (1785–1787).

Table 2 Banchi Pubblici napoletani: Income Account 1788

TOTAL EARNINGS (interest and intermediation margins) (A)(*)	ducats 577.546
wages and pensions	230.889
administrative expenses	89.925
TOTAL operating expenses (B)	320.814
Gross profit (C) = (A)-(B)	256.732 (100)
Beneficience (D)	163.982 (63,9%)
Profit (**) accruing to capital (C) - (D)	**92.750** **(39,1%)**

* *Totale attivo:* earnings from banking activity and from managing the patrimony of the *luoghi pii* and *Case Sante*
** *Avanzo netto*

institutions, while the remaining 40 per cent is the Net Profits accruing to the banks (*Avanzo Netto*). The banks' Net Profits were used to increase the banks' patrimonial assets.

Operating Costs are 59 per cent of Total Earnings: this is a remarkably good cost/earnings ratio, comparable to today's performance.

The *Scheda Galanti* does not provide any direct information on the value of the charities' patrimonial assets, but reports their earnings from these assets. These earnings amount to 275,355.00 ducats; a flow that, discounted as perpetuity at the rate of 2 per cent, gives a capital value of more than 13 million ducats. This result is in line with Tortora (1882, p. 244), who reports that in 1788 the amount of deposits was 24 million ducats, while the banks' patrimonial assets were no less than 13 million ducats.

This evidence shows that the public banks devoted a substantial share of their earnings to the charitable activities of their mother institutions, and their operations were remarkably efficient. It also confirms what was stressed above, namely that the charities' patrimonial assets were the solid foundation on which the Neapolitan population built its trust in the public banks.

The accounting procedures did not formally separate credits and debits from charitable giving, but these were accurately treated as independent in the *Scheda Galanti*. Therefore, this accounting system enabled the administrators to distinguish between the commercial and the philanthropic activities of the two institutions (the charity and the bank), pretty much as it happens today with the two separate accounting systems pertaining, respectively, to the Banking Foundations and the commercial banks.

The available data also illustrate another interesting aspect of the ancient Neapolitan banking system, notably the size of its activity. These data suggest that the public banks performed a substantial, pervasive financial function in the Neapolitan Kingdom. To the purpose of illustrating this point, we elaborate on the data for 1620 and 1788 (see Costabile and Nappi in this volume, and Filangieri 1940, respectively).

In 1620, the daily wage (measured in grana) in the building industry and in agriculture was equivalent to 5.429 grams of silver. The ducat in that year contained 24.95 grams of silver and the monetary circulation amounted to 2,746,756.00 ducats, equivalent to 68,531,562.00 grams of silver and corresponding to 12,623,239.00 working days. The number of working days per year in the building industry and in agriculture was 325 and 200 respectively (Malanima 2013). These figures correspond to 63,116.00 and 36,066.00 working units virtually employed, respectively, in the agricultural sector and in the building industry. Assuming that each employee had four dependents, the banking sector would have provided its financial services to several hundred thousand people (between 180,330 and 315,580).

Let us now consider the year 1778: the amount of loans (***depositi impiegati ad utile***) was 8,995,375 ducats, equivalent to 224,425,259 grams of silver. Since the wage per day was at that time 40 grani = 7.76 grams of silver (Malanima 2013), we find a potential stock of 28,920,781 working days. Thus, given the number of working days in agriculture and in the building industry referred to above, potential employment would have been between 144,603 and 88,987. Given our hypothesis on the number of dependents, the population benefitting from the banks' services would have been between 723,015 and 444,935.

For reference, the population in the city of Naples amounted to 408,992 persons in 1791 and 341,743 persons in 1821 (De Renzi 1826). This suggests that the public banks' services were not limited to the population of the city of Naples but were also extended to other parts of the Kingdom.

5 Mutualism, Philanthropy and Modern Banking

What can we learn today from this old story? Certainly, credit is now—in terms of instruments and organization—a different business, but many features of the old experience of the public banks of Naples are modern and still instructive. The most important one is the dual nature of the Banking Foundations introduced by the Amato-Carli Act that, similarly to the old Neapolitan banks, places them in between the 'public' and the 'private' domains. This dual nature is highlighted by their shifting between the two domains: they were labelled 'public' until 1998 and 'private' thereafter. In 2003, two sentences of the Supreme Court (Corte Costituzionale) granted them the right to produce their own charters. Although the Banking Foundations are subject to the supervision of the Treasury Ministry, their governance is the responsibility of several statutory stakeholders representing the interests of the communities in which they operate. In short, today we have for-profit banks providing Foundations with most of the resources they use for their philanthropic purposes.

All this may be considered the result of a general political decision to put an end to the direct role of the state in the banking system. As we said above, it is unclear to what extent the solution of resuming—although in a different juridical setting—the model and nature of the public banks has been a deliberate choice. That result was probably unintentional, mainly a side effect stemming from the need to find a way for putting a large and strategic share of the nation's wealth in private, but socially well-identified hands: the so-called social-private sector (*privato sociale*), rather than conferring that wealth to the 'atomistic' market, at least not immediately. The most important consequence of that decision was to confer upon the Foundations the essential role of protecting the major Italian banks from real contestability in the market. In turn, as 'patient shareholders' of for-profit banks, while exerting a decisive stabilizing influence on a strategic sector of the economy, the Foundations benefit from the revenues from their banks' credit activity.

In a more general perspective, the Italian society experienced the sudden birth of a brand new and influential sector in the national arena. Considering the long-term institutional inertia and the entropy of the system, the rise of these Banking Foundations may be considered the main and most influential novelty of the last 40 years.[4]

The above analysis has considered the origin of the Neapolitan banking system and has argued that the privatization and consolidation process in the 1990s brought to a new life the philanthropic dimension of banking through the leading role assigned to the Foundations in the governance of the large Italian for-profit banks.

Today, two distinct models of mutualistic companies operate in the Italian credit market: one is inspired by a revised, modern version of the Neapolitan public banks; the other is the cooperative model. In the latter, cooperative banks limit their mutualism to the interests of the cooperative members. In this case, mutualism, while fuelled by profits, does not have a philanthropic motivation. By contrast, the philanthropic model of mutualism has two main objectives: firstly, to promote the so-called social-private sector (*privato-sociale*) and secondly, to reduce the extent of credit rationing, especially towards small- and medium-sized firms. This model of mutualism permeates the largest Italian banks to some extent at least, because of the social orientation of their shareholders, the Banking Foundations. Moreover, as this paper has argued, thanks to their nature of 'patient shareholders' only marginally affected by the short-termism typical of managerial companies, the Foundations have acted as a stabilizing factor in the Italian banking system and contributed to limit the degree of contestability of the largest banks.

It should be also noticed that the enduring relevance for modern banking of the 'public bank model' is not limited to the Italian experience. For instance, it inspired a recent reform in Spain, where the Amato-Carli model was used as the reference framework for the law 26/2013, which privatized the Spanish savings banks (Ortiz, 2014; Sanchez-Calero Guilarte, 2014).

[4]It must be observed, though, that the uneven distribution on the national territory of the eighty-nine existing Banking Foundations has definitely contributed to make the Italian economic dualism worse.

In the light of these considerations, it is unfortunate that the 'public bank model' is conspicuously missing in the international literature on banking. For instance, the rich historical and analytical framework developed by Calomiris and Haber (2014) ignores the resilient, five-hundred-year-old model of the Neapolitan public banks, which overcame many crises, went through many different political and institutional regimes and is still alive. Definitely, mutualism and philanthropy deserve a major place in any analysis of the 'Game of Bank Bargaining', namely of the alternative models of political/institutional/economic coalitions that shape the world of banking.

References

Barra, Christian, Sergio De Stefanis, and Giuseppe Lubrano Lavadera. 2016. Risk and Regulation: A Difference-in-Difference Analysis for Italian Local Banks. *Finance Research Letters* 17: 25–32.

Calomiris, Charles W., and Stephen H. Haber. 2014. *Fragile by Design: The Political Origins of Banking Crises and Scarce Credit.* Princeton, NJ: Princeton University Press.

Colino Mediavilla, José L., and José C. Gonzalez Vasquez (eds.). 2014. *Las Cajas de Ahorros y la prevencion y tratamiento de la crisis de las entitades de credito.* Granada: Editorial Comares.

Desai, Meghnad. 2006. *The Route of All Evil. The Political Economy of Ezra Pound.* London: Faber and Faber.

De Renzi, Salvatore. 1826. *Miasmi paludosi, contagi ed epidemie.* Napoli: dalla Tipografia Vara.

Filangieri, Riccardo. 1940. *I banchi di Napoli dalle origini alla costituzione del Banco delle Due Sicilie: 1539–1808.* Napoli: Tipografia degli Artigianelli.

Galanti, Giuseppe Maria. 1789. *Nuova descrizione geografica e politica delle Due Sicilie.* Tomo Terzo, Napoli: presso i Soci del gabinetto Letterario.

Gesell, Silvio. 1958. *The Natural Economic Order*, Revised English edition. London: Peter Owen Ltd.

Giannola, Adriano. 2009. Bank Mergers and Credit Allocation Among Italian Regions. In *The Banks and the Italian Economy*, ed. Damiano Silipo, 125–133. Heidelberg: Springer.

Giordano, Luca, and Antonio Lopes. 2015. Competition Versus Efficiency: What Drives Banks' Spreads in Italian Banking System? *Academic Journal of Economic Studies* 1 (2): 93–119.

Keynes, John Maynard. 1936. *The General Theory of Money, Interest and Prices.* London: Macmillan.

Malanima, Paolo. 2013. Prezzi e Salari. In *Il Mezzogiorno prima dell'Unità. Fonti, dati, storiografia*, ed. P. Malanima and Nicola Ostuni. Soveria Mannelli: Rubbettino.

Ortiz, Maria Lidon L. 2014. Los supestos de transformciones previstos en la ley 26/2013 de Cajas de Ahorros y fundaciones bancarias. Problemas de interpretacion y de integration. In *Las cajas de ahorros y la prevención y tratamiento de la crisis de las entidades de crédito*, ed. Colino Mediavilla and Gonzalez Vasquez. Abelote, Granada: Comares.

Pound, Ezra. 1973. *Selected Prose 1909–1965*. London: Faber and Faber.

Rocco, Michele. 1785–1787. *De' banchi di Napoli e della loro ragione*, 3 vols. Napoli: Fratelli Raimondi.

Sanchez-Calero Guilarte, Juan. 2014. Las crisis de las Cajas y la respuesta legislativa. In *Las cajas de ahorros y la prevención y tratamiento de la crisis de las entidades de crédito*, ed. Colino Mediavilla and Gonzalez Vasquez. Abelote, Granada: Comares.

Stefani, Maria L., Valerio Vacca, Daniele Coin, Silvia Del Prete, Cristina Demma, Maddalena Galardo, Iconio Garrì, Sauro Mocetti, and Dario Pellegrino. (2016). Le banche locali e il finanziamento dei territori: evidenze per l'Italia (2007–2014). Banca d'Italia, *Questioni di Economia e Finanza*, n. 324, marzo.

Tortora, Eugenio. 1882. *Raccolta di documenti storici e delle leggi e regole concernenti il Banco di Napoli*. Napoli, R. Stab. Tipografico del cav. Francesco Gianni.

Index

L. Costabile and L. Neal (eds.), *Financial Innovation and Resilience*, Palgrave Studies in the History of Finance,
https://doi.org/10.1007/978-3-319-90248-7

O

P

Kolibri 360 GmbH
Ferdinand-Jühlke-Straße 7
99095 Erfurt, Deutschland
produktsicherheit@kolibri360.de